W9-AGH-806

FORE▶SHADOWS

OF WRATH and REDEMPTION

WILLIAM T. JAMES General Editor

HARVEST HOUSE PUBLISHERS
Eugene, Oregon 97402

Cover design by Terry Dugan Design, Minneapolis, Minnesota

FORESHADOWS OF WRATH AND REDEMPTION
Copyright © 1999 William T. James
Published by Harvest House Publishers
Eugene, Oregon 97402

Library of Congress Cataloging-in-Publication Data
    Foreshadows of wrath and redemption / William T. James, general editor.
        p.   cm.
    Includes bibliographical references.
    ISBN 1-56507-976-0
    End of the world—Biblical teaching. 2. Bible—Prophecies—End of the world.
    I. James, William T., 1942-   .
    BS649.E63F67   1999
    236'.9—dc21   98-43131
                                                        CIP

Printed in the United States of America

      99   00   01   02   03   04   05 /BP/ 10 9 8 7 6 5 4 3 2 1

This book is dedicated to Dr. John F. Walvoord, whose faithful scholarship in God's Holy Word on behalf of his Lord continues to inspire, instruct, and enlighten all of us who strive to attain and disseminate prophetic insights during these last days.

Acknowledgments

Jesus Christ is the whole purpose for this book because the testimony of Jesus is the spirit of prophecy (Revelation 19:10).

Because we believe we stand at a critical time very near the end of the Church Age, each contributing author to *Foreshadows of Wrath and Redemption* prays that this volume will lift the Lord Jesus high in order that God's Holy Spirit draws all men, women and children to Him for salvation and for spiritual edification.

My profound thanks to these, my wonderful brothers and my sister in Christ, whose generous giving of their immense gifts and talents was done so at great sacrifice because of their tremendously busy schedules. That God will bless and reward them is my grateful, thankful prayer.

A special thanks to my good friend and Christian brother Mike Hile, for his many kindnesses and generosities in helping me as we travel while trying to do God's will and work. His new book, *Timeline 2000: Does God Have a Plan for Mankind?* is a much welcomed addition to my personal library, and I highly recommend that volume for everyone who desires a deeper look into God's prophetic Word.

I continue to draw special sustenance from my good friends Gail Blackburn and Scott Curtis, who provide encouragement in many forms and in many ways. Such friendships are made in heaven, and I do not consider them lightly.

Angie Peters, my daughter-close coworker in these efforts on behalf of our Lord, brightens my life in so many ways. My love and thanks to Angie, to her husband, Kurt, and to their children, Lindsey and Nick, for all they continue to mean to me. Angie is not only a top-of-the-line editor, but a writer of great talent. Her book, *Celebrate Home: Great Ideas for Stay-at-Home Moms,* continues to inspire readers who desire practical and spiritual insights into family life and raising children.

All my love to Margaret, who always seems to know exactly the right things to say and do at precisely the right time in making our home a love-filled buffer against the sometimes abrasive world outside. She and our sons, Terry and Nathan, mean everything to me.

My friends at Harvest House never cease to amaze me with their spiritual acumen, quality of workmanship and marketing skills in producing books that honor Christ. My sincere thanks to each Harvest House associate for contributions made to *Foreshadows of Wrath and Redemption.*

Without our readers, the process of book writing and production would be pointless. My thanks to every person who takes precious, fleeting time out of his or her life to read this book. May God bless your reading of these chapters and make your life all He created it to be for His honor and His glory.

CONTENTS

PART 3
PAUL PREDICTS PERILOUS TIMES

Daniel's Last-Days Flood

William T. James

Planet Earth wobbles toward a foreboding future under the fear-filled eyes of nervous world-watchers. However, the portentous events filling today's headlines thrillingly echo Daniel the prophet's words within spiritually attuned ears: "… and the end thereof shall be with a flood…" (Daniel 9:26).

The book of final prophecies that Daniel was told to "…shut up… and seal… even to the time of the end" seems to now be open, its contents spilling across our newspapers' front pages and our television screens (see Daniel 12:4). No previous generation has experienced the number, frequency and intensity of signals so similar to things prophesied to be witnessed by the generation alive at the consummation of human history. Daniel's last-days flood indeed seems to be deluging the planet while the prophet's words in Daniel 12 resound hourly.

Knowledge now doubles every two years. With the advent of the Internet and other communication technologies, that pace continues to increase at a rate impossible to comprehend or harness.

We run to and fro at breakneck speed. We do so literally through travel that enables us to cover millions of miles of space in just a matter of days. We do so electronically, our communications running like lightning in a fraction of a second to every point on earth—and even to distant worlds.

Jesus' words about the signs of the times just before His return at the time of Armageddon are becoming reality before our eyes as we move through our daily lives. False christs, false prophets, wars and rumors of wars and all the other signals our Lord said will be happening concurrently in birth-pang fashion convulse our world with continuing regularity.

Israel, pressured from all sides to accept absurd demands in a satanically inspired pseudo-peace process; Russia and its neighbors positioned precisely as Ezekiel 38 and 39 prophesy; China gaining strength and exerting increasing hegemony over the Rising Sun regions from which the "kings of the east" will come; the European Union poised to become the colossus that will produce the "ten kings" power base of Revelation 17:12,13, from which the Antichrist will launch his drive for world conquest: The nations of prophecy appear ready to play out the final, violent scenes of this Earth Age.

Mankind grows worse and worse, just as the apostle Paul prophesied. Perilous times are here as the fierce, heady, high-minded lovers of pleasure more and more dominate societies and cultures. Current ecumenical movements to bring all religious systems together into one configuration prove Paul's prediction that endtime man will have a "form of godliness, but [deny] the power thereof" (2 Timothy 3:5).

Man's intellect continues to produce technology that Antichrist will no doubt use to subdue, control and ultimately force all people to worship him or be killed.

Foreshadows of Wrath and Redemption examines in-depth the signs that Jesus and the prophets foretold would prevail during the seven-year tribulation period (see Revelation 6–19). Moreover, the vast body of evidence herein presented points to the stunning fact that many signals foreshadowing the coming wrath of God are observable today!

Last Days Deluge

No matter which way we look on earth's horizon, we see thunderheads of the approaching end-time storm. Despite rosy predictions by politicians, scientists, religionists and philosophers that earth's Golden Age lies just over the next hill or just around the next bend, we hear rumblings and see the lightning that signal ominous things to come.

While it is true that an infinitely magnificent golden future lies just beyond earth's stormy horizon, such a future will not be produced by fallen mankind, but by Jesus Christ upon His return to put down satanic rebellion and establish His kingdom. Human beings will never produce heaven on earth. A brief examination of the direction the humanistic flood is sweeping this generation documents that we are gushing down a sin-darkened ravine toward apocalypse.

False Christs, False Prophets, Great Deception

Proof abounds that we live in a time marked by false christs, false prophets and deception. Deceived victims number in the thousands. For example, consider the Jim Jones Guyana massacre, the David Koresh Waco debacle and the deluded cult members who thought they could hitch a ride on a spacecraft hidden behind the Hale-Bopp comet. Benjamin Creme still proclaims Lord Matreya to be the coming christ. Dozens of lesser-known false christs and their false prophets deceive growing numbers of people who seek to fill the void only the true Christ can fill. These luciferically empowered death cults, most of which claim apocalyptic prophecies as their foundational doctrines, are making shocking headlines more and more.

If there is any question about the fact that many people are already deeply involved in the end-time deception, consider the billions of dollars spent on the psychic hotlines. Modern-day soothsaying has produced an industry that currently generates more than $5 billion annually. Hollywood and music industry celebrities glowingly report personal encounters with demon forces through psychic counselors who introduce them to spirit guides, personal angels or other benign-sounding—but evil—spiritual entities.

Far more troubling than these devilish activities, however, is the subtle evil that deludes and corrupts ever-increasing numbers of people, including many within the body of Christ. The ravening wolves in sheep's clothing of Matthew 7:15, like Satan himself, stalk about the earth—even among Christ's fold—seeking whom they may devour. They preach and teach a feel-good message that promises anything and everything the deluded, spiritually ignorant who listen with "itching ears" desire. The false teachers feed their flocks the garbage that they are good people who deserve only the best despite the fact that God's Word plainly teaches that "there is none that doeth good, no, not one" (Romans 3:12). Those who sit under such abominable false teaching have their egos stroked to the point they themselves become as God in their own minds. The gospel they hunger for and are given is not the *Christ-centered* gospel of blood atonement for the sin that separates them from God the Father, but a gospel that evicts God's Son, Jesus Christ, so they can sit upon the throne of their own lives.

The true joy and peace these deluded flocks yearn for eludes them because they overtly or unwittingly believe they can achieve tranquility through self-effort. Like the geopolitical world that time after time fails at making peace, people under the influence of false teachers can never find lasting inner peace because they reject the Prince of Peace, Jesus Christ, for whom and by whom all things were made.

Unity is the catchword of the hour for the ecumenical movement taking place in America and around the world. Therein lies what looks to be the heart that pulses within the growing beast known as *apostasy.* Disagreement and division equates to intolerance, bigotry and hate in today's world where we must all strive to get along.

Of course, this attempt to make peace is pure sophistry. Those who propose unity that fits within the world system's definition of the word exclude biblical Christianity that demands moral accountability to the true God of heaven through His Son, Jesus Christ. Jesus said He came not to bring peace, but division (see Luke 12:51). He said this not because His journey through physical life was to be lived as a troublemaker, but because He knew the prideful, sinful hearts of the creation called man. Christ came to earth in the flesh as both God and man to seek and to save that which was lost (all mankind). Many people would believe and accept Christ as God's Way of salvation; unfortunately, many more would not believe and would march down the broad way to destruction.

Humanism, the instrument used by Satan to enslave fallen mankind, calls for a unity that appeals to fallen man's arrogance and pride. The devil's seducing words, "You shall be as gods," echo and reverberate today with ecumenists' promises that man, through his own effort, can build an earthly utopia. Tragically, the body of Christ, the church, is being drawn into this luciferic quagmire.

Movements are afoot under the guise of bringing Christ's body together that have at their cores the vile heresy that instructs Christians to not allow *form* of worship to separate them. This sort of theology claims that all Christians must unite so God's work can go on and God's kingdom can be produced here on earth as it is in heaven.

Such high-sounding phraseology and heady appeal sounds wonderfully irrefutable and, indeed, is to many irresistible. But form of worship becomes the irreconcilable problem when compromise of the gospel of Jesus Christ must be entertained for the purpose of achieving unity. The world religious system from which springs the ecumenical avalanche currently crashing down upon Christianity demands that we all *just get along* and that we accept *all* belief systems within Christianity as equally true and acceptable in the eyes of God. But the Scripture says, "For there is one God, and one mediator between God and men, the man, Christ Jesus" (1 Timothy 2:5). Nothing and no one satisfies the holiness of God in the matter of forgiveness of sin. Jesus Himself said, "I am the way, the truth, and the life: no man cometh unto the Father, but by me" (John 14:6).

True unity in the sense that God accepts unity comes *only* through His Son Jesus. Manmade systems, even high-sounding

manmade religious systems, do not meet the Almighty's specifica-
tions—or even come close to meeting them.

The current call for unity among all believers that comes from
the ecumenical movements of our time are antithesis to the true
unity demanded by God the Father as witnessed by God the Son's
prayer found in John 17. Consider those words of Jesus to those
who believe in Him, then ask yourself: Is this the same Jesus
claimed by the ecumenists who say God accepts all belief systems?

> These words spoke Jesus, and lifted up his eyes to heaven, and said,
> Father, the hour is come; glorify thy Son, that thy Son also may glo-
> rify thee. As thou hast given him power over all flesh, that he should
> give eternal life to as many as thou hast given him [verses 1,2].

> And this is life eternal, that they might know thee, the only true God,
> and Jesus Christ, whom thou hast sent. I have glorified thee on the
> earth: I have finished the work which thou gavest me to do [verses 3,4].

> And now, O Father, glorify thou me with thine own self with the glory
> which I had with thee before the world was. I have manifested thy name
> unto the men who thou gavest me out of the world: thine they were, and
> thou gavest them me; and they have kept thy word [verses 5,6].

> Now they have known that all things whatsoever thou hast given me are
> of thee. For I have given unto them the words which thou gavest me;
> and they have received them, and have known surely that I came out
> from thee, and they have believed that thou didst send me [verses 7,8].

> I pray for them: I pray not for the world, but for them which thou
> hast given me; for they are thine. And all mine are thine, and thine are
> mine; and I am glorified in them. And now I am no more in the world,
> but these are in the world, and I come to thee. Holy Father, keep
> through thine own name those whom thou hast given me, that they
> may be one, as we are [verses 9-11].

> While I was with them in the world, I kept them in thy name: those
> that thou gavest me I have kept, and none of them is lost, but the son
> of perdition; that the scripture might be fulfilled. And now come I to
> thee; and these things I speak in the world, that they might have my
> joy fulfilled in themselves [verses 12,13].

I have given them thy word; and the world hath hated them, because they are not of the world, even as I am not of the world. I pray not that thou shouldst take them out of the world, but that thou shouldst keep them from the evil. They are not of the world, even as I am not of the world [verses 14-16].

Sanctify them through thy truth: thy word is truth. As thou hast sent me into the world, even so have I also sent them into the world. And for their sakes I sanctify myself, that they also might be sanctified through the truth. Neither pray I for these alone, but for them also who shall believe on me through their word [verses 17-20];

That they all may be one; as thou, Father, art in me, and I in thee, that they also may be one in us: that the world may believe that thou hast sent me. And the glory which thou gavest me I have given them; that they may be one, even as we are one [verses 21,22]:

I in them, and thou in me, that they may be made perfect in one; and that the world may know that thou hast sent me, and hast loved them, as thou hast loved me. Father, I will that they also, whom thou hast given me, be with me where I am; that they may behold my glory, which thou hast given me: for thou lovedst me before the foundation of the world [verses 23,24].

O righteous Father, the world hath not known thee: but I have known thee, and these have known that thou has sent me. And I have declared unto them thy name, and will declare it: that the love wherewith thou hast loved me may be in them, and I in them [verses 25,26].

Jesus Christ *is* the dividing line of truth versus falsehood. An individual human being is either for Him or against Him, the Scripture says. The world system, because it is fallen from man's rebellion in the Garden of Eden, opposes God and His Son, Jesus Christ. True unification or, better stated, "reunification," with the true God of heaven comes only through His beloved Son who died on Calvary's cross, the Lord Jesus Christ. Unity of any other sort is unacceptable in God's perfect eternal economy.

Today's talk of unity is anti-Christ at its black, festering core. This end-time onslaught of false teaching and false prophecies is rapidly moving this generation through great delusion toward the prophesied apostasy of 2 Thessalonians 2:3. It foreshadows the coming wrath of God.

Wars and Rumors of Wars

War has been a continuing plague within human interaction since the day Cain slew Abel. Rumors of wars are always with us because, as James wrote, "From whence come wars and fightings among you? Come they not hence, even of your lusts that war in your members?" (James 4:1).

The world's concept of peace is never true peace, but merely a lull between episodes of warfare. When so-called peace is enforced, threats of wars and murmurings of hostilities bubble just below the surface of civility. Jesus, in His Olivet Discourse on final prophecies, however, was talking about warfare that will come with greater frequency and ferocity the closer the end of this earth age comes. Wars, followed by rumors of wars, will come much like contractions increase for a woman who is about to give birth.

We do not have to go back very far in the historical record to document that we live in an age of such convulsive activity. Wars on a global scale are the ultimate manifestations of man's fallen nature, which cannot find peace apart from Christ's atonement. Natural man harbors violence capable of producing great destruction. One-on-one violence, families warring against each other, gang warfare in our cities, ethnic group against ethnic group—all these confirm that ours is a generation witnessing one of the key final prophecies foretold by Jesus Christ.

The frightening fact that mankind now possesses, through nuclear weaponry, the capability to destroy all life on earth is proof that God's prophetic Word is truth (see Mark 13:20). Recent resumption of nuclear testing, first by India, then, in retaliation, by Pakistan, foreshadows things to come. Diabolical regimes, particularly those in the Middle East, threaten devastation upon the whole world as their technology improves and progresses toward the point when missile delivery systems will be capable of hitting their nearest neighbors and *every* continent on earth. Not only do these tyrant-led governments seek nuclear capabilities, but they already possess warheads that can contain biological agents such as anthrax and other virulent, life-threatening microentities; nerve agents of great destructive potential; and other agents even more deadly that could be unleashed at any moment. Only the staying hand of God has thus far prevented wars of world-ending proportions. There is coming a time when God will remove His restraining hand and mankind's love affair with war and killing will bring the human race and all other flesh to the point of extinction. Remember, Jesus said that if He did not return, "no flesh should be saved" (Mark 13:20).

Thankfully, God Almighty will not permit His creation to be utterly destroyed by man. The Lord Jesus Christ will intervene and put an end to the violence. All who harbor murderous, warring intentions within their hearts will be locked forever in outer darkness when Christ judges and rules. *True* peace will at last permeate the planet as the Lord of lords and King of kings sits upon the throne of the millennial earth.

Famines, Pestilences, Earthquakes

Reports from around the world indicate that earthquakes, famines, pestilence and other phenomena are noticeably on the increase. Planet Earth seems to be suffering from labor contractions through geophysical and environmental upheavals of many sorts. Earthquakes, volcanoes, floods, droughts, hurricanes, typhoons, cyclones and tidal waves have, of course, always been an integral part of life on this planet. Instantaneous reporting of natural disasters also plays a part in adding to the perception that such phenomena are coming with greater frequency and intensity. Statistical studies by seismologists and other scientists show marked increases and troubling trends just within the past several decades. (See chapter 3 for a more in-depth look.) Documentation and research data tell the story that we live in an era of highly unusual geophysical turbulence.

To add to the turmoil are the discoveries of new viruses and bacteria, such as ebola and eboli, that threaten entire populations around the world. Pestilences of many sorts are on the rise. AIDS and other diseases also point to the probability that we live in a time in which the final prophecies of God's Word are beginning to unfold.

God's Word tells us that the Pharisees scolded Jesus while He rode the little donkey into Jerusalem, ordering Him to make the people stop praising Him as their Messiah. Jesus answered the Pharisees, saying that if the people remained silent, the very stones would cry out. Could it be that the more rebellious people become in our day, and the more this generation denies Jesus Christ, the more we are seeing all creation cry out His praise?

Signs in the Sun, Moon and Stars

When gigantic comet fragments slammed into Jupiter a few years ago and the resulting planetary carnage was recorded by earth's most powerful telescopes for all to see, concerns began to rise. What if such a thing happened to this planet? God's Word seems to indicate that something similar will happen when a mountainous flaming object crashes into one of earth's oceans. Jesus apparently was speaking about that future event and others equally catastrophic when He said in Luke 21:26 that men's hearts will fail them with fear for things they see coming upon the earth.

Since that Jupiter event, Hollywood has created a number of productions dealing with comets and meteors striking the earth. Science fiction has made the leap to reality with governments now jointly working on plans to use nuclear weapons to intercept such potentially catastrophic visitors while they are still far out in space.

Another "heavenly" phenomenon is on the rise. UFO sightings have become commonplace. Roswell, New Mexico, has become a household name because a puzzling crash of something took place in 1947. Quasi-documentaries and full-blown news reports direct our attention to the stars almost nightly. A recent report from Arizona said that hundreds of people, including airline pilots, saw gigantic UFOs, which then left the area at a high rate of speed when pursued by Air Force jets.

We have for many years been entertained by aliens, extraterrestrials and so forth. People report being buzzed, beeped, burned, abducted and probed by strange, small, gray creatures with large heads and big eyes. On a more logical level—and one more documentable—we view scenes on a daily basis that would have, until the late 1960s, been considered spectacular. Now space shuttles taking off and returning to earth, people in space suits walking on the outside of space stations and mechanical rovers moving about the surface of a planet more than 100 million miles away have become almost routine. We have, as a generation, indeed witnessed fearful signs in the sun, moon and stars.

Jesus, however, prophesied occurrences that will truly stagger those people alive on earth when the final prophecies about the sun, moon and stars come to pass. The book of Revelation has much to say about this. For example, the sun is prophesied to become as dark as sackcloth, the moon is predicted to turn blood red. The stars are prophesied to fall and the powers of heaven will be shaken.

It is not far-fetched to consider whether the many unusual things transpiring in our night skies (and even during daylight hours) might be the foreshadows of a great delusion that will come upon earth dwellers as prophesied in 2 Thessalonians: "And for this cause God shall send them strong delusion, that they should believe a lie" (2:11).

When the rapture of the church occurs, might the Antichrist and his system of propaganda proclaim that extraterrestrials or some great cosmic force has abducted those who disappeared—for the betterment of earth? While many who study prophecy feel it to be a bit too speculative to conjecture on such matters, we must conclude that because we are seeing strange signs in the sun, moon and stars, including weird sightings, the idea that Antichrist forces might offer such an explanation is within the realm of possibility.

In that vein, it seems likewise within the realm of possibility that the Lord's words, "as it was in the days of Noah, so it will be at the coming of the Son of Man," include fallen angels or demonic beings once again interacting with humanity like when, some biblical students believe, the "sons of god" took as wives the "daughters of men" (see Genesis 1–4).

Although much of the reporting of abductions and alien contact are mere Hollywood hype to generate interest in movies about aliens and extraterrestrials, it is still prudent to ask: Could such hyperbole help set up end-time mankind for the great satanic lie that will delude a large multitude of people during the time of apocalypse?

Distress of Nations with Perplexities

Economic factors plague nations of today's world, causing stresses and distresses for governments and citizenries alike. Technologies needed to compete in the growing global marketplace separate the "have" nations from the "have-not" nations as never before. Those who can afford the technologies continue to widen the gap between themselves and the poorer nations. Conflicts stem from such problems and grow to fully blossomed resentments and hatreds. Such economically depressed regions become ripe for the plucking by wicked regimes who use the seething discontent to build power bases, promising not only relief from poverty but, ultimately, great prosperity.

Great masses of people today are in poverty. China, India, most of Africa, South America, Central America, Mexico, vast areas of Russia and the former USSR eastern-bloc nations all harbor great populations of extreme deprivation. Most of these regions call upon the United States for assistance. For example, the International Monetary Fund (IMF) is expected by the world community to fund Russia's failing economy with "loans" amounting to billions of dollars. The world stock markets went wild in August 1998 when Russia's economy went into free-fall with the ruble losing most of its value. When that nation's leaders demanded billions to prop up Russia's economy, they were refused. This set in motion fears that the communists in the Duma might have a vehicle for moving toward a return to controlling power.

The ultimate fear, of course, revolves around the 22,000 nuclear warheads in Russia's arsenal. It is feared that the individual bosses controlling provincial power spheres might begin selling these weapons—or at least the enriched uranium from them—to tyrant states such as Iraq and Iran in order to gain funds to build their own provincial militaries.

What is not often revealed to the American public is the fact that the IMF is funded for the most part by the United States. America, however, is in bankruptcy for all practical purposes because of national debt that, despite what the economic planners say, is impossible to ever pay off. A smaller and smaller core of productive workers more and more support a welfare class that pays no taxes but to whom the government insanely contemplates giving tax breaks in the form of monetary rebates out of "fairness."

Revelation 13:14 tells the results of nations gone mad with distresses. The one called Antichrist will come to power offering peace and prosperity through brilliant stratagems that will restore order, particularly economic order. Obviously, the number and mark system of *electronic funds transfer* through computers will be part of this system for control purposes. That control will quickly turn into enslavement.

In order for us to sense the distress of nations to come, we have only to consider the growing concern over the year 2000 (Y2K) computer problem. Government, business and financial leaders express grave misgivings about their abilities to deal effectively with the *millennium bug.* So intertwined is the computer with our daily lives that it is no stretch at all to imagine a crisis of monumental magnitude caused by system failures in America and around the world. Likewise, it is easy to believe that an austere system of computer controls might be conceived and implemented to restore order.

We are seeing in our day foreshadows of the distress and perplexity of nations that will befall mankind during the time of God's wrath.

The Nations in Prophecy

Israel

World attention focuses on Israel today while most earthly powers seem to be arrayed against that nation. Despite the fact that Israel is infinitesimally small compared to the vast Middle East region, not just the PLO and Arab leaders such as Syria's Assad, but all leaders of all nations seem to be insisting that this tiny state give up even more land in the false peace process. Prophetic Scriptures state that conditions will become increasingly worse for Israel until the one called Antichrist, indwelt by Satan himself, perpetrates unparalleled persecution upon the Jews who are alive at the time the final prophecies come to pass.

America travels a dangerous path through the current administration's insistence that Israel give up more land to further a peace agenda. Economic pressures and threats of discontinuance of support in other areas is a dangerous game. More dangerous for America than for Israel, however. God says in His Word: "I will bless them that bless thee, and curse him that curseth thee" (Genesis 12:3). America's longevity as a powerful influential nation could well be linked to its treatment of Israel during these critical days ahead. Although the United States was instrumental in helping modern Israel come to birth in 1948, *God* gave that nation its new life just as the prophet Ezekiel foretold in the Ezekiel 37 account of the "valley of dry bones." God Almighty needs no help in protecting and sustaining those He chooses to protect and sustain.

America's leadership—at least the leadership within the current administration—seems to be of the opinion that American dollars should speak the final word on the Mideast peace process. The U.S. economy swells pridefully in a bubble of prosperity that apparently makes some feel this is a nation impervious to the economic destitution that afflicts much of the rest of the world. But the Lord hates a proud look (see Proverbs 6:16,17), and those who entertain such delusional notions should heed the words of George Santayana: "Those who cannot remember the past are condemned to repeat it." All we have to do is recall that one day in 1929 instantly changed the way of life for millions of people in America.

Israel is God's prophetic timepiece. It behooves us to keep close watch on that nation's intricate movements within the geopolitical mix. Each day Israel's interaction with the other nations of earth seems to move this generation one tick closer to that moment when Israel signs the "covenant with death and hell" (Isaiah 28:18). To be part of those exerting pressure that will ultimately force Israel into the deadly pseudo-peace pact with Antichrist (see Daniel 9:27) is to risk the direct wrath of a righteously jealous God. Israel's increasingly troubled interaction within the turbulent world of geopolitics is proof that foreshadows of God's wrath continue to boil ominously.

Russia

Post-Soviet Russia is more unstable than ever, harboring potential for military action that most expert observers of foreign affairs refuse to acknowledge. The Russian army continues to suffer collective depression since its fall from being the most powerful military machine on earth. Russian officers long for a return to those glory days. But the problem is bigger than that. Reliable sources report that Russian generals are barely in control of their troops, many of whom are alcoholics or drink heavily to forget their terrible plight. Most troops live at the poverty level or below, and their families often go without adequate food, clothing and housing. A number of Russian officers have committed suicide because their situations are no better than those of the troops under them. With Boris Yeltsin in poor health as of this writing, and his control over the Russian government uncertain because of the tremendous pressures being brought to bear upon him by the communists in the Duma, the Ezekiel 38 and 39 prophecies could come to pass in the very near future.

These passages indicate a horde led by *Gog,* the chief prince of Rosh (Russia), will storm over the *mountains of Israel to take great spoil.* The attack will take place in the *latter times* and will be opposed only by a note of protest from a Western power bloc of unknown composition.

Alliances formed between Russia and the pan-Islamic union seem to fit the pattern of the prophesied Gog-Magog force that God Himself will bring into the Middle East toward Israel. The one the Scriptures call *Gog* will no doubt conceive the "evil thought" when he considers the vast oil and mineral riches as well as the warm water ports of that region. It is interesting that at present there is great anticipation in some quarters of major oil strikes near the southeast end of the Dead Sea. The current situation points to the fact that the whole region to the extreme north of Israel is a tinderbox that could kindle a fire of aggression at any moment. This could spark one of the major prophecies given in God's Word (read the Gog-Magog references in Ezekiel 38 and 39).

While Russia appears to be struggling to be a responsible world citizen and to achieve status equal to its position when it led the USSR, it nonetheless throws fuel on the fire of raging hostilities in the Middle East and elsewhere by selling weapons—including nuclear arms—to even the worst of tyrants in power today. Russia's membership in the G-8 and NATO cannot disguise the fact that much of its leadership continues to think like those who harshly ran the Soviet empire. Neither should America's leaders be deceived into thinking Russian missiles, both land-based and submarine-based, are pointed in directions other than toward the United States. Russia is a very hungry bear upon which the wise should keep a wary eye.

Rising Sun Nations

China and the other nations of the Orient have always seemed mysterious, even unknowable, to most of us in the Occidental world. Not so as of late. China in particular seems to be aggressively pursuing contact with the West for the obvious purposes of obtaining Western technology and gaining Western markets. At the same time, China is building a military of superpower class. No other nation in the region more aptly fits the description implied within the biblically prophetic term "kings of the east."

Controversy abounds about the possibility of problematic activities by foreign governments and citizens at the very highest levels of American government. The troubling questions range from influence-peddling through political contributions to overt espionage involving such nations as China and Indonesia, as well as others. At the very moment President Bill Clinton met with Chinese Communist leaders in Tiananmen Square, where hundreds of student protestors were murdered in prodemocracy demonstrations a few years ago, evidence was building at home in the United States that administration-approved sales of military-applicable missile and satellite technologies to China pose a direct threat to America's security. These serious allegations, if true, might hasten the formation of the military force scheduled to storm out of that vast Oriental region of the world to do battle at Armageddon.

European Union

With the implementation of the Maastricht Treaty January 1, 1999, which marked Europe's coming together as a single economic power, a major final prophecy seems to be on the brink of fulfillment. Nebuchadnezzar's dream of the huge metallic man statue and Daniel's interpretation of the king's dream could soon take on tremendous significance for our generation. (See Daniel 2.)

The European Union (EU) in one day became a stupendous economic power. And because money rules this world, the EU also became the world's greatest power. Experts predict that Europe will now control approximately 46 percent of the world's bond market, with America controlling about 32 percent. Certainly the changes and restructuring taking place throughout the world are staggering. The reviving Roman Empire is in evidence everywhere in the world today. The "ten kings" power base, which Antichrist will enjoy according to Revelation 17:12,13, might be very near completion by the time the euro, Europe's single monetary unit, is instituted.

Whether these ten kings are ten nations out of the revived Roman Empire, ten gigantic world trading blocs or something else, the Maastricht factor will cause dynamic rearrangement in global economic power spheres. Whether those rearrangements bring about stability or chaos remains to be seen. It is fascinating to consider these world-shaking matters in light of Revelation 13 and the fact that planet Earth is on the brink of a new millennium. We can see the foreshadowing of those ten kings who will give their power and authority to the beast. (See Revelation 17:12,13.)

Present-day power brokers make decisions from their elevated positions in the economic stratosphere of world finance. At the risk of being dubbed a conspiracy nut, I believe it is reasonable to give credit where credit is due. Those who are behind the world bank are the same globalist elite who are in the highest echelon of the Tri-Lateral Commission, the Council on Foreign Relations, the International Monetary Fund and so on. These organizations and people control the forward motion of earth's money movement. They speed it up, they throttle it back. They manipulate and cajole. Most likely it is from this strata that the ten kings of Revelation 17:12,13 will come. They no doubt will believe they have almost a divine right to control finance because they alone have the intellectual power as well as the economic power to act in the best interest of mankind. These people, whoever they are at the time the prophecies of Revelation 13 are played out, will no doubt be in complete agreement with the man they believe to be the greatest world leader ever to appear on the scene—the beast of Revelation. They will give all their economic power and governmental authority to him.

More and more, it appears that now might be the time in human history when Antichrist's platform of power is being constructed. From that power base, he will speak great prideful words that promise peace and prosperity to a desperate and chaotic generation of earth dwellers. Developments within New Europe and the world economic power circles in general might well be contributing to what is looking like the last-days flood predicted by Daniel the prophet.

Perilous Times

In 2 Timothy 3, Paul makes predictions characterizing individuals who will populate the world during an era he describes as "perilous times." He paints a bleak picture indeed. Those people are predicted to, according to Paul's writing, grow worse and worse, deceiving and being deceived. While we might have trouble believing that mankind can get much worse based upon the horror stories coming out of the world news sources, Jesus foretold that the last seven years of man's history just before His return will be more terrible than any time ever known on earth. Our daily newspapers and nightly newscasts report murders, rapes, thefts and every other type of crime, but what we are seeing today is but a precursor of a truly savage era.

Vast documentation could easily be accessed to prove that this present generation of earth dwellers has among its numbers those who are lovers of self, proud, boasters, blasphemers, undisciplined, fierce, heady, high-minded, without natural affection, lovers of pleasure more than lovers of God, having a form of godliness but denying the power thereof. We are already experiencing in this day the types of heinous behavior God's Word says will dominate during the time of apocalypse.

Man's inhumanity to man makes mockery of the much bally-hooed theory of evolution, which is almost a religious system worshiped by the pseudo-intellectuals of our time. People are not getting better and better, as the evolutional model projects, but are growing worse and worse just as God's Word prophesied. We did not come from an amoebic-type spot of slime that crawled out of a primordial swamp. Man has not metamorphosed from a single cell and evolved through all these various stages of evolution to the point we are now—allegedly—the highest order destined to progress toward godhood and perfection. We were created perfectly by the Creator of all things, Jesus Christ preincarnate, but since the rebellious act of disobedience and the fall in the Garden of Eden, humanity is becoming more and more debased.

Sin-induced insanity is evident everywhere. Southern Sudan, for example, has become so bad that, according to reliable sources, hundreds of thousands of people, particularly Christians, have been murdered for their faith. Such things as crucifixions, live burials, and children being murdered so that the killers can harvest, then sell, their organs around the world are apparently part of everyday life in that region. The United Nations and even America seem to be turning a blind eye. Apparently it has become so bad that refugees from Sudan have fled to Ethiopia for relief.

Again, Jesus foretold that times worse than any ever experienced in our history will occur during the great tribulation. This is an awesome prediction when considered against the background of the historical record that reveals the horrors of millions of martyrs falling in the time of the Dark Ages, Hitler's regime, Stalin's purges, and Mao's genocide.

Developing Antichrist Technologies

All we have to do in order to realize the swiftness with which technology is advancing is to consider that the computer we buy today for our home or business is well on its way to being obsolete by the time we learn how to use it. It is hard to imagine how computers and collateral technologies can advance much beyond their current sophistication, but that is what people have said throughout the ages about every revolutionary invention. Revelation 13 clearly prophesied the use of computers and other devices for controlling people that will be advanced far beyond even the amazing current technology. Those rapidly advancing technologies foreshadow troubling times ahead for earth's inhabitants. For example, triangulation tracking through computers and low-orbit global positioning satellites, ostensibly for assisting police in their work to fight crime, can locate objects, animals or people with astounding accuracy. Biochip sensors are already being used by implanting transponders beneath the skin to keep tabs on fish, birds and other wild as well as domestic animals. It's even possible that some parents have had such devices implanted in their children to thwart possible kidnapping attempts. Implanting microchips that contain complete financial, medical and personal information dossiers is already within the realm of possibility.

Antichrist's system of such intrusion will be infinitely greater in scope, according to Revelation 13. The beast's control technology is one of the major prophecies destined to contribute to the perilous times predicted by Paul. (Read chapter 13 for an in-depth look at where that developing technology stands at present.)

Rescue from the Flood

Although God promised mankind that He would never again destroy the world by a water flood (Genesis 9:12-17), Jesus nonetheless said of the very end of human history: "But as the days of Noah were, so shall also the coming of the Son of man be" (Matthew 24:37). Daniel the prophet said, "...and the end thereof shall be with a flood..." (Daniel 9:26), equating the deluge of events that would bombard end-time man symbolically to a literal flood. Those prophesied terrors of judgment are scheduled to cascade like a horrendous avalanche upon this anti-God, anti-Christ world of unbelievers during the last seven years that will consummate human history.

All authors in this book truly believe we are presently at a critical moment in God's prophetic timeline. Our collective desire is to hold God's magnifying glass over the issues and events of our day, exposing them to the light of God's unerring truth and His Holy Word, the Bible, so that many people will be drawn by God's Holy Spirit to Jesus Christ—the only true source of salvation. Jesus said, "And when these things begin to come to pass, then look up, and lift up your heads; for your redemption draweth nigh" (Luke 21:28).

Each person who accepts Jesus Christ as Savior and Lord, whether he or she has died during this Church Age or is living when Christ calls us to meet Him in the air at the rapture, will escape God's terrible judgment during the seven-year tribulation period. For if you "confess with thy mouth the Lord Jesus, and...believe in thine heart that God hath raised him from the dead, thou shalt be saved" (Romans 10:9)—saved from the wrath to come (see 1 Thessalonians 5:9).

Accept Christ this moment—then you need not fear the stormy end-time events flooding this generation. Jesus will bring peace to your heart that will dissipate those foreshadows of wrath and highlight the foreshadows of redemption—injecting your soul with a taste of heaven, your joyous, eternal destination.

▼ ▼ ▼

Part 1

Jesus' Olivet
Forewarnings

CHAPTER 1

False Christs, False Prophets, Great Deception

Ed Hindson

For more than a year, David Koresh had predicted an armed confrontation with federal agents. He even nicknamed his compound "Ranch Apocalypse." In a paranoid frenzy, the Branch Davidians had bought or bartered for $200,000 worth of weapons, thousands of rounds of ammunition and a grenade launcher. The initial FBI raid had been met with such a flurry of bullets that federal agents decided to send heavily armed tanks against the compound to break through the walls and insert massive injections of tear gas into the buildings starting at 6:04 A.M., April 19, 1993.

The tank incursions were met with volleys of gunfire. Inside the compound, the Branch Davidians donned gas masks and prepared for an apocalyptic confrontation with the "enemies of God." FBI spokesman Bob Ricks explained, "We were hoping by the infusion of gas into that compound that the women would grab their children and flee."[1] Instead, they all "bunkered down," put on gas masks and tried to withstand the siege.

The tanks rammed the building five times between 6:04 and noon. At 12:05, flames erupted from the opposite ends of the compound and were whipped by 20 to 30 mile-an-hour winds. Within minutes the entire compound was ablaze. By 12:18, the watchtower collapsed. Shortly thereafter, the ammunitions room exploded in a ball of fire. And by 12:28, the second floor was engulfed in flames and the roof collapsed. The blazing flames and dark smoke billowed across the Texas sky. Only nine of Koresh's followers managed to escape or survive the fire. Arguments persisted for some time as to whether the inferno was the result of a mass suicide, an accident or an act of desperate self-destruction. But the whole terrible mess was the end result of a false prophet whose deceived followers perished for a lie.

A false prophet is one who contradicts the true message of Christ, as well as one whose predictions fail to come true. David Koresh was guilty on both counts. A typically self-deceived extremist cult leader, Koresh perished with nearly 90 of his followers in the flames of Ranch Apocalypse. And in Matthew 23:27-33, Jesus Christ warned there is a worse fate for false prophets: They will not escape the fires of hell!

Jesus spoke often of false prophets and spiritual deception. He told His disciples that spiritual truth could be recognized by its fruits. Then He added, "Not everyone who says to me, 'Lord, Lord,' will enter the kingdom of heaven....Many will say to me on that day, 'Lord, Lord, did we not prophesy in your name, and in your name drive out demons and perform many miracles?' Then I will tell them plainly, 'I never knew you. Away from me, you evildoers!'" (Matthew 7:21-23). One might expect false prophets and extremist cults to arise from non-Christian religions that reject Jesus Christ. But when false cults arise from within Christianity, it is especially disturbing. The New Testament, however, is filled with warnings about heretics, false prophets and false prophecies. Even in apostolic times, the apostle John wrote, "Dear children, this is the last hour; and as you have heard that the antichrist is coming, even now many antichrists have come....They went out from us, but they did not really belong to us" (1 John 2:18,19).

Masters of Deceit

The Bible describes Satan as the "father of lies" (John 8:44). He is pictured in Scripture as the ultimate deceiver; his name means "accuser." He is the accuser of God and His people (Revelation 12:10). He is opposed to God and seeks to alienate people from the truth. He misled the fallen angels (Matthew 25:41; Revelation 12:4). He tempts men and women to sin (Genesis 3:1-13; 1 Timothy 6:9). He denies and rejects the truth of God and deceives those who are perishing without God (2 Thessalonians 2:10). Ultimately, he "inspires" the false prophets and the very spirit of antichrist (1 John 2:18-23).

The Bible clearly warns us that in the last days people will "abandon the faith and follow deceiving [*seducing* (KJV)] spirits and things [*doctrines* (KJV)] taught by demons" (1 Timothy 4:1). These false teachings will come through hypocritical liars whose minds have been captured by Satan's lies. Thus, the process of spiritual deception is clearly outlined in Scripture:

The term *angel* (Greek, *angelos*) means "messenger." God's angels are His divine messengers (Hebrews 1:14; Revelation 1:1), and His true prophets and preachers are called the angels of the churches (Revelation 2:1,8,12,18; 3:1,7,14). By contrast, Satan is pictured as a fallen angel, the leader of other fallen angels and the one who deceives the whole world (Revelation 12:9). He is revealed as the ultimate power behind the Antichrist and the false prophet, who deceives mankind with false religion (Revelation 13:14). Thus, the messengers of deceit are Satan-inspired false prophets and teachers whose messages are the very spirit of antichrist (1 John 2:18).

The Process of Deception

The lure of false doctrine is that it presents itself as the truth. It appears as a corrective measure to established doctrine. It is propagated by those who are certain they have discovered some new revelation of truth or a better interpretation of old, established truth. Either way, they are convinced they are right and everyone else is wrong.

That is Satan's oldest trick. He appeals to our *self-conceit* and leads us into *self-deceit*. When he first approached Eve, Satan questioned the integrity of God's command and appealed to her selfish desire to be like God. It was that same desire that had led to his own fall in the first place. And there is something selfish enough in all of us to want to believe that we can know what no one else knows. C.S. Lewis said,

> What Satan put into the heads of our remote ancestors was the idea that they could "be like gods."... And out of that hopeless attempt has come nearly all that we can call human history... the long terrible story of man trying to find something other than God which will make him happy.[2]

One does not have to look hard to find expression of self-centeredness in most cult leaders: Father Divine said he was God. David Koresh claimed to be Jesus Christ. Sun Myung Moon says he is "Lord of the Universe." Joseph Smith claimed to receive angelic revelations. Mary Baker Eddy believed her book, *Key to the Scriptures,* was inspired of God. Herbert W. Armstrong claimed his church was the only one on earth proclaiming "the very same gospel that Jesus taught and proclaimed."

Once the false teacher falls into the illusion that he or she alone is God's messenger and has a corner on His truth, spiritual deception is inevitable. Mary Baker Eddy, the founder of Christian Science, was so convinced she was right that she said, "Today the healing power of Truth is widely demonstrated as an imminent, eternal science....[Its] coming as was promised by the Master is for its establishment as a permanent dispensation among men."[3] She believed that her "discovery" of Christian Science fulfilled the promise of Jesus' second coming!

In the preface to her *Key to the Scriptures,* Mrs. Eddy said of herself, "Since the author's discovery of the might of Truth in the treatment of disease as well as of sin, her system has been fully tested and has not been found wanting."[4] It is difficult to imagine the sincerity of such self-conceit and spiritual arrogance. The only logical explanation is that she really thought she was right.

Once *spiritual deception* sets in, it leads to *spiritual darkness.* It is not long before the deceived cult leader begins to espouse heretical doctrine. Since he or she acknowledges no one else as God's spokesperson, traditional and orthodox concepts may be challenged or even disregarded. Pride and arrogance are the sins that lead a person to become spiritually deceived. These sins take us to the second stage of spiritual deception. Satan tempts us with our own self-centeredness and lures us into spiritual darkness with the bait of our own pride. We really want to believe we are right and everybody else is wrong. The Bible calls it the "pride of life" (1 John 2:16 NASB).

Having been hooked by our arrogance, we are reeled in by our ignorance. Most people who fall into the trap of false doctrine are ignorant of the implications of their views. Hank Hanegraaff illustrates this in his epic work *Christianity in Crisis.*[5] In exposing serious doctrinal flaws, Hanegraaff states that many sincere preachers get off the theological track, but don't know enough theology to realize their error.

The problems arise when false teachers love their erroneous teachings to the point they will not repent of them even when their error is exposed. This is what leads to *spiritual blindness.* The willful rejection of the truth results in the mind being blinded by Satan. The

Bible says, "They are darkened in their understanding and separated from the life of God because of the ignorance that is in them due to the hardening of their hearts" (Ephesians 4:18). Scripture further explains that Satan himself is the source of spiritual darkness: "The god of this age has blinded the minds of unbelievers, so that they cannot see the light of the gospel of the glory of Christ, who is the image of God" (2 Corinthians 4:4).

Once theological error falls into "ecclesiastical cement" it is virtually impossible to eliminate it. When false doctrine is accepted by an organized religious body, it will be perpetrated by a false defense (apologetic) based upon a false premise. If I honestly believe my dog is a reincarnation of my Uncle Joe, I will look for every possible proof of Uncle Joe's personality in my dog's behavior. When a whole group of followers accept false doctrine as truth, they will organize it, categorize it and systematize it. But that doesn't make it true!

The Cultic Paradigm

All cult logic is built on the same faulty premise: "We alone know the truth." Believing themselves to have discovered truth that is unknown to others, cultists assume they have a corner on that truth. The cultic paradigm works like this:

> We alone know the truth of God;
> therefore,
> we alone are the people of God.

Other variations of the cultic paradigm derive from this original premise. For example, if we alone know the truth, then all others are in error. If we alone are the people of God, then all others are heretics. If people reject our message, they are rejecting God's message. If people persecute us, they are persecuting the cause of God because our cause is God's cause. Since we are right, and others are wrong, our church is the only true church.

Basic Traits

While schismatic cults exist in every religion from Lubavitcher Jews to Muslim extremists, they all have certain characteristics in common.

> **Extrabiblical Revelation:**
> "We have a special message from God."

Every religious cult has a sacred book translation, set of writings, key to interpretation, and perhaps visions, dreams or voices to validate its beliefs. Muslims believe the Koran is God's final revelation to man through the Prophet Muhammed. Mormons look at *The Book of Mormon* as equally inspired as the Bible. Jehovah's Witnesses recognize only their New World Translation of the Bible. Seventh-day Adventists recognize Ellen G. White as an inspired prophet of God. Christian Science reveres Mary Baker Eddy's *Science and Health with Key to the Scriptures* as divinely inspired.

While some cultic religions have gone so far as to produce and sanction their own sacred books, others have not. Instead, they claim allegiance to the Bible, but insist that their interpretation is the only spiritually valid understanding of Scripture. The Way International founder Victor Paul Wierwille claims, "God spoke to me audibly, just like I'm talking to you now. He said he would teach me the word as it had not been known since the first century."[6] By contrast, *The Way* magazine condemns the so-called Christian church as being built essentially upon manmade doctrine and tradition.[7] Thus, Josh McDowell and Don Stewart conclude, "The Way International believes Victor Paul Wierwille has the only true interpretation of the Scriptures and is the only one who can lead fellow Bible students out of the confusion in which traditional Christianity has engulfed them."[8]

The Children of God (COG), also known as the Family of Love, recognize David Berg as "prophet and King" and his "Mo letters" as

God's truth. Berg himself has said, "My letters mean exactly what they say, literally, and they don't need explaining away, spiritualizing or reinterpreting by any one."[9] One of Berg's early prophecies concerned an impending earthquake in California in the early seventies that never came to pass, yet he was revered by COG members as "God's prophet and King." Later revelations of sexual relations with his own daughters and other cult members only caused Berg to use his letters to defend his practices.[10]

The Church of Bible Understanding, originally known as the Forever Family, is an example of a Bible-based cult. Founded in 1971 in Allentown, Pennsylvania, and headed by Stewart Traill, this religious group uses orthodox Christian terminology loaded with very unorthodox meanings. Cult observers Una McManus and John Cooper state that Traill's "understanding" of the Bible and its concealed meanings ("figures") are accepted as authoritative for cult members. They note that the group has "declared war on the powers of this world, including government, police, schools, parents, and churches."[11]

The Church of Armageddon, also known as the Love Family, looks to the vision of its members, including founder Paul Erdmann (also known as "Love Israel"), as its divine authority. Members renounce all worldly traditions of matrimony and are considered to be married to one another.[12]

In each of these examples, the words, visions or writings of a human leader are made equal to the Bible. In some cases they are looked upon as being of even greater authority than Scripture itself. Whenever someone claims to have a new revelation from God, he or she is making the same claim Muhammad made for the Koran and Joseph Smith made for *The Book of Mormon.*

Presumptuous Leadership:
"I know what is best for you."

Not every cult leader is dangerous, but every one is presumptuous. Cult leaders think they alone have God's ultimate message for mankind. Therefore, in their minds, it becomes an absolute necessity that they deliver God's message at all costs and eliminate whatever opposition they face in doing so. Branch Davidian cult leader David Koresh's demand that his 58-minute "message to the world" be aired on radio in Waco, Texas, is typical of such a mind-set.

Early descriptions of David Koresh's and Jim Jones' backgrounds show striking similarities: broken homes, parental neglect, desire for power and control, excessive sexual appetites and the constant demand for loyalty and allegiance from their followers. Jim Jones and David Koresh may be extreme examples of dictatorial cult leaders, but they are not that far removed from the excessive behaviors of Sun Myung Moon, who dictates the marriages to total strangers of thousands of his followers, or David Berg, who authorized incest within the Children of God. Like this statement from the egotistical Reverend Ike, who said, "You can't lose with the stuff I use," the blasphemous and extravagant claims of deluded cult leaders are incredible. Here are just a few:

Judge Rutherford (Jehovah's Witnesses): "Jesus Christ has returned to earth A.D. 1914 to establish the Theocratic Millennial Kingdom" (*The Kingdom,* 1933). The world is still awaiting this revelation.

Mary Baker Eddy (Christian Science): "Death is an illusion" (*Science and Health,* 584:9). She succumbed to that illusion on December 3, 1910.

Father Divine (Peace Mission): "I am God Almighty...the Holy Spirit personified...the Prince of Peace" (*New Day,* July 16, 1949). "God" (George Baker, alias Father Divine) died in 1965.

Elijah Muhammad (Black Muslims): "Wallace Farad [Muslim version of Father Divine] is God himself! He is the one we have been looking for the last 2,000 years" (*New York Herald Tribune,* April 3, 1963). Wallace Farad (alias Allah) disappeared in 1934 and was never seen again.

Elizabeth Clare Prophet (Church Universal and Triumphant): "I am that I am" (*Teachings on the Path of Enlightenment*). She claims to be the channel of the "Great White Brotherhood" of "Ascended

Masters." She and her followers are awaiting the end of the world in Montana.

Meher Baba (Sufism Reoriented): "I am Jesus Christ personified" (*Parvardigar*). Baba died on January 31, 1969.

Sun Myung Moon (Unification Church): "Jesus Christ will return by being born in the flesh in Korea as Lord of the Second Advent and True Parent of the world family" (*Divine Principle,* pp. 501ff.). Moon considers himself to be the Messiah incarnate.

David Berg (Children of God): "Forget not thy King.... Forsake not His ways, for He hath the key, even the Key of David! Therefore, thou shalt kiss the mouth of David. For thou art enamored of my words and thou art in love with me, thy Savior!" (*The Kingdom: A Prophecy,* August 20, 1971, Lo. No. 94). Berg is revered as King, Father and David by his followers.

John Robert Stevens (The Walk): "We are going to turn and become the savior of the Church" (*Living Word,* July 6, 1975). Steven's followers denounce all churches but their own as the "harlot of Babylon."

Herbert W. Armstrong (Worldwide Church of God): "We grow spiritually more and more like God, until at the time of the resurrection— we shall then be born of God—we shall then be God" (*The U.S. and British Commonwealth,* p. 9).

David Koresh (Branch Davidians): "I am the Lamb of God" (*People,* March 15, 1993, p. 41). He died April 19, 1993.

> **Exclusive Salvation:**
> "We alone are the people of God;
> all other are lost."

This one criteria separates cults from denominations. Various Christian denominations may differ on their methods of ordination, their mode of baptism or their form of church government, but they generally don't consign each other to hell because of those differences. Cults, on the other hand, are always convinced they are the only ones going to heaven. All others are lost, damned, heretical or have the mark of the beast!

Jehovah's Witnesses believe that the Church Age ended in 1914 with the return of Christ to earth. Therefore, they do not meet in churches, but in Kingdom Halls. They say that only Jehovah's faithful witnesses (the 144,000) know and believe the truth—all others are lost. They clearly teach that only faithful Jehovah's Witnesses (both the "remnant" and the "other sheep") will survive the battle of Armageddon and see the salvation of Jehovah.[13]

Mormons believe they alone are the "latter-day saints" of God. Brigham Young said, "Every spirit that does not confess that God has sent Joseph Smith, and revealed the everlasting gospel to and through him, is of antichrist."[14] Speaking of non-Mormon Christian churches, Mormon apostle Orson Pratt said, "They have nothing to do with Christ, neither has Christ anything to do with them, only to pour out upon them the plagues."[15]

Seventh-day Adventists believe that the third angel's message in Revelation 14 requires the observance of Saturday Sabbath-keeping in order to guarantee eternal life. They allow that some Christians may live and die in ignorance of the third angel's message, and thus be given another chance to receive it at a special resurrection. But all who refuse will suffer annihilation.[16]

Christian Science founder Mary Baker Eddy said, "A Christian Scientist requires my work *Science and Health* for his textbook… because it is the voice of truth to this age… uncontaminated by human hypotheses."[17] In the glossary of *Science and Health,* the true church is defined as "that institution which affords proof of the apprehension of spiritual ideas and the demonstration of divine science."[18] Since Christian Science views itself as unerring and divine, it presumes that all other churches are erroneous.

Spiritualism declares it is the "highest message of truth which we have as yet grown to grasp."[19] Sir Arthur Conan Doyle said, "Spiritualism is the greatest revelation the world has ever known."[20] But Spiritualism (or spiritism), with its emphasis on communicating with departed spirits, has always opposed every major doctrine of Christianity (inspiration of the Bible, deity of Christ, the virgin birth, the atonement, and the resurrection) as anathema. Lord Dowling, a strong spiritualist advocate, said, "The doctrine of the Trinity seems to have no adherent in advance circles of the spirit world."[21]

Swedenborgians believe that Christ returned in the eighteenth century when their founder received what they claim to be the key to the interpretation of Scripture. They also believe Christ designated them alone to be the "New Jerusalem."[22] Following the highly speculative ideas of Emanuel Swedenborg, this small but influential cult claims to be the church signified by the New Jerusalem of the apocalypse. The rest of professing Christianity is viewed as "perverted from the truth."[23]

The Worldwide Church of God, under Herbert W. Armstrong and Garner Ted Armstrong, denounced all trinitarians as false prophets. They denounce all other churches as preaching a false gospel and a false Christ. They accuse others of "stupendous errors," "false conceptions," and "spiritual blindness."[24] Today, under the leadership of Joseph Tkach, the Worldwide Church of God has repudiated the Armstrong view.

The Unification Church (Moonies) teaches that Sun Myung Moon is the second messiah ("Lord of the Second Advent") sent to complete the work of salvation begun by Jesus Christ. Moon says of himself and his church, "No heroes in the past, no saints or holy men in the past, like Jesus or Confucius have excelled us."[25] Emphasizing his church exclusively, Moon claims, "We are the only people who truly understand the heart of Jesus, and the hope of Jesus."[26]

Once the process of spiritual deception reaches the point where the cultists believe they alone are God's people, then it follows logically that whatever they believe must be God's truth. By contrast, then, all who disagree with them are viewed as lost or deceived. Their belief that they have an exclusive corner on truth leads them to think they also have an exclusive corner on salvation.

> **Limited Eschatology:**
> "Jesus is coming only for us;
> we alone will be spared."

It was this "we are right; all others are wrong" mentality that enabled the followers of David Koresh to surrender their wives and daughters to him for sexual purposes. It also opened the door for them to contradict the clear teaching of Jesus against self-retaliation and take up arms to kill people in the name of God. It was this same mentality that provoked Muslim extremists from the Al-Salam Mosque in Jersey City, New Jersey, to bomb the World Trade Center in the name of God.

Christian-based cults have often begun as a result of some prophetic date-setting scheme. In most cases these eschatological prognosticators were sincere in their belief that Christ would soon return. However, when things did not work out the way they expected, they soon devised other explanations for their foiled mistakes.

In 1870, Charles T. Russell became influenced by Adventist teacher Jonas Wendell in Pittsburgh, Pennsylvania. Sparked with a renewed interest in the second coming of Christ, Russell organized a Bible class, began teaching and started publishing a magazine called *Zion's Watchtower and Herald of Christ's Presence*. By 1881, Russell incorporated Zion's Watchtower Tract Society. By 1886, he began publishing a seven-volume series entitled MILLENNIAL DAWN, later called STUDIES IN THE SCRIPTURES.

Following the ideas of N.H. Barbour, Russell initially taught that Christ would return spiritually, not physically, in 1874 and finish the end-time harvest by 1914, the dawn of the millennial age. By correlating historical events with the length of the corridors in the Great Pyramid of Egypt, Russell confirmed his 1874 date for the beginning of the tribulation. Modern Jehovah's Witnesses reject Russell's calculation in favor of 1914. Cult expert Ronald Enroth observes, "To accommodate the change, a new edition of Russell's STUDIES (1923) simply added forty-one inches to the corridor's length in order to locate the starting point for the final years of earth's existence in 1914."[27]

Since there was no visible appearance of Christ in 1914, Jehovah's Witnesses believe He revealed Himself only to His faithful witnesses (the 144,000). Initially, Jehovah's Witnesses emphasized that when that number was complete (presumably around 1918), Christ would reveal to the world that He was already here. Today, they teach that there are two classes of followers: 1) The "congregation of God," the true church of Jehovah, and 2) the "great crowd" or "other sheep." The first group is limited to the 144,000 and will live in heaven, while the latter group is larger and will live on earth after Armageddon.[28]

Jehovah's Witnesses teach that they are the 144,000 "associate kings" who will rule with Christ in the millennium. They believe they are the only ones who know the truth that Christ returned on October 1, 1914, and ended the Church Age and the rule of nations. Hence, they recognize no church but their own and will not salute the flag of any nation. They also believe they alone will survive the battle of Armageddon and enter the millennium as God's true people.

Mormons also believe they hold a special place at the time of Christ's return. Calling themselves the Latter-day Saints, Mormons believe the time of the end is at hand and will culminate in the regathering of Israel in Jerusalem, the regathering of Ephraim (Mormons) at Zion (Independence, Missouri), and the regathering of the ten lost tribes to Zion. Mormons believe they will build the Temple of God in North America and recapture Zion from the Reorganized Church of Latter-day Saints (who hold title to the temple property in Independence after a split from the group that went on to Salt Lake City).

Mormons also believe they will be regathered first since Joseph Smith was a "pure Ephraimite," and the Ephraimites (Mormons) now hold the priesthood, having received the "fullness of the everlasting gospel" in these last days. They also believe that only faithful

Mormons will enter the celestial kingdom (God's highest eternal order) and live eternally with their wives and children and continue to procreate more children in that celestial state. In other words, Mormons believe they hold center stage in God's eschatological program.

Moonies believe that all humanity will literally be saved by Sun Myung Moon, "Lord of the Second Advent." Even departed Christians will return to earth and serve the new messiah in the "True Family" of eternity. "Everybody who ever lived," notes Jack Sparks in *The Mind Benders,* "good, bad, and indifferent—will participate in that great unified family formed around Moon, his wife and his children." Sparks then adds, "What malarkey! This is one of the most amazing schemes a human being has ever devised to deceive people and to bring them under oppressive domination."[29]

Notice again how one lie leads to another: We alone have the truth; we know what is best for you; we alone are the people of God; we alone will be in heaven. It is this kind of logic that sets up the ultimate conclusion: *All who are against us are against God.* Once the cultist is thus deceived, he or she becomes willing to do almost anything to protect the group from the enemy.

> ### Persecution Complex:
> "The world is against us because we have the truth."

One does not have to look far to find plenty of examples of the cultic-persecution complex. David Koresh carried a Glock 9mm pistol and kept an arsenal of deadly weapons at his disposal because he believed the "agents of Satan" were about to attack him and launch the final battle of Armageddon.[30] Expecting a soon-to-come apocalypse, Koresh's Branch Davidians fortified their Mount Carmel complex outside Waco, Texas, to prepare for the end of the world.

Sheik Oman Abdel-Rahman told his Muslim followers to "kill the enemies of God in every spot to rid it of the descendants of apes and pigs fed at the tables of zionism, communism and imperialism."[31] Like a true cult leader, Abdel-Rahman assumes that his enemies are God's enemies as well.

There is little difference in the attitude of many of the more traditional or institutionalized cults. Down deep, they know they are different or out of step with traditional beliefs, so they expect to be rejected. Think of the abuse and rejection Mormons and Jehovah's Witnesses must experience as they go door to door to peddle their beliefs. "Jesus warned us that we would be persecuted," they say, almost inviting more persecution.

Institutionalized cults may have been started by fanatics, but as they grew, their leadership diversified and with time came to develop theological explanations for why they are persecuted. But in today's extremist cults, where the leader has a small but radical following, any rejection of the leader may result in direct hostility.

A nomadic cult founded by Jimmie T. Roberts of Kentucky has no name and wanders from place to place, often eating out of garbage cans. Nicknamed "the garbage eaters," they have left in their wake a trail of broken homes, battered women and abused children.[32] Believing that children are too young to know God, they assume little ones are "ruled by Satan." This mentality then assumes that unruly children are agents of the devil and need to have the devil beaten out of them.

Jim Jones was so paranoid because of his sinful lifestyle and unlawful activities that he knew intuitively he was in trouble. So he devised a scheme of moving around the country to avoid police investigators. Finally, when he wanted to avoid the federal government, he moved his flock to Guyana. There in the sticky South American jungle, he armed his men with guns, laced everyone's Kool-Aid with cyanide, and prepared for an inevitable confrontation with the outside world—a confrontation that cost the lives of more than 900 people.

Spiritual deception is a gradual, subtle process. Satan, the great deceiver, convinces the cult leader that he has found the truth no one else has ever discovered. Armed with this egotistical ammunition, the cultist begins to weave a web of religious deception. He first falls victim to it himself, then he convinces others that he is right and manipulates their resources to further spread his message. In time, this leads to oppressive organizational controls to ensure this process continues.

God is against false prophets whose spiritual delusion causes them to invent their own message apart from God's truth. The Bible presents them in seven categories:

1. *Self-deceived.* Some false teachers may be sincere, but they are still wrong. They have deceived themselves into believing their messages are true. As Jeremiah points out, their messages come psychologically from within their own minds and are not from God.

2. *Liars.* Some false prophets are deliberate liars who have no intention of telling the truth. The apostle John says, "Who is the liar? It is the man who denies that Jesus is the Christ. Such a man is the antichrist—he denies the Father and the Son" (1 John 2:22).

3. *Heretics.* These are people who preach heresy (false doctrine) and divide the church. Of them John said, "They went out from us, but they did not really belong to us" (1 John 2:19). The apostle Peter said, "There will be false teachers among you. They will secretly introduce destructive heresies.... These men blaspheme in matters they do not understand" (2 Peter 2:1,12).

4. *Scoffers.* There are some who do not necessarily promote false teaching so much as they outright reject the truth of God. Of them the Bible warns, "In the last days scoffers will come, scoffing and following their own evil desires" (2 Peter 3:3). The apostle Paul calls them "lovers of themselves ... boastful, proud ... conceited" (2 Timothy 3:2,4). Jude calls them "grumblers and faultfinders" (verse 16).

5. *Blasphemers.* Those who speak evil of God, Christ, the Holy Spirit, the people of God, the kingdom of God, and the attributes of God are called blasphemers. Jude calls them godless men [who] "speak abusively against whatever they do not understand....They are clouds without rain ... trees, without fruit ... wild waves of the sea ... wandering stars" (Jude 10,12,13). The apostle Paul says that he himself was a blasphemer before his conversion to Christ (1 Timothy 1:13).

6. *Seducers.* Jesus warned that some false prophets will appear with miraculous signs and wonders to seduce or deceive the very elect "if that were possible" (Mark 13:22). Our Lord's implication is that spiritual seduction is a very real threat even to believers. This would account for the fact that a few genuine, but deceived, believers may be found among the cults.

7. *Reprobates.* This term means "disapproved," "depraved," or "rejected." Paul refers to those who have rejected the truth of God and turned to spiritual darkness. Consequently, God has given them over to a "reprobate mind" (Romans 1:28 KJV). They have so deliberately rejected God that they have become "filled with every kind of wickedness" (verse 29). As a result, they are "God-haters" (verse 30), whose behavior is "senseless, faithless, heartless, ruthless" (verse 31). These people are so far gone spiritually that they know it and don't care!

In Jesus' own prophetic message, the Olivet Discourse (Matthew 24–25), He warned, "Watch out that no one deceives you....Many will turn away from the faith ... and many false prophets will appear and deceive many people.... False Christs and false prophets will appear and perform great signs and miracles" (Matthew 24:4,10, 11,24). Our Lord warned His disciples—and us—of the possibility of spiritual seduction by false prophets and teachers, especially as the end of the age approaches.

▼ ▼ ▼

Wars and Rumors of Wars

Daymond R. Duck

People have been fighting each other ever since the first two children of Adam and Eve started disagreeing with each other. Their first child, a son named Cain, killed their second child, a son named Abel (Genesis 4:8). And that was the beginning of man's assault against man. As we well know, this single act of violence has progressed to include the deaths of thousands in countless wars. Although earlier wars probably occurred, the earliest conflicts recorded in the Bible took place during the life of Abraham (see Genesis 14:1-16). When four kings of the East and their armies attacked the wicked city of Sodom, overcame its defenders and captured his nephew Lot, Abraham quickly gathered 318 men trained for war. They followed the kings, overcame them and released their captives—winning a great victory. Since that time, many wars have been waged—and we can be sure war will continue to be a part of life until the end of the age (see Daniel 9:26).

War Is the Result of Human Actions

Not a single day has passed since WWII without the drums of war beating somewhere on earth. The church, the United Nations, peace treaties, peacekeeping missions, peace-promising politicians, peace marchers, peacemongers, peaceniks and multitudes of sincere peace-loving people have not been able to silence them. The record is truly distressing. Those who ask why need look no further than the Bible for an answer. The apostle James said, "From whence come wars and fightings among you? come they not hence, even of your lusts that war in your members? Ye lust, and have not: ye kill, and desire to have, and cannot obtain: ye fight and war..." (James 4:1,2).

War is the result of human beings acting on their lusts. People need to be regenerated through faith in Jesus Christ, but without regeneration they yield to the wicked desires of their hearts. And the Bible makes it plain that giving in to those desires leads to war. When human beings reject the only solution, Jesus Christ, the only alternative is war. "There is no peace, saith my God, to the wicked" (Isaiah 57:21). This insightful revelation from God is very important. It means that human beings are caught up in a great struggle, a struggle between light and dark, good and evil, the ways of Christ versus the ways of Antichrist; a struggle with righteousness pitted against sin, truth pitted against untruth, honesty against deceit, faithfulness against unfaithfulness, the way of God versus the way of Satan. Whether we know it or not, opposing principles are constantly warring within us and forcing us to choose sides. Choosing the wrong side leads to war—war between families, races, religions and nations. To satisfy their lusts, some human beings are willing to do any vile thing a depraved mind can think of. The willing submission of many individuals to the unregenerate desires of their hearts is ravaging the world.

In 1990, Saddam Hussein, lusting after money and power, invaded Kuwait and touched off the Persian Gulf War. That same kind of lust and violent action threatens to ignite war all over the

Middle East today. In *Forewarning: Approaching the Final Battle Between Heaven and Hell,* Chuck Missler writes,

> The Middle East is a cauldron ready to boil over. Egypt wants the southern Negev; the Palestinians want all of Israel and Jordan; Syria wants all of Lebanon, Jordan, Israel, and the West Bank; Turkey wants part of Iraq; Iran wants part of Iraq and hegemony in the Persian Gulf; Iraq wants Kuwait and whatever parts of Saudi Arabia it can get; Yemen also wants part of Saudi Arabia; and everyone is desperate for water.[1]

Bible prophecy declares that the Russian lust for Israel's gold, silver, cattle and goods will ignite the earth-shaking battle of Gog and Magog (see Ezekiel 38 and 39). The Antichrist will lust after a world government, uproot three nations to get it, and bring in the last Gentile world kingdom (Daniel 7:24). The false prophet will lust after a world religion, impose the infamous "mark of the beast" to achieve it, and cause many to be cast into the lake of fire (Revelation 13:11-18; 14:9-11). China will lust after control of the Middle East, move across the dried up Euphrates River to seize it, and touch off the terrible battle of Armageddon (Revelation 9:14-16; 16:12-14). Acting upon our lusts leads to war.

Supernatural Beings Influence Our Actions

Supernatural phenomena is one of today's hot topics, as evidenced by a steady stream of books and movies about visitations, UFOs and the spirit world. Society's fascination with satanism, witchcraft, divination, demons and angels is dramatic. The use of psychics, a worldwide phenomenon, reaches from individuals to small-town police departments, the FBI, the CIA, the top brass of the military, the White House and on up to the most influential people in the world. In *Fast Facts on False Teachings,* Ron Carlson and Ed Decker report that an estimated 50 to 60 million Americans are involved in some form of the occult.[2]

Many Christians ridicule these things, but it is a mistake to lightly brush them aside. The Scriptures are saturated with teachings about the involvement of the unseen world in the affairs of human beings. Consider these well-known examples of visitations for the good of humanity: God visited the earth to talk with Adam and Eve in the Garden of Eden (Genesis 2:15-17); He came again to talk with Moses in flames of fire from the burning bush (Exodus 3:1-5); He came again to lead the Hebrews in a pillar of cloud by day and a pillar of fire by night (Exodus13:21,22); He appeared to the Hebrews at Mt. Sinai (Exodus 19:20-25); Jesus, Moses and Elijah visited three of the disciples on the mount of transfiguration (Mark 9:2-7); Jesus spoke from heaven when Paul was converted on the road to Damascus (Acts 9:3-6); the Holy Spirit came down like a dove when Jesus was baptized (Mark 1:9-11); the Holy Spirit came again when the 120 believers were praying in the upper room on the day of Pentecost (Acts 2:1-4); an angel visited Joseph before Jesus was born (Matthew 1:18-25); the angel Gabriel visited Mary about the same time (Luke 1:26-38); and multitudes of angels visited the shepherds to announce the birth of Jesus (Luke 2:8-14). The list could go on and on because earth has been visited by the supernatural over and over again, including the great 33-year visitation of Christ when He lived here on earth as a human being. He had always existed, but He took on the form of a man and visited this earth so He could qualify as a perfect sacrifice for the sins of the world (Philippians 2:5-8). Without that we would have no hope. Without the indwelling presence of the Holy Spirit we would not be saved.

Many Scriptures also refer to the unseen world's involvement in the affairs of government. One good example is when God sent Moses to tell Pharaoh to let the children of Israel go. Pharaoh refused, so God sent a variety of plagues and forced Egypt's leader to release the people (Exodus 5–12). One interesting aspect of the story occurred when Aaron cast down his rod before Pharaoh. God performed a miracle and changed it into a slithering serpent. Then Satan got involved and Pharaoh's wise men duplicated the miracle (Exodus 7:10-13). Supernatural involvement offers the only credible explanation for those acts.

Another example of supernatural involvement in governmental affairs occurred when a "watcher and holy one" came to earth from heaven "to the intent that the living may know that the most High ruleth in the kingdom of men, and giveth it to whomsoever he will, and setteth up over it the basest of men" (Daniel 4:17). The "watcher and holy one" saw to it that King Nebuchadnezzar was afflicted with a mental illness and lost his kingdom until he acknowledged the Most High God seven years later (Daniel 4:29-37).

And then there was the time when King Belshazzar tried to prove that he wasn't afraid of anything or anyone, including Almighty God. He sent for the holy vessels taken by Babylon from the temple in Jerusalem and desecrated them by drinking wine from them. Suddenly the mysterious fingers of a man's hand appeared and wrote on the wall. God was intervening to put an end to the haughty king and his kingdom (Daniel 5).

The Almighty intervened again when King Herod foolishly let the Jewish people believe he was a god. The angel of the Lord smote King Herod so that he died a repulsive death (Acts 12:20-23). In yet another instance, Satan stepped in when King David took a census in Israel. The Bible says, "Satan stood up against Israel, and provoked David" to do it (1 Chronicles 21:1).

Members of the vast unseen world have also been involved in wars on earth. Upon entering the Promised Land, Israel's first target was the ancient city of Jericho. The people of Jericho prepared by retreating behind the city walls and shutting the gates. Instead of attacking them, the children of Israel simply marched around the city and went back to their camp. They did the same thing every day for six days. On the seventh day, they marched around the city seven times, the priests blew their trumpets, the people gave a shout, the walls of Jericho fell and the children of Israel took the city (Joshua 6:1-16). On another occasion, the angel of the Lord called Gideon to lead the children of Israel in their struggle against the Midianites. The angel had Gideon reduce his 32,000-man army to just 300 men. Then he had the 300 men attack the 135,000 Midianites with, of all things, pitchers, lamps and trumpets. The larger and well-armed Midianite army panicked and fled (Judges 7).

The unseen world was involved in war again when the king of Syria decided to eliminate Elisha the prophet for spying against

him for the king of Israel. The king took a large army and surrounded Elisha's village. Elisha's servant spotted the enemy troops
and was terrified, but Elisha calmed him by saying, "They that be
with us are more than they that be with them" (2 Kings 6:16).
Elisha prayed and God revealed an unseen army that was protecting him and his servant. When the large Syrian army came in
to attack, God's invisible army smote them with blindness (2 Kings
6:8-23).

On yet another occasion, the great army of King Sennacherib of
Assyria was soundly trouncing all the militaries around him. He
took his experienced troops and surrounded the city of Jerusalem.
But before he could attack, an angel passed through his camp and
killed 185,000 of his men (2 Kings 19:32-36).

Then there was the time when King Jabin of Canaan built 900
chariots of iron and used them to oppress the seemingly defenseless
children of Israel. After the Israelites repented of their sins, God
called a faithful woman named Deborah to deliver them. He had
her assemble an army on the high ground at Mt. Tabor. King Jabin's
900 chariots of iron rolled out along the Kishon River and prepared
to attack, but God sent a great rain causing the river to suddenly
overflow its banks and the chariots and men were washed away.
Then the children of Israel attacked from the high ground and won
a great victory (Judges 4–5).

All of this has significance for Christ's second coming and the
battle of Armageddon, when Jesus returns at the end of the tribulation period with the unseen armies of heaven. The battle of
Armageddon will really be a war between the armies of the earth
and the armies of heaven led by the Lord Jesus Christ (Revelation
19:11-19). The powerful weapons of mankind will not work in a
war with beings from the spirit world.

It does not score points in the secular court of public opinion, but
most Christians are aware of the fact that the Bible teaches that
supernatural beings are influencing the human race. Most Christians know that a fallen angel, Satan, appealed to the lusts of two
vulnerable human beings, Adam and Eve, and caused the corrup-
tion of the entire human race (Genesis 3:1-7). Most Christians

believe the church began when the Holy Spirit came to baptize people into the body of Christ (Acts 2:1-4). It may not be fashionable in the secular world to believe in the Holy Spirit, fallen angels, demons and other such beings, but the Bible says they are real and they have a vested interest in what goes on in this world. Although many educated people scorn the idea, it is important to understand that the war-producing struggle between good and evil in the heart of man is actually the result of a greater struggle between forces in the supernatural realm. The Bible even teaches that this struggle will heighten as we approach the end of the age. The apostle Paul said, "The Spirit speaketh expressly, that in the latter times some shall depart from the faith, giving heed to seducing spirits, and doctrines of devils" (1 Timothy 4:1). Seducing spirits have caused a lot of trouble in the world, but they are going to be an even greater problem in the days to come.

The prophet Daniel actually called this struggle between supernatural forces in the unseen world "a great war." He had been fasting and praying for three weeks when he had a vision of Christ, fell into a deep sleep, and was touched by a good angel from the supernatural realm. The good angel told Daniel that he had been trying to reach him, but the prince of Persia had prevented him from getting through. He said he made it only because another angel named Michael helped him. He also said he would have to go back and fight against the prince of Persia. Then the prince of Greece would come (Daniel 10).

Daniel's vision means there was a literal king of Persia who ruled in the physical realm. It also means there was a demonic prince of Persia who ruled in the spiritual realm. The same thing can be said for Greece: a physical king of Greece ruled in the natural realm and a demonic prince of Greece ruled in the spiritual realm. Furthermore, God had assigned an angel named Michael to rule over Israel in the spiritual realm, and he assisted the good angel in his struggle against the demonic prince of Persia. This provides conclusive evidence that Satan has a spiritual kingdom that includes a group of fallen angels called demons. It does not mean that Satan has demons behind every door or under every bed, but it does mean that he has fallen angels who are real and often influence the natural world in a negative way. Their evil effect on the vile passions of man is often responsible for war.

This is consistent with the teachings of Jesus, who spoke of Satan's kingdom and referred to him as the prince of this world (John 12:31; 16:11; Matthew 12:22-29). It is also consistent with the teachings of Paul. He said, "We wrestle not against flesh and blood, but against principalities, against powers, against the rulers of darkness of this world, against spiritual wickedness in high places" (Ephesians 6:12). The apostle called Satan the prince of the power of the air (Ephesians 2:2) and the god of this world (2 Corinthians 4:4). Many of the world's best scholars understand this to mean that Satan has a kingdom governed by a system of powerful fallen angels who influence the lusts of people on this earth. Their evil influence on the lusts of unregenerate man fuels the fires of war.

It may not be a popular concept, but the temporary rule of Satan over unclean spirits is something the world must contend with. Powerful unseen forces have a lot to do with world events now taking place. The spiritual realm will do much to make the headlines during the great tribulation. Jesus compared the end of the age to the days of Noah (Matthew 24:37), whose days were marked by the "sons of God" marrying the "daughters of men" (see Genesis 6:1-4). That bewildering concept is nothing to sneeze at. The list of scholars who believe the "sons of God" refers to fallen angels is impressive (see also Job 1:6; 2:1). If they are right in their interpretation, the end of the age will be marred by the massive involvement of fallen angels in the affairs of the world.

We know with certainty that the Antichrist will come forth with the power of Satan and give honor to the "god of forces," who also happens to be Satan (2 Thessalonians 2:9; Daniel 11:38). We also know that Satan will open the abyss and release millions of demon-possessed locusts, who will be led by a fallen angel king named Abaddon (Revelation 9:1-12). We even know there will be war in heaven with God's angels fighting Satan and some of his fallen angels. Satan and his loathsome followers will be cast down to this earth (Revelation 12:7-12). And we know that demon spirits from the mouths of the satanic trinity will go forth to summon the kings of the earth to the bloody battle of Armageddon (Revelation 16:13-16). Astute scholars can infer different meanings from these Scriptures, but one thing is clear: The Bible definitely teaches that fallen angels and/or demonic spirits will wreak havoc and cause war on this earth at the end of this age.

The End of the Age

The prophets of old predict a spooky scenario for the end of the age. Useless ear-tickling talk about peace will abound, but terrible weapons will be in the bloody hands of violent people. The idea of world government will turn sour, the lusts of power-hungry villains will be great, demonic activity will multiply and the end of the age will actually be a time of war for the whole earth. Here is a random look at some of the Bible prophecies.

Israel

God gave all of the Promised Land to the Jews, and He gave it to them forever (Genesis 13:15; 17:20,21; 26:1-5; 28:22). He will not allow the Jews to swap "land for peace" and get away with it for very long. He will not let the Arabs—or any nation, group of nations or world government—take the land away from Israel and go unpunished. He intends for Israel to possess East Jerusalem, the temple mount and a whole lot more; no one can do anything about that (see Ezekiel 47:21-23). The beautiful land belongs to Israel and because God is God, the issue is settled forever. Those trying to divide that land are making a terrible mistake. Although no doubt skilled in war, they are setting up a confrontation with God they cannot hope to win.

Israel is the "rod of God's inheritance" and the Jews are God's "battle axe and weapons of war." God will use them to "break in pieces the nations" and to "destroy kingdoms" (see Jeremiah 51:19,20). Think about that! Israel is a weapon, and God is the one who wields it. He will use that little nation to chop up and destroy the big nations of the world. People skillfully destroy each other today, but they know nothing about the precision of God's war machine.

And what about Jerusalem? God says He will "make Jerusalem a burdensome stone for all people; all that burden themselves with it shall be cut in pieces, though all the people of the earth be gathered together against it" (Zechariah 12:3). Jerusalem is the one city on the face of this earth that God intends to use to judge the world. He will bring the armies of the world against it, and they will be crushed. Even if every army on earth unites against Jerusalem, they will all be crushed. Jerusalem has supernatural protection; God will destroy every army that attacks His chosen city (Zechariah 12:9).

Having said that, we need to understand that everything is not going to be a pretty bed of roses in Israel when the end of the age arrives. Concerning the entire nation, God said, "It shall come to pass, that in all the land, saith the LORD, two parts therein shall be cut off and die; but the third shall be left therein" (Zechariah 13:8). Concerning the holy city, He said, "I will gather all nations against Jerusalem to battle; and the city shall be taken, and the houses rifled, and the women ravished; and half of the city shall go forth into captivity, and the residue of the people shall not be cut off from the city" (Zechariah 14:2). These Scriptures mean that veteran armies are going to attack Israel again and again. Eventually, two-thirds of those Jews who live outside Jerusalem will perish, but one-third will never perish. One-half of Jerusalem will be captured, but the other half will never be taken.

Dr. David Jeremiah says, "The land of Israel has been the nerve center of the world since the time of Abraham. When Jesus Christ came to earth, Israel became the truth center of the world. There is coming a day in the future (the millennium) when the land will be the peace center of the world. Today, as we look at that small piece of real estate in the Middle East, it is the storm center of the world."[3]

The current peace process will produce a temporary and unworkable false peace. Soon after that worthless document is ratified by the deceitful Antichrist and his band of lying cohorts, war will erupt. Israel and Jerusalem will be in the middle of the storm. Why?

Because the world refuses to recognize the sovereignty of Israel's God, and He intends to vindicate His holy name by showing the world that no one can defeat this tiny nation.

Russia

Ezekiel 38 and 39 record an amazing prophecy yet to be fulfilled. A great power, almost always identified as Russia by prophecy experts, will organize a coalition of nations in the last days and come forth from the north parts to attack the little nation of Israel (Ezekiel 38:16). Good prophetic scholars are clearly divided on the exact time of the attack. Some writers, including this one, place it at least three-and-a-half years before the tribulation period. Others place it at the tribulation period midpoint. Regardless of the timing, almost all agree that a terrifying day is coming when Russia and several of its allies will mount a poorly planned and ill-fated attack against Israel.

Keep in mind the fact that war, as mentioned earlier, is the tragic result of lust. The prophet Ezekiel reveals that the Russian leader will think an "evil thought" and attack Israel "to take a spoil and a prey" (Ezekiel 38:10,12). He will desire to possess Israel's silver, gold, cattle and goods (see Ezekiel 38:13). Also keep in mind the fact that a powerful archangel called Michael has been assigned to protect Israel (Daniel 10:21). This means that Russia and its allies will take a great army with a huge reservoir of terrible weapons and expect to win an easy victory over the chosen people. But their war plans will fail to consider the unseen world, the anger of God and the awesome power of Michael and his great army of mighty angels (Ezekiel 38:19). The Russian coalition will be composed of many mighty people of war, but they will be mere mortals who cannot prevail against the handpicked angels in God's unseen world.

Suddenly there will be a great earthquake—an earthquake so violent it will be felt the world over. Every animal and every human being on earth will be shaken. Experienced troops in the terrified Russian coalition will fight each other. While they are furiously destroying themselves, the angels of God will drench them with rain, hail, blood, fire and brimstone (Ezekiel 38:20-22). Five out of every six coalition troops will die (Ezekiel 39:2). Liberal preachers and theologians have a problem with this, but it will be the judgment of God upon barbarian nations wrongly trying to destroy His special people, the Jews.

Too many people ignore the fact that God can use war for His own good purposes. He can be provoked into setting up devastating battles. When the people in the Northern Kingdom of Israel turned against God and refused to change their ways, He used the Assyrians to destroy their kingdom. When the inconsiderate people in the Southern Kingdom of Judah made the same mistake, He used the Babylonians to destroy their kingdom. When the spiritually blind people of Jesus' day refused to accept Him as the Messiah, He used the Romans to destroy their nation. He uses war to soften hearts, to spark repentance, to influence worship and to save souls. He will use the defeat of Russia and its allies to cause a great revival in many nations (Ezekiel 38:23).

What do we say to those who want to cast aside this prophecy—the people who say Russia is no longer a threat and America is the world's only superpower? They argue that the once evil empire would never attack Israel. But God *always* fulfills His Word; that Russia still wants to be a superpower; that Russia is still preparing for war; that Russia says she has to keep her nuclear forces prepared so she can implement alliance commitments; and we remind you that Russian President Boris Yeltsin warned the world on February 5, 1998, that an American attack on Iraq could lead to a world war. Despite all the changes in Russia, the nation still has more than a million soldiers; several hundred intercontinental nuclear missiles; several hundred bombers; several hundred fighter planes; several thousand tanks; several dozen submarines and more. Many in the intelligence community say Russia still has an appetite for war, and some are predicting a Russian attack on Israel before the year 2000.

Persia (Iran)

Scripture makes it crystal clear that this ancient nation will be one of the main end-of-the-age contributors to the Russian coalition of nations (Ezekiel 38:5). Tehran's Islamic fundamentalist government has many agreements with Russia and bitterly opposes any agreements with Israel. Iran is adamant in its opposition to the Middle East peace process and gives fervent support to terrorist organizations operating against Israel. It is using the bulk of its vast profits from the sale of oil to acquire Scud B and Scud C missiles from North Korea, cruise missiles from China, nuclear and biological weapons from Russia, and it was expected to have long-range missiles capable of hitting Israel with nuclear and biological warheads by the end of 1998. The Iranians are practicing for war. They believe they can temporarily seal off the Straits of Hormuz, blockade U.S. warships, stop the flow of oil and cause harm to those who might support Israel. They even seem to believe that a strong coalition of Arab nations could quickly defeat Israel.

The nation of Iran demonizes anyone who does not worship Allah. It persecutes and kills Christians and Jews alike. And it fails to consider the possibility that Israel could be under the supernatural protection of God and His mighty angels. Get out the long black robes of mourning. The Iranians, their Islamic religion and their false god, Allah, are going to suffer a great defeat. Multitudes of eager young men will delight in the opportunity to go off to war against Israel. They will believe they can rapidly march into the Holy Land and push Israel into the sea. But they will die an embarrassing death on the mountains of Israel. And their bodies will become food for the ravenous birds and wild beasts of the field (see Ezekiel 39:4).

Libya

Another nation headed for certain defeat as a member of the Russian coalition is Libya (Ezekiel 38:5). This mostly Arab nation was a NATO ally until about 1981, when the nation turned away from the West and began to strengthen its ties with "the evil empire." Because of its involvement in and support for terrorist activities, Libya is currently suffering under United Nations sanctions. But Russia claims the nation is being falsely accused by the

West and is giving Libya badly needed technical and military assistance. With Moscow's help, Libya is building what CIA Director John Deutch calls "the world's largest underground chemical weapons plant." In recent months, Iraq's leader, Saddam Hussein, and Libya's Muammar Qadhafi have become very friendly. The Libyan leader is helping Saddam hide his outlawed weapons of mass destruction from United Nations inspectors, and the Iraqi leader is returning the favor with stockpiles of deadly weapons and sensitive military technology.

Libya will also lose many troops and weapons as a member of the Russian coalition, but that will not end the suffering in that godless nation. At least two other gloomy prophecies will be fulfilled during the tribulation period. One prophecy says Libya will join a group of African nations, including Ethiopia and Egypt, in another attack on Israel. That coalition will also meet with disaster (Jeremiah 46:8-10). Another prophecy says the Antichrist will move his great army into the Middle East. At some point he will decide to protect his southern flank by attacking Egypt and Libya. He will easily defeat them (see Daniel 11:43).

Cush (Ethiopia and/or Iraq and/or Sudan)

Another loser in the Russian coalition of nations is an ally that some Bible translations call Cush and others call Ethiopia (Ezekiel 38:5). Some authorities say this refers to Iraq and, perhaps, Sudan. Others say it is a reference to the modern nation of Ethiopia.

Iraq's population is about 80 percent Arab. Roughly 95 percent are Muslim, so anti-Semitism is a big problem. This nation of warmongers has "El-Hussein" improved Scud missiles, Katyusha rockets, 115mm cannons, and it seems to be on the brink of developing nuclear weapons. Most Iraqi missiles can be fitted with chemical and biological warheads. The nation has VX nerve gas, mustard gas, anthrax, smallpox and other biological agents. According to the Jewish Minister of Defense, Iraq has enough poison gas to kill every man, woman and child in Israel. It has already used chemical weapons on its own people, the Kurds. It is developing, building and storing weapons of mass destruction in both Libya and Sudan. Its poorly trained and equipped air force was badly crippled in the Gulf War, but the Russians have helped rebuild it. They have also sold Baghdad large quantities of weapons. Iraq owes Moscow a big debt. Even if Iraq does not join the doomed Russian coalition in the battle of Gog and Magog, Bible prophecy still predicts a turbulent future for the nation. Isaiah predicts a tribulation period attack by the Medes (modernists call them the Kurds) (Isaiah 13:4-6; 17; 18). Jeremiah predicts that God will overthrow the famous Iraqi city of Babylon as He did Sodom and Gomorrah (Jeremiah 50:40). The apostle John says the city will be destroyed in one hour (Revelation 18:8-10,17,19). Isaiah and the apostle John both predict that it will become the home of wicked, unclean spirits (Isaiah 13:19-22; Revelation 18:1-2).

The modern nation of Ethiopia has a very large Muslim population with a built-in hatred for Israel. In recent years the Ethiopian government has adopted many socialist policies and developed strong ties with both Russia and Iran. It has a large army, a small air force and a small navy. It will probably join the Russian coalition and lose most of its military. Even if it doesn't, its future is still not good. When the Antichrist attacks Egypt and Libya during the tribulation period he will also bring the Nubians into submission (Daniel 11:43; Ezekiel 30:4-9; Zephaniah 2:12). The Nubians are from Sudan, Ethiopia and possibly Djibouti.

Sudan is showing the same signs as the other nations scheduled to join the doomed Russian coalition. This sprawling nation has been transformed into a militant Islamic state. Its military is trained and equipped by Iran. It supports the PLO and many terrorist organizations opposed to the existence of Israel. Having strengthened its ties with Iraq, it is helping Saddam Hussein hide his Scud missiles and chemical and biological weapons from United Nations inspectors. Sudan has also jointly built a chemical weapons plant with Iraq on Sudanese property. The nation has used mustard gas on its own citizens, murdered 1.5 million Sudanese Christians and may be responsible for the disappearance of 1 million more. Sudanese citizens are forced to convert to Islam, and some are even being sold into slavery. Churches there are being burned, and Christian pastors are literally being crucified. Can anyone question why God would use the Antichrist to conquer this nation of wicked Nubians during the tribulation period?

Gomer (Germany)

Not all Bible scholars agree, but many think that Gomer is Germany (see Ezekiel 38:6). It is hard to believe that Germany will join the Russian coalition in an attack on Israel, but the nation does have a bad military history and the unimaginable will happen. When the Berlin Wall fell and the East and West were unified, many hard-line communists were brought into the new government. Treacherous enemies of the West are still holding high positions and Germany, a hard-working industrialized nation, has developed strong ties with Russia, Iran and Iraq. Some German companies have given substantial help to both Iran and Iraq for their chemical and biological weapons programs. Passionate German anti-Semitic groups are increasing in both number and size. Attacks on Jewish shelters, shrines and property are steadily increasing. Germany, now with the largest army in Western Europe, is deploying troops outside its country for the first time since WWII—and it is not unusual for this militaristic nation to act independently of its European Union allies.

Togarmah (Armenia and/or Turkey)

The identity of Togarmah is confusing and debatable, but it is probably Armenia and/or Turkey (see Ezekiel 38:6). Surrounded by three hostile neighbors—Turkey, Iran and Azerbaijan—the small, often-conquered nation of Armenia is vulnerable to their lusts. So its fearful government maintains strong ties with Russia, supports that nation and looks to it for protection. That may be enough to drag her into the Russian coalition.

Turkey is also in a difficult position. Following WWI, the nation embraced a Western-type of government. Following WWII, it was strategically important to the West as a barrier to Russia. During the

Persian Gulf War, it was an ally providing badly needed air bases for U.S. planes. For years it was welcomed as a member of such Western organizations as the European Economic Community (EEC), the Council of Europe and NATO. But all that has changed. Turkey has been rebuffed in its efforts to join the EEC. Its only option seems to be to seek other allies, so it is looking toward some of those nations that were members of the old Soviet Union. Our once faithful friend may well go down with the Russian-led coalition on the mountains of Israel.

Sheba and Dedan (Saudi Arabia)

Sheba and Dedan, cities in Saudi Arabia, question why the Russian coalition of nations is invading Israel, but they do nothing to assist God's chosen people (see Ezekiel 38:13). Joining their verbal opposition to this hideous attack will be the merchants of Tarshish, who most commentators believe to be Great Britain, and another group of nations called "all the young lions," who most commentators identify as the English-speaking nations coming out of Great Britain—in particular, the United States and Canada. No other specific prophecies are mentioned about the future of Saudi Arabia, but the oil-rich nation will be included in the final world war.

Syria

Another unfulfilled prophecy concerns the fiery destruction of Syria's capital, Damascus. Isaiah said, "Behold, Damascus is taken away from being a city, and it shall be a ruinous heap. The cities of Aro-er are forsaken: they shall be for flocks, which shall lie down, and none shall make them afraid" (Isaiah 17:2). A few historians say this has been fulfilled, but they are wrong because Damascus has never ceased to be a city. "The cities of Aro-er" refers to the suburbs of Damascus. That area has not been forsaken and is not at rest, so we can expect a future war. Concerning the question of when, prophecy experts have long been aware that Russia's allies in the battle of Gog and Magog do not include Syria and Egypt. Many experts think the omission of these nations could mean they will be defeated before then. Some even think their defeat may be what actually triggers the battle.

A war with Syria seems to be shaping up. After the nation of Israel came back into existence in 1948, Israeli farmers began to farm land and establish villages in disputed areas along the Golan Heights between Israel and Syria. The Syrians tried to stop that by using the high ground of the Golan Heights to fire down upon the settlements below, but that didn't work. The situation got tense, tempers flared and Syria attacked Israel. That set off the Six-Day War of 1967. Israel won the war, captured all of the Golan Heights and established more farms and villages.

Today, Syria is insisting that Israel return control of the Golan Heights. But the nations are still in a stalemate. Israel refuses to return the land without a peace treaty with Syria. And Syria refuses to sign a peace treaty as long as Israel holds the land. Neither side will give in. The prospects for peace are dim; reports of an impending war are common. The reckless Syria has already begun to get ready by digging bunkers on its border with Israel, moving large numbers of well-armed troops into strike positions and upgrading its forces in several ways. For example, it is spending billions of dollars on weapons and has tripled the size of its military in the last two decades. It has acquired Scud B, Scud C and Russian-made SS21 missiles that can deliver chemical and biological warheads. It has acquired multiple launchers so it can fire its missiles in a barrage. It has a sizeable air force and a large army with hundreds of tanks. It has two factories operating at peak capacity producing deadly biological weapons. Syria has thousands of bombs containing nerve gas that can be dropped from planes, and it may soon receive nuclear weapons from Iran. This is putting a lot of pressure on Israel. It is not hard to find experts who say war is inevitable. When it comes, Israel will respond with an overwhelming force. There will be nothing left of Damascus except a ruinous heap of ashes.

But the prophecies are not all negative. Syria's afflictions will eventually bring a spiritual change in the nation. God's chastening will "yield the peaceable fruit of righteousness." The nation will finally turn to Christ, form an alliance with Egypt and Israel, bless God and serve Him during the millennium (Isaiah 19:23-25). This is a good example of how bad news often has a happy ending.

Lebanon

War with fiery destruction is also coming to the beautiful mountains of Lebanon. The prophet Zechariah said, "Open thy doors, O Lebanon, that the fire may devour thy cedars. Howl, fir tree; for the cedar is fallen; because the mighty are spoiled: howl, O ye oaks of Bashan; for the forest of the vintage is come down" (Zechariah 11:1,2). Today, the world recognizes Lebanon as a sovereign nation, but the northern part of the country is occupied by Syrian forces. The government is controlled by Syrian-backed puppets who can't do anything without Syrian approval. In essence, the nation is nothing more than a Syrian province. As Syria goes, so goes Lebanon. So the war between Syria and Israel will be like the vortex of a fiery whirlpool that sucks in helpless Lebanon. The same planes that bomb the city of Damascus will also bomb military targets in the mountains of occupied Lebanon—the base of operations for some of the most barbaric and dangerous terrorist groups in the world. With Syrian permission and support, they routinely attack Israeli soldiers and targets. Their actions have already provoked several clashes with the Israeli army.

Edom, Moab and Ammon (Jordan)

The kingdom of Jordan is the most moderate in the Middle East, the friendliest to Israel and a mixed bag in Bible prophecy. Some prophecies reveal that Jordan will become the possession of Israel before the tribulation period begins (Jeremiah 49:1,2; Obadiah 1:15-19). Others indicate that the ancient Jordanian city of Petra (the children of Ammon) will escape the destructive clutches of the Antichrist during the tribulation period (Daniel 11:41). It is just speculation, but one scenario could be for Israel to get into a war and be forced to expand her borders for protection—by occupying the land of Jordan. At some point, the Antichrist would move in, disarm Israel, break his covenant to protect Israel and, as a result, many of the Jews would have to flee to Petra. That will be the only place on earth to escape his clutches. (*Note:* The word *Edom* is used in different ways in the Scriptures. It refers to Arabs who lived in the area of modern day Jordan, and sometimes it refers to all Arabs.)

Egypt

Next to Israel and the Revived Roman Empire, there is more prophecy in the Bible about the poor, dry, windswept nation of Egypt than any other. The nation's short-term future looks bleak, but its long-term future looks rosy. One prophecy indicates that God will use war to make a large part of Egypt desolate for 40 years (Ezekiel 29:8-12; also see Joel 3:19). There is debate over whether this has already been fulfilled. Those who think not point to the fact that all animals and all humans will completely avoid the area. That has never happened. So many expect a future nuclear attack with radioactive fallout that will make the area desolate.

But there is wide agreement on several other amazing prophecies. One prophecy states that Egypt will lose a war and suffer greatly before the tribulation period arrives (Ezekiel 30:1-6). Another prophecy indicates civil war in Egypt, with the government being overthrown and the nation coming under the hand of a cruel leader (Isaiah 19:1-15). The Nile River will be diverted, the old riverbed and all the irrigation canals will dry up and the crops will die. Another prophecy has the large Egyptian army going north and being defeated near the Euphrates River (Jeremiah 46:1-10). Another prophecy specifies that the Antichrist will attack and subdue Egypt during the tribulation period (Daniel 11:42). And then there is the good news: Egypt's calamities will cause the nation to turn from gloom to glory, from the crescent to the cross, from Allah to Jesus. God will heal the torn nation so that many of its citizens will serve Him during the millennium (Isaiah 19:16-25).

In 1978, Egypt and Israel signed the heralded Camp David accords. In exchange for peace, Israel gave the Sinai back to Egypt.

The Jews also abandoned several settlements and military bases. Even though Egypt agreed to peace, the nation still opposes Israel in many ways. Some of its leaders still refer to Israel as an enemy. "Land for peace" has not worked and normalization of trade and tourism is nonexistent. In many ways the situation is growing worse, not better. A great struggle is going on in Egypt for the heart and soul of the people. Islamic radicals are very strong and have made several attempts to oust President Mubarak—even trying to assassinate him. Their extremism and propensity for violence has forced Egypt to harden its attitude toward Israel. It could even lead to civil war.

Military experts say Egypt possesses nuclear weapons and agree that Cairo has chemical and biological weapons. The nation is also purchasing missiles to deliver them. Its future is laced with war, and these kinds of weapons will bring a quick and violent response.

Philistines (Palestinians)

Psalm 83 contains an interesting prophecy that seems to apply to the end of the age. This song of Asaph identifies a group of Middle Eastern nations who say, "Come, and let us cut them off from being a nation: that the name of Israel may be no more in remembrance" (Psalms 83:4). This psalm seems to apply to the end of the age because the nation of Israel has been neither unified nor sovereign since the Northern and Southern kingdoms split. Since the eighth century B.C., Israel has been a divided nation, a conquered nation or a scattered nation.

But prophecy indicated that Israel would come back into existence (as it did in 1948) and be surrounded by many nations who would be its enemies. The Palestinians (PLO) are included among the list of enemies. Psalm 83 turns into a prayer calling for their destruction. That will happen; the only question is who will do it? Will it be Israel when it comes under attack and lashes out? Or will it be the Antichrist who will move into the Middle East and overthrow many countries (Daniel 11:41)? This psalm calls for the unstoppable judgment of God to fall as it has in the past...which does not bode well for the Palestinians.

The Palestinians have a wonderful opportunity to get on the right side, but they never seem to make the right choice. Every time a Syria, or an Iraq, or an Iran threatens war against Israel, the PLO sides with Israel's enemies. Instead of trying to stop terrorism against Israel, as they have agreed to do, they often appear to be supporting it. Instead of changing the articles in their Charter calling for the destruction of Israel, as they have agreed to do in the Oslo accords, they seem determined to keep them. Also, in violation of the Oslo accords, they are constantly threatening to declare a Palestinian state. Instead of encouraging peace, they encourage demonstrations. Instead of creating an atmosphere of friendly and peaceful relations, they often threaten another Intifada. And instead of collecting some of the illegal weapons possessed by Palestinian extremists, they are often out distributing more weapons. They offer up a lot of flowery talk about peace, but all their actions appear to be preparations for war.

Medes (Kurds)

Although approximately 10 million strong, the Kurdish people have no country to call their own. Most live in Iran, Iraq and Turkey. A few live in Armenia and Syria. Descendants of the Medes, they have a long history of war. Struggling for a nation of their own, they are often betrayed, abused and attacked by armies in the countries in which they live. Turkey wants them destroyed, Iran wants to force them into Islam and Saddam Hussein has used chemical weapons against them. According to the Bible, they will reappear as the tribulation period approaches and join other nations in a successful attack on Babylon (Isaiah 13). It's very interesting that powerful politicians in the United States are calling for America to arm and train Kurds so they can overthrow Saddam Hussein.

The United States

The United States did not exist as a nation when the Scriptures were written. That probably explains why the nation is not mentioned by name in Bible prophecy and why the nation's prophetic future is such a big question. America's future is a matter of speculation. And the speculation has produced a variety of opinions:

1. The United States is prophetic Babylon (Isaiah 13,21,47; Jeremiah 50–51; Revelation 17–18).

2. The United States is one of "the young lions" (Ezekiel 38:13).

3. The United States is "the eagle's wings" (Daniel 7:4).

4. The United States is "the great eagle" (Revelation 12:14).

5. The United States will become a second-rate power before the tribulation period arrives because of economic, military and/or monetary collapse.

6. The United States will become a second-rate power before the tribulation period arrives because so many citizens will be raptured.

7. The United States will abandon its role as a world leader because of problems or a military defeat.

8. The United States will be destroyed before the end of the age arrives.

We can be sure of one thing: The United States will not glide through the tribulation period unscathed. For example, American involvement in NATO is an ominous sign. This once valuable organization is being transformed into the world's police-enforcers of United Nations resolutions. That makes America the military arm of the emerging world government. Closely connected to this is the NATO Expansion Treaty currently being considered by the United States Senate. This treaty commits the United States to defend Europe's NATO nations. The problem with this is that Bible prophecy teaches that Europe will take over the world government and be involved in many wars during the tribulation period. With the United States tied to defending the Revived Roman Empire, Europe's wars will be America's wars—and Europe is going to fall. We also cannot ignore the general prophecies that apply to every nation. Three of them are as follows:

1. Every nation and every army will be involved (Isaiah 34:2).

2. Every nation except Israel will cease to exist as a nation (Jeremiah 30:11; 46:28).

3. Every army will be brought to the battle of Armageddon (Revelation 16:14).

We also know that the history of Israel clearly proves that God will not allow wicked nations to exist forever. When a nation feeds on the academic baloney of political correctness and secular humanism instead of the Bread of Life, it is destined for a moral holocaust. When a nation becomes so broad-minded and tolerant that it will accept anything but true Christianity, it is heading for certain destruction. The moral decline of the United States makes us a nation at risk. We may experience the greatest and most embarrassing collapse ever witnessed in human history. Among other things, the United States should repent of its sins, try to get on the side of God, refuse to sign the NATO Expansion Treaty, break ranks with the United Nations and rapidly give unwavering support to Israel (Genesis 12:3). But this is not likely to happen, and individuals can do very little except pray, repent of their own sins and make their own salvation through Christ sure.

The Kings of the East (China and others)

The kings (plural) of the East are thought to be China and her allies (perhaps Japan, North Korea, India, Pakistan and/or others). Many prophetic scholars think the organization called the Pacific Rim nations may signal the alignment of this large end-of-the-age power. It will kill one-third of the earth's population and move into the Middle East when the Euphrates River dries up (Revelation 9:14,15; Daniel 11:44). It will go there to attack the Antichrist, but join the whole world in the bloody war with Christ at the battle of Armageddon (Revelation 16:12).

China, one of the worst nations on earth for persecuting Christians, operates state-run churches for propaganda and show while forbidding evangelism and forcing faithful churches underground. Teaching the inerrancy of the Scriptures, Bible prophecy, the Olivet Discourse, the book of Revelation, the second coming of Christ and more are prohibited. Abortion, forced abortion and forced sterilization are common. Female infanticide (the killing of baby girls because sons are preferred) and harvesting organs (the execution of human beings to obtain their vital organs) is rampant. Communism and humanism are the politically correct choices. All of this is the result of seduction by evil spirit forces. It will come back to haunt the physical world in a very real way.

America's attempts to open China's economic markets are turning that nation into a powerful military force. United States trade is providing China with the funds and technology to modernize and strengthen one of the largest and most dangerous armies on earth. It is simultaneously increasing China's need for oil and its interest in the all-important events of the Middle East. Beijing is pouring billions of dollars into military modernization and now has nuclear weapons, chemical weapons, missiles, attack submarines and more. It has become the world's largest supplier of technology to third-world countries and most especially to Israel's enemies. The acquisition of Hong Kong gave China added economic, political and technical strength. The acquisition of missile technology from the Clinton administration is a threat to the whole world and may be responsible for triggering another nuclear arms race. Also, China's lust for the island nation of Taiwan is a growing problem. Japan is steadily increasing its ties with China and is now investing more money there than in any other nation on earth, including the United States. Many Japanese investors who are hesitant to spend money in Russia because of the instability there are turning to China.

Other threats will come from India and Pakistan, who have both tested nuclear weapons in recent months. They are now mounting nuclear warheads on missiles. Pakistan is an Islamic Republic, and there is widespread concern that some of its nuclear weapons will find their way into the Middle East.

The Revived Roman Empire
(The European Economic Union)

A large number of nations in Europe (Portugal, Spain, Ireland, England, Netherlands, France, Belgium, Luxembourg, Sweden,

Finland, Denmark, Germany, Italy, Greece, Austria and possibly Poland, Hungary, Czechoslovakia and others) are uniting to form what many believe will be the largest and most powerful group of nations on earth. This is the long-awaited Revived Roman Empire, the unfortunate group that will produce the satanically inspired Antichrist (see Daniel 9:26).

But the uniting of Europe is not the only thing we see on the world's far-reaching and infallible prophetic radar screen. We also see an elite group of powerful bankers, industrialists and politicians constantly working to transform the United Nations into a powerful world government. They openly admit they hope to achieve this goal near the beginning of the next millennium. Bible prophecy indicates that their new world government will quickly be divided into the ten toes—ten divisions with ten powerful kings or rulers—on Nebuchadnezzar's famous statue (see Daniel 2:42-44).

Following the rapture, a charismatic leader in Europe will make a foolish agreement with Satan to obtain power, a throne and great authority (Revelation 13:2). With satanic help, this leader will rise to power in Europe and soon take over three of the new world government's ten divisions (Daniel 7:8,24). Then the other seven divisions will be turned over to him, and he will transform his newly acquired world government into a very powerful and evil world force. He will move his great army into the Middle East where he will get caught up in several wars and finally be destroyed (Daniel 11:41-45).

It should be interesting to watch the development of unity in the previous long list of European nations that are going to be involved in these tragic wars before their combined army is defeated.

Armageddon

The war of all wars will take place at the end of the tribulation period. No one will be able to sit on the sidelines. Demonic spirits will lure vast multitudes from all over the world to a plain near the Mountain of Megiddo in the northern part of Israel for what they will believe to be a final battle with Israel. This unity will be a grave mistake because, in reality, they will be gathering to meet the judge of all mankind, Jesus Christ. They will gladly assemble to fire their weapons at Israel, but God is in control and they will find themselves standing before the all-powerful Lord of lords and King of kings. The result will be so terrible the Bible pictures these people as being thrown into the winepress of God's wrath. Their sudden death will produce more than little patches or small pools of blood on the ground. The Bible says their demise will produce a river so great the blood will be up to the horses' bridles for about 180 miles (Revelation 14:20; 16:12-16; 19:11-21).

We are not talking about a scrimmage, military exercises or war games. We are talking about a great battle when Jesus will pour out His incredible judgments upon the armies of the world because of the sins of all mankind and the mistreatment of His people, Israel. All the armies of the world will be there thinking they will easily win a great battle, but Jesus will return to fight for His people (Zechariah 14:3-12).

We already see the Jews gathering back in their land. The world already views Jerusalem as "a cup of trembling" and "a burdensome stone" for all people round about (Zechariah 12:2-11). These are signs that the tribulation period and the ultimate battle of Armageddon are rapidly approaching. The final siege of Jerusalem will bring Jesus into the war. When it comes, the massacre will be terrible, but it will also bring an end to wickedness for a long, long time.

The Christian View of War

Jesus said, "Blessed are the peacemakers: for they shall be called the children of God" (Matthew 5:9). Peacemaking is the high calling of those who seek to enter the kingdom of heaven. It involves loving our enemies, praying for those who spitefully use us and turning the other cheek.

But the Old Testament offers several examples where God commanded war. And Christians know that peacemaking is not always possible. The apostle Paul said, "If it be possible, as much as lieth in you, live peaceably with all men" (Romans 12:18). Whenever possible Christians should seek peace. When that is not possible, war is viewed as something similar to applying the death penalty on a national scale. Christians are not in favor of war, but they understand that war can be forced upon them.

The vast majority of Christians believe in a Bible-based concept called the "just war." This idea was started by St. Augustine in the fifth century A.D. Basically it says that most wars are wrong, some wars cannot be avoided and some wars are necessary. It even spells out some of the conditions for waging war. A few are as follows:

1. *Last resort*—War must be the last resort. All nonviolent options must be exhausted or war cannot be justified.

2. *Just cause*—War can be fought in self-defense, to right a wrong, to redress an injury and for other similar just causes.

3. *Likelihood of success*—War can only be fought if there is a real chance of success because there is no way to justify death and destruction in a hopeless war.

4. *End result*—War can only be fought if the end result will be better than the conditions that would exist if there was no war.

5. *Ultimate goal*—The ultimate goal of war should be to establish justice, reestablish peace, improve the lives of people, and so on. Otherwise the war is wrong.

6. *Excessive or unnecessary force*—Only that force which is needed to attain the ultimate goal should be used. When the ultimate goal is reached, the war should stop.

7. *Civilians*—Innocent civilians should not be targets in war. Unless their deaths are the unavoidable result of an attack on a military target, it cannot be justified.

A small number of Christians are pacifists who believe all war is contrary to God's will. Their main doctrine is appeasement and acquiescence, which is unscriptural. The Bible does not teach that meekness means weakness. Moses killed a man before he fled Egypt the first time. When he returned, he faced down Pharaoh, the most powerful man on earth. He went up on Mt. Sinai to meet God and receive the Ten Commandments. He descended from the mountain and found some of the ungodly worshiping a golden calf. He had them killed. He was sometimes opposed by multitudes, but he always stood his ground. He was a man of courage, but the Bible calls him "meek, above all the men which were upon the face of the earth" (Numbers 12:3).

Jesus was also meek (Matthew 11:29). He made His triumphal entry into Jerusalem "meek, and sitting upon a donkey" (Matthew 21:5). But when He entered the temple and saw that the Jews had turned God's house into a place of profit instead of a place of prayer, He poured out the changers' money, turned over their tables and drove them out with a scourge (John 2:13-17).

The point is that Christians should be meek before God, humble in His presence and submissive to His will. But Christians should also fight against wrong.

The End of War

Few people, including most world leaders, know or care what the Bible says about the power and influence of spiritual forces. Some seem to believe in spiritual forces, but they are more interested in the occult than the forces of good. They hear not the voice of God, obey not His commands and totally ignore His many warnings of a coming seven-year period of judgment.

Our wise God has always known that it would come down to this, that people would be seduced by the powers of darkness; that people would ignore Him; that people would not want to know what the Bible says about abortion, homosexuality, pornography and the like; that people would not want to know what the Bible says about worshiping false gods and goddesses; that people would hate Israel and persecute and kill Christians who tell them they are sinning. That is why He made this determination approximately 2500 years ago: "My determination is to gather the nations, that I may assemble the kingdoms to pour upon them mine indignation, even all my fierce anger: for all the earth shall be devoured with the fire of my jealousy" (Zephaniah 3:8).

Just keep in mind the fact that good comes from everything God does. When He completes His terrible judgments the world will finally have rest and peace, joy and singing (Isaiah 14:1-8). The nations will "beat their swords into plowshares, and their spears into pruninghooks: nation shall not lift up sword against nation, neither shall they learn war any more" (Isaiah 2:4). Praise God and amen!

▼ ▼ ▼

CHAPTER 3

Famines, Pestilences, Earthquakes

William T. James

Almighty God's seismograph far exceeds in capability any instrument human scientists have or ever will devise. It forecasts the single greatest earthquake this planet will ever suffer and forewarns of catastrophic geophysical and astrophysical phenomena. Famines and pestilences of every description, including plagues that produce terrible sores on human flesh, plagues that involve supernatural insects that attack human beings, gigantic hailstones and other huge objects from space that will impact earth causing the oceans of earth to turn into a blood plasma-viscosity because all life in the seas will die—God's seismograph predicts all these things and more. For example, God forewarns us that the sun will apparently go nova, becoming dark while at the same time heating the earth to many times hotter than normal and causing the moon to appear blood red. According to God's Bible—God's seismograph—there is coming a time when this planet will be totally engulfed by fire and destroyed.

There is, however, no reason to be fearful of these coming calamities. The great and loving God of heaven has provided a way to escape these terrifying cataclysms. As a matter of fact, His way is the one and only way to avoid those terrors and the horrors of hell. His name is Jesus Christ.

Scoffers and the Last Days

Prophecies given within God's Holy Word, the Bible, predicted precisely the mindset that will mark the generation alive at the very end of the age. Second Peter 3:3,4 says, "Knowing this first, that there shall come in the last days scoffers, walking after their own lusts, and saying, Where is the promise of his coming?" Words of mockery and derision from scoffers blast at fundamentalist, pre-millennial truth from every quarter. The primary hue and cry of late against rapture teaching, and pretribulation rapture teaching in particular, hisses in serpentlike fashion from the lips of those who speciously claim that "the rapture theory" was invented by a woman in the early 1800s who claimed she was given the doctrine in a vision.

In my involvement in interview programs around the nation, I've found, much to my sadness, accumulating evidence that scoffing at the futurist view of biblical prophecy, and at pretribulation rapture teaching in particular, is like a swelling tsunami that threatens to sweep the very heart of God's Word from this generation. Thankfully that cannot happen. No cataclysm, tidal wave or other force can quench the fire of God's Word. The Bible has stood the test at every critical point in history, and it continues to stand great testing today. Prophecies that are beginning to come to pass before the eyes of this generation continue to prove with every passing day that interpreting the prophetic Word in an absolutely literal way rather than allegorically, symbolically or, as the praetorists insist, as history already accomplished, is the Holy Spirit-directed way.

Many people who question the legitimacy of the pretrib rapture view do so because they are genuinely concerned, confused and searching for answers. Some ask earnest questions with open minds despite their misdirected belief in a post-millennial, amillennial or other hybrid view. The scoffers do not include these people, but rather those whose voices first begin to refute rapture teaching with derisive laughter that quickly degenerates to hostility and even anger when they are confronted with truth from Holy Scripture.

Regardless of their best attempt at interpretation, gross error or heretical "walking after their own lusts," if those who scoff have truly accepted Christ as their Savior and Lord, they will be instantaneously delivered at the rapture from the wrath to come (read 1 Thessalonians 5). Those scoffers who truly refuse to accept that Jesus Christ paid for their sins on that cruel cross at Calvary will remain on earth to endure the most terrible period of human history mankind will ever suffer. (See chapter 15, "Rapture Before Wrath" by Thomas Ice, for an in-depth look at the rapture and all it will entail.)

Treasuring Up Wrath

No greater horrors occurring in the history of man can be imagined than those atrocities involved in the many genocidal purges that have taken place on this fallen planet. Such purges have been perpetrated upon many races and classes throughout the ages. Let us consider for the moment some of those that have taken place just within the last 100 years.

This quickly closing millennium contains a historical record filled with powerful testimony validating the truth in God's Word: "Evil men and seducers shall become worse and worse" (2 Timothy 3:13). Man's inhumanity to his fellow man continues to tramp bloody, murderous footprints across the unfolding pages of our daily lives as witnessed by our local, national and world news reports. Indeed, mankind today collectively demonstrates a hardened and impenitent heart. And God's Word forebodingly warns, "...Thy hardness and impenitent heart treasurest up unto thyself wrath against the day of wrath and revelation of the righteous judgment of God" (Romans 2:5). God's warning states further, "But unto them that are contentious, and do not obey the truth, but obey unrighteousness, indignation and wrath, tribulation and anguish, upon every soul of man that doeth evil" (Romans 2:8,9).

God spoke to all the beastly tyrants who have perpetrated their bloodthirsty genocide. His finger of condemnation seems to point particularly at the dictators of the twentieth century: "These, having not the law, are a law unto themselves: who show the work of the law written in their hearts, their conscience also bearing witness, and their thoughts the meanwhile accusing or else excusing one another in the day when God shall judge the secrets of men by Jesus Christ according to my gospel" (Romans 2:14-16).

The world's foremost geopolitical scholars and historians readily acknowledge that the twentieth century has been the bloodiest of all. Peter and Patti Lalonde write in their book *The Edge of Time,* regarding Jimmy Carter's National Security Council director Zbigniew Brzezinski:

> In the opening pages to his book *Out of Control: Global Turmoil on the Eve of the 21st Century* ... Brzezinski refers to the twentieth century ... as the century of "megadeaths, mega being a factor of 10^6." He explains that while the figures of megadeath he provides are estimates: "... what is important is the scale and not the exact numbers. It is the scale—so unprecedented that it becomes almost incomprehensible.... In brief, this century's wars extinguished no less than approximately *87,000,000 lives,* with the numbers of wounded, maimed or otherwise afflicted being beyond estimate." Mr. Brzezinski then proceeds to give figures in the millions for the atrocious killings committed "in the name of doctrine" by despots like Hitler, Lenin, Stalin, and Mao. In conclusion to his chapter, he calculated that 170 million human beings had lost their lives as a result of war and genocide so far in the twentieth century, an estimate that, in his own words, is "perhaps somewhat low."[1]

While most human beings on planet Earth would never desire to inflict genocidal atrocities on their fellow beings, such horrors committed by the beasts among us through the ages indicate just how deceitful and desperately wicked the human heart is and how far that wickedness will go if unchecked by God's Holy Spirit. The unbridled conscience of man inevitably leads to an insatiable thirst for blood. Is it any wonder that when the Holy Spirit is "taken out of the way" (2 Thessalonians 2:7), the last great dictator of human history will bring mankind to the point of total annihilation at Armageddon?

The cup of God's indignation and wrath certainly must be very near full to overflowing, even just considering twentieth-century man's inhumanity to man. And remember, people get the kind of leadership they allow and, therefore, the kind of leadership they deserve. This is true of any people during any age.

Christ Unseals the Scrolls

John the apostle suddenly found himself in the throne room of God witnessing what surely must of been the most spectacular scene ever observed by human eyes. He was summoned by Christ Himself: "After this I looked and, behold, a door was open in heaven: and the first voice that I heard was as it were of a trumpet talking with me; which said, Come up here, and I will show thee things which must be hereafter" (Revelation 4:1).

The old prophet was awed by what he saw as reported through his account of God's throne room and the astonishing heavenly activity (see Revelation 4). A book was brought forward by an angel who looked in vain to find one who could unseal the scroll. John was greatly saddened and distressed because no one could be found to unseal the book and he wept bitterly. Then one of the heavenly elders comforted John and said, "Weep not: behold, the Lion of the tribe of Judah, the Root of David, hath prevailed to open the book, and to loose the seven seals thereof" (Revelation 5:5).

Jesus Christ then took the scroll from God the Father and all in heaven bowed before the Son of God and worshiped Him and praised Him alone as worthy to break the seal and open the book (Revelation 5).

The Wrath of God Unleashed

The fullness of God's wrath now begins to overflow His cup of indignation. Christ's bride, the church—all born-again believers in Jesus Christ as the only way to salvation—has been removed from planet Earth. Christians of the Church Age now fall down before the

Lamb of God with all other heavenly beings while Jesus opens the book of the apocalypse. Keep in mind that this is the unfolding of God's wrath upon a wicked and rebellious generation of earth dwellers right from the first seal Christ opens. Twenty-one judgments follow in a series of seven seals, seven trumpets and seven vials or bowls over a period of seven earthly years. This truth is essential to an understanding that Christians of the Church Age will be taken home to the Father's house *before* this last seven years of judgment and wrath begins (read John 14).

The Lord prophesied during His Olivet Discourse (Matthew 24–25) shortly before His crucifixion about this terrifying time on planet Earth. Some argue that the first three-and-one-half years of this seven-year period will be mankind's own doing. However, mankind can do nothing if God does not allow it. When the Almighty takes His hand off this world—when the restrainer of 2 Thessalonians 2:7 is removed from His present office of restraint—wicked man will have his own willful way. The result will be anarchy, chaos and the most powerful terrorizing the weak. Man will get his wish in establishing a world based upon the hellish evolutionary theory. It will indeed be the survival of the fittest—or, perhaps more correctly stated, the survival of the most vicious.

Nature, too, will go wildly uncontrolled as the very stones cry out against man's refusal to acknowledge Jesus Christ as King of kings and Lord of lords. Thus, that first three-and-one-half years of the apocalypse will be as much God's wrath as will the last three-and-one-half years when His wrath falls from the cup of His indignation with more profusion and greater concentration.

Jesus addressed His disciples' question, "What shall be the sign of thy coming, and of the end of the world?" (Matthew 24:3): "Jesus answered and said unto them, Take heed that no man deceive you. For many shall come in my name, saying I am Christ; and shall deceive many. And ye shall hear of wars and rumors of wars: see that ye be not troubled: for all these things must come to pass, but the end is not yet. For nation shall rise against nation, and kingdom against kingdom; and there shall be famines, and pestilences, and earthquakes, in various places. All these are the beginning of sorrows" (Matthew 24:4-8).

Jesus was speaking of a specific time—the time of *sorrows*. This, I believe, refers to the beginning of the apocalypse or the tribulation. Ed Hindson and Daymond Duck dealt with false christs, false prophets, great deception and wars and rumors of wars in the first two chapters of this book. Let us now look at famines, pestilences and earthquakes in terms of what we see happening today—the foreshadows of the coming wrath—and what God's Word warns about the wrath itself.

It is perhaps good to further emphasize a few facts about the unsealing of the book. Dr. John Walvoord, the preeminent prophecy scholar of our day, gives us a good basis from which to consider matters concerning God's unfolding wrath. The Son of God, introduced as a Lamb that had been slain, holds in His hands a book having seven seals (Revelation 5). "This," Dr. Walvoord says, "will be the important means of revelation of future events in Chapter 6." This book, Dr. Walvoord explains,

> ...is not a book such as is common in our modern civilization, but rather is a scroll rolled on a roller such as they used at that time. In the vision, this roll of parchment is represented as having writing on both sides. On the edges of the roll, there are seals so placed that as it is unrolled it is necessary to break the seals one at a time. As each seal is broken, the scroll reveals another event that is prophetic of the coming time of Tribulation.[2]

"As chapter six begins," Dr. Walvoord continues, "the apostle John...sees the lamb, the Lord Jesus Christ, opening one of the seals. When the first seal is opened it begins a tremendously significant series of events. They picture a period of time of unprecedented trouble for the entire world."[3]

Dr. Walvoord, in answering the question concerning what the seals refer to and what events are here portrayed, states further:

> Many expositors of the book of Revelation believe that the next event in the prophetic program of the present age will be the coming of the

Lord for His church. This is called the Rapture, or the translation, of the Church. This could occur at any time.

After the rapture of the church has taken place, the last seven years of Israel's program described in Daniel 9 will unfold. This future period of approximately seven years will be climaxed by Christ's returning in power and glory to establish His kingdom in the world.

This coming of Christ is pictured in the nineteenth and twentieth chapters of Revelation. The seven years between the Rapture and the time that Christ comes back to the earth is the period which is before us in this book of Revelation beginning in Chapter 6.

As the seals are broken and the parchment is unrolled, the events to be fulfilled are revealed in graphic detail. The question might well be asked at this point why one should study this portion of Scripture. If, as a matter of fact, the saints will be in glory as Christians, why should we study this Scripture predicting a period that does not directly relate to us?

The answer is this: God has given this revelation by way of warning and informs us how this present age is going to end. As we study these terrible judgments as they are unfolded in the book of Revelation, they present to us God's prophetic foreview of the great climax of world history as it will take place in the terrible year just before Christ comes back in power and glory....[4]

Dr. Walvoord then presents an interesting analogy that might give us a clue as to why this present generation is witnessing an increase of frequency and intensity of unusual phenomena on many fronts:

As the first seal is opened, John in his vision hears the noise of thunder. It seems that the noise of thunder is a symbolic presentation of a coming storm. On a warm summer day, one can hear thunder in the distance even though the sun is still shining where he is. On the distant horizon, however, the dark clouds can be seen. The roar of thunder in the distance is the beginning of a storm. That seems to be the symbolism here. For the passage speaks of the noise of the thunder....[5]

Prophetic Tremors on the Rise

God's seismograph forewarned nearly 2,000 years ago of the end-time quaking we are beginning to experience today. The many upheavals are already progressing like a degenerative disease in most all areas of human affairs, whether considering socioeconomic, geopolitical, religious or technological matters, whether involving things pertaining to the geophysical and astrophysical, or maybe even what the New Agers call the paranormal.

To bring it back for a moment to Dr. Walvoord's analogy, the storm front is approaching and we hear the rumbling. Dr. J. Vernon McGee, in analyzing Revelation 8, which pictures a time of "silence in heaven" following the storm front that initially slams planet Earth following the rapture of the church, brings into focus for us how the distant rumblings we hear now, or if you will, these prewrath tremors we feel at present, will eventually affect mankind.

He says that this "heavenly hush" is but a brief lull in judgment activity indicating not the exhausted patience of God but rather the carefully measured reluctance of God, who is slow to anger, slow to judge: "This silence marks the transition from grace to judgment...."[6]

We are not at this present hour in the midst of the lull just before the seventh seal is opened, of course. That time of silence is scheduled to take place within the great apocalyptic storm itself, the tribulation period. We are, however, in a lull of sorts. A calm or stillness that permits this generation to hear the distant thunder warning of that approaching end-time storm. I am convinced we are in the midst of a time when God is gently, lovingly, trying to get the attention of mankind. Through His great, though not infinite, patience He is letting this generation feel the vibration of His righteous anger in order to call every person to repentance.

Last Days "Seismic" Activity

Global warming, "El Niño," a hole in the ozone layer, destruction of the rain forests, and many other ominous-sounding words and phrases have recently been made part of contemporary lexicon.

Although much of the furor around these issues are the rantings and ravings of environmental fanatics who want the American government to throw billions of dollars their direction so they can build power bases to influence people, it cannot be denied that there are portentous signals all around us.

Famines

Few scenes on television are more troubling than those showing tiny children in the throes of starvation. Many of us, if we are honest, admit that we've hurriedly changed channels and tried to erase from our minds the pictures of the little ones whose bellies are distended and whose skeletons, through emaciation, strain against ulcerated skin. America as a land of plenty is far removed from these distant places of deadly famine, and we prefer to keep it that way. There is coming, God's Word says, a time of such tragedy that it will afflict *every* area and most every person on the planet.

Following the first two horsemen of the four horsemen of the apocalypse, we read:

> And when he had opened the third seal, I heard the third beast say, Come and see. And I beheld, and, lo a black horse; and he that sat on him had a pair of balances in his hand. And I heard a voice in the midst of the four beasts say, A measure of wheat for a penny, and three measures of barley for a penny; and see thou hurt not the oil and the wine (Revelation 6:5,6).

Considering that Jesus, in His Olivet Discourse, said that this time of future tribulation would be the most terrible that earth dwellers would ever suffer, this third horseman account of famine during the apocalyptic era is indeed terrifying. People alive at the time will not be able to simply change channels or look the other way. They will be experiencing it in every sense. No matter where they live, it will be *their* tiny children with distended stomachs, pasty skin and emaciated bodies who will be looking up at them for food that cannot be found. This will be no ordinary famine—if there is such a thing—but starvation on a scale beyond our ability to imagine.

The first two riders of the apocalypse will have set the stage for this, the greatest famine in human history. Antichrist, who will have come on the scene promising peace and prosperity, will under satanic direction make life more miserable than ever for all of those who inhabit the earth. The red horse of war will prove once and for all man's absolute inability to institute world peace. The aftermath of the unprecedented devastation caused by the many conflicts raging around the globe will cause agricultural production to fall off and the resultant shortages will make prices inflate astronomically.

Dr. John Walvoord, in commenting on this era, states that in order to understand the vision of verses 5 and 6, we must first realize the worth of "penny," translated in the NIV, NKJV and NASB as denarius. Walvoord explains:

> In the wage scale of that time, it was nothing uncommon for a person to receive one denarius for an entire day's work. In other words, it was that which a common laborer would receive for a day's toil. For such a coin, one measure of wheat, or three measures of barley, could be purchased. The explanation seems to be this: A measure of wheat is approximately what a laboring man would eat in one meal. If he uses his penny to buy barley, which is cheaper grain, he would have enough within an entire day's wages to buy three good meals of barley. If he bought wheat, which is a more precious grain, he would then be only able to buy enough for one meal. He would not have enough left to buy either oil or wine. Oil and wine were considered essential in biblical times. The oil was used for shortening and the wine was a common beverage. To put it in ordinary language, the situation would be about the same as predicted. That one would have to spend a day's wages for a loaf of bread, and that one would not have enough money left to buy even an inexpensive beverage. What is portrayed here is a time of famine when life will be reduced to the barest necessities. Famine is almost always the aftermath of war.[7]

The third horseman riding the black horse of famine, then, sets up the horrible scene that follows—the pale horse of Revelation

6:8—when literally billions die while the wrath of God falls on incorrigible mankind.

All the famines of past generations will seem as nothing compared to this horrible era. The fourth horseman account says that many more will die by the violent acts of their fellow human beings, by beasts of the earth and simply by death (presumably mass starvation).

God's Word has much to say about famine. For example, see Genesis chapters 12 and 41; Ruth 1:1; 2 Samuel 21:1; 1 Kings 18:2; 2 Kings 6:25 and chapter 7; and Luke 4:25. However, we do not have to go back to biblical times to examine the terror within the human condition termed *famine*.

A Reuters news service story recently reported that the results of the 15-year Sudanese civil war threatens more than 700,000 people of southern Sudan with starvation.

> Hundreds of thousands of people in southern Sudan are facing severe famine. The rebel Sudan People's Liberation Army has made military progress against government forces this spring and the hostilities have made farming difficult. Relief agencies warn they are underfunded and ill-equipped to deliver food to an area the size of western Europe. Hundreds of people have died, and without urgent help, thousands more will perish, aid officials say.[8]

Hoofbeats of the black horse upon which rides the horseman of famine precariously balancing the scales already send seismic shock waves across vast areas of our globe. One recent story reports prices of staple goods in Indonesia rising 50, 70, even 200 percent, and a *Time* magazine article reports:

> Vietnam faces a stagnant economy, rebellious farmers, soured foreign investors, a rapidly expanding labor pool, and even the ravages of el niño. Predictions of drought in some parts of the country, flooding in others, have farmers scurrying to pagodas to pray for spiritual intervention. "This is our most serious crisis within a decade," says reform-minded economist Li Dang Dong.[9]

Droughts, floods, fires and smoke-related damage have adversely affected hundreds of thousands of agricultural areas in Asia. These and collateral problems caused by rebellious, angry people in the areas affected are taking their toll on food production across the world. Even the Americas are now on the verge of what seems to be a precursor period to the third horseman judgment of the apocalypse. Wildfires are, as of this writing, destroying vast rainforests of Central America and Mexico and sending destructive choking smoke to our nation, and the resultant effects are incalculable.

People become dangerously desperate when they are threatened by food shortages. One interesting observation along these lines in the southern state where I live at least is seeing what happens during the months of January and February when the weather forecasters warn of ice storms or even snow. The moment the forecasts are issued, people rush to the supermarkets to gather food to see them through, even though ice storms and snow storms in this area last only a few days at most. People become outright hostile and threatening to their neighbors in these situations, and grocery shopping becomes a rather risky business during these times.

If such a small, almost insignificant problem can cause such a crisis whereby people go temporarily insane and fight each other in supermarkets, what might a truly monumental food shortage crisis do to our so-called civilization?

One such crisis might very well loom on the horizon. Much continues to be written and said about the year 2000 (Y2K) problem. Could the computer glitch that many experts tell us cannot be fully avoided produce a food distribution crisis of major proportions?

However, the looming problem has the attention of many analysts, secular and nonsecular. (Noah Hutchings addresses the Y2K problem in-depth in chapter 14, "The Y2K Worry.")

Airplanes that will not fly, automobiles that will not run, telephones, television, computers that will not operate, electric power grids that fail. Experts fear these and many more problems because computers will read 00 as the year 1900 instead of 2000. But these would pale in comparison to food distribution problems just in the United States alone. The panic that might ensue when the supermarket shelves empty and American stomachs start rumbling could bring on anarchy. The potential certainly exists for a crisis of frightening dimensions. And even this possibly catastrophic situation would be nothing compared to the prophesied famine to be produced by the third rider of the great tribulation.

Pestilence

Jesus said in Matthew 24:7 that the tribulation period will be marked by pestilence. I believe the Lord, when prophesying pestilence during the great tribulation, meant that the coming pestilence will far exceed in dimension and virulence any such tragedy that has ever afflicted previous generations. Since, as we have been analyzing, indicators of our day strongly point to the fact that we are sensing other prewrath seismic activity, it should be interesting to note whether pestilence might be included in the quaking.

Just as famines in Jesus' Matthew 24 prophecy apparently coincide with the third rider who rides the black horse of Revelation 6:5, pestilence coincides with the rider on the fourth horse. Dr. Walvoord analyzes:

> In verses seven and eight, the fourth seal is opened, and the voice of the fourth beast is heard to say, "come and see." John writes, "And I looked, and behold, a pale horse, and his name that sat on him was Death and Hell followed with him. And power was given unto them over the fourth part of the earth, to kill with sword, and with hunger, and with death, and with the beasts of the earth."

> This is a very important step in the prophetic unfolding, for here is a terrible divine judgment on the world. The horse described as pale in color is more accurately pictured as a livid green horse. The rider on this horse is called Death and Hades, the abode of the dead, follows after him. Power is given to this rider over a fourth part of the earth to kill with the sword with hunger and with death and with the beasts of the earth....[10]

These judgments are truly awesome if we consider today's world population. Well over 1 billion people would die in that terrible era of future judgment if today's world population figures remained the same. Dr. Walvoord further states:

If one-fourth of the earth's population were destroyed in a single judgment from God, it would represent something far more terrible than anything this world has ever known since the time of the flood when God destroyed the whole human race with the exception of Noah and his family....The fourth seal of the book of Revelation makes clear that the prophecy does not deal with trivial things. But it is describing a period of world history that is awful beyond any word. It is prophesying a time when God is going to bring judgment on the world as He has never brought judgment on the world to this hour. It is a time of unprecedented judgment.[11]

One-fourth of the world's population at that time will perish by sword (war and homicide), hunger (famine), death (apparently by aging and every other cause), and by beasts of the earth. It is the latter death-dealing term that presents some fascinating possibilities regarding Jesus' prophecy about apocalyptic pestilence.

The fourth horse upon which the horsemen of death and hell ride is aptly called pale. Actually, it denotes a *chloros,* a sickly green color like that of human corpses if left unattended by mortuary science. When the pale horse gallops across the world scene literally billions of people will have already died because of the preceding judgments. Undoubtedly the decomposing, uninterred bodies will themselves contribute greatly to millions and millions of additional deaths when the fourth seal is broken.

"Beasts of the earth," including domesticated pets and other animals, will devour the corpses and scatter them as well as attack and kill many helpless, half-alive human beings. However, the term "beasts of the earth," according to some astute observers, might harbor an even more ominous connotation. Noted author, lecturer and Bible teacher Chuck Missler notes, "... This fourth horseman, although he is generally viewed as [indicating pestilence]...may reflect far more than just conventional diseases. Don't assume that the beasts of the earth are necessarily large enough to be seen with the naked eye.[12] Missler also points out the fact that the four horsemen of Revelation 6 seem to closely parallel Jesus' prophecies in Matthew 24—wars and rumors of wars, famines, pestilences, earthquakes and so on. And when Jesus states that if He did not return at the time of Armageddon "there should no flesh be saved," the Lord could have been referring to, in addition to other things, a frightening plague running rampant upon the planet.

Earthquakes

Jesus, the Lion of the tribe of Judah, said shortly before He was crucified that earthquakes will be a significant sign of the great tribulation. The Lord obviously meant earthquakes of unprecedented seismological dimension. The apostle John, awed in the presence of God and the heavenly hosts, watched as the glorified Christ, who alone was worthy to do so, unsealed the sixth seal. John recorded, "And I beheld, when he had opened the sixth seal and, lo, there was a great earthquake; and the sun became as black as sackcloth of hair, and the moon became as blood; and the stars of heaven fell unto the earth..." (Revelation 6:12,13).

God's wrath at that future time of judgment will be obvious even to the most hardened rebel. No doubt the great earthquakes of the time will open fissures when God Himself applies pressure to the tectonic plates crushing against one another. The prophecy in Revelation 6 forewarns of one specific earthquake of unparalleled magnitude. Most likely, that earthquake will cause a rift within the planet that will unleash tremendous volcanic activity.

The sun becomes dark, the moon turns blood red and heavenly bodies fall to earth. This is a tremendous time of geophysical and astrophysical catastrophes combining to constitute the greatest judgment yet to befall incorrigibly wicked mankind. Ash and sulfuric dioxide gases undoubtedly will explode into earth's atmosphere. Life on earth will become increasingly tenuous and the atmosphere will choke all creatures who draw breath while they stumble through a supernaturally darkened world.

Earthquakes we see and hear reported today, as devastating as they are in many cases, will seem as nothing compared to the quakes of the apocalypse. However, just as God is giving mankind today a hint of His coming wrath in every area of human affairs, He is also, through the intensity and frequency of earthquakes taking place, calling lost people to turn their hearts toward Him.

Seismic activity around the globe has exploded over the past two decades. Of course, part of this eruption stems from the fact that reporting earth tremors has improved and proliferated. The truth remains that seismologists continue to document increasing numbers of earthquakes. It is as if Jesus' words, "There shall be ... earthquakes in divers [various] places" (Matthew 24:7), were given to those alive at the end of the twentieth century as a foreshadowing of things to come.

Since the 1906 San Francisco quake, the intensity and frequency of tremors continue to mount. Reports of tremblers come in almost hourly. It seems no geographical area is immune from earthquakes these days. The following assessment by prophecy scholar Jack Van Impe presents some fascinating statistics on earthquake activity in history:

> History shows that the number of killer quakes remained fairly constant until the 1950s, averaging between two to four per decade. In the 1950s, there were nine, in the 1960s, there were 13, in the 1970s, there were 51, in the 1980s, there were 86. From 1990–1996, there have been more than 150.[13]

While increased seismological monitoring has made it appear that earthquake activity is on the rise, it is equally accurate to say that this generation has witnessed more earthquake activity than any other generation. Jesus' prophecy predicting that there will be mounting evidence that will indicate "a time of sorrows" (birth pangs) has been absolutely validated in our time. Jesus, by and for whom all things were created, prophesied through the prophet John two future earthquakes of staggering magnitude. The first of those yet future quakes will, despite its devastation, have a positive effect: "And the same hour was there a great earthquake, and the tenth part of the city fell, and in the earthquake were slain of men seven thousand; and the remnant were terrified, and gave glory to the God of heaven" (Revelation 11:13).

God will apparently use that future earthquake to manifest the truth of who He is. While 7,000 men—and that apparently refers to men of great reputation—will die as a result of the quake, many others will turn their hearts toward God in repentance. God's love is plainly shown even through His terrible wrath. He still calls rebellious people to repentance during this time of horrendous judgment.

The Quantum Quake

God's seismograph, through His omniscience, has registered prophetically the earthquake of all earthquakes. From the Bible we learn that this future quake will have instant worldwide ramifications and bring in its wake the full measure of God's wrath upon blasphemous mankind:

> And the seventh angel poured out his vial into the air, and there came a great voice out of the temple of heaven, from the throne, saying, It is done. And there were voices, and thunders, and lightnings; and there was a great earthquake, such as was not since men were upon the earth, so mighty an earthquake, and so great. And the great city was divided into three parts, and the cities of the nations fell.... And every island fled away, and the mountains were not found. And there fell upon men a great hail out of heaven, every stone about the weight of a talent [perhaps 100 pounds]; and men blasphemed God because of the plague of the hail; for the plague was exceeding great (Revelation 16:17-21).

Dr. John Walvoord says of this most powerful quake:

> The cities of the world fall, their magnificent structures being reduced to rubble. Great changes take place in the topography of the world at large. Every island is described as fleeing away, and mountains disappear. On top of this wholesale destruction visited upon the entire world, there comes a great hail out of heaven.... If this verse is interpreted literally, it pictures a desolation by this hail of that which remains from the destruction of the earthquakes. In spite of this great judgment, men still blaspheme God and fail to repent.

> The destruction described in the seven vials of the wrath of God to be poured upon the earth at the climax of the Tribulation is only the

beginning, however. The whole world is to be brought to the bar of justice before the King of kings and Lord of lords as He returns to rule. The dramatic presentation is designed to impress the reader with the fact that there is no safety apart from salvation in Christ, there is no escape of divine judgment apart from receiving the One who bore the judgment of sinners when He died for them on the Cross.

The study of these terrible judgments of divine wrath upon a wicked world should point us to the wonder of the grace of God who can take those who are sinners by nature and by choice and yet wonderfully save them and deliver them and make them fit objects for the grace and blessing of God.

The Word of God is plain: Salvation is the divine offer for all those who will trust in Christ, and judgment must be the lot of those who spurn divine grace.[14]

Those Not Subject to God's Wrath

Plainly, the things we have looked at involve the wrath of God Almighty, which will be fully poured out during that future time of apocalypse. Dr. Walvoord's commentary precisely points to God's one and only plan to keep you and me from that future time of righteous judgment. God's Word says in 1 Thessalonians 5:3: "For when they shall say, peace and safety; then sudden destruction cometh upon them, as travail upon a woman with child; and they shall not escape."

The entire world at present is crying "peace and safety." The journalistic and diplomatic eyes of the world are on that little city called Jerusalem and on Israel because the powers-that-be blame that nation for refusing to give in to the Palestinian Liberation Organization's (PLO) demand that Israel give up more and more land for peace. Note the pronoun used in this prophecy: "When *they* shall cry peace and safety." The Scripture here, I believe, separates the lost, unbelieving world from those who believe in Christ. When "they" cry peace and safety, then sudden destruction comes upon "them" and "they" shall not escape. Notice the pronoun usage in verses 4 and 5 of 1 Thessalonians 5: "But ye, brethren, are not in darkness, that that day should overtake you as a thief. Ye are all the children of light, and children of the day: we are not of the night, nor of darkness." And now look at verse 9: "For God hath not appointed us to wrath, but to obtain salvation by our Lord Jesus Christ." "We" Christians of the Church Age are saved by the marvelous grace of God. We will not come under His wrath either during the tribulation period or following the great white throne judgment (during which time the awesome judgment of God will be meted out).

Some who believe that the rapture of the church will take place at midtribulation rather than in the pretribulation era base their theory on the premise that God's wrath doesn't begin falling until three-and-a-half years into the apocalypse. But Jesus Christ, the Lion of the tribe of Judah, opens the seals, one through seven, as depicted in Revelation 6. Because Jesus Christ is God, the judgments that flow from those seals are God's judgments, thus His wrath. Since Christians, as is plainly stated in 1 Thessalonians 5:9, are not appointed to wrath, but to salvation through Jesus Christ, they will escape the time of the apocalypse—all of it (see Revelation 3:10).

The famines, pestilences and earthquakes of our daily headlines foreshadow that unimaginable time of God's wrath. The birth pangs that will produce the apocalypse convulse this world hourly. Therefore, it is more important now than ever before that we who are God's children through His grace gift, Jesus Christ, work to bring lost people to the Lord while at the same time looking for "that blessed hope, and the glorious appearing of the great God and our Saviour, Jesus Christ" (Titus 2:13).

▼ ▼ ▼

CHAPTER 4

Signs in the Sun, Moon and Stars

Chuck Missler

Jesus warned us that

there shall be signs in the sun, and in the moon, and in the stars; and upon the earth distress of nations, with perplexity; the sea and the waves roaring; men's hearts failing them for fear, and for looking after *those things which are coming on the earth:* for the powers of heaven shall be shaken (Luke 21:25,26, emphasis added).

Cosmic Threats?

When gigantic fragments of the Comet Shoemaker-Levi 9 crashed into the planet Jupiter in July of 1994, almost every significant telescope watched the awesome collisions. Ever since, concerns have been expressed regarding what would be the result of a similar collision on planet Earth. Our entertainment media, armed with the latest digital special-effects technologies, has begun a spate of asteroid collision films highlighting the difficulties in dealing with an unwelcome trajectory of such debris.

Comets are essentially dirty snowballs composed of ice, stones and flaming gases. They are less solid than asteroids, but their greater speeds offset their lesser mass. They are apparently of relatively recent origin or they would decay before they reach the earth. Approximately 650 comets have been scientifically recorded, the largest being about 42 miles in diameter. Approximately five new comets are discovered each year and billions may be beyond the farthest planets. There are also innumerable asteroids, some of which are of substantial size. "Eros" is 13 miles long, about the size and shape of Manhattan. "Juneo," 120 miles; "Vesta," 240 miles; "Pallas," 300 miles. "Ceres" is 480 miles in diameter (it would not fit in the state of Texas). The earth's atmosphere protects us from the smaller asteroids. However, if they are larger than 50 meters (half the size of a football field), they pack about 10 megatons of energy, comparable to some of our larger warheads. These larger asteroids are expected to near the earth about once per century. In 1972 the earth narrowly missed a 10-megaton impact.[1]

Despite the widespread presumptions (of which we all are guilty) that our universe is uniform, stable and linear, all one has to do is look through a set of binoculars at the moon or examine the planets via photographs returned by our space probes to see that our solar system is obviously a rough neighborhood. It is quite apparent that the history of our solar system has been characterized by collisions and catastrophes of all sorts.

The earth accumulates about 100 tons of extraterrestrial material every day under a constant rain of interplanetary debris. Most meteoroids enter the atmosphere and burn up unnoticed. Some survive the fiery heat of entry and are slowed down by air friction to a speed of about 200 miles per hour, and what is left hits the ground as a meteorite. If it weren't for the constant reworking of the earth's surface by erosion and plate tectonics, our own planet would be as densely cratered as the moon. There are currently more than 100 craters on the earth, some ranging up to 80 miles in diameter.

Near-Misses and Hits

In October 1992, the media broke the news that our planet was in danger of being hit by a comet.[2] Fortunately, supplemental observations revealed that no collision is likely for centuries, at least until eight more orbits are completed.[3] The comet "Swift-Tuttle" passes near the earth about every 130 years, each time a little closer. It is unusually large and travels at 125,000 miles per hour. On January 23, 1982, an asteroid almost a third of a mile in diameter passed within 2.5 million miles of the earth without being observed. It was discovered *a month later*.[4] And on March 22, 1989, a closer near-miss ("1989 FC") missed us by only six hours (400,000 miles)!

A famous example of an asteroid that hit the earth came down in Tunguska (central Siberia) on June 30, 1908, devastating more than 2,000 km[2] of forest. The Tunguska region is so remote that it wasn't explored until 17 years later. Had it been a comet, it probably would have exploded at a higher altitude and done no damage. Had it been composed of denser iron, it would have reached the ground making a large crater. It was apparently a rocky asteroid, about the size of a city office building, that decelerated and exploded at an altitude of five miles. In 1994, scientists found tiny fragments of this rocky object imbedded in tree resin at the impact site. The meteor crater near Winslow, Arizona, was formed by just such a metallic meteorite, with the same 15-megaton energy as Tunguska. Experts estimate that such impacts happen about once every 300 years on the earth's surface, but only once every millennium on land.

Even relatively modest-sized asteroids can result in substantial long-term impacts. A tsunami from a Tunguska-class object could produce widespread destruction and even devastate continental coastlines. Some scientists attribute the extinction of prehistoric species to cosmic collisions of the past.[5] Polar instability (they have moved thousands of miles) and numerous magnetic reversals may have been triggered by such collisions.[6] (This is the type of event which may have been involved with the "Long Day" of Joshua [see Joshua 10:13].[7])

In 1991, the discovery of a crater (named Chicxulub) under Mexico's Yucatan peninsula is conjectured by some to have resulted in the extinction of the dinosaurs. The size of this asteroid has been estimated to have been over six miles in diameter and its energy estimated at over 100 million megatons—5 billion Hiroshima atomic bombs![8]

Defensive Measures

The Planet Crossing Asteroid Survey, coordinated by Jet Propulsion Lab, is intended to be an international program to track asteroids near the earth. (Asteroids are deemed more hazardous than comets since they are far more elusive and almost invisible until they have already passed.) Those objects whose orbits cross ours are called Apollo objects. NASA reports that there are almost 4,000 such objects more than half a mile across,[9] and astronomers estimate that about 80 of them are on courses that could lead to collisions with the earth.[10]

NASA has proposed constructing Spaceguard, a system of six new telescopes around the world, for the specific purpose of identifying threatening asteroids.[11] However, it has been estimated that even with this facility, 10 percent of threatening asteroids would still get through undetected. (Even comets coming in from the far reaches of the solar system for the first time would not be perceived until 6 to 12 months before impact.) A space-based solution may have to be undertaken and may be another justification for an international effort. NASA has also studied the problems of interception and deflection,[12] but this proves to be an even more formidable task than the Strategic Defense Initiative because asteroids travel fast and can be very large. Also, breaking one up into chunks may not deflect the chunks adequately. One of the strongest proponents of defensive measures is Dr. Edward Teller.[13] At the recent "International Technical Meeting on Active Defense of the Terrestrial Biosphere from Impact by Large Asteroids and Comets" at the Livermore National Laboratory, he strongly advocated serious commitments to develop a meaningful program.[14]

Alien Encounters?

Perhaps even more disturbing are the almost systematic increases in the reports of encounters with what many believe are alien spacecraft. People report having been buzzed, beeped, burned and even abducted and probed by strange creatures occupying strange craft. In recent years these accounts have included reports by more than a dozen NASA astronauts that they, too, have seen strange extraterrestrial vehicles that have also been simultaneously tracked on radar.

A few decades ago such reports were restricted to lone couples driving on back country roads in the middle of the night. In more recent years it has become almost commonplace to have thousands of people view the phenomena for hours over major cities in Mexico, Korea, Europe and Israel, as well as in Phoenix, Arizona, and Washington, D.C. These strange encounters have been increasingly the subject of serious scientific inquiry, and they appear to involve crafts that are tracked on radar and leave tangible traces on the ground such as radiation. Yet they also appear to defy physical laws as we know them by exceeding the speed of sound without sonic booms, executing sharp turns at incredibly high speeds, and even seeming to materialize or dematerialize at will. Compounding the extensive confusion on this subject, UFO encounters are also the subject of considerable disinformation, hoaxes and government intervention (and possible cover-ups). Even the Vatican, with an intelligence network second to none, has confirmed their existence.

Are these crafts from outer space? Or are they from another dimension? Increasingly, the most committed scientists, as exemplified by J. Allen Hynek of the United States and Jacques Vallee of France, have concluded that they appear to be hyperdimensional and probably demonic.[15]

Perhaps most disturbing of all are the frequency and consistency of reports by people who believe they have been abducted and intrusively examined by the occupants of strange crafts. These tales are too bizarre to accept, but too frequent and consistent to ignore.

Some polls have suggested that this activity may involve over 1 percent of the U.S. population!

Scientific conferences at places like the Massachusetts Institute of Technology (MIT) have been convened by professionals who are at a loss to explain—or deal with—those who relate such encounters. The purported abductees have been profiled as above average intelligence with no prior psychiatric history, and yet they clearly appear to be the victims of a traumatic event of some kind. To add to the mystery, the reported medical examinations administered seem to be preoccupied with investigations of the human reproductive processes. After personally dealing with almost 100 such cases, Dr. John Mack, formerly head of the Department of Psychiatry at Cambridge Hospital, Harvard University, shocked the professional scientific world when he announced publicly that he believes that the beings are real and they appear to have an agenda of establishing a hybrid race.[16]

The Biblical View of Aliens

Is there the possibility that these encounters may be a prophetic link with the strange events recorded in Genesis chapter 6?

> And it came to pass, when men began to multiply on the face of the earth, and daughters were born unto them, that the sons of God saw the daughters of men that they were fair; and they took them wives of all which they chose.
>
> ...There were giants [Nephilim—NIV] in the earth in those days; and also after that, when the sons of God came in unto the daughters of men, and they bare children to them, the same became mighty men which were of old, men of renown (Genesis 6:1,2,4).

This strange passage describes the bizarre circumstances that led to the extreme disaster of the famous flood of Noah. The term translated "the Sons of God" is, in the Hebrew, בְּנֵי־הָאֱלֹהִים, bene-ha'elohim, which is a term consistently used in the Old Testament for angels.[17]

When the Hebrew Torah, which, of course, includes the book of Genesis, was translated into Greek in the third century before

Christ (giving us what is known as the Septuagint Translation), this expression was translated *angels.*[18] This carries great weight since this translation was benefitted by the best experts at that time, and their translation was the one most widely quoted by the writers of the New Testament. Also, the *Book of Enoch* also clearly treats these strange events as involving angels.[19] Although this book was not considered part of the "inspired" canon, the *Book of Enoch* was highly venerated by both rabbinical and early Christian authorities from about 200 B.C. through about A.D. 200, and is useful to authenticate the lexigraphical usage and confirm the accepted beliefs of the period.

The biblical passage refers, clearly, to *supernatural beings* intruding themselves upon the planet Earth. (There are alternative interpretations of this, which we will examine shortly.) "The daughters of men" (הָאָדָם בְּנוֹת, b*e*noth ha'adam, literally, "the daughters of Adam") refers to the natural female descendants of mankind. (Notice that no particular genealogical history is specified.) These errant, supernatural "alien" beings apparently mated with human women and produced unnatural *superhuman* offspring! The term translated *giants* is from the Hebrew, נְפִילִים, n*e*philim, and literally means "the fallen ones" (from the verb *nephal,* to fall). In the Septuagint translation, the term used was γίγαντες, *gigantes,* or "earth-born."[20]

The Heroes of Mythology

These unnatural offspring, the *Nephilim,* apparently were monstrous and have also been memorialized in the legends and myths of every ancient culture on planet Earth. These also seem to be echoed in the demigods of Greek legends and fables.[21] Throughout Greek mythology we find intercourse between the gods and women which yielded half-god, half-man *Titans,* demigods or heroes that were partly terrestrial and partly celestial.[22] Hercules is but one example. The seductions attributed to Zeus include Thetis, Dione, Leda, Metis and Europa.[23] Some scholars even attribute some of the ancient monuments, such as the Great Pyramid near Cairo, to these ancient giants. There are also some attempts to link the Great Pyramid to the peculiar "face"[24] on the planet Mars.[25]

Why was the presence of the *Nephilim* so great a threat that God would resort to such an extreme measure as a worldwide flood?

The Gene Pool Problem

In Genesis 6:9, we encounter another strange reference: "These are the generations of Noah: Noah was a just man and perfect in his generations, and Noah walked with God." The word for "generations" is well understood since it is frequently used to refer to genealogies, but what does "perfect in his generations" mean? The word translated "perfect" is תָּמִים, *tamiym*, which means "without blemish, sound, healthful, without spot, unimpaired." This term is used of physical blemishes.[26] This suggests that Noah's genealogy was not tarnished by this intrusion of *fallen angels.* It seems that this adulteration of the human gene pool was a major problem on planet Earth, and Noah was among the few left who were not thus contaminated.

Fallen Angels?

The "angel" view of this classic Genesis text is well documented in both the ancient Jewish rabbinical literature as well as the writings of the early church. In addition to the Septuagint Translation, the venerated (although noncanonical) *Book of Enoch,* the Syriac Version of the Old Testament as well as the *Testimony of the 12 Patriarchs,*[27] and *The Little Genesis,*[28] confirm the lexigraphical usage and the extant beliefs of the ancient Jewish scholars. It is clear that the learned Philo Judaeus understood the Genesis 6 passage as relating to angels.[29] Josephus Flavius also clearly represents this view:

> They made God their enemy; for many angels of God accompanied with women, and begat sons that proved unjust, and despisers of all that was good, on account of the confidence they had in their own strength, for the tradition is that these men did what resembled the acts of those whom the Grecians call giants.[30]

The early church fathers understood the expression "sons of God" in accordance with the ancient interpretation as designating angels. These included Justin Martyr,[31] Irenaeus,[32] Athenagoras,[33] Psuedo-Clementine,[34] Clement of Alexandria,[35] Tertullian,[36] Commodianus,[37] and Lactantius[38] to list a few. It was also espoused by Martin Luther and many more modern exegetes, including: Koppen, Twesten, Dreschler, Hofmann, Baumgarten, Delitzsch, W. Kelly and A.C. Gaebelein.

The "Lines of Seth" View

Yet many able scholars hold a different view. Some students of the Bible have been taught that this passage refers to a failure to keep the "faithful" lines of Seth separate from the worldly line of Cain. The idea is advanced that after Cain killed Abel, the line of Seth remained faithful, but the line of Cain turned ungodly and rebellious. The "sons of God" are deemed to be referring to the line of Seth; the "daughters of men" referring to the line of Cain. The resulting marriages blurred the separation between them. (Why the resulting offspring are called the *Nephilim* is still without any clear explanation.)

The "sons of Seth and daughters of Cain" interpretation obscures the intended grammatical antithesis between the sons of God and the daughters of Adam. Attempting to impute this view to the text flies in the face of the earlier centuries of understanding of the Hebrew text among both rabbinical and early church scholarship. Substantial liberties must be taken with the literal text to impose this view. Furthermore, the term "daughters of Adam" does not denote a restriction to the line of Cain, but indicates that many of *Adam's* descendants seem to have been involved. In fact, these "daughters" are the same as those referred to earlier in the same sentence! And what about the "*sons* of Adam?" Were they innocent? Why were they not spared in the judgment?

Perhaps even more to the point, procreation by parents of differing religious views does not produce unnatural offspring. Believers marrying unbelievers may produce "monsters," but hardly superhuman, unnatural children. The lexigraphical antithesis clearly intends to establish a contrast between the "angels" and the women of the earth.

It should also be pointed out that most conservative Bible scholars reject the "Sethite" view.[39] Among those supporting the angel view are: G.H. Pember, M.R. DeHaan, C.H. McIntosh, F. Delitzsch, A.C. Gaebelein, Arthur W. Pink, Donald Grey Barnhouse, Henry Morris, Merrill F. Unger, Arnold Fruchtenbaum, Hal Lindsey and Chuck Smith.

New Testament Confirmations

In biblical matters it is essential to always compare Scripture with Scripture. The New Testament appears to confirm the angel view in its comments concerning the judgment of these fallen angels. Both Jude and the apostle Peter comment on these issues. In 2 Peter 2:4,5 we read:

> For if God spared not the angels that sinned, but cast them down to hell [*Tartarus*], and delivered them into chains of darkness, to be reserved unto judgment; and spared not the old world, but saved Noah the eighth person, a preacher of righteousness, bringing in the flood upon the world of the ungodly...

Even Peter's vocabulary is provocative. He uses the term *Tartarus*, here translated *hell*. This is the *only* place this Greek term appears in the Bible. *Tartarus* means "dark abode of woe"; "the pit of darkness in the unseen world." As used in Homer's *Iliad*, it is "as far beneath hades as the earth is below heaven...."[40] In the Greek mythology, some of the demigods, Chronos and the rebel Titans were said to have rebelled against their father Uranus and, after a prolonged contest, they were defeated by Zeus and condemned into *Tartarus*.

Peter's comments even establish the time of the fall of these angels to the days of the flood of Noah, both here and in his earlier epistle:

By which also [Christ] went and [proclaimed][41] unto the spirits in prison; which sometime were disobedient, when once the longsuffering of God waited in the days of Noah, while the ark was a preparing, wherein few, that is, eight souls were saved by water (1 Peter 3:19,20).

The epistle of Jude[42] also alludes to the strange episodes when these "alien" creatures intruded themselves into the human reproductive process:

And the angels which kept not their first estate, but left their own habitation, he hath reserved in everlasting chains under darkness unto the judgment of the great day. Even as Sodom and Gomorrah, and the cities about them in like manner, giving themselves over to fornication, and going after strange flesh, are set forth for an example, suffering the vengeance of eternal fire (Jude 6,7).

The allusions to "going after strange flesh," keeping "not their first estate," having "left their own habitation," and "giving themselves over to fornication," seem to clearly fit the alien intrusions of Genesis 6.

It is interesting that the word translated *habitation,* οἰκητήριον, *oiketerion,* refers to the heavenly bodies from which they had disrobed. This term appears only twice in the New Testament, each time referring to the body as a dwelling place for the spirit.[43] The "giving themselves over to fornication and going after strange flesh" seems to have involved their *leaving* their earlier "first estate," that is, the body they were initially "clothed with."

The Capabilities of Angels

We know relatively little about the nature, essence, powers or capabilities of angels. We know they seem to have no problem materializing into our space and time. They spoke as men, ate meals,[44] took people by the hand[45] and were capable of direct combat. One was responsible for the death of the firstborn in Egypt.[46] Another killed 185,000 Syrians.[47] (You don't mess around with angels!)

Angels always seem to appear as men,[48] because they are always rendered in the masculine. Remember, they were attractive targets for the homosexuals of Sodom.[49] The New Testament indicates that many of us may have encountered angels without discerning any uniqueness: "Be not forgetful to entertain strangers: for thereby some have entertained angels unawares" (Hebrews 13:2).

But some people regard Christ's comments regarding marriage in heaven as disqualifying the "angel" view of Genesis 6:

> But they which shall be accounted worthy to obtain that world, and the resurrection from the dead, neither marry, nor are given in marriage: neither can they die any more: for they are equal unto the angels; and are the children of God, being the children of the resurrection[50] (Luke 20:35,36).

In heaven there is no need for procreation. Marriage is a human institution to prevent the extinction of the race by death. This statement by Jesus Christ makes no comment on the *capability* for sex or other mischief of the *fallen* angels. They can fall; they can aspire to degeneracy. What limits their technologies? Some ancient traditions attribute to the disclosures of angels the various arts and sciences of the ancient world.[51]

Post-Flood Occurrences

Regarding the *Nephilim,* Genesis 6:4 also includes the haunting phrase, "and also after that." Apparently these strange events were not confined just to the period *before* the flood. There seems to be some recurrence of these things that resulted in unusual giants appearing in subsequent periods later in the Old Testament narrative, specifically the giant-races of Canaan.

A number of tribes such as the Rephaims, the Emims, the Horims and the Zuzims (also known as Zamzummims) were giants.[52] The kingdom of Og, king of Bashan, was the "land of the giants."[53]

When Moses sent his 12 spies to reconnoiter the land of Canaan, they came back with the report of giants in the land.[54] (The term used was *Nephilim.*) Their fear of those terrifying creatures resulted in their being relegated to wandering in the wilderness for 38 years.

When Joshua and the nation Israel later entered the land of Canaan, they were instructed to wipe out every man, woman and child of certain tribes.[55] That strikes us as disturbingly severe, but it seems that in the land of Canaan, there was again a "gene pool problem."

These Rephaim, Nephilim and others seem to have been established as an advance guard to obstruct Israel's possession of the Promised Land. Was this also a stratagem of Satan? Later, we find Arba,[56] Anak and his seven sons (the "Anakim") also as giants, along with the famed Goliath[57] and his four brothers.[58]

The Destiny of the Nephilim

Most students of the Bible tend to assume that the demons of the New Testament are equivalent to the fallen angels. Angels, however, have the ability to materialize, physically touch people, share meals, and so on (except those presently bound in *Tartarus*). In contrast, the demons appear to desperately seek embodiment.[59] Angels and demons seem to be quite different creatures.

The Nephilim, the unnatural offspring, are apparently not eligible for resurrection.[60] The bodies of the Nephilim, of course, were drowned in the flood. What happened to their spirits? Could these disembodied spirits be the demons of the New Testament? These may well have continued through the *dæmones incubi* of the Middle Ages and may also be recurring through the UFOs of today. Are the increasing number of abduction reports a recurrence of this kind of intrusion?

Is it possible that these strange occurrences may fulfill end-time prophecies? In Daniel 2 we encounter Nebuchadnezzar's famous dream that Daniel interprets as an overview of all Gentile empires from then until the time when God establishes His own. There are four, as expressed in the four metals of the image in his dream: gold (Babylon), silver (Persia), brass (Greece), and iron (Rome). The fourth is described as later emerging in a second phase: the iron mixed with miry clay. (This same pattern is confirmed in a later series of visions given to Daniel directly, as recorded in Daniel 7.)

Daniel's portrayal suggests that these pieces will ultimately recombine into some final form before the end. This theme is echoed in many other passages and is one of the reasons that many Bible commentators have, for centuries, looked for an ultimate revival of the Roman Empire, in some form, at "the time of the end." This final empire, represented by the ten toes of iron mixed with miry clay, is the subject of many passages dealing with the final climax. It will be in the days of the ten toes that the "stone cut without hands" will smite the image and set up God's own government upon the earth. This "stone," which the builders rejected, is, of course, the Lord of lords, Jesus Christ.

The Return of the Nephilim?

Even our common expression "the idol has feet of clay" comes to us from Daniel's classic passage. But just what is represented by the "miry clay"? It seems to be strangely mixed (but not completely) with the iron in the dream. The term "miry clay" is from an Aramaic root meaning clay made from dust. There is a strange allusion when Daniel explains:

> And whereas thou sawest iron mixed with miry clay, *they shall mingle themselves with the seed of men:* but they shall not cleave one to another, even as iron is not mixed with clay ... (Daniel 2:43, emphasis added).

Daniel switches to a personal pronoun—*they* "shall mingle themselves with the seed of men." This is extremely suggestive when viewed in light of the warning of our Lord that "As the days of Noah were so shall also the coming of the Son of man be" (Matthew 24:37). Just who are "mingling with the seed of men"? Who are these non-seed? Could this be a hint of a return to the mischief of Genesis 6? Are "aliens" and their hybrid offspring part of the political makeup of this emergent world empire? Are the UFO incidents part of a carefully orchestrated demonic program to lead us toward a political agenda? It staggers the mind to contemplate the potential significance of Daniel's passage and its implications for the future global governance.

Jesus opens and closes this confidential briefing to His disciples with an emphasis on guarding against deception: "Take heed that no man deceive you" (Matthew 24:4). He further emphasizes that, "There shall arise false Christs, and false prophets, and shall shew great signs and wonders; insomuch that, if it were possible, they shall deceive the very elect" (Matthew 24:24). This means our intellect and scientific information is no protection against the times that are coming. Only our position in Jesus Christ and our spiritual preparation will avail. *Are you prepared for the days ahead?* Indeed, our Lord has warned us that it will be a terrible time:

> Men's hearts failing them for fear, and for looking after those things which are coming on the earth: for the powers of heaven shall be shaken (Luke 21:26).

▼ ▼ ▼

CHAPTER 5

Distress of Nations with Perplexity

Gary Hedrick

And there will be signs in the sun, in the moon, and in the stars; and on the earth distress of nations, with perplexity, the sea and the waves roaring (Luke 21:25).

When the disciples asked Jesus when He would be coming back, He responded with a series of remarkable signs and trends[1] that He said would characterize the period immediately before His second coming. The Lord entered these reference points into the prophetic record so the terminal generation—that is, those of us who are alive on earth when the end-time drama commences—will be able to monitor the progression of events right up to the end of the age.

The apostle Paul wrote, "But you, brethren, are not in darkness, so that this Day should overtake you as a thief" (1 Thessalonians 5:4). Every generation of believers, like the first-century congregation at

Thessalonica, has been admonished to be expectant and watch for the day of the Lord.

However, we have always known that only one generation would actually survive to witness these events firsthand. The Bible outlines a number of prophetic indicators that will be reflected in world conditions as the time of His return draws near. None of these indicators, by itself, is prophetically significant. They only become significant when they happen simultaneously, with unprecedented frequency and intensity. Jesus said, "So you also, when you see *all these things,* know that it is near—at the doors!" (Matthew 24:33, emphasis added).

Technically, because the rapture is an imminent event and is not associated with any specific prophetic sign, it can happen at any time. However, the prophetic trends Jesus said will characterize the world *after* the rapture, during the tribulation, will surely become evident even *before* this seven-year period commences. In fact, a trend, by its very nature, develops over an extended period of time. It does not happen suddenly.

The Olivet Discourse

Preterists and other nonmillenarians claim the Olivet prophecy was fulfilled in its entirety nearly 2,000 years ago when the Romans destroyed Jerusalem in A.D. 70. Even references to the sun, moon and stars (Matthew 24:29; Luke 21:25), they say, are not literal but figurative. Interpreters such as John Gill point to obscure Jewish sources referring to the "sun" symbolically as the kingdom of the house of David, the "moon" as the Sanhedrin and the "stars" as the rabbis, or teachers of Israel. They suggest that the kingdom ("sun") was darkened, the Sanhedrin ("moon") stopped giving its light (for example, stopped handing down legal decisions) and the teachers of Israel fell from their positions of leadership—and it all happened in A.D. 70.

One problem with this approach is that it is simply not consistent with traditional Jewish interpretation. The Babylonian Talmud mentions the "sun, moon and stars" 13 times and in 11 of those instances it refers to literal heavenly bodies. The Soncino edition of the Talmud uses "sun, moon and stars" in a figurative sense only twice and neither of those references pertains to the Davidic kingdom, the Sanhedrin or the rabbis.[2]

Another problem is that the Olivet prophecy climaxes with the second coming of the Messiah: "Then they will see the Son of Man coming in a cloud with power and great glory. Now when these things begin to happen, look up and lift up your heads, because your redemption draws near" (Luke 21:27,28). Who is naïve enough to believe that Christ returned in A.D. 70? The Son of Man did not return to earth in power and glory, the Jewish people were not rescued and the promise of Zechariah 14:11, that Jerusalem would never again be destroyed, was not fulfilled. Quite to the contrary, the land was overrun by the Romans in A.D. 68–70, Jerusalem and the temple were burned to the ground, and the Jewish people were scattered to the four winds.

There is only one tenable position—that many elements of the Olivet Discourse await a future fulfillment during the coming tribulation period and subsequent return of the Messiah to planet Earth.

A World in Distress

One of the trends prophesied in the Olivet Discourse is "distress of nations, with perplexity." The Greek word translated *distress* comes from a verb meaning "to squeeze" or "to compress." In classical Greek, this word was used to describe a "cattle squeeze," a contraption whose sides could be pushed inward to hold an animal in position while the farmer administered medication.

This imagery from an ancient farm suggests an interesting analogy. As we approach the time of the end, the nations will be increasingly wicked and out of control. We see this even in the Old Testament messianic prophecies, including: "Why do the nations rage, and the people plot a vain thing? The kings of the earth set themselves, and the rulers take counsel together, against the LORD and against His Anointed, saying, 'Let us break Their bonds in pieces and cast away Their cords from us'" (Psalm 2:1-3). So how does the Lord respond to this rebellion of the nations? David tells us, "He who sits in the heavens shall laugh; the LORD shall hold them in derision. Then He shall speak to them in His wrath, and distress them in His deep displeasure: 'Yet I have set My King On My holy hill of Zion'" (verses 4-6).

It is difficult to imagine a more appropriate description of the world today than the one presented in Psalm 2. David prophesies that the rulers of the earth will "take counsel together." All we have to do is look around us and see that there are more international organizations in the world today than at any other time in history. There are regional and global alliances, trade agreements, economic treaties, and on and on it goes. Yet the international community in our generation continues to be plagued by ethnic conflict, anarchy and colossal power struggles.

Unseen powers are at work behind the scenes that no one seems to understand. World leaders themselves are pawns in a global board game—a game in which their moves are orchestrated by people and organizations motivated by lust for power, position and monetary gain. There is no room for the Lord in the world's halls of power. The international scene, then, is evolving just as the prophets said it would. The Lord is allowing the nations to back themselves into a corner where the problems of the world seem overwhelming. This is the Lord's way of "squeezing" an out-of-control world and holding it tightly in place while He administers a sobering dosage of His wrath and judgment.

Getting Ready for the Anti-Messiah

One of the most mysterious characters mentioned in the prophetic Scriptures is the end-time political leader known as the Antichrist. Actually, this unusual title comes to us from the Greek New Testament, where it appears as *antichristos* (1 John 2:18,22; 4:3; 2 John 7). The prefix *anti* means "against" or "opposed," and *christos* is the Greek equivalent of the Hebrew *mashiach,* or "anointed one." So it literally designates someone who is diametrically opposed to God's Anointed One, the Messiah. In the Hebrew

New Covenant, or *Berith haChadashah,* the Antichrist is known as *Tzoror haMashiach,* or Enemy of the Messiah.

The apostle John explains that a spirit of antichrist has been active in the world for at least 2,000 years: "Little children, it is the last hour; and as you have heard that the Antichrist is coming, even now many antichrists have come, by which we know that it is the last hour" (1 John 2:18). Near the end of this age, a political leader will rise to prominence on the world scene. Although he is portrayed in Scripture as a very charismatic and persuasive individual, he will also be the very incarnation of evil. He will embody the pervasive spirit of antichrist that has been active since the first century. Since the prophets intimated that he would come from the same ethnic stock as the people who destroyed the temple in A.D. 70, we expect him to be a Roman or European (see Daniel 9:26). He will come from somewhere in the Mediterranean world, or roughly the geographical area that corresponds to the ancient Roman Empire.

This evil, end-time political leader is known by a number of biblical names, including the little horn (Daniel 7:8); a king with "fierce features" (8:23); "the prince who is to come" (9:26); the abomination of desolation (9:27; Matthew 24:15); "the man of sin" and "the son of perdition" (2 Thessalonians 2:3); "the lawless one" (2:8); "the beast" (Revelation 11:7; 13:1ff.); and, of course, "the Antichrist" (anti-Messiah) (1 John 2:18).

In Christian eschatology, as well as in Jewish tradition, the Messiah is a divinely anointed Deliverer who comes to rescue His people, Israel, in the midst of a great military calamity. Once the enemies of Israel are vanquished, He establishes a worldwide kingdom of peace and prosperity for all nations:

> Now it shall come to pass in the latter days that the mountain of the LORD's house shall be established on the top of the mountains, and shall be exalted above the hills; and all nations shall flow to it.
>
> Many people shall come and say, "Come, and let us go up to the mountain of the LORD, to the house of the God of Jacob; He will teach us His

ways, and we shall walk in His paths." For out of Zion shall go forth the law, and the word of the LORD from Jerusalem.

He shall judge between the nations, and rebuke many people; they shall beat their swords into plowshares, and their spears into pruning hooks; nation shall not lift up sword against nation, neither shall they learn war anymore (Isaiah 2:2-4).

The anti-Messiah will oppose God's end-time program in every way he can. He will take steps to consolidate his own power base so he can bring the nations together and form a counterfeit kingdom. He will oppose God's King, Jesus Christ, by setting himself up as a king.

Webster's *Ninth New Collegiate Dictionary* explains the Greek derivation of the prefix *anti* and says it means "... of the same kind but situated opposite, exerting energy in the opposite direction, or pursuing an opposite policy." How interesting! According to Webster's, the prefix *anti* suggests something opposite, but still "of the same kind." The anti-Messiah and the true Messiah are both deliverers. They are both redeemers, and both are known as kings. But they have vastly different motives and opposing agendas. The true Messiah is led by the Spirit of God; the anti-Messiah is controlled by the forces of darkness. The true Messiah will establish God's kingdom on earth; the anti-Messiah will attempt to establish a satanic kingdom on earth.

How will the Antichrist elevate himself to a position where he wields so much political power on earth during the tribulation? There are several answers to this question. *First, the Bible explicitly says the Antichrist will be supernaturally empowered by Satan.* Describing his vision of the "beast," or Antichrist, the apostle John wrote, "The dragon [Satan] gave him his power, his throne, and great authority" (Revelation 13:2; cf. 12:9). Like the serpent in the Garden of Eden, he will be a Machiavellian character in every way—calculating, cunning and crafty.

Second, the Antichrist will possess extraordinary powers of oratory. The prophetic Scriptures tell us that "he was given a mouth speaking great things and blasphemies" (Revelation 13:5; cf. Daniel

7:8,11,20,25; 11:36). He will be able to sway the masses with his engaging personality and convincing words.

Third, the Antichrist will be perceived as a miracle worker. The apostle Paul wrote, "The coming of the lawless one is according to the working of Satan, with all power, signs, and lying wonders, and with all unrighteous deception among those who perish, because they did not receive the love of the truth, that they might be saved" (2 Thessalonians 2:9,10). Prophetic scholars continue to debate the question of whether the Antichrist will have the ability to work genuine miracles. Will his "lying wonders" be nothing more than clever sleight of hand, perhaps using laser technology, holographic images or other deceptive techniques? It is a moot question, however, because the result is the same whether the miracles are genuine or not. Many people will assume that the Antichrist's miracle-working powers come from God. Unfortunately, they will be wrong (cf. Matthew 7:21-23).

Fourth, God will allow the Antichrist to possess these uncanny powers of persuasion and leadership. "And for this reason God will send them strong delusion, that they should believe the lie" (2 Thessalonians 2:11). Over and over again, John says "it was given to" the beast to do these remarkable things. In other words, he is permitted to carry out his tribulation program. God even allows him to "make war with the saints and to overcome them" (Revelation 13:7). It is true that the Antichrist's authority comes from the dragon, or Satan (verse 4), but we also know that all authority in heaven and on earth has been given to Jesus Christ (Matthew 28:18). This means even the devil exercises authority only by the permissive will of Almighty God!

Fifth, the restraining influence of the Holy Spirit will be removed during the tribulation. The Holy Spirit lives in believers (1 Corinthians 6:19). So, when the church is caught up in the rapture (prior to the commencement of the tribulation), the Holy Spirit will also be removed. There will be no more "salt" or "light" left in this old world (cf. Matthew 5:13-16). In a very real sense, this will allow Satan and his minions full reign on earth. "And now you know what is restraining, that he may be revealed in his own time. For the mystery of lawlessness is already at work; only He who now restrains will do so until He is taken out of the way. And then the lawless one will be revealed, whom the Lord will consume with the breath of His mouth and destroy with the brightness of His coming" (2 Thessalonians 2:6-8).

Sixth, the international community will be prepared to accept a leader who demonstrates an ability to deal effectively with the world's mounting problems. As we enter the twenty-first century, the nations of the world are increasingly distressed and perplexed, just as Jesus prophesied in His Olivet Discourse. Economic and political problems, military emergencies, not to mention the world-wide expansion of Islamic fundamentalism and related security issues, will add to the frustration of world leaders. That is why they will be receptive to the Antichrist's message of "peace and safety" (1 Thessalonians 5:3).

Many Christians think of the Antichrist as a ruthless dictator who will seize power, enslave the masses and transform the world into a global police state. However, I think this is largely a misconception—at least in the beginning. The prophets compare the kingdom of the Antichrist to the ancient Roman Empire (Revelation 13:1; Daniel 7:23-25), and historians tell us that the empire was hardly a police state. There was a period of military conquest, obviously, but for much of its 1,000-year reign the Roman Empire was actually a relatively loose confederation of nations. The Romans often allowed local kings and rulers to remain in power and serve as governors. Nations were actually clamoring to join the empire because Roman citizens enjoyed many social, economic and political benefits not available to noncitizens.

The Antichrist, then, probably will not use gestapolike tactics to seize power. Instead, he will mesmerize the nations, like the snake-charmer from India who holds a cobra under his spell by playing a flute. The Antichrist's "flute" will be his silver-tongued oratory and uncanny ability to forge alliances and solve problems. Evidently, what puts the Antichrist on the map politically, at first, is a seven-year, comprehensive Mideast peace agreement that he arranges (Daniel 9:27). The agreement might include permission for

Orthodox Jews to construct a temple on Mount Moriah, possibly in exchange for a Palestinian State in the West Bank. Whatever form the agreement takes, the Antichrist will no doubt will be acclaimed as a hero for succeeding where so many before him have failed. It is not difficult to imagine him being awarded the Nobel peace prize for such an achievement.

First, however, he will focus on consolidating his own base of power, which will very likely be in Europe. Again, many scholars conclude that he will arise from this part of the world because Daniel said the Antichrist would be descended from the same people who destroyed Jerusalem and the temple in A.D. 70 (Daniel 9:26)—namely Romans or Europeans. Furthermore, the Antichrist is portrayed by John as a beast "rising up out of the sea" (Revelation 13:1), a reference to the Mediterranean world and the geographical area occupied by the ancient Roman Empire.

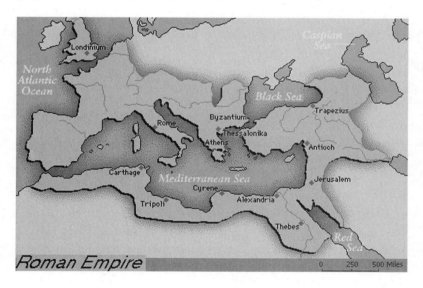

Interestingly enough, our generation has seen the nations of this region coalesce into a United States of Europe. In fact, the prestigious financial publication *Strategy and Business* recently published an advisory under the title "Business Expectations and

Strategy for the United States of Europe."[3] Skeptical readers should note that this information did not originate with religious fanatics delirious with millennial fever. The article's coauthors were Franco Modigliani, winner of the 1985 Nobel Memorial Prize in Economic Science and professor at the Massachusetts Institute of Technology, and Hossein Askari, director of the Institute for Global Management and Research and chairman of the International Business Department at George Washington University.

Here, in part, is what Modigliani and Askari reported to their clients in the global financial community:

> The economic size and significance of the 15 countries that make up the European Union are indisputable. The combined 1995 gross domestic product of these countries was estimated at $8.4 trillion, exceeding that of the United States ($7 trillion). This means that Europe is the largest single market on the face of the globe.

Effective January 1, 1999, 11 European Union (EU) member states adopted a common currency (known as the "euro") under an agreement that binds their economies irrevocably together. The euro will be gradually phased in until the transition is complete on January 1, 2002, making the union even stronger. Without question, the EU has become a world superpower in its own right. The Antichrist will likely use this platform (the EU) to launch his political career. From there he will use his negotiating skills and charisma to extend his influence, sway the masses and subdue his foes (Daniel 7:23,24). He will take advantage of deteriorating world conditions to maneuver himself into a position of global leadership.

Earth: A Planet in Trouble

The Earth Council is an international, nongovernmental organization (NGO) created in September 1992 "to promote and advance the implementation of the Earth Summit agreements."[4] These summits, held in 1992 and 1997 in Rio de Janeiro, Brazil, brought together leaders from more than 100 nations to discuss ways of advancing "the mutually reinforcing goals of sustainable development: environmental health, economic prosperity, social equity, and general well-being" for all the inhabitants of planet Earth. Yet the Earth Council acknowledges that it has made little headway in improving the planet's plight since the first summit in 1992. Here are the facts:

- *More than 100 nations are worse off today than they were 15 years ago.* Some 1.3 billion people have daily incomes of less than $1, and 60 percent of humanity lives on less than $2 per day.

- *The gap between the richest and poorest 20 percent of the world's people has doubled* over the past 30 years, from 30-fold to 60-fold.

- *Approximately 1.5 billion people live with dangerous air pollution; 1 billion live without clean water; and 2 billion without sanitation.*

- *Eighty percent of direct foreign investment in the developing world goes to only a dozen countries,* all classified as "middle income" with the exception of China. Just 5 percent goes to Africa and 1 percent to the 48 least-developed nations.

- *The debt burden on the developing world continues to mount, now reaching $2.1 trillion.* Sub-Saharan Africa's debt payments are larger than its expenditures on health and education, even though 63 percent of adults in this region—currently more than 20 million people—are infected with HIV. Experts say this tragic AIDS epidemic is so pervasive and so advanced that entire populations are in danger of being wiped out.

- *Less than a quarter of the world's population consumes three-quarters of its raw materials and produces 75 percent of all solid waste.* A child born in the United States will have 30 times more impact on the earth's environment during his or her lifetime than a child born in India, according to the Earth Council's report.

The U.S. Center for Refugees reports that one of the critical issues of the twenty-first century will be the growing refugee crisis. Millions of families worldwide have been driven from their homes in areas ravaged by war and political turmoil.

Worldwide Refugees and Displaced Persons

Africa	2,944,000
Europe	2,020,000
The Americas & the Caribbean	616,000
East Asia & the Pacific	535,000
Middle East	5,708,000
South & Central Asia	1,743,000
World Total	**13,566,000**

Taken from the *1997 World Refugee Survey* published by the U.S. Center for Refugees
1717 Massachussetts Ave., NW, Suite 701, Washington, DC, 20036

Terrorism in the Twenty-First Century

Yet another problem the world faces as we enter the next millennium is that of global and domestic terrorism. Militant Islamic and other terrorist groups can strike without warning virtually anywhere in the world. While it is true that a majority of Muslim people, particularly Sunnis, do not endorse such deadly tactics, the unfortunate reality is that a sizable and very violent Muslim minority believes martyrdom during the course of carrying out a terrorist act is "the pathway to paradise."

Over and over again, the State of Israel has been the target of brutal and cowardly terrorist attacks. Radical Palestinian groups have indiscriminately murdered and mangled men, women and children by detonating pipe bombs on buses and in public places in Jerusalem and Tel Aviv. Libya has been linked to terrorism in various parts of the world, and so has Syria. Northern Ireland has suffered at the hands of terrorists for decades.

The bombing of the World Trade Center in New York City on February 26, 1993, showed that we are not safe from these attacks—even on American soil. The mastermind of the bombing, Ramzi Yousef, confessed to the FBI that he "sought to punish the United States for its continued aid to Israel."[5] Yousef fled the country after the bombing, but was arrested in Pakistan in February 1995, and extradited to the United States. This was not his first brush with the law; he had previously been convicted for his role in a plot to create

"48 hours of terror in the sky" by bombing a dozen U.S. passenger jets. Yousef allegedly said he hoped the blast in New York City would topple one tower on top of the other, which could have cost 250,000 lives.

On April 19, 1995, the attack on the Murrah Federal Building in Oklahoma City by white supremacist, antigovernment terrorists shocked the nation yet again. In the deadliest mass murder in American history, 168 men, women and children perished. Apologists for the "Christian Patriot Movement" claimed the attack was in retaliation for the horrible extermination of the Branch Davidians in Waco, Texas, two years earlier to the day, by out-of-control government agents.

In February 1998, two men were arrested in a Nevada medical laboratory and charged with possessing a biological agent—in this case, anthrax—for use as a deadly weapon. According to law enforcement authorities, the pair may have planned to release the substance in the New York City subway system. One of the men allegedly had bragged about having enough anthrax to wipe out much of the population of New York City.

Experts say the threat of biological terrorism is very real. Somewhere, sooner or later, it will happen, and we are not ready:

> "A monumental task lies before us," Dr. D.A. Henderson told the International Conference on Emerging Infectious Diseases.

> Biological agents are the ultimate "stealth" weapons—invisible and virtually undetectable. Scientists said easily obtained materials could be used to unleash pandemics of ebola, anthrax and smallpox, and the world's nations, including the United States, are not fully prepared for such an event.

> "The specter of the biological weapon's use is an ugly one, every bit as grim and foreboding as the picture that has been painted of a nuclear winter," said Henderson, of the Johns Hopkins University School of Public Health. "It is not 'if' but 'when'... and I hope we're going to be prepared."[6]

Needed: A Man with a Plan

Occasionally, we hear someone say, "We don't need a Messiah. Humankind can pull itself up by its own bootstraps. We haven't done all that badly so far." Tell that to a child in Africa who has lost his entire family to AIDS, lives on the streets, and whose belly is swollen from malnutrition. Tell it to a mother and father in the former Soviet Union who have lost their factory jobs and cannot buy food or clothing for their kids. Tell it to the young children of a mayor in South America who was gunned down, along with his wife, by drug smugglers while corrupt law enforcement officials looked the other way. Tell it to Palestinians and Israelis in the Middle East who are tired of living in the cross fire of hostile factions on both sides.

The evidence is clear: This old world is in trouble. (See the following chart, "Prelude to the Tribulation.") Increasingly there is a sense of desperation and frustration among the nations as one political scheme after another is doomed to failure. Any leader who can offer substantive solutions to the world's many problems will be enthusiastically received and hailed as a great deliverer or messiah. This is what the prophets said long ago, and it could happen in our generation.

▼ ▼ ▼

PRELUDE TO THE TRIBULATION:
Distress of Nations with Perplexity

REGION	COUNTRIES AFFECTED	NATURE OF CRISES	VOLATILITY RATING*
Eastern Europe	The Czech Republic, Poland, Romania, Bulgaria, Belarus, Ukraine, Slovakia, Hungary	The government of Belarus is becoming more totalitarian, prompting the opposition press to compare the Belorussian president to Stalin. The Ukrainian economy is propped up by huge loans from the International Monetary Fund. Experts fear that former Soviet nuclear arsenals could be dismantled by cash-starved governments and sold to the highest bidder.	★★★
Balkans	Slovenia, Croatia, Bosnia and Herzegovnia, Serbia, Yugoslavia	Conflicts between government forces and rebels have resulted in massive casualties. Serbian leaders have been indicted on charges of genocide. In 1995, NATO deployed a 60,000-person, multinational peace-keeping force in the region to stop fighting between Bosnian Serbs, Muslims and Croats, but isolated fighting continues.	★★★
Western Europe	England, Ireland, Scotland, Spain, Portugal, France, Austria, Belgium, Netherlands, Germany, Scandinavian Countries, Switzerland	The 15 nations of the European Union comprise the greatest unified economic bloc in the world. They continue the trend of consolidation by adopting a single currency in 1999. The Lomé Convention extends the EU's influence beyond Europe to include 70 affiliated nations in Africa, the Caribbean and the Pacific.	★
Mediterranean	Greece, Turkey, Cyprus, Italy	Political analysts express concern that Turkey's secular government might be overthrown by Islamic extremists. A 13-year-old war between Kurdish rebels and the Turkish army continues as Kurdish refugees flee to Italy in droves. Greece and Turkey continue to be at odds over the divided island of Cyprus. Italy pins hopes on the new European common currency (euro) to pump new life into its faltering economy.	★★

*Four stars means very volatile

PRELUDE TO THE TRIBULATION:
Distress of Nations with Perplexity

REGION	COUNTRIES AFFECTED	NATURE OF CRISES	VOLATILITY RATING*
Russia	Russian Federation	The transition from a collectivist economy to a free, market-based economy has created many hardships in Russia. Westernization has brought unemployment, inflation, corruption, prostitution and an organized crime syndicate known as "the Russian Mafia." The streets of major cities are unsafe and anti-Semitism is on the rise.	★★★
Caucasus	Armenia, Georgia, Azerbaijan	The resignation of Armenia's president in 1998 was a disturbing blow against peace and ethnic harmony in the Caucasus. "Christian" (i.e., Orthodox) Armenia is at war with its larger and richer Muslim neighbor, Azerbaijan. In April 1998, the U.S. and Britain jointly undertook a secret operation to remove nuclear material from Georgia because of the volatile political situation there.	★★★
Central Asian Republics	Kazakhstan, Turkmenistan, Tajikistan, Uzbekistan, Kyrgyzstan	All five states have faced severe economic, social, ethnic and political problems since the breakup of the Soviet Union in 1991. Unemployment and political instability plague the region. Democracy has taken hold only in Kyrgyzstan, and to a lesser extent in Kazakhstan. Tajikistan's near civil war with a coalition of Islamic and pro-democracy groups has badly damaged its economy and left it heavily dependent on Russia.	★★★

*Four stars means very volatile

PRELUDE TO THE TRIBULATION:
Distress of Nations with Perplexity

REGION	COUNTRIES AFFECTED	NATURE OF CRISES	VOLATILITY RATING*
Baltic States	Lithuania, Latvia, Estonia	Relations between the Baltics and their much larger neighbor Russia are strained. Russian officials, in fact, have accused Latvia of "genocide" against ethnic Russians living in Latvia. The region suffers from the same economic problems as the rest of the former Soviet Union.	★★
Middle East	Israel, the Arab States, portions of northern Africa (Egypt, Libya)	The on-again, off-again Mideast peace process continues to falter. Palestinian leaders undercut the Oslo Accords by refusing to delete references to the destruction of the State of Israel from their charter. The Iraqi nuclear and biological weapons program continues in open defiance of UN prohibitions. Islamic terrorist organizations based in the Middle East continue their campaign of Jihad ("Holy War") around the world.	★★★
Africa	Rwanda, Sudan, Somalia, Angola, Congo, Burundi, South Africa, Kenya, Ethiopia	Much of Africa is in political and economic turmoil. Millions are starving under corrupt military dictatorships. Millions more are threatened by an out-of-control AIDS epidemic in Sub-Saharan Africa.	★★★
Indian Subcontinent	India, Sri Lanka, Pakistan, Bangladesh, Afghanistan	A "new Islamic order" has been introduced in economically troubled Pakistan while neighbor India continues to struggle with an eight-year rebellion in Kashmir. Both India and Pakistan possess nuclear weapons and have conducted recent tests in defiance of international bans. Bangladesh, one of the poorest nations in the world, is ravaged by floods and famine.	★★½

*Four stars means very volatile

PRELUDE TO THE TRIBULATION:
Distress of Nations with Perplexity

REGION	COUNTRIES AFFECTED	NATURE OF CRISES	VOLATILITY RATING*
Asia/Pacific Rim	China, Taiwan, North and South Korea, Japan, Australia, New Zealand, Indonesia, Burma, Cambodia, Vietnam	China, the most populous country on earth with 1.2 billion people, absorbed Hong Kong in 1997 and now has its sights on tiny island neighbor Taiwan. With much of the rest of the region still reeling from recent economic setbacks, China—officially both communist and atheistic—is set to continue expanding its influence well into the next century. North Korea, one of the world's last communist dictatorships, cannot feed its own people due to the massive amount of resources it diverts into ballistic missile and nuclear weapons programs.	★★★
The Americas	Canada, United States, Mexico, Central America, South America	Several countries in Latin America are plagued with political insurrection and terrorism. Powerful drug cartels control corrupt government officials and the influence of communist factions is growing. Illegal immigrants pour across the U.S. border to escape the poverty and homelessness that are rampant throughout much of Mexico, Central America and South America. In the U.S., metropolitan areas are ravaged by racial strife and gang violence.	★★★

*Four stars means very volatile

Part 2

Ezekiel and John Prophesy the Fate of Nations

Chapter 6

Israel on the Spot

Zola Levitt

If it weren't for the Bible, it would certainly be hard to explain why Israel is considered so important in the world today. Indeed, when we look at nations with populations comparable to Israel's, we find they are only rarely in the news as would be expected. For example, Benin, Paraguay and Denmark have their ups and downs like all nations, but the goings-on in such relatively small places is of little concern to the world leaders, the media and the man on the street. David Bar-Illan, senior advisor to Prime Minister Benjamin Netanyahu of Israel and his media spokesman, bemoaned the fact that his boss was known worldwide while he himself could not even name the prime ministers of comparable-sized nations around the world.

Media attention is what makes a prime minister or a nation famous or infamous in today's world, and for some reason (known only to God) Israel gets much more than its share. While a handful of reporters cover European capitals, there are 400 newspeople, TV commentators and the like in Jerusalem every day! While entire revolutions take place in countries ten times Israel's size with minor media coverage, CNN virtually stops its news day to report that the orthodox and the secular Jewish people are arguing again on some Israeli street. The *Dallas Morning News,* a reliable critic of Israel along with so many of its sister newspapers in this country, ran a picture of so-called strife while covering some neighborhood disagreement in the Holy Land in which there were zero casualties. The front-page story was accompanied by a huge photograph of the factions that were arguing. Page 13 of the same paper recorded seven murders over the same weekend in Dallas.

The *New York Times,* our "newspaper of record," keeps up a steady drumbeat of criticism of this allied democracy no matter what else in the world is happening. I think that if a world war broke out, the *Times* editor would order his reporters to keep a front-page space open for its usual Israel coverage—whatever else might be happening!

Media attention in the modern world simply means negative coverage, since the media tends to feature the world's troubles. Cynicism, negativism and some sort of nether drama marks our media these days. They are turning into entertainment organizations desperate to draw a crowd to whom they hawk the products of their advertisers. The crowd is evidently better drawn by the sort of negative news that is part and parcel of the human condition. Witness the litany of robberies, killings, fires, and so on reported on the local TV news each night in every American city. The media could cover the good works of their cities every night just as it could cover the fact of Israel's miraculous restoration, in one generation, that evolved into a progressive modern democracy. But news editors favor the tried and true; bad news about good people always sells.

There might be an even more sinister idea at work in the media's negative coverage of the news. Wars are a boon to any media. CNN charged triple the going rate for commercials during its coverage of the Persian Gulf War, and sponsors lined up to pay those prices. It did not escape the notice of the editorial board that real conflict—bombs, people dying in the streets, big fires—provided a huge audience like no local robberies and murders could. What if they could arrange their own wars? This almost science-fiction concept may be unconsciously at work today. Coverage of what the media views as trouble spots—Bosnia, Ireland, Africa, and oddly enough, Israel—is in place just in case some spark ignites a real shooting war. And needless to say, coverage of the news in such places aims to exacerbate their situations. Hence the "plight" of the Palestinians and Israel, the "hopelessness" of the arguments in Ireland. We might say that the media are continually publishing introductions for war in the hope that some war will commence where their people are in place. Then the media accomplishes its major purpose, its reason for being: It makes big money.

We must keep in mind that the media are not some public service but simply profit-making businesses that charge substantial fees for the coverage provided. In *Forewarning* and *Foreshocks of Antichrist* I pointed out that the media are likely supported by petrol dollars since makers of oil-based products buy a great deal of advertising. If the makers of cars, cosmetics, gasolines and so forth are not pleased with the sort of coverage they receive in the media—if it does not somehow support Arab oil interests—then they may buy less advertising space. And so we have a profit-making business covering an ordinary day-to-day life situation in Israel in a most negative and provocative way for greater profits.

For its part, Israel goes along, the only democracy in the Middle East achieving wonderful things. Its per capita income is now comparable to that of England and greater than that in the largest Arab oil-producing states, including Saudi Arabia. As a result the Arabs of Israel, the only Arabs privileged to live in a democracy in the Middle East, are profiting as well and have a standard of living hardly imagined by Arab people elsewhere. (The Egyptian government issues precious few visas for its citizens to visit Israel even though this is perfectly allowable under the Camp David peace accords and Israelis visit Egypt every day in huge numbers. I believe the government of Egypt doesn't want its citizens to see how well the Arabs of Israel are living. They fear an absolute revolution when people see their cousins in the Holy Land driving cars, drinking clean water, having doctors in their villages and schools and so on.)

The international solution to Israel's success seems to be to cut the place in half, give the Jewish people less land and somehow bring peace by dividing one of the smallest nations in the world. Certainly it is the division of the world's available land into smaller and smaller parcels with different governments that causes the rash of "wars and rumors of wars" of the latter half of this century. When the United Nations was founded in the late 40s, there were less than a hundred nations, and at this point there are close to two hundred. Having more nations simply provides the situation where "nation will rise against nation."

Israel must be the most obvious example of creating new boundaries that create new troubles. If Saddam Hussein of Iraq could complain that the British mapmakers drew a boundary cutting off the province of Kuwait from Iraq then what would Israel say? Iraq has a murky history emanating from about the time of the Arab conquest of Mesopotamia more than 1,000 years ago, but Israel started out as one nation under Jewish leadership 35 centuries ago! History and archaeology show this to be Jewish land from the Mediterranean to past the Jordan River, and from the deserts of the south to northern borders that exceed the Galilee and Golan Heights on the north. But even though the formal boundaries of Israel are about half the size of what they were in biblical times, world leaders, and especially Arab leaders, demand that even this small area be cut in half again and an equal portion be given to those who have sworn to drive Israel into the sea.

"It Is Written"

Why is all this happening to Israel? The best of all reasons is that prophetic Scripture says it will happen. While the world press dithers over Israel's supposed intractability with the peace process or bad treatment of the Palestinians or a wrong-headed prime minister, the real reason is that Israel must be maneuvered into a position where it will be "hated of all nations" (Matthew 24:9).

It is well to remember that close to 100 percent of end times prophecy concerns that tiny nation, and the biblical signs of the end pertain especially to Israel. The Olivet Discourse of our Lord— His answer to the disciples' question, "What will be the sign of Your coming and of the end of the world?" (Matthew 24:3)—details phenomena that are global in scope but of particular concern to those in the Holy Land. The Lord addresses His disciples as Israelites in particular when He observes, "He that shall endure unto the end, the same shall be saved" (verse 13).

It is the Jewish people gathered in Israel at the time of Armageddon who must endure "unto the end"—that is the second coming of the Lord—to be saved. At the time, "they shall look upon me whom they have pierced, and they shall mourn for him as one mourneth for his only son.... In that day there shall be a fountain opened to the house of David and to the inhabitants of Jerusalem for sin and for uncleanness" (Zechariah 12:10; 13:1).

It is imagined that the Jews are receiving some sort of favor or second chance due to their salvation at the second coming, but they are saved by seeing the Lord come out of heaven to stop that mad battle raging in Jerusalem. Since He is coming back to the earth exactly in their midst where they stand back to back in their nation's capital ("And his feet shall stand in that day upon the mount of Olives..." [Zechariah 14:4]), they simply see Him come and they believe. Undoubtedly, Gentile soldiers engaged in Armageddon who look up and see Him are saved as well. After all, anyone looking up into the sky and seeing a heavenly figure riding a white horse with a robed army behind Him and an identification on that robe reading "King of kings and Lord of lords" will believe, and that's all there is to that. They believe by seeing, but this is after the age of grace when we believe in "things not seen."

Besides that piece of evidence that the signs of the end are given in particular to Israel, Matthew 24:15,16 advises, "When ye therefore shall see the abomination of desolation, spoken of by Daniel the prophet, stand in the holy place (whoso readeth, let him understand:) then let them which be in Judea flee into the mountains" rather than try to cope with the Antichrist. The advice presupposes that the Jews are pretty much gathered in Jerusalem at that dramatic time. I belabor the point that Israel is concerned in Matthew 24 because that discourse is often taught in reference to the church and erroneously leads to the church having to endure the tribulation. But obviously Israel is singled out for instructions because it is deeply involved in end-times prophecy.

We know that the start of the tribulation period is signaled by the Antichrist's peace covenant with Israel, and it is obvious that we are being prepared for such news day by day. The "peace process" has conditioned the world to imagine that there is some drastic situation in Israel that badly needs some international agreement to settle it. To look at the world objectively, it is clear that peace covenants are needed much more in other trouble spots where there are real conflicts going on and not in Israel, which is suffering from something more like a common ghetto problem. But to satisfy the prophecy, world opinion is being manipulated to where the Antichrist's seven-year offer will be most welcome. Even the Israelis, I think, will sign that covenant in a hopeful spirit out of necessity at the time it is offered. (The necessity will not be the need to make peace, but simply pressure from the United Nations and certain powerful members to come to some accommodation with the Arabs.) The media will immediately trumpet the idea that peace has at least been achieved in Israel only to be proved as wrong as when we trumpeted the same thing about Ireland in 1998. We can all recall the glad ceremonies and triumphant dinners and toasts that preceded the worst bombing in the history of Irish terrorism.

The Antichrist's false peace will last longer than the Irish false peace by three years or so. At the midpoint of the tribulation, at exactly three-and-a-half years after the signing of the covenant, the Antichrist will perform that "abomination of desolation, spoken of by Daniel the prophet" (Matthew 24:15) and proclaim himself God in the tribulation temple! (The temple may have been built as one of the stipulations of the original peace covenant, but in any case, it will be standing on Mount Moriah at the midpoint of the tribulation.) The Antichrist will "cause the sacrifice and the oblation to cease" (Daniel 9:27) as he reneges on his agreement. And that, in a sense, begins Armageddon. I believe it is from that point that the king of the East begins to mobilize the most fearsome army the world has ever known. China and possibly other Far Eastern powers will march 200 million men all the way to Israel evidently to challenge the Antichrist, who they do not believe is God. The Chinese communists, after all, are atheists and believe that no one is God, and the huge number of Chinese Moslems (outnumbering the ethnic Chinese) will take the Antichrist to be a total pretender since he is not Allah. And finally military-minded China will simply note that the Israelis did not believe the Antichrist had supernatural powers since they bolted (taking the Lord's advice). And so the Chinese and other Far Easterners will be motivated to vanquish the pretender, the Antichrist in Jerusalem who claims to be the God of Israel.

A visit by a 200,000,000-man army will do Israel little good. This will be the most difficult-to-handle tour of Israel ever undertaken, and the land and the people will suffer.

Anti-Semitism: A Sign of the End

Anti-Semitism is the motivating factor of the Antichrist, as it is of all of those who counterfeit or simply cannot accept the simple gospel of the Lord. Jesus Christ, the Messiah of the Jews, said that if you're not for Me, you're against Me, and the Antichrist is certainly first among those who are against Him and His people at the end. It is amazing that just a generation after the Holocaust anti-Semitism is obvious again in the world today. In the United States and elsewhere, the Jews, for reasons hard to understand, are despised with special derision. From American country clubs to Swiss banks to Oriental imaginings of Jewish-caused economic problems, hatred of Israel and the Jewish people is a normal state of affairs in this world. And increasing anti-Semitism is a true symptom of the end of the age.

Anti-Semitism has a long history, much of it chronicled in Scripture. Moses' pharaoh, Nebuchadnezzar, Antiochus and Titus received scriptural credit for their hatred, or were prophesied about in Scripture, but hatred of the Jews did not let up after biblical times. The coming of the Moslems in the seventh century A.D. was the beginning of a perennial prejudice against Israel as virulent today as it ever was. The Crusades, the Inquisition and general discrimination against Jewish communities throughout Europe and Russia kept the chosen people moving from place to place in hope of respite. Finally in the United States, and seemingly only there, did the soles of their feet find rest, and there they prospered.

But even in America, anti-Semitism has been a latent but effective force against God's chosen. We could take for granted a certain amount of anti-Jewishness in the church, particularly in the "liberal" churches. It was these very denominations who punished the Jews in Europe throughout the Middle Ages. One does not normally find aversion to the Jews among Bible-reading people, but occasionally the biases of the denominations seem to infect the true believers.

When my son Aaron went to a Christian high school, a teacher said one day that Christianity did not start in Israel, but actually in Greece. When I spoke to the teacher, I reminded him that Jesus Christ is Jewish, and so were all of His disciples and all of His apostles. Jesus came to this earth and declared to His disciples, "Go not into the way of the Gentiles, and into any city of the Samaritans enter ye not: But go rather to the lost sheep of the house of Israel" (Matthew 10:5,6).

Obviously, errors are creeping into our Christian universities and colleges. A textbook called *A Survey of the New Testament,* by Robert H. Gundry, is in use at Dallas Baptist University and Criswell College.

Let me highlight a few of the errors being taught in this book:

> • *"'And they glorified the God of Israel' (Matthew 15:31), shows that the 4,000 whom Jesus now feeds are Gentiles."*
>
> This idea on the part of the one who said, "I am come only unto the lost sheep of the house of Israel" (Matthew 15:24) is followed by a vain attempt to create a non-Jewish following of Jesus. The author

goes on, *"Together then, with the preceding Gentile woman and, earlier, the centurion and the Magi, they represent the great mass of Gentiles who are flocking into the church of Matthew's time."*

There was no church in Matthew's time, nor any "great mass of Gentiles" saved in the Gospels, though they are to come in considerable numbers later on.

- The author subscribes to Replacement Theology: *"Matthew writes his Gospel for the Church as the new chosen nation, which at least for the time being has replaced the old chosen nation of Israel."*

- *"Luke was probably a Gentile... his name is Greek. His facility in using the Greek language also suggests that he was a Gentile."*

The same things were true of Paul, certainly a Jew and a "pharisee of Pharisees." (This and other points are contradicted by our excellent study by Dr. McCall entitled "Was Luke a Gentile?" which appears in the March 1996 issue of the *Levitt Letter*. You can read it on our website at www.levitt.com.)

The author promotes an anti-Israel Replacement Theology doctrine, and he appears to misunderstand the mission of Jesus Christ, who came, as He said, to bring the Kingdom to Israel. If secular colleges are bothered by PC (political correctness), Bible colleges need to watch out for PD (Progressive Dispensationalism), the doctrine behind these distortions.

There are plenty of other questionable textbooks in our seminaries, and many other seminaries that have fallen into this sort of doctrine. I believe Replacement Theology teaches a bias against the Jews and their homeland. And so among what should be the best friends of Israel that America contains, a false doctrine based on anti-Semitism flourishes.

Ultimately, the Antichrist will bring the most horrific anti-Semitism the Jews have ever experienced. It is important to the Antichrist's counterfeit of Jesus that he be accepted as *the* Messiah, and he evidently attempts to make that happen. He is rebuffed by Israel, which has a long history of rejecting false messiahs (and the real Messiah), and so he ultimately enters the temple itself and proclaims himself Almighty God! At this, the Jews flee, and the doom of Armageddon is sealed.

Many teach that Israel will accept the Antichrist as their messiah, but this is nowhere indicated in Scripture. The fact that they sign a peace covenant with him is an act of far less magnitude than accepting him as messiah, of course. They have been signing peace agreements for years now, and the Antichrist's will seem to them to be just a longer term, more serious attempt to settle Middle East turmoil. Their mere acceptance of his treaty terms does not amount to accepting him spiritually. It is quite possible that they are rightly suspicious of him from the beginning, but they want so badly to have peace—and possibly to have some arrangement whereby they can rebuild the temple—that his covenant will seem acceptable at the time. But when he later reveals himself as a true counterfeit of God, they will have no more of him. And that, of course, sets the stage for the world mobilization for that cataclysmic battle.

Who Is the Antichrist?

I've been asked who the Antichrist is in speaking engagements more than almost any other question these days. I tend to be asked to speak to biblical churches who are reasonably well taught where prophecy is concerned, and the members of those churches realize that the Antichrist is very likely alive and mature today. Some folks make educated guesses, but they've been doing that since the beginning. The various popes, Hitler, Henry Kissinger and so on have been selected, among others, for this very special dishonor. (Kissinger has been a suggestion for some 25 years because he is Jewish.) Today, many people think the Antichrist is to be a Jew. This is almost universally believed in the churches, but there is no evidence for that idea. The scriptural sanction for this theory is Daniel 11:37: "Neither shall he regard the God of his fathers, nor the desire of women, nor regard any god: for he shall magnify himself above all." It is rendered this way in the NIV: "He will show no regard for the gods of his fathers or for the one desired by women, nor will he regard any god, but will exalt himself above them all."

The second translation is the accurate one. The Hebrew word used for God is not *Elohim*, but *elohai*. The difference is crucial. Elohai means *gods* in the sense of idols. The verse states that the Antichrist will not worship the idols his father worshiped. The King James translators, living in particularly anti-Semitic times in England, must have fallen into temptation to use the ancient Jewish expression "God of his fathers." This indictment of the Antichrist being Jewish has persisted for all these centuries. (The King James translators' aversion to Judaism is obvious again in Acts 12:4, where they substitute Easter for Passover.)

The idea that the Antichrist is a Gentile is easier to support. All biblical persecutors of the Jews were Gentiles, from the pharaohs to the foreign kings to the caesars. Also, Israel undertakes a formal covenant with the Antichrist. If he were one of their own, they probably would not have to actually sign a document. The policies of Prime Ministers Rabin, Peres and Netanyahu were accepted by their fellow Jews without the necessity of formal documents. But dealings with Gentile powers such as the United States, the Arabs, or the Oslo peace accords were contractual matters more like the Antichrist's upcoming covenant.

There is also a lack of logic in assuming that this major anti-Semite would persecute his own people. It really is difficult to imagine a Jewish person blaspheming to the extent of claiming to be the God of Israel. But who among the world's Gentiles the Antichrist may be, I just don't know.

Where Do We Stand?

There are many renditions of end-time events and many educated guesses as to the motivations of the characters. Suffice it to say that the construction we just looked at fits with scriptural fact. Other factors not foreseen at this time may change some of the motivations, but I feel that this scenario fits well with what we understand now.

So where do we stand? Today's society is as much on the verge of the end of the age as the newspapers say it is. While there's no

biblical sanction for imagining the end to be at the change of millennium, it should surprise no Bible student if it were. There are
any number of factors urging this point of view, including the sat-
isfaction of all of the Lord's warnings in Matthew 24:4-14. The anti-
Semitism, which the Antichrist will utilize to justify his ultimate
raid of Israel, and the idea that some peace covenant must be made
in Israel are in place. The analogy of a stage play with pieces of a set
and certain actors being in their right places for the culmination of
a play is often used, and it is very appropriate. Around that stage,
besides what I have already mentioned, are global economic problems; alliances very similar to that described by Ezekiel in his invasion of Gog and Magog; a powerful European confederacy; a rising
of the king of the East to a position where he could conceivably
attack the Middle East; the proliferation of nuclear, chemical and
biological weapons; the hostility of world Islam to democracy; the
apostasy of the "liberal" churches. All these conspire to make it
seem like the world has either gone haywire or is simply con-
forming to our Lord's sad picture of the end of the age.

If these are not forewarnings, then we are misunderstanding
either the world situation or Scripture. Each one of us needs to
deeply consider his or her position with God at a time like this.

I have always believed that prophecy is placed in Scripture not
only for the edification of the saints but also as a tool of witness.
Surely a common-sense appeal in a world like the one we live in
now is justified. Sometimes when I speak in churches, I am
impressed to give an invitation—not so much an emotional appeal
accompanied by stirring hymns, but rather a simple, straightfor-
ward "don't be foolish" presentation of the gospel.

In view of all of the forewarnings, this is the best time we have seen
so far to expect the Lord's imminent arrival. With that in mind, make
your peace with Him and reserve your place in a much finer, more
peaceful, more wonderful life on earth to come.

▼ ▼ ▼

CHAPTER 7

Russia on Edge

Tim LaHaye

This is what the Sovereign LORD says: I am against you, O Gog, chief prince of Meshech and Tubal… (Ezekiel 38:3).

More than 2,500 years ago, God gave the prophet Ezekiel an astonishing prophecy to give to the world, one that would be fulfilled in "the latter days." Many Bible scholars feel that prophecy, found in Ezekiel 38 and 39, is being fulfilled in our lifetime. The prophecy involved a then-unknown nation that would become powerful in "the latter days" or end times. Incredibly, that prophecy, regarding the nation of Russia and her many allies in the Arab nations of the world, began to be fulfilled during the Bolshevik Revolution of 1917, shortly after Israel began gathering back into the Holy Land.

Prior to Ezekiel 36 and 37, which predicted the regathering of the nation Israel into her homeland, Ezekiel had issued many prophecies against the longstanding enemies of Israel—the Assyrians, Egyptians, Chaldeans, Babylonians and lesser city states that include Tyre and Sidon. Then suddenly, in chapters 38 and 39, the prophet threw a historical hand grenade into the prophetic mix by singling out the totally unknown nation of Russia, referred to as "Magog," a nation mentioned only twice in all the Bible up to that point in Old Testament history.

Even after that prophecy, Russia remained obscure for two millennia! The Babylonians and Assyrians passed off the scene of history and were replaced by the Medo Persians, Greeks and Romans, just as another great Hebrew prophet of that era, Daniel, had predicted. Now all of those nations are extinct, and Russia, until recently, was a superpower. The thrilling part is that Russia's rise to power occurred in the last 70 years.

If that doesn't sound incredible to you, it should. You can be sure that skeptics would ridicule the Bible if Russia were not on the world scene today as the global community runs wildly toward its planned one-world government and, ultimately, to Armageddon itself. But what I find so significant is that this prophecy came immediately *after* the prediction of Israel's regathering (Ezekiel 36–37), as though the two prophecies were related. And they are! For both Israel's rebirth as a nation and Russia's ascension as a major player on the world scene were outgrowths of World War I. The first World War, as I explain in my book, *Are We Living in the End Times?* was a fulfillment of our Lord's own prophecy of the first sign (or "birth pain") of His "coming and of the end of the age" (see Matthew 24:1-8). It was more than coincidental that of the 15,000 wars in human history, the one unique enough to be a "sign of the end" (World War I) plus the "super sign of the end" (as some call Israel being regathered into the land) plus Russia's rise to being a dominant player on the world scene all had their beginnings in the years spanning 1914 to 1917. Add the fulfillment of other signs that originated during that same timeframe, and we realize that was a most significant time in human history. It was the beginning of the "birth pains" that would increase like a woman in travail until the tribulation itself begins—just seven years prior to the glorious appearing of Christ to this earth.

Note that Russia didn't burst on the world scene at the same time Israel became a nation. However, it is very significant that Russia has broken all records in mankind's long history of its inhumane treatment of its fellow man. For it was in communist Russia that Satan seemed to inculcate all the evils of the ages in his grand scheme to control the world. Using the power of government, its agencies, money and other influence, Russia spread the most deadly atheistic ideology the world has ever known. Dr. Zbigniew Brzezinski, former National Security Advisor for President Jimmy Carter, called this communist-dominated century the most barbaric in all human history. In his book *Out of Control,* he wrote, "During the twentieth century, no less than 167,000,000 lives—and quite probably in excess of 175,000,000—were deliberately extinguished through politically motivated carnage....This is more than the total killed in *all* previous wars, civil conflicts, and religious persecutions throughout human history."[1]

If you examine his list, you would find that the inhumane ideology called communism, primarily fostered from Russia, was the foremost cause for these deaths. For decades, the hard-core, world-conquest communists conducted world congresses on communism in their country for delegates from China, India, North Korea, Asia and every other nation in the world, including the United States. These congresses were little more than indoctrination programs that showed delegates how to return home to overturn existing governments and impose that atheistic form of socialism, or communism, on their homelands. This ideology, which has been a fire in the minds of godless people for more than 200 years, finally found its resting place in the former Soviet Union and now resides big-time in Russia and many other countries to which it has been transported. There is no more satanically inspired evil in today's world. Former U.S. President Ronald Reagan was right when, in 1983, he shocked the world by calling Russia "an evil empire."

Do not be deceived by the fall of the Soviet Union. Communism *is not* dead. It is still on its relentless path of satanically inspired world domination, just as the Bible prophesied it would in the end time. In fact, if Russia is going to do what the prophets predicted, which we will discuss in this chapter, it better get to it soon or the nation will be discarded for other satanically inspired centers like

Beijing, China. (But I predict Russia will fulfill this prophecy sometime in the next decade.)

The Coming Destruction of Russia

No rational person takes pleasure in the destruction of an entire
nation, not even when that destruction is an act of judgment by a
righteous, sovereign God. Russia is unquestionably the nation identified in the prophecies of Ezekiel 38 and 39. But it is not sufficient
just to say that Bible scholars for several hundred years have interpreted those chapters as referring to Russia. We must be more
explicit than that, for ascertaining the proper identity of "Gog" and
"Magog" is essential to the interpretation of this passage. Therefore
I suggest three reasons that confirm the identity of the nation predicted to invade Israel in the last days.

Russia's Philosophy

God said through the prophet Ezekiel, "Son of man, set thy face
against Gog, the land of Magog, the chief prince of Meshech and
Tubal, and prophesy against him, and say, Thus saith the Lord GOD;
behold, I am against thee, O Gog, the chief prince of Meshech and
Tubal" (Ezekiel 38:2,3 KJV). We have already seen in the Bible that
God is against "Magog" (the country) and "Gog" (the chief prince
of the country). Why would a loving God who has always been *for*
mankind be *against* this nation? Because the nation is against *Him*.
Magog exhibits her antagonism toward God by opposing humanity,
the especial object of God's love; defying God's Word; and, above all,
antagonizing God's people, the nation of Israel. Philosophically and
religiously, the nation of Russia qualifies in every way. It is anti-
God, anti-human, anti-Bible, and anti-Israel. But there is another
reason for recognizing Magog as Russia.

Russia's Geographical Location

A second significant reason to identify Russia as Magog is its geographical location. The Bible usually describes geography in relation to Israel. For example, "south" means south of Israel; "north"

signifies north of Israel. The only likely exception would come in this instance because Ezekiel was in Babylon when he spoke the prophecy. A case could be made that the prophet may have meant "north of Babylon" when he said, "You will come from your place in the far north" (Ezekiel 38:15) (for that is where the prophet was when God gave him this prophecy), or, "I will bring you from the far north and send you against the mountains of Israel" (Ezekiel 39:2).

Etymological Evidence

Etymology, the study of linguistic changes and the history of words, is a third way to support the identity of the nation in Ezekiel's prophecy. *Magog* is an ancient name for the nation now known as Russia. Gog, as we've noted, merely means "the chief prince of Magog," or more literally, the chief prince of "Meshech and Tubal."

Genesis 10 helps to establish the identity of these people. Magog was the second son of Japheth who, according to Josephus, the great Jewish historian, settled north of the Black Sea. Tubal and Meshech were the fifth and sixth sons of Japheth, and their descendants settled south of the Black Sea. It is believed that these people intermarried and became known as Magog, the dominant tribe. The name *Moscow* derives from the tribal name *Meshech;* and *Tobolsk,* the name of the principal state, comes from *Tubal.* The noun *Gog* is from the original tribal name *Magog,* which gradually became *Rash,* then *Russ,* and today is known as *Russia.*

Bible scholars anticipated Russia becoming a dominant power in the end time even when it was literally a nonentity as a nation. Early in this century Russia was still a second-rate influence in the affairs of nations; in 1905 tiny Japan defeated Russia in the Russo-Japanese War.

Why Will Russia Attack Israel?

I will turn thee back, and put hooks into thy jaws, and I will bring thee forth, and all thine army, horses, and horsemen, all of them clothed with all sorts of armour, even a great company with bucklers and shields, all of them handling swords: Persia, Ethiopia [Cush], and

Libya [Put] with them; all of them with shield and helmet; Gomer, and all his band; the house of Togarmah of the north quarters, and all his bands; and many people with thee. Be thou prepared, and prepare for thyself, thou, and all thy company that are assembled unto thee, and be thou a guard unto them. After many days thou shalt be visited: in the latter years thou shalt come into the land that is brought back from the sword, and is gathered out of many people, against the mountains of Israel, which have been always waste: but it is brought forth out of the nations, and they shall dwell safely all of them. Thou shalt ascend and come like a storm; thou shalt be like a cloud to cover the land, thou, and all thy bands, and many people with thee.

Thus saith the Lord GOD; it shall also come to pass, that at the same time shall things come into thy mind, and thou shalt think an evil thought: and thou shalt say, I will go up to the land of unwalled villages; I will go to them that at rest, that dwell safely, all of them dwelling without walls, and having neither bars nor gates, to take a spoil, and to take a prey; to turn thine hand upon the desolate places that are now inhabited, and upon the people that are gathered out of the nations, which have gotten cattle and goods, that dwell in the midst of the land. Sheba, and Dedan, and the merchants of Tarshish, with all the young lions thereof, shall say unto thee, Art thou come to take a spoil? hast thou gathered thy company to take a prey? to carry away silver and gold, to take away cattle and goods, to take a great spoil? Therefore, son of man, prophesy and say unto Gog, Thus saith the Lord GOD; in that day when my people of Israel dwelleth safely, shalt thou not know it? (Ezekiel 38:4-12 KJV).

During the past 80 years, Russian diplomats and foreign policy strategists have proven that they are much smarter than their Western counterparts. It seems like every time diplomats engage them in conference, the people lose land, friends, people or rights. What would make a former superpower like Russia at the end time abandon the path of diplomacy and attack the nation of Israel? There are three possible reasons.

1. *Russia's Longstanding Hatred*

History clearly shows that the Jews cannot be intimidated by the Russians or anyone else. We can be certain that the Russians are not pleased with Israel's four military victories since 1949. It is highly possible that the Russians will finally decide they cannot defeat the Israelis through their Arab allies without personally engaging them on the field of combat. This decision could be the one that summons them to march against Israel.

2. *Plunder, Spoil, and Wealth*

In Ezekiel 38:12,13 we read,

"I will plunder and loot and turn my hand against the resettled ruins and the people gathered from the nations, rich in livestock and goods, living at the center of the land." Sheba and Dedan and the merchants of Tarshish and all her villages will say to you, "Have you come to plunder? Have you gathered your hordes to loot, to carry off silver and gold, to take away livestock and goods and to seize much plunder?"

These verses seem to suggest two important possibilities. One is that the economic conditions of Israel are destined to improve and those of the Soviet Union will deteriorate. We have already seen that, as a result of the peace treaties made between the Jews and the Arabs, Israel will experience a time of phenomenal material blessing, making her an object of greed on the part of the Russian rulers and their Arab allies. In fact, today Israel's gross national product exceeds $100 billion annually. This is ten times that of the nation's five closest Arab neighbors.

The future is not so bright for Russia. One way in which God has manifested His displeasure with Russia as a nation during the past eight decades lies in her total economic failure under communism. The Crimea was known under the czars as "the breadbasket of the world." The wheat harvested there was bountiful and more than sufficient for the needs of the Russian people, and large quantities were exported to other nations of Europe.

Since the Russian Revolution, however, that nation's severe weather has worsened, producing some of the harshest winters on record. Russia has become notorious for poor wheat crops—partly because of the weather and partly because of the lack of motivation among the Russian people under communism. Reports from Russia that scientists have desperately tried to manipulate the weather are probably fraudulent. If they are true, they give evidence that the scientific endeavors have not worked—and have even made the situation worse. Economic judgment from God is destined to continue, bringing the need to purchase increasing quantities of foreign grain.

3. *God's Sovereign Will*

The primary reason Russia will invade Israel is that God has decreed it. Ezekiel 38:3,4,8 declares:

> This is what the Sovereign LORD says:... I will turn you around, put hooks in your jaws and bring you out with your whole army—your horses, your horsemen fully armed, and a great horde with large and small shields, all of them brandishing their swords...After many days you will be called to arms. In future years you will invade a land that has recovered from war, whose people were gathered from many nations to the mountains of Israel, which had long been desolate. They had been brought out from the nations, and now all of them live in safety.

Ezekiel 39:2 adds, "I will turn you around and drag you along. I will bring you from the far north and send you against the mountains of Israel." Ezekiel 38:10 states: "This is what the Sovereign LORD says: On that day thoughts will come into your mind and you will devise an evil scheme." The attack on Israel is conceived and mobilized by Almighty God. This implies that God will stir the Russians' greedy plan, fulfilling Ezekiel 38:4, "I will put hooks in your jaws and bring you out."

In studying these two chapters of Ezekiel, I sense that God will pour out His wrath upon Russia not only to demonstrate His power, but also to heap judgment on those who have persecuted human beings, especially Israel.

The prophetic scenario is plain: Russia does not have Israel as her primary target. Russia's major objective has admittedly been world conquest. One way in which the communists have been consistent for the last 80 years is in their implacable movement toward that primary objective. God has proclaimed that He raises up whom He will and puts down whom He will (Ezekiel 21:26; Daniel 4:34,35). Even at the end time, when Russia reigns as a superpower, God will still be in control, for He is able to "put hooks in her jaw" and lead "her" to obey His will.

Russia's Allies in the Attack on Israel

From a careful study of ancient and modern national players in the Middle East region, we learn that a dominant leader called Gog, described as the "chief prince of Rosh," is going to arise and lead Russia into a vast northeastern confederation of nations including Iran, Ethiopia and other African nations, Germany, Armenia, possibly Turkey, conceivably some Oriental countries and whoever else can be included within the statement, "and many peoples with thee." This group of nations, headed by Russia, will advance against Israel in the last days.

The Russian Invasion of Israel

Some 2,500 years ago the Hebrew prophet Ezekiel described in considerable detail the circumstances under which communist Russia and her hordes of anti-Semitic nations would attempt to invade the little nation of Israel. (See Ezekiel 38:4,8,9,15,16.) There are two legitimate ways to interpret the kind of weapons used in this prophecy—literally and symbolically. Bible-believing scholars can be found on either side.

A literal interpretation of the passage suggests that modern methods of warfare will someday become obsolete, and man will return to primitive weapons. That is not as far-fetched as it may appear. For years, electronic scientists have reportedly been working on long-range heat-ray devices that would have the capacity to render metallic surfaces so hot they could not be touched. If such an invention were produced by the West, Russia could not invade Israel with tanks, bazookas and modern weaponry. It would have to resort to horses. Metal weapons would be replaced with wooden; these would not be wooden swords and spears as used in ancient days, but implements fashioned with enormous strength out of basic wood materials, seasoned with resin, or lignostone, or other chemically treated woods that already are used industrially and have an amazingly long burn life.

If, on the other hand, the passage is to be taken symbolically, the prophet Ezekiel is merely describing implements of war in terms meaningful to his contemporary audience. We must always remember that the Bible was written to specific people at a specific time and must therefore relate to them. If the prophet 2,500 years ago had referred to tanks, half-tracks, aircraft carriers and airplanes, no one would have understood what he meant.

Regardless of which approach we take in interpreting this passage of Scripture, we know that Russia will mount a massive military attack on Israel, and only God will be Israel's defense. God's supernatural intervention will save her.

"The Hordes" Who Join the Invasion

Russia almost never does anything alone. We have already seen that when it pursued a goal unilaterally, as in Afghanistan, it got bogged down in an endless war. That is usually not Russia's style. Instead, it prefers to supply the military technology and money to its satraps such as the Palestine Liberation Organization, Cuba, Syria and Egypt. Consequently, when Russia comes down to invade Israel, she will use the Middle East hatred of the Jews to her advantage and inveigle these nations to help in the fighting. This will probably be the most massive invasion army assembled in the history of the world—all in opposition to Israel, a nation of less than 5 million people. For the first time since World War II, Israel will be betrayed by its friends.

Two Confederations of Nations

I am convinced that the invasion described by Ezekiel is not the battle of Armageddon, the warfare between Jesus Christ and the nations described in Revelation 16. First, at this time there will be two leagues of nations: the northeastern confederation that invades with Russia, and the western confederation that has befriended Israel in the past. Second, in Ezekiel's account, only a certain number from the armies of the world will march against the Jews. In the battle of Armageddon, armies will come from all the countries of the world against Christ—not Israel. Yet, while this warfare will not be the real battle of Armageddon, to the participants it will seem like it.

We have already identified some of the nations of the Northeastern Confederation that will join Russia. The western confederation of nations also appears in Ezekiel's prophecy. "Sheba and Dedan and the merchants of Tarshish and all her villages will say to you, 'Have you come to plunder? Have you gathered your hordes to loot, to carry off silver and gold, to take away livestock and goods and to seize much plunder?'" (Ezekiel 38:13).

Who are these nations that greet force with diplomacy? Little doubt the western confederation comprises the democracies of the West, principally the United States, Great Britain and Canada. "Sheba and Dedan and the merchants of Tarshish" were the seafaring Phoenicians, many of whom migrated to Europe, particularly the British Isles and Spain. These countries, the colonizers of the seventeenth and eighteenth centuries, provide the only vigorous anticommunist spirit in the world today.

The King James version renders "Tarshish and her villages" in verse 13 as "Tarshish, with all the young lions thereof." For this reason, many Bible scholars identify America, Canada, Australia and other western democracies as the "cubs" of Great Britain and Spain, the colonizers of the West. Certainly that is historically valid. Therefore, this probably does identify the nations of the prophecy.

It stands to reason that Russia does not take the entire world in its war against Israel. At a time when two confederations of nations exist—basically communist versus anticommunist—Israel is allied with the anticommunists, as it is today. Unfortunately for Israel, instead of meeting communist force with force, the western democracies will meet the invasion with diplomacy. This historically represents the weak response of the democracies in both the world wars and in almost every conflict since.

Instead of sending help at the moment when Israel needs support, its allies will send a diplomatic note (perhaps through the United Nations) that essentially inquires of Russia and her hordes, "What are you going to do in little Israel—loot and carry away silver and gold and seize many riches?" This may be the most breathtaking, dramatic moment in the history of modern Israel. Until that time, that tiny nation could depend at least on the United States.

God Delivers Israel

The scenario that develops at this point in our prophetic story is exciting. Confronted by overwhelming forces from Russia and forsaken by her friends, Israel will turn to God, and He will do for modern Israel what He did for ancient Israel. As the God over all forces, He will deliver Israel from the hands of her oppressor. As certain as it is that Russia and her Middle East hordes will come down against Israel, so it is that God will destroy the invading forces and deliver Israel supernaturally. And the prophet doesn't leave us in doubt as to the methods God will use in this destruction. It is noteworthy that this is not the first time they will have been used by the Almighty, for all of them have precedence in the Old Testament.

A Mighty Earthquake

In my zeal and fiery wrath I declare that at that time there shall be a great earthquake in the land of Israel. The fish of the sea, the birds of the air, the beasts of the field, every creature that moves along the ground, and all the people on the face of the earth will tremble at my presence. The mountains will be overturned, the cliffs will crumble and every wall will fall to the ground (Ezekiel 38:19,20).

Evidently, the Russians and their hordes are allowed to begin an airborne invasion while the infantry launches a ground assault. But at a strategic moment, God generates a powerful and destructive earthquake that causes people to tremble at His presence. This catastrophe will manifest the power of a supernatural God. Earthquakes were, of course, used by God in ancient days; Amos 1:1 and Zechariah 14:5 recount the terrible earthquake that rocked the land of Palestine in the days of Uzziah, king of Judah. It was no doubt a special intervention of God that caused that earthquake.

Jesus predicted that earthquakes would be one of the signs of His return and the end of the age (Matthew 24:7,8). The record shows that we have experienced an alarming increase in earthquakes during the past several decades. (Read chapter 3: "Famines, Earthquakes, Pestilences" for more information.) We should also remember that the book of Revelation predicts that during the first quarter of the tribulation, a mighty earthquake will create havoc throughout the entire world (6:12-17). Another earthquake in the middle of the tribulation will rock the city of Jerusalem (Revelation 11:13), and still another at the end of the tribulation could well be the mightiest earthquake ever to shake the earth (Revelation 16:17-21). Consequently, it is not unreasonable that God might use His power to create earthquakes in defense of Israel when Russia's armies come against her.

The Sword of the Lord

> I will summon a sword against Gog on all my mountains, declares the Sovereign Lord. Every man's sword will be against his brother (Ezekiel 38:21).

Nothing shakes man from his independence and false sense of security like an earthquake, particularly one having the magnitude that God will provide for Israel's deliverance. And because Israel is no match for the invading hordes of military personnel about to devour it, the Lord will confuse its enemies, and they will do battle with each other. If they are using tanks, they will train them on each other. If they are using airplanes, they will dogfight against their own planes. Or if, as discussed earlier, they have reverted to more primitive weapons of warfare, Israel's enemies will skirmish among themselves rather than against their originally intended foe. One precedent for such an incredible event appears in Judges 7:8-22, where the story is told of a large army becoming so confused that the soldiers attacked each other and fled in fright from a mere 300 Israelites.

Plague and Bloodshed

> I will execute judgment upon him with plague and bloodshed...
> (Ezekiel 38:22).

History shows that plagues have often accompanied the wanton killing of human beings in battle. Human carnage, blood and the remains of a battlefield breed disease. But in the case of Russia's invasion of Israel, the plague seems to be something uniquely manipulated by God to further destroy the effectiveness of the enemy. The next judgment to befall the invaders is a plaguelike pestilence that causes much bloodshed. Pestilence associated with the aftermath of war is similar to that foretold by our Lord in Matthew 24. Those who survive the earthquake and the hand-to-hand combat will certainly perish in the plague.

Floods

> ... I will pour down torrents of rain, hailstones and burning sulfur on him and on his troops and on the many nations with him (Ezekiel 38:22).

The portion of the invading force left after the earthquake, the fighting and the plague will be destroyed by hailstones and burning sulfur. For those who interpret Ezekiel 38:22 literally, there are Old Testament precedents both in the destruction God rained down on Sodom and Gomorrah and in some of the battles of Israel. For example, Joshua 10:11 states that when Joshua's armies fought against the Amorites, "The Lord hurled large hailstones down on them from the sky, and more of them died from the hailstones than were killed by the swords of the Israelites."

This final stage in God's judgment on the invaders could create not only a muddy terrain that would bog down any military advance, but also flooding conditions that would imperil human life.

Burning Sulfur

The use of burning sulfur as a means of judgment recalls the destruction of Sodom and Gomorrah, with both earthquake and fire and brimstone (burning sulfur). The troops who survive the other four judgments will die as a result of the falling sulfur. No wonder God says in Ezekiel 39:4: "On the mountains of Israel you will fall, you and all your troops and the nations with you."

These five judgments of God will result in the annihilation of the armies of Gog and their allies. This will undoubtedly be the greatest holocaust fulfilled in a single day in the history of the world…. But there is more.

God Destroys the Spies "in the Isles"

"Persia, Cush and Put will be with them, all with shields and helmets, also Gomer with all its troops, and Beth Togarmah from the far north with all its troops—the many nations with you" (Ezekiel 38:5,6). As a special demonstration to the world of God's omnipotence, Ezekiel gives the unusual prophecy that God will not only destroy the entire army of Magog, but He will also consume with fire those who "live in safety in the coastlands." Bible scholars understand the word *coastlands* to mean "the nations"; some older translations render it "in the isles."

Who would qualify as those who live in nations not involved in the conflict? They could be individuals who live in safety or security on islands, or this could refer to uninvolved coastland nations. The verse probably refers to the many communist/socialist spies and sympathizers who live in the western democracies who regularly take advantage of their freedom by pursuing subversion for the cause of world socialism. Such spies or communist infiltrators

occupy many key positions throughout America—in the bureau-
cracy, universities and colleges and the media—and subvert the
minds of our citizens. One national magazine has said there are
more Marxist professors in American colleges and universities than
any other country in the world.

These people who have spent much of their adult life betraying
the country that gives them freedom and safety will suddenly be
consumed by fire. The United States will not have to reactivate the
House Committee on Un-American Activities to administer justice.
Rather, the God who knows "the thoughts and intents of the heart"
will judge these traitors by fire. We can only imagine the number of
vacancies that will occur in one day in the federal and state governments and in the 3,000 universities and colleges of America. In
all likelihood, this same judgment will create similar vacancies in
Canada, Australia and the British Isles. At the United Nations,
divine fire judgment will suddenly fall and reveal the identity of
those who really are communist/socialist spies or sympathizers.
Such an event will create electrifying headlines.

The World in Chaos—Time for the Antichrist

Can you imagine the chaos into which the world's nations will be
plunged the day after God destroys not only the invading armies of
Russia, but also the communist spies in the western world? On the
one hand, the skeptical attitude of the secular humanists toward
the existence of God will suddenly be confronted with irrefutable
evidence of a supernatural God. There will be absolutely no other
explanation for these events. In addition, many trusted leaders in
key positions of influence will have been destroyed by fire because
they were traitors to their country.

Probably the greatest result of this chaos will be the transition of
surviving western democratic leaders into positions as dominant
world leaders. The threat of worldwide communism will have been
destroyed in a single day, leaving Israel and the western confederation of nations in a world-dominating position.

We cannot be certain what will occur politically immediately after this awesome event. But I believe that the rising tide of interest in world government under the guise of "the new world order" will suddenly find little opposition. With communism removed as a world threat, the socialistic, humanist politicians of the world may naturally assume that a one-world government—within either the United Nations or its replacement—should provide the solution to this planet's ills. All this will prepare the way for the Antichrist to consolidate the nations in preparation for the day when he signs a covenant with Israel and ushers in the great tribulation period spoken of so frequently by our Lord and the Hebrew prophets.

Of this we can be certain: All the world will momentarily stand in awe of the supernatural God in heaven who, after 1,900 years of silence, has spoken in terms that even the most unbelieving can understand. Hopefully, millions of honest souls will seek the Savior during this time, resulting in what could be the greatest soul harvest of all time.

When Will Russia Be Destroyed?

Whenever we discuss the future events of Bible prophecy, someone immediately asks, "When will this take place?" Admittedly, Bible teachers do not concur as to the "when" of the destruction of Russia. But for at least four reasons, this event cannot be fused with the battle of Armageddon.

1. *Armageddon is not directed against Israel, but constitutes an attack on the part of the world's nations against Christ (see Revelation 16:12-21; 19:11-21).*

The deception of the Antichrist and his insane hatred of Jesus Christ at the end of the tribulation period will culminate with his bringing together—even from the Orient over the dried-up River Euphrates— hordes of people against Jesus Christ, the coming King—but not Israel. That the Antichrist will utterly fail is clearly predicted in Revelation 19. However, this Scripture passage should not be confused with Ezekiel 38 and 39, which to even a casual reader plainly states that Israel is the object of Gog and Magog's hatred. These two attacks are unique and distinct, and I believe they will occur at least ten or more years apart.

2. *No one-world government is functioning during the events in Ezekiel 38 and 39.*

The destruction of Russia, as revealed by God to His prophet, will come at a time when, as we have already seen, Israel is the central focus of two confederations of nations. These two confederations, the northeastern confederation of Russia and her hordes versus the western democracies that do not come to the aid of Israel, cannot coexist in the one-world government predicted by our Lord and His prophets for the seven-year tribulation.

3. *Gog comes from the North, the Antichrist from Europe.*

Gog the prince and Magog the country are predicted to come from the "north parts" (Ezekiel 38:15). According to Daniel 7:8,24,26, the Antichrist comes out of Rome, a mixed blood of Romans, Greeks and possibly Jews.[2]

4. *It takes seven years to burn the implements of war* (Ezekiel 39:8-10).

Armageddon occurs at the end of the tribulation period just before the millennium. This in turn, according to 2 Peter 3, begins with a renovation of the earth by fire. It is certain that the Jews will not spend the first seven winters of the millennium burning the implements of war left over from the tribulation.

Considering these four reasons, we can conclude only that Ezekiel 38 and 39 are not to be confused with Armageddon. Instead, they occur ten or more years earlier, prior to the tribulation period.

When Does Israel Burn War Implements?

In Ezekiel 39:8-10, we find that after Russia has been supernaturally destroyed, "those who live in the towns of Israel will go out and use the weapons for fuel and burn them up.... For seven years they will use them for fuel." Obviously, the Israelis are not going to pile all the war implements together and make an enormous bonfire. They will use the weapons for firewood for seven seasons instead of gathering wood from the forests.

Two facts stand out in bold relief. First, Israel will enjoy seven years of peace *after* Russia is destroyed; second, for seven winters the Israelis will be reminded of God's supernatural intervention on their behalf as they burn the implements of war. It is vitally important that we locate these seven years chronologically, because they are the key to the period in which Russia will be destroyed.

God has not left us without information regarding His plans for the future. The Next Major Prophetic Events chart (page 166) reflects the major events accepted by almost all scholars who hold a pretribulationist view of prophecy. The chart specifies that the Antichrist breaks his covenant with Israel during the latter three-and-one-half years of the tribulation. According to Revelation 12, this event will unleash the harshest anti-Semitic persecution the world has ever known—a fiery furnace arranged for the Jews by the Antichrist. Russia will have to be destroyed *at least* three-and-one-half years *before* the tribulation begins, for the Jews to have seven years in which to burn the implements of war.

On the Seven Years of Burning chart (page 167) this detail has been added with the thought in mind that there is no reason necessitating the Jews' burning the weapons during the first three-and-one-half years of the tribulation. The entire seven-year period of burning could occur *before* the tribulation begins, but there is no way to be certain of this. We can only speculate as to whether the seven-year period occurs entirely before the tribulation; we know it cannot extend beyond the tribulation.

What About the Rapture?

Most premillennial scholars place the rapture of the church before the tribulation. The biggest misconception of some pretribulationists is that the second coming of Christ for His church (the rapture) and the beginning of the tribulation period are simultaneous. They may be, but no passage of Scripture requires it. We must remember that the tribulation is not started by the rapture of the church, but by the signing of the covenant between the Antichrist and Israel.

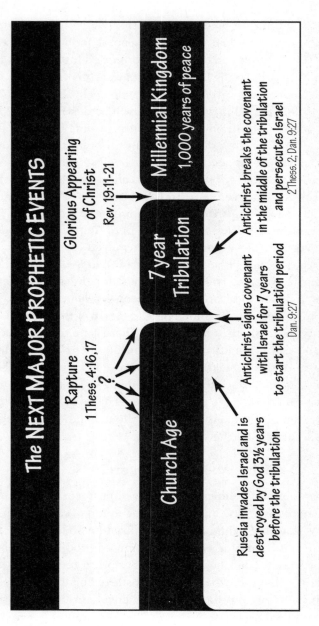

The Next Major Prophetic Events

Rapture
1 Thess. 4:16,17

Glorious Appearing
of Christ
Rev. 19:11-21

Church Age

7 year Tribulation

Millennial Kingdom
1,000 years of peace

Russia invades Israel and is destroyed by God 3½ years before the tribulation

Antichrist signs covenant with Israel for 7 years to start the tribulation period
Dan. 9:27

Antichrist breaks the covenant in the middle of the tribulation and persecutes Israel
2 Thess. 2; Dan. 9:27

Whether the rapture of the church takes place before the peace treaty is signed, only God knows. It probably will not, so that the church can serve as soul harvesters after God reveals His presence by destroying Russia.

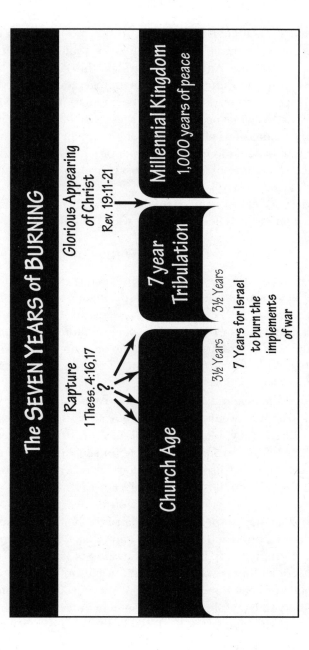

The Seven Years of Burning

Church Age

Rapture
1 Thess. 4:16,17
?

3½ Years

7 Years for Israel
to burn the
implements
of war

**7 year
Tribulation**

3½ Years

Glorious Appearing
of Christ
Rev. 19:11-21

Millennial Kingdom
1,000 years of peace

The whole seven years of burning could come before the tribulation begins. It cannot be in the millennium, for the earth is renovated by fire (2 Peter 3:10-13). The Jews are persecuted during the last 3½ years of the tribulation, so at least the first 3½ years of that burning will be in the Church Age. Before or after the rapture? No one knows.

Admittedly, 1 Thessalonians 4:17,18 and 2 Thessalonians 2—which describe the rapture, the tribulation and the revelation of the man of sin or the Antichrist—parallel the signing of the covenant. But it is important not to tie them together. The rapture could take place several years prior to the tribulation period. The closer we get to the actual occurrence of these events, however, the more we are inclined to believe they could happen in close succession. If they do occur in close proximity or simultaneously, the church will still be on earth when Russia invades Israel and is destroyed by God.

Remember: Any chronology of the rapture and the invasion of Israel is speculative and should be given wide flexibility.

When Will God Destroy Russia?

Having considered the possibilities for the seven years when the implements of war are burned, we can speculate on the possible time of the invasion of Israel and the subsequent destruction of Russia. Although we know they will take place a minimum of three-and-one-half years before the tribulation, no one can predict when the tribulation will occur; *the exact time of our Lord's return is known only to God.*

I believe that the next major event on the prophetic calendar will be the peace treaty between Israel and the Arab world. This cessation of hostilities may likewise signal a short time of peace throughout the whole world. For example, in speaking of the end time and the coming of Christ, 1 Thessalonians 5:2,3 says that the day of the Lord will come "while people are saying, 'Peace and safety.'" Further, "Destruction will come on them ... and they will not escape." This indeed suggests that before the holocaust known as the tribulation period, a time of peace and safety will encompass this earth, interrupted only by Russia's invasion of Israel.

The generation that saw Israel become a nation will not pass away until the Lord has come, according to Matthew 24. So signs of peace and safety in Israel should appear soon in order that the false period of prosperity that precedes Russia's invasion can begin to take shape. It is impossible to say when such an eventuality will come. What can be predicted, however, is that Russia will be destroyed before the Antichrist arrives on the scene and signs his covenant with Israel. There is no simple and dogmatic answer to the question of whether Russia's destruction comes before Christ's return. The Bible does not offer conclusive evidence, and my suggested answer should be regarded as somewhat speculative.

The rapture may occur in any of four possible time sequences: before Russia is destroyed, immediately afterward, long afterward, or simultaneously with the signing of the covenant between the Antichrist and Israel.

I personally believe Christ's return will occur after Russia is destroyed, as I explain more fully later. I am convinced that the destruction of Russia will appear as a supernatural event that will cause all the world to know that God has acted. During the aftermath of this catastrophe, millions of people will seek the Lord. In fact, the greatest soul harvest in the history of mankind may result from that moment of divine retribution. If so, there will be a need for harvesters. Because this event takes place before Israel's conversion and the sealing of the 144,000 during the first half of the tribulation, who will be better equipped to do the harvesting than the church of Jesus Christ and its worldwide host of missionaries?

The Results of God's Destruction of Russia

I will display my glory among the nations, and all the nations will see the punishment I inflict and the hand I lay upon them [Gog, the chief prince of Russia, and the spirit of the evil one that indwells him, along with Russia and her allies] (Ezekiel 39:21).

For 1,900 years the God of the universe has been silent—at least in ways our sophisticated world can understand. The apostle Peter warned: "First of all, you must understand that in the last days scoffers will come, scoffing and following their own evil desires. They will say, 'Where is this "coming" he promised? Ever since our fathers died, everything goes on as it has since the beginning of creation'" (2 Peter 3:3,4).

The secular humanist intellectuals of our day are among the greatest scoffers the world has ever known. Unless they see a world-wide flood, a Moses who rolls back the Red Sea, the ten plagues of Egypt, the daily manna sent down from heaven to feed three million Jews, the closed mouth of Daniel's lions or the fiery furnace that cannot destroy the three Hebrew children they will not believe in a supernatural God.

It is easier for these skeptics to look up at the stars and announce "accident," survey the marvels of nature and proclaim "spontaneous life," analyze the amazing human body and conclude "evolution" than to profess God. The Bible calls such people fools: "The fool says in his heart, 'There is no God.' They are corrupt, their deeds are vile; there is no one who does good" (Psalm14:1).

We have already noted two of God's purposes for destroying the invading armies of Russia and their allies:

1. To judge Magog (Russia) and Gog (the chief prince of Russia and the spirit that drives all evil leaders).

2. To save the nation of Israel politically and spiritually.

Now we should examine the most important reason of all: *"And the nations will know that I am the LORD"* (NASB). Eight times in Ezekiel 38–39 God announces that this is His true purpose in destroying the invading forces of Russia (see 38:16,20; 38:23; 39:6; 39:7; 39:21; 39:22; 39:27,28). God, in remaining generally silent for the past 1,900 years, has chosen to make the skeptics believe in Him by faith rather than by physical demonstration. The destruction of Russia will be a striking exception.

The Most Memorable Day in Modern History

This world has known many memorable days: the creation of the earth, the flood in the days of Noah, the death and resurrection of Jesus Christ. Since then, nothing in the physical world shows the irrefutable hand of God in terms that the most sophisticated unbeliever can understand. When our Lord walked on the earth, He performed such mighty miracles that even His greatest enemies had to acknowledge that He was endowed with supernatural power. People who saw Him walk on water, calm the troubled storms, multiply a boy's lunch to feed thousands of people, heal all manner of diseases, cast out demons, and even raise the dead were forced to admit, "No one could perform the miraculous signs You are doing if God were not with You."

Infallible Miracles vs. Ordinary Miracles

God has for nearly 20 centuries chosen in His sovereignty to require that man believe in Him through His printed and spoken word and through the power of the Holy Spirit. During this period of time, the Lord has performed millions of ordinary miracles (for example, miraculous healings and other life-saving interventions). But to my knowledge, at no time has He provided an infallible proof miracle—one that would force even the greatest skeptic to acknowledge the supernatural existence of God. However, one day God *will* perform an infallible proof miracle: the destruction of Russia's invading armies on the mountains of Israel.

The Coming Harvest

Through the tremendous communication technologies that continue to develop, every country of the world will receive the electrifying news that God has destroyed Russia's invading hordes.

The aftermath of such an event can only fulfill the purpose of God when the millions of souls who have been deceived by secular humanist philosophy suddenly realize that a supernatural God reigns over the universe. I have no question that literally multiplied millions will be driven to their knees to call upon the name of the Lord. Those who have heard the gospel prior to that time may spontaneously look to the Lord for salvation. Others will need the printed page—the Word of God, church services, television and radio programming and personal witnessing.

I find that many unsaved souls are becoming intrigued by Bible prophecy today and are more open to accepting the claims of Christ. As a result of reading the *Left Behind* series of prophetic novels about the end times (Tim LaHaye/Jerry Jenkins), many readers are receiving Christ and many others are rededicating their lives to winning others to Him. The reasons are threefold, I believe: 1) the realism with which the events are depicted; 2) the dawn of the new millenium; and 3) the obvious signs of the Lord's soon return. As one writer says, "These are indeed the times of the signs!" If we are seeing such incredible results already, can you imagine the number that would respond to the Savior as a result of Russia and its hordes being destroyed in an obvious display of supernatural power on the mountains of Israel?

The Opposite of Revival

We must not be confused about these future events. They are not harbingers of a worldwide revival. In fact, nothing in the prophetic Scriptures indicates that the world will get better and better at the end time. Instead, it teaches quite the opposite—that "perilous times shall come" (2 Timothy 3:1 KJV).

In the same way that the skeptical Pharisees of Jesus' day observed His supernatural demonstrations of power and rejected Him, so millions of people will spurn the truth after God's striking intervention in that day. We may hope and pray that more than a billion souls will call upon the name of the Lord, but what about the other three to four billion people on the earth? Very likely, the majority will heed the lying devices of Satan and begin to explain away those supernatural events. In the final analysis, it is not enough just to believe in the supernatural power of God; one must repent of his sins and surrender his will to God. And that humble gesture clashes with man's innate sense of pride.

No human being can long entertain the conflict of mind between what he truly believes and what he does. For example, many people reject the Lord today, not for lack of evidence, but for love of sin. As Peter has warned, "Scoffers will come ... following their own evil desires." And rather than give up self-love to follow their beliefs, many will change their beliefs to justify their lusts.

During the crucial days after this memorable moment in world history, there will be two realms of action: the political and the spiritual. Politically, as we have already seen, the world will amalgamate into a universal kingdom and prepare for the reign of the Antichrist. How long that will take no one knows; it is doubtful whether it will extend to more than a decade.

In that same era, many people will come to grips with the spiritual significance of the events and welcome salvation, but the majority will not. The current status of people who will witness the events of that day determines in large part what they will do. If they have already heard the gospel countless times and have not responded to it, they likely will not respond this time either. Abraham said to the rich man in Luke 16:31: "If they do not listen to Moses and the Prophets, they will not be convinced even if someone rises from the dead." Probably the billion or so people who I pray will respond to Christ will be those who are being deceived now about the existence of God or who have never heard the truth.

> If [we] confess with [our] mouths, "Jesus is Lord," and believe in [our] hearts that God raised him from the dead, [we will be] saved. For it is with [the] heart that [we] believe and are justified, and it is with [the] mouth that [we] confess and are saved (Romans 10:9,10).

It May Be Later Than We Realize

As we approach the dawn of a new millennium, the nation of Russia is falling on hard times. In spite of the massive bailouts and handouts from their many liberal socialist friends in our government and on Wall Street, that nation's tightly controlled communist-type of economy is plunging the nation into dire poverty. Many Russians still do not have adequate jobs, housing and food, which is always a formula for a revolution or a takeover by a dictator. Popular hard-core communists, including General Alexander Lebed, are waiting for the opportunity to become leaders of Russia if Yeltsin should stumble, die or resign. These leaders would undoubtedly lead the country in a more militant and aggressive manner. General Lebed is very popular with the 55 million Muslims of the country and could easily wield the force to go down and attack Israel.

Regardless of who the Russian leader is, no economist sees any way the Russian economy can improve without the grant of more freedom, which communists are usually unwilling to give. Consequently, Russia has lost its superpower status due to economic troubles, and will, if continuing in its present direction, soon become a third-world country without the resources to fulfill the prophecies of Ezekiel. How long can the soft-core communist leadership or even a hard-core replacement continue? Only God knows—perhaps ten years or so; but, unless there are massive changes in the country soon, it will be too late. By then Russia will be so bankrupt it will not be able to fulfill its prophetic destiny, which means one thing loud and clear: Very soon Russia can be expected to seize the moment and look greedily on the little nation of Israel. The Russians would fan anti-Semitic fervor among their Arab allies and fulfill the attack of Ezekiel 38 and 39, as predicted 2,500 years ago.

Late in 1997, one of the most reliable Middle East sources of information, *The Intelligence Digest,* actually predicted that Russia and its Arab friends would attack Israel within 18 to 36 months. Conditions have arisen that have lengthened that time frame temporarily, but the fact that people are even thinking about it publicly is most significant. One thing you can count on is that Russia and its allies will soon go down to attack Israel. The Bible predicts it— and the time could be very close at hand. And so could the rapture of the church, either before or after it takes place. Make sure you are ready in either case!

▼ ▼ ▼

CHAPTER 8

Rising Sun Nations on the Move

Tim LaHaye

The emergence of China onto the world scene as a powerful geopolitical force to be reckoned with during this generation has the attention of all the world leaders. It is not only the largest country of the world, with a population of 1.2 billion (almost five times that of the United States), but that vast empire is led by the most ruthless communist leaders. And they are looking hungrily at their Asian neighbors—Taiwan, India and the Philippines. They know the rest of the world is too cowardly to stand up to them with more than word threats. If they are not stopped, they will conquer the world, for communists are trained to envision imposing their brand of socialism on the entire globe.

Thanks to American capitalists who have invested heavily in developing this backward nation merely to gain incredible profits, China, which otherwise would never have been able to compete economically on the world scene, is experiencing its first real growth in hundreds of years. If allowed to go unchecked, those investors, or their grandchildren, will live to regret such profit-motive investments without demanding internal social reforms that would have granted basic freedoms to the Chinese people. It will be interesting in the years ahead to see Russia and China contend for supremacy in the area. Without realizing it, they both could be fulfilling Bible prophecy.

The rise of China to such a dominant world political force during the past decade has enormous significance from a prophetic point of view. Many students of prophecy believe it signifies a trend that world geopolitical conditions are shaping up for the world's last great conflict described more than 1,900 years ago by the apostle John when he wrote: "And the sixth angel poured out his bowl upon the great river, the Euphrates; and its water was dried up, that the way might be prepared for the kings from the east" (Revelation 16:12).

These "kings from the east" have befuddled Bible prophecy scholars for many years, for few mentioned anything about them—until the communist takeover of China during World War II. Since then it has become apparent that this nation has a prophetic role, however minor it may be, in end-time events. Although China has been content to stay within its vast borders for thousands of years and live pretty much to itself, its communist dictators have changed all that. They seem to have the same obsession that characterized communists before them—world conquest.

America: Communist China's Primary Target

One hundred-eighty years ago Napoleon Bonaparte said, "When China awakens, the world will tremble." You don't have to be a prophet to recognize that the time of trembling has already come to Asia and, within one decade, will probably come to the whole world.

No longer is China, with the world's largest population, the paper tiger it has been for almost 5,000 years. In our lifetime, it has startled the world and frightened many in the military complex with her enormous economic and military potential. Many observers recognize that within 10 or, at best, 20 years, China could very well threaten the entire world even more than the Soviet Union did just a decade ago. China already has nuclear weapons— or soon will—and has a delivery system feared by every country in the Orient. This country is trafficking in arms beyond belief by buying them from Russia and any of the former impoverished satellite countries that will sell them. Then it turns around and sells that which it doesn't want to keep to any of the oil-rich allies that can afford them (such as Iran, Iraq or even India).

China recently regained Hong Kong. Now its aggressive demand for Taiwan and the Sprately Islands indicates it has a strategy to control all of Asia. Whoever controls the Spratelys not only controls the oil check points to the oil dependent countries of the East, including Japan, Taiwan and the Philippines, but also Australia, Indonesia and Singapore—where 50 percent of the world's population lives. Basing claims to these almost uninhabitable islands to centuries old documents, China is probably more interested in the suspected rich oil fields under them than their location because no country can prosper today or in the foreseeable future without oil.

But China is not just interested in the Orient. In 1997, the Chinese almost negotiated an incredible coup in the Americas. First, it was disclosed that they had leased an important pier in Long Beach, California, that was being vacated by the U.S. Navy. The pier was to be used for the government-owned Chinese Ocean Shipping Company (COSCO) to help speed imports into the United States. Our balance of payments with China already shows a deficit of $50 billion and is expected to go as high as $70 or $100 billion, a tribute to American capitalists whose concern for profits exceeds their concern for the safety of our country.

Another amazing effort was China's attempt to gain a foothold in the Panama Canal area when the United States withdraws from that region before the turn of the century. With long-term leases at each end of the canal, China could virtually control the shipping through the canal. Some military experts believe this could force the United

States to have two separate navies because warships could no longer be sent to support our naval forces from one ocean to the other without China's permission. At this writing, neither of these negotiations have been finalized, but it does show the long-range goals of the Chinese government.

Keep in mind that China is not controlled by democracy-loving liberals like most countries in the world. Chinese leaders are among the most dedicated communists in the world. They are not "agrarian reformers" or "progressives," as our media tried to represent them a few years ago. Rather, they are a ruthless group of elite leaders who have stolen the opportunity for freedom from the 1.2 billion freedom-loving Chinese people, and they have never wavered in their plan to use China as a military platform from which to conquer the world. The events of the next two decades, if indeed we have that long, will prove that point.

It is obvious that the obsession of America's leadership to appease these ruthless communists will strengthen their position and weaken ours. Many American leaders have never been able to deal successfully with communists in general, much less with Oriental communists. Our leaders have assumed when strong communist leaders become dictators or "presidents" of their countries that they become nice people whose word can be trusted or, for that matter, whose signatures on treaties can be trusted. History shows that is a naïve concept. In recent years only former President Ronald Reagan, who regarded communism for what it really is ("an evil empire"), understood them. He dealt with diplomacy backed by force, which is why the Soviet Union finally collapsed.

Appeasement seems to be the watchword of the present leadership in our country. For this reason the World Bank, which is controlled and financed by American taxpayers, has financed the Chinese economy until all experts expect it to challenge our own economy for world markets in 10 to 20 years. When I was in Beijing in 1995, I read the English version of the *Asian Press* and saw the Chinese government bragging about the fact that they had obtained the highest loans from the World Bank of any country on earth. Twenty-two billion dollars! For several years they allowed

American companies to buy 25 percent of corresponding companies in China to gain capital. If you were to drive through Beijing you would no doubt be dumbfounded by the names of countless American companies that have affiliates in China. This, of course, has contributed to our enormous trade deficit that has provided China untold billions to support its socialistic economy.

Further evidence that China has indeed awakened from her centuries-old economic slumber includes a recent TV special that reported that seven of the ten tallest buildings in the world are in China. (Not exactly ideal places to be during the enormous earthquakes prophesied for the coming tribulation period.)

The Greatest Political Scandal in American History

In a desperate attempt to be reelected in 1996, the Clinton campaign took millions of dollars in illegal campaign donations. Much of it allegedly came from the Chinese Communist government. It is reasonable to ask, "What concessions were promised the communist leaders of China in return?" Even though 55 witnesses have fled the country, having pleaded the Fifth Amendment in refusing to testify before Congress, it is reasonable to assume that special favors were promised in return for the early campaign contributions. (Historically, using government money as bribery is an accepted path for China to use to obtain national communist objectives.) Renewal of "Most Favored Nation" (MFN) trading status, which the president asked for and received in 1997, was obviously one communist objective. (Clinton did this in spite of the fact that he ridiculed George Bush in 1992 for granting the same trading preferences.)

One possible payoff that U.S. veterans find most odious is that the Clinton Administration rejected the U.S. Marines' request to occupy the aforementioned strategic pier in Long Beach, California, yet subsequently leased it to the Chinese Communists instead. Prophecy writer and political analyst John Wheeler, Jr., described the incident:

In 1996, Clinton and his top aides met with Long Beach officials to urge the city to make the deal with the Chinese Ocean Shipping Company (COSCO), which promises to infuse fresh money into the cash-strapped local economy. The Chinese would rent the port facility for $14 million per year.

The huge 600-ship merchant fleet has long been suspected of various illegal activities by U.S. authorities. In 1992 the Federal Maritime Commission fined COSCO $400,000 for providing illegal kickbacks in violation of the 1984 U.S. Shipping Act.

In 1996, U.S. Customs agents intercepted a shipment of 2,000 AK-47 assault rifles aboard the COSCO ship *Empress Phoenix*, which was docked at Oakland, Cal. The weapons were shipped by the Poly Technologies Group and were intended for sale to street gangs in Los Angeles. The main problem with allowing the Chinese to operate a port terminal in the defense-rich environment of Long Beach involves national security.

"I am astonished that we would be providing COSCO, a known tool of the Chinese People's Liberation Army, with a beachhead anywhere in California, but especially in Long Beach," said the Heritage Foundation's Asian expert, Richard Fisher. "I can't even begin to imagine the degree or amount of under-the-water, on-top-of-the-water and land-based surveillance that would be needed to ensure that COSCO did not use this port for intelligence gathering, insertion or recovery of agents, or other forms of espionage," Fisher said.

Rep. Gerald Solomon (R-NY), chairman of the House Rules Committee, urged Attorney General Janet Reno to appoint a special counsel to investigate the plan. "Everywhere we turn, we see China taking active measures to compromise, infiltrate, neutralize or otherwise undermine American economic and security interest," Solomon said. "Is this what China is getting in return for its big contributions to Clinton and DNC campaign coffers?"

A Chinese-American entrepreneur named Johnny Chung made more than 50 visits to the White House during Clinton's first term. Chung took six Chinese officials—one of whom was a COSCO adviser—into the White House in 1996.

Chung donated $366,000 to the Democrats during that period, including a $50,000 contribution he hand-delivered to Hillary Clinton's aide Margaret Williams at the White House, in violation of federal law. The money was later returned to Chung.[1]

This agreement looks every bit like a political payoff for illegal Chinese government donations to the Democratic Committee during the '96 elections. In 1997, outcries from irate citizens and veterans groups alerted the U.S. Congress, and they prevented the Chinese lease of the Long Beach Navy pier. In the meantime, the red-carpet treatment extended to the new dictator of China in October 1997 could also be considered a payoff. Such a welcome at the White House is usually reserved for kings and potentates of friendly nations. Many observers worry that still other secret agreements must be met that will further compromise the military and industrial security of the United States. The sale of highly technical missile guidance systems that the Chinese needed to launch their satellites is also hard to understand because it allows the Chinese leaders to aim their missiles not only at friendly neighbor countries like Japan and Taiwan, but even at some locations in the United States.

"One-worlders," a group including Bill Clinton and his administration team members, do everything they can to bring about a one-world government which, they believe, is the only solution to this war-torn world in which we live. At present, the primary objective of the world planners is to enable China to enter the twenty-first century as a major player on the world scene of nations. One-world-order proponents don't lack patriotism; rather, their patriotism just happens to be misdirected to their beloved one world order. Little do they realize they are playing into the hands of the world planners who will usher in the government of the Antichrist just prior to the tribulation.

Of one thing we can be certain: China is not going to go away. Americans who have a long history of trusting socialists and communists fail to recognize the present leaders of China as the real threat they are to the world—and 1.2 billion people cannot be ignored! More importantly, John the Revelator saw them as players on the world scene in the end times.

China and the Bible

The Bible says very little about China. In fact, the reference to China, "kings of the east," includes more than just China. That phrase really means "kings of the rising sun," which would include Japan and possibly other Asian countries. As Dr. John Walvoord, a scholar and writer considered to be the dean of prophecy scholars living today, writes of this expression:

> There has been some tendency to take the expression "the kings of the east" literally, "the kings of the sunrise"—as referring specifically to Japan where the rising sun is a symbol of its political power. However, it is more natural to consider the term, "rising sun" as a synonym for east.[2]

Some Bible teachers suggest that "the Sinites" referred to in Genesis 10:17, and again in the prophecy of Isaiah 49:12, are where the "land of Sinim" is located. After God scattered the Sinites from the Tower of Babel, they evidently settled in the East in what we know today as China. Then they became isolated from the rest of the world.

After the great flood, those earliest settlers carried with them the stories of creation and the one true God. Early missionaries to China pointed out the truth of God in the Chinese pictographic language. My brother-in-law, a missionary to Taiwan for more than 20 years, told me the Chinese name for God is "ShangTi," which is made up of two pictographic symbols: "above" (or heavenly) and "emperor." Together, they mean "Heavenly Emperor." In a country that worships many gods, it is interesting that the earliest of Chinese characters (going back as far as 4,500 years) indicate that they recognized one God above all the emperors and other gods. Chuck Missler gives other illustrations of Chinese pictographs:

> For example, the word "boat" is made up of three Chinese characters: vessel, eight and mouth, which could be a carry over from the eight mouths on the ark. The word "beginning" (of sin) combines the

pictographs for "woman, secretly and mouth." The Chinese word for "devil" combines four words: motion, garden, man, and privately. Even more obvious is the word for "desire or covet." It is made up of two trees and the symbol for woman. Doubtless there are many other Chinese characters that could be traced to Genesis before the Tower of Babel.[3]

Another interesting factor students of China find is that the most ancient Chinese calendars are seven-day calendars. Given their pagan background, we can only speculate that this, too, is a carry-over from the book of Genesis. Geographically, the Euphrates River, one of the first rivers mentioned in the Bible, has served for centuries as the natural dividing line between East and West. It is evident to Bible scholars that Judaism and Christianity had an enormous impact on the world west of the Euphrates River, but very little influence on the East. Instead, the master deceiver has condemned the billions of souls of the peoples of the East with a succession of false religions such as Buddhism, Hinduism, Taoism and combinations of all of them. The dragon, the official symbol of China, overpowered the primitive biblical teachings possessed by the first settlers with the polytheistic pantheism they have today. The idea that "god is all and all is god" is really a rejection of the God of the Bible.

The early settlers of Asia carried with them the account of the one true God and His early acts of creation, the Garden of Eden, the fall and the worldwide flood in the days of Noah. Unfortunately, the devil, the deceiver of the minds and souls of mankind, made the Orient his chief capital for the religions of Babylon. Religion in Rome was Babylonian mysticism mixed with Christianity. China has the pure religion of Babylon—polytheism—the worship of many gods.

Joseph Lam, born to missionary parents who spent most of their lives in China, believes the national symbol, the dragon, is the true symbol of the god of China. In the book of Revelation, our Lord called Satan a "liar and deceiver." The apostle John calls him a dragon and predicts that when he is cast out of heaven, he will deceive billions of people into taking the mark of the beast and worshiping his image

(Revelation 13). During the tribulation, that old serpent the devil will lead billions to reject Christ and worship himself. It is not difficult to see how, at the end of the tribulation period, the master deceiver of the souls of man will easily deceive "the kings of the east" and their followers into making the long trek west to the Meggido Valley to do battle with the King of kings. Already steeped in humanistic religions for centuries, and currently controlled by humanistic communists with an obsession for world conquest, their vision of spreading their might and culture over the entire world will make them easy targets for one last gigantic deception—Armageddon.

China Suffered the Effects of Israel's Sin

When God performed a biological miracle on the loins of Abraham and Sarah over 3,500 years ago, He created a nation He intended to be his "torchbearers" to bring the light of His grace and truth to the whole world. His blessing on the nation during the early reign of Solomon that caused the queen of Sheba to say "the half was not told me" (1 Kings 10:7) indicates that God wanted to use Israel as a powerful testimony to the peoples and nations of the world that He blesses those who obey Him. Unfortunately, Solomon later disobeyed God and permitted his wives to bring in their pagan worship. After his death, many Israelites followed them into paganism, so many that God finally permitted a pagan nation to take them into captivity, and their lamp was almost extinguished. Instead of being a nation blessed of God, the centuries showed they had incurred the curse of God for their disobedience. The rejection of their own Messiah was, of course, the last straw, and they were driven from the land for 1,800 years.

In all probability, one of the areas of the world God intended the Israelites to evangelize was east of the Euphrates. Joseph Lam reminds us:

> King Solomon traded with China. The ancient Silk Road super-highway went from the New Testament port of Antioch to Changan (Sian). Silk routes also went by sea from Jerusalem to Ningbo in the

Tang and Song dynasties. The caravan land routes went through Baghdad and connected with nearly all the ancient capitals from Babylon to Khanbalik (Beijing).[4]

Had Israel only been faithful to God instead of worshiping idols, there would have been plenty of ways to get the message behind those vast mountain passes.

China's Anti-Christian Obsession

The story of missionary efforts in China during the eighteenth century is a heroic tale, but not nearly as successful as in other countries where the people were not so exposed to demons and spirits of devils. After more than 100 years of courageous missionary efforts, there are estimated to be 60 million Christians in China. We all rejoice at this number of born-again souls, but that is only one-half of 1 percent of the population. Few countries boast of more continuous persecution of Christians than China—even today. It has long seemed that the U.S. State Department and the current administration are blind to the human rights violations of Christians throughout the world, especially in China. Much more than politics is involved. A satanic struggle rages in the Orient today between the spiritual "powers of the air"—Satan against the Spirit of God.

When I was in Beijing, I secretly interviewed several Christians who know what it is like to be persecuted and to live under the constant threat of persecution. Several of those I talked with indicated they first heard the gospel over shortwave radio, through which the Spirit of God witnessed to their empty hearts. Several were former Buddhists, another a committed communist. All admitted emptiness in their hearts prior to turning on the shortwave radio to gospel broadcasts out of Hong Kong. There is something satanic to the opposition that Christians are subjected to behind the Bamboo Curtain. While in their country, I learned they had two kinds of churches: 1) the approved, or "mainline," churches that had to agree not to teach the forbidden doctrines of the inerrancy of Scripture and the second coming of Jesus Christ (two doctrines Satan has always opposed!); and 2) the underground, or house churches, that teach the whole Bible until the worshipers are discovered and imprisoned. It is in these house churches where thousands are coming to Christ each week. Joseph Lam puts it in perspective:

> In the West, we think of bomb-making instructions on the Internet as dangerous. Not to the dragon. To him, the "most dangerous" message on the Internet is the "Second Advent of Christ." The soon return of Christ is the message the thought-police most want to censor out. In fact, in many areas the police are registering modems and even fax machines in order to keep the end-times message of Christ's return from being circulated. You see, Chinese Christians believe passionately that Christ is coming again, not just someday—but "in this generation." The dragon knows he must stop this Apostolic message of hope. If somehow he can stop these New Testament-style Bible studies, he knows he will cripple Church growth in China.

The kingdom of God and the Second Coming of Christ are the rarest sermon topics preached in China's government-controlled pulpits…. The dragon persecutes the house churches because he is terrified of the end-times gospel they preach. This message liberates the people from bondage to their control and so it has to be denounced as "antirevolutionary" superstition.

- Christians are consistently forbidden the right to do any public evangelism of any kind. Private worship is reluctantly permitted but gospel preaching is banned.

- Directives to the state-controlled churches warn pastors not to preach the message of Revelation.

- Pastors in congregations of the "Three Self Patriotic movement" skip liturgical readings about the second coming of Christ such as Hebrews 9:28 and Revelation 19; 22:20,21.

- Sunday School teachers are not allowed to discuss the "day of the Lord" predicted in both the Old and New Testaments.

- The Olivet Discourse, recorded in three of the four gospels, is forbidden (the most important outline of prophecy in Scripture).

- Many Chinese hymns of advent, missions, judgment and the millennial reign of Christ are no longer sung in registered Chinese churches. Such music isn't politically correct.

Lam concludes, "Nothing so upsets the dragon as the mention of Christ's return, and nothing so comforts the Chinese church and missions."[5]

I could not help thinking that in America, where pastors have the freedom to preach anything they please, thousands of churches never hear that second coming message. Not because they are forbidden by government, but because they have been tricked by seminary professors into thinking it is confusing or not relevant for today. Satan uses different tactics in different cultures—anything that will produce silence on the blessed hope of Christ's soon return. Why? Because there is no more spiritually motivating teaching in the entire Bible!

A 200-Million-Man Army?

As early as May 21,1965, the author of a *Time* magazine article on China threw a hand grenade into the laps of prophecy preachers by stating that the Chinese had the potential of yielding an army of "200 million troops."[6]

That specific number identically coincided to the one found in Revelation 9:16, which predicts that 200 million horsemen would be unleashed and go out to slay "one-third of men" at the blowing of the sixth trumpet judgment during the tribulation period. This reference triggered an outbreak of speculation that found some suggesting that the 200 million would come with the kings of the east to do battle with Christ at the consummation of the end of this age known as the battle of Armageddon.

There is no question that the armies of the Orient that come to that battle at the very end of the tribulation will be enormous, due to the incredible population of those countries. However, this definitely does not describe the Revelation 9:16 army. Consider the following reasons:

1. That army goes out during the sixth seal, which occurs near the middle of the tribulation; the Revelation 16:12 army goes out at the end of the tribulation.

2. The 200 million in Revelation 9:16 are not humans; they are demons, doing things that man cannot do. They have a supernatural effect on the earth.

3. That army kills one-third of the world population, or approximately one-and-a-half-billion people, from the Euphrates to the Holy Land. There aren't that many people in the entire region. In addition, Revelation 9 has a worldwide view. They must have a worldwide mission to find that many people to kill.

4. The *Time* magazine article included all the men and women under arms in China, including their local militias or defense forces. There is no way in this world the communist government could risk committing all its military and armament to the Middle East, for they know their freedom-hungry citizens would revolt before they got back. Besides, the logistics of moving an army of 200-million people from the Orient across the Euphrates and the Arabian Desert to the little land of Israel seems impossible, even with today's modern means of transportation. That would consist of four times as many troops as were utilized in all of World War II—and that stretched from the South Pacific through Europe and into the Near East and lasted more than five years. This battle is accomplished in a matter of days. To involve 200 million people in such a short period of time would be impossible.

For these and other reasons, it is not realistic or scripturally necessary to assume that the armies of Revelation 16:12 are synonymous with those of Revelation 9:16. It is more likely that when the Euphrates River (the natural boundary between East and West for 1,600 miles) is "dried up," the "kings of the east" will march a sizable army across to battle with the King of kings. That army will probably be more like three to five million people strong. Remember, they will be joined in the valley of Megiddo by huge armies from all over the world, and while that valley is vast (as Napoleon has said, "the most ideal natural battlefield in the world"), even it has a limit to how many people it can hold.

When Will These Things Be?

The significance of the rise of China to the point that it is becoming a principal player among the nations of the world at this strategic time in history has not been lost on perceptive prophecy expert Dr. John Walvoord. Seeing the prophetic significance of China's rise to prominence back in 1967, he wrote:

> The fact that the rise of Asia has occurred in our twentieth century with so many rapid and unexpected developments is another evidence that the world is moving toward its final climax and the end of the times of the Gentiles. In Asia, as in other parts of the world, the stage is being set for the final drama in which the kings of the east will have their important part.[7]

If Dr. Walvoord were writing on that subject today, he might be inclined to say the curtain is about to rise. I am convinced that the rise of China to world prominence economically and militarily in our day is, prophetically speaking, a most significant event. We are the first generation that has witnessed the sleeping giant of China reach the potential of fulfilling this prophecy. No one doubts that unless something drastic and unforeseen occurs soon, China will gain control of most of the countries of the East, with whom it shares many religious and cultural similarities. That China could be led in these very days by her master, the dragon, "that old serpent, the devil," the deceiver of man, to so rebel against God that it would join the armies of the world in opposition to the coming of Jesus Christ is realistic. What is needed to bring China to that capability? Very little! Just the deceiving spirit forewarned by John the Revelator. China is almost there today and could gain control of the entire Orient in 10 or, at most, 20 years.

And remember, this does not take place until seven years *after* the rise of the Antichrist, which follows the rapture of the church. That is more than enough time to prepare to fulfill Revelation 16:12! And it is one more reason we have to believe Christ may return for His church in our generation.

▼　▼　▼

CHAPTER 9

European Union on the Brink

Arno Froese

If we take into consideration science and technological development, particularly concerning travel and communication, there is no doubt we are living in the most exciting time in human history.

Empire One

Based on the Bible, man is about 6,000 years old. During the first 4,000 years, we saw mighty civilizations arise, attaining a high level of intellectual capacity and building an amazing infrastructure philosophically, politically, economically and militarily. Even today, ruins of ancient Babylon testify to the greatness of past days.

Empire Two

Babylon was the first Gentile world empire. Then came the Medo-Persian Empire, which achieved unprecedented greatness. The biblical book of Esther describes some of the glorious days of that kingdom. Ezra, Nehemiah and other prophets write about the great Persian king who allowed the temple to be rebuilt in Jerusalem.

Empire Three

If we want to know more about the Grecian Empire, we only need to look at our own Constitution and our governmental system to quickly discover the influence of Greek culture and civilization. A closer look at Washington, D.C., for example, reveals an astonishing number of buildings precisely patterned after Greek architecture. The influence is undeniable. And most scholars agree that the New Testament was originally written in Greek.

Empire Four

The last Gentile world empire, Rome, most certainly has not vanished. Not only do we have amazing buildings and structures dating from the empire's times as evidence of Rome's great culture, but the Roman government of democratic philosophy and freedom of religion is evidenced in virtually all western civilized nations. For example, the United States was built on biblical as well as Roman principles. We will see more about that later in this chapter.

Governments Authorized by God

At this point, I need to emphasize that *all* nations, regardless of their religion or political structure, are built on biblical principles. The law in every country on the face of the globe tells its citizens, "Do not steal, lie, cheat, kill, commit adultery," and so on. No nation, regardless of what type of government, encourages or permits violations against the fundamental principles of the Ten Commandments. As a matter of fact, if a government encouraged murder, theft, lying, disregard of authority of parents, adultery and the like, it would, within a generation, cease to exist.

Four Thousand Years with No Change

If we combine the four mentioned empires and analyze the first 4,000 years in human history, we must confess that not much has changed in relationship to our day. They plowed the ground with beasts of burden, they planted seed in the same manner and brought in the harvest by hard labor, sometimes assisted by an animal.

Even the last 1,800 years saw very little change, although some mechanical tools were employed in agriculture, warfare and communication. But the fundamentals of that civilization were not significantly different from the first 4,000 years.

The Last Two Centuries

The beginning of notable change, although virtually unknown to the public, began in the mid-1700s with the first workable steam engine, which France and England played a major role in developing. Not until the end of the 1800s, when Etienne Lenoir of France assembled the first internal combustion engine and Karl Benz of Germany completed the first automobile in 1885, did a change begin to take place. For all practical purposes, the Industrial Revolution became visible only at the beginning of the twentieth century.

Parallel in time, Italian Guglielmo Marconi was successful in transferring communication over a wireless telegraph. That was another major contribution to the development of modern communication through the airwaves. Hundreds, thousands, even tens of thousands of others could be named in this process, but these are some of the earliest signs of the new civilization. For the first time in history, man could travel without a ship, a horse, a mule or a camel. People were able to accomplish work with mechanical devices, using energy not based on human or animal muscle power. They began to communicate across vast distances in moments, not based on audible sound or written letter.

Also important to mention is air travel, which developed parallel to the internal combustion engine. Pioneering work, as far back as 1783, paved the way for airplanes with several successful flying machines in 1810, 1842, 1866, 1878 and 1890. Even a steampowered plane with a crew was in the air in 1894. From that time on, hundreds, even thousands, of scientists and engineers were busy the world over improving and developing better transportation by land, sea and air.

Equally important, communication was being developed with astonishing speed. The major contributor of implementing ideas was, no doubt, the new country—the United States of America. But no individual country could really claim superiority, except to say that most developments were developed within the European civilization, which, of course, was solidly established on three continents: Europe, America and Australia. Today, the USA leads in avionics, computers and communication.

Now and Then

I have listed these relatively recent inventions to show that until the middle of the 1800s, the world was much the same as it was in the beginning. Man had to sweat to earn a living. The only reliable and practical help he had were the beasts of burden—the horse, donkey, mule, ox and camel. But by the middle of the 1800s, everything began to change with explosive speed.

For the first time in history it became possible, due to transportation and communication, to fulfill Scriptures such as Revelation 13:3: "and all the world wondered after the beast." Before that time, it had been impossible for "all the world" to wonder after someone because the continents were separated by time and distance and even oceans. Before the 1900s, Revelation 13:8 could not have been fulfilled: "And all that dwell upon the earth shall worship him."

We may not yet fully realize the significance of global communication. On one hand, it benefits mankind, but on the other hand it also provides for the fulfillment of negative Bible prophecy. Regarding communication, Peter Lalonde writes:

> ... The pope encourages the media in this "noble" effort [to covertly modify public perception]. On World Communications Day, he exhorted media leaders to transmit a "message of trust" to the world and reminded them that their "task" seems to go beyond human possibilities: informing in order to form [public opinion].

> However, although the causes may often seem noble, the surreptitious implanting of ideas into the mass consciousness through the power of modern media is cause for serious concern. This is especially true when the media present a preprogrammed anti-American, pro-globalist perspective.

For example, when Ted Turner was criticized for outright distortions in his much-publicized special, "A Portrait of the Soviet Union," he responded, "When you paint a portrait, you can paint whatever you want; I didn't say it was a true picture."[1]

But we also need to keep in mind that we all benefit from the new global communication system. Many ministries are taking advantage of new technology to preach the precious, liberating gospel to all parts of the world.

I mention these things so we will definitely realize that we are living in an exciting time, a time during which technological progress is making fulfillment of many Bible prophecies a possibility. And, actually, the technology itself is a fulfillment of Daniel 12:4: "But thou, O Daniel, shut up the words and seal the book, even to the time of the end: many shall run to and fro, and knowledge shall be increased."

Visible Fulfillment of Bible Prophecy

While mankind's achievements are remarkable, one specific event outshines all others in history, save the Word becoming flesh: the reestablishment of the nation of Israel in the Promised Land. Our forefathers searched the Scripture diligently and studied the promises that spoke of the return of the Jews to the land of Israel, yet during the years since the destruction of the Temple in A.D. 70 by Rome, it was impossible for the Jews to return and build their own nation. When we observe these developments in the light of Bible prophecy, we understand why it was necessary for the civilized world to change into an industrialized and computerized global society. This all was necessary to accommodate the fulfillment of the prophetic Word.

The Peculiar People

The Jews have always been a peculiar people among the nations of the world. No matter where they settled, it wasn't long before they established themselves successfully and proved they were a step ahead of the rest of the people. While no prophetic fulfillment was visible, such as their return to the land of Israel, the Jews remained an example of fulfillment of Bible prophecy to the Gentiles.

Frederick the Great one day asked one of his close counselors to prove the existence of God. The counselor answered: "The Jews, your majesty, the Jews." The uniqueness of the Jews was eloquently penned by no less than author Mark Twain in 1899:

> If the statistics are correct, the Jews represent merely one percent of humanity—an irrelevant spark in the light of the Milky Way.

> Normally speaking, the Jews should hardly be heard of, and yet we heard and hear of them again and again.

> They can rival any people on Earth for fame, and their significance in economy and trade are in no ratio to their population.

> Their contribution to the list of great names in literature, natural science, art, music, finance, medicine and profound learning is just as amazing.

> They have done extremely well in this world—with their hands tied behind their backs. They could rightly be proud of themselves.

> The Egyptians, Babylonians and Persians came into power, filled the Earth with their glory, but perished.

> The Greeks and Romans followed, made a lot of noise, and then disappeared. Other nations arose, their torches burned for a while and then they were extinguished, and today they sit in the twilight or are completely disappeared.

> The Jews saw it all. They beat them all, and are today what they always were, showing no decay, no aging, no weakening, no decline of energy, no blunting of their wideawake dynamic spirit.

> Everything is mortal except the Jew. All other powers perish, but he remains. What is the mystery of his immortality?

The Bible answers Mr. Twain's question in Deuteronomy 14:2: "For thou art an holy people unto the LORD thy God, and the LORD hath chosen thee to be a peculiar people unto himself, above all the nations that are upon the earth." Furthermore, in Deuteronomy

15:6 we read, "For the LORD thy God blesseth thee, as he promised thee: and thou shalt lend unto many nations, but thou shalt not borrow; and thou shalt reign over many nations, but they shall not reign over thee." One day, the Jews will no longer be dependent on foreign aid, but they will graciously "lend unto nations."

Israel Shall Reign

The Jews will also "reign over many nations." That has not taken place yet. Although someone may argue that this was fulfilled during the time of David and Solomon, we cannot deny that these promises go much further because they are spoken by the Eternal One, and Israel as a nation is eternal. Let's reconfirm this fact through additional Scripture: "And all people of the earth shall see that thou art called by the name of the LORD; and they shall be afraid of thee" (Deuteronomy 28:10). This verse clearly says "all people of the earth"! We must admit that it has never happened. At the height of Israel's glory, under King Solomon, the Bible makes this statement, "And there came of all people to hear the wisdom of Solomon, from all kings of the earth, which had heard of his wisdom" (1 Kings 4:34).

They came to hear the wisdom of Solomon, but Israel did not reign over them; neither were these people afraid of Israel because they came voluntarily in peace.

When John the Baptist was born, his father Zacharias expressed the desire of the Jewish people for the fulfillment of those prophecies. Luke 1:71 reads: "That we should be saved from our enemies, and from the hand of all that hate us." Note that Zacharias was not giving us his desires or opinions. What the Bible says is that "Zacharias was filled with the Holy Ghost, and prophesied" (Luke 1:67). This shows that the Jews had enemies and many hated them. This rejection of the Jews has been painfully experienced for thousands of years. Until this very day, Zacharias' prophecy has not been fulfilled. Plenty of enemies still surround Israel, and the Jews are still hated by the majority of the world's population.

Conditional Blessings

Certain blessings were also given to the Jews conditionally upon their obedience to the Lord's commandment: "And the LORD shall make thee the head, and not the tail; and thou shalt be above only, and thou shalt not be beneath; if that thou hearken unto the commandments of the LORD thy God, which I command thee this day, to observe and to do them" (Deuteronomy 28:13). We all know that Israel was not obedient. The Jews rebelled against God and the negative fulfillment took place. For example, in Deuteronomy 28:15-19,25, 37,64:

> But it shall come to pass, if thou wilt not hearken unto the voice of the LORD thy God, to observe to do all his commandments and his statutes which I command thee this day; that all these curses shall come upon thee, and overtake thee: Cursed shalt thou be in the city, and cursed shalt thou be in the field. Cursed shall be thy basket and thy store. Cursed shall be the fruit of thy body, and the fruit of thy land, the increase of thy kine, and the flocks of thy sheep. Cursed shalt thou be when thou comest in, and cursed shalt thou be when thou goest out....

> The LORD shall cause thee to be smitten before thine enemies: thou shalt go out one way against them, and flee seven ways before them: and shalt be removed into all the kingdoms of the earth....

> And thou shalt become an astonishment, a proverb, and a byword, among all nations whither the LORD shall lead thee....

> And the LORD shall scatter thee among all people, from the one end of the earth even unto the other; and there thou shalt serve other gods, which neither thou nor thy fathers have known, even wood and stone.

Unconditional Blessings

It is important to emphasize that in spite of terrible persecution and dispersion God repeatedly promised that He would gather the Jews from all the nations back to their homeland: "then the LORD thy God will turn thy captivity, and have compassion upon thee, and will return and gather thee from all the nations, whither the LORD thy God hath scattered thee" (Deuteronomy 30:3).

Moses, just before he died, summarized God's view of Israel: "Happy art thou, O Israel: who is like unto thee, O people saved by the LORD, the shield of thy help, and who is the sword of thy excellency! and thine enemies shall be found liars unto thee; and thou shalt tread upon their high places" (Deuteronomy 33:29).

Israel Cast Away?

Some people say that "Israel was cast away; they ceased to be a nation. Since the birth of the church, Israel has been replaced by the spiritual calling of the church from among the Gentiles." Let's investigate this statement so we won't be misled regarding Israel's future. The prophet Jeremiah clears up any misunderstandings when he says, "Thus saith the LORD, which giveth the sun for a light by day, and the ordinances of the moon and of the stars for a light by night, which divideth the sea when the waves thereof roar; the LORD of hosts is his name: If those ordinances depart from before me, saith the LORD, then the seed of Israel also shall cease from being a nation before me for ever" (Jeremiah 31:35,36).

Even though Israel was not a visible identity as a nation, it nevertheless existed even during that time of dispersion. When you get up in the morning and see daylight, and in the evening, the moon and the stars, or if you are at the coast and hear the roar of the ocean, then you can be assured that Israel lives!

Jews Are Prophetic

Do you wonder why I write about the Jews and Israel when my chapter is titled "European Union on the Brink"? I do so because it is absolutely necessary to understand that God called a man named Abraham and chose a special people through him. That promise was confirmed to Isaac, Jacob and the 12 tribes of Israel. From these people, Jesus—the Word of God who became flesh and dwelt among us—came.

We can't talk about prophecy without targeting the prophetic nation of Israel. Only through the Jews will God establish peace on earth. Only through the Jews can people be saved, as the Lord Jesus confirmed, "Salvation is of the Jews" (John 4:22). That settles the matter as to where salvation comes from!

Realizing these facts, we immediately begin to understand that the devil, the opposer of God, the father of lies, is forced to imitate the Creator. So don't be surprised that the devil must bring about a people called by his name.

The God of This World Rules

What I am going to write now may be very offensive and certainly will hurt the pride of many nationalists, whether they be Americans, Canadians, French, Italians, Germans, Austrians, Russians, Chinese or others. But I must say it because the truth is that all the nations on earth are under the jurisdiction of Satan, the great imitator.

The Bible says that the world is ruled by the prince of darkness, "the god of this world." That, however, does not diminish God's authority; He still stands above all the nations of the world, in spite of the fact that He has given the direct rulership temporarily to Satan.

So, it stands to reason that the devil must attempt to bring about a new world society that will challenge Israel and, finally, challenge the Lord Jesus. Now, we understand what Psalm 2:1-3 says, "Why do the heathen rage, and the people imagine a vain thing? The kings of the earth set themselves, and the rulers take counsel together, against the LORD, and against his anointed, saying, Let us break their bands asunder, and cast away their cords from us."

The center of this new global world is now being built on the richest and most sophisticated continent on earth—Europe.

The Other "New Nation"

A simple fact often overlooked is that from among the nations of the world, God has graciously chosen those who come by faith to Jesus and become children of God. They are God's new holy nation. This "new nation" is present in the midst of all people around the globe. Just as the Jews were scattered across all the nations of the world, but are now returning to their own land, the church of Jesus Christ, the new nation, is scattered abroad, too. It is living among the children of the world in the midst of the crooked and perverse nations. But we, too, will return to "the land" where we belong—Beulah Land—in the presence of our Lord! This will take place at the moment of the rapture, when we will be taken up to Him in the twinkling of an eye at the last trump of God.

Unconditional Grace

It is essential to realize that God's promises to Israel and to the church are unconditional. We have just seen that some promises were based on the condition that Israel would obey the commandments of the Lord. They failed to fulfill that condition; thus, they were unable to receive the fulfillment of the promises God had given them. However, that does not change the eternal "I will" of God: "And I will make of thee a great nation, and I will bless thee, and make thy name great; and thou shalt be a blessing: and I will bless them that bless thee, and curse him that curseth thee: and in thee shall all families of the earth be blessed" (Genesis 12:2,3).

This is distinctively clear. When God addresses Abraham, He speaks about "a great nation" and "all families of the earth." Note that God did not say, "If you will hear my voice, follow my commandment and do as I tell you." This promise was based exclusively on the will of God.

The Roots of the Church

Let's take a look at the relationship between Israel and the church. In Romans 11:13, the apostle Paul takes great pain to emphasize that he addresses the Gentiles: "For I speak to you Gentiles, inasmuch as I am the apostle of the Gentiles, I magnify mine office." In the beginning of the chapter, Paul identifies himself as "an Israelite, of the seed of Abraham, of the tribe of Benjamin" (11:1). Note that he does not say, "I am a Christian." Why not? Because we are all one in Jesus. "There is no difference between the

Jew and the Greek: for the same Lord over all is rich unto all that call upon him" (Romans 10:12).

Paul also writes of his physical nation and asks, "Hath God cast away his people?" What is the answer? "God hath not cast away his people which he foreknew" (Romans 11:2). Then in verses 15-18, he begins to explain:

> For if the casting away of them be the reconciling of the world, what shall the receiving of them be, but life from the dead? For if the first-fruit be holy, the lump is also holy: and if the root be holy, so are the branches. And if some of the branches be broken off, and thou, being a wild olive tree, wert graffed in among them, and with them partakest of the root and fatness of the olive tree; boast not against the branches. But if thou boast, thou bearest not the root, but the root thee.

These few verses clearly demonstrate Israel's continuing existence.

We should not be confused regarding Israel's position and the position of the church. Paul further explains, "For I would not, brethren, that ye should be ignorant of this mystery, lest ye should be wise in your own conceits; that blindness in part is happened to Israel, until the fulness of the Gentiles be come in" (Romans 11:25). Only when the fullness of the Gentiles, meaning the number of believers to be added to the church, will verse 26 take place, "And so all Israel shall be saved...."

Never must we be so naïve to think that God has rejected Israel and replaced her with the church. The erroneous conclusion is being made that all the promises given in the Old Testament now belong to the church. Unfortunately, this teaching is widely accepted among the established Protestant denominations and reinforced under the leadership of the Roman Catholic Church. This false doctrine is easily refuted because the prophets clearly write about the return of the Jewish people from the dispersion to the land of Israel, giving an abundance of literal geographic references. Some Scriptures raise even more difficulties with the concept of the church replacing Israel. Jeremiah 30:7 is a good example: "Alas! for that day is great, so that none is like it: it is even the time of Jacob's trouble; but he shall be saved out of it." If we were to apply this Scripture to the church, we obviously have a problem because it doesn't say, "Israel's trouble" but "Jacob's trouble." This is addressed to Israel because "Jacob," which in English means "supplanter or deceiver," still has the "Jacob" nature. Even until this very day, the Jews have not yet experienced a conversion, but all who belong to the church have.

We can say with reasonable assurance that when the Bible says Israel, the Jews, or Hebrews, it is referring to the biological descendants of Abraham, Isaac and Jacob. Quite often the word *Gentile* is found in the Scripture in opposition to Israel or the Jew. Further, we read in Jeremiah 30:11 about Israel and the nation, "For I am with thee, saith the LORD, to save thee: though I make a full end of all nations whither I have scattered thee...."

The Covenant to the Church

What about the unconditional covenant for the church? Jesus, the author and finisher of our faith, has this to say:

> I have glorified thee on the earth: I have finished the work which thou gavest me to do. And now, O Father, glorify thou me with thine own self with the glory which I had with thee before the world was. I have manifested thy name unto the men which thou gavest me out of the world: thine they were, and thou gavest them me; and they have kept thy word. Now they have known that all things whatsoever thou hast given me are of thee. For I have given unto them the words which thou gavest me; and they have received them, and have known surely that I came out from thee, and they have believed that thou didst send me.

> I pray for them: I pray not for the world, but for them which thou hast given me; for they are thine. And all mine are thine, and thine are mine; and I am glorified in them. And now I am no more in the world, but these are in the world, and I come to thee. Holy Father, keep through thine own name those whom thou hast given me, that they may be one, as we are....

> Father, I will that they also, whom thou hast given me, be with me where I am; that they may behold my glory, which thou hast given me: for thou lovedst me before the foundation of the world" (John 17:4-11,24).

That is the Lord's plan for the church. Will He fulfill His intention? We do not need to belabor the answer because our salvation is exclusively and unconditionally based on His grace. We haven't earned it; we don't deserve it; we are not able to keep it through our own efforts. In spite of our rebellion, disobedience and unfaithfulness, Jesus is faithful. He is gracious, and He will bring to pass that which He has promised. Paul exclaims, "For I know whom I have believed, and am persuaded that he is able to keep that which I have committed unto him against that day" (2 Timothy 1:12).

The church will not be brought into His presence and glorified because we are such great people who have worked so diligently for the Lord and faithfully kept His Word. If that were the case, we would never stand a chance. We will only be glorified because our Lord saved us. All that which we have committed unto Him, He will keep: "If we believe not, yet he abideth faithful: he cannot deny himself" (2 Timothy 2:13).

Only to Him Belongs Honor

In Revelation 4:10,11, we can see a wonderful picture of the fact that the Lord has brought His promises to pass: "The four and twenty elders fall down before him that sat on the throne, and worship him that liveth for ever and ever, and cast their crowns before the throne, saying, Thou art worthy, O Lord, to receive glory and honour and power: for thou hast created all things, and for thy pleasure they are and were created."

There will be no place for anyone to exclaim: "Look what I did!" "I earned this crown!" "I have been faithful!" or "I received my just reward!" No, not at all. We will cast our crowns before the throne and exclusively give Him all the glory!

Revival or Apostasy?

I strongly disagree with the many statements published today prophesying of a great revival sweeping the land and thereby preparing the church for the coming of the Lord. The "Kingdom Dominion" teaching insists that the Christian's involvement in the political process will prepare the United States for an unprecedented Christianizing of the nation so that the entire government will be run exclusively by Christians. As a result, so the teaching goes, peace, justice and righteousness will be established for all people. If that were to happen, then indeed the Lord could congratulate us when He comes. But it will not happen. The Bible gives us a picture opposite of that worldwide revival view.

Jesus actually asks, "When the Son of man cometh, shall he find faith on the earth?" (Luke 18:8). Those who place their hope in the success of the church on earth will be greatly disappointed. But all who put their trust exclusively in the already accomplished work of the Lord Jesus on Calvary's cross are preparing themselves for the great day of the marriage supper of the Lamb, as we read in Revelation 19:7,8: "Let us be glad and rejoice, and give honour to him: for the marriage of the Lamb is come, and his wife hath made herself ready. And to her was granted that she should be arrayed in fine linen, clean and white: for the fine linen is the righteousness of saints."

Have you noticed how the Lamb's wife made herself ready? To her "was granted fine linen." She did not produce the righteousness that is necessary to appear before the Lamb. We didn't earn it; we didn't deserve it; we couldn't produce it. It was, is and always shall be "granted" unto us! The church and Israel's choosing is based on the eternal unconditional promises of God.

The European Union

With our new understanding of the position of Israel and the church, let's now take a look at the Gentile world. Fundamentally speaking, there are three major groups of people, four superpowers, and five continents.* The three groups of people are:

- Europeans
- Asians
- Africans

---

* Note: In the USA and a few other countries, the counting of the continents is different, but internationally, only five are recognized, as we can see, for example in the five rings of the symbol of the Olympic Games.

The four superpowers are:

- Babylon
- Medo-Persia
- Greece
- Rome

The five continents are:

- Europe
- Asia
- Africa
- America
- Australia

It is interesting to realize that Israel lies in the center of the three groups of people: Europeans, Asians and Africans. Israel is separated from Europe by the Mediterranean, from Africa by the desert and from Asia by the great Euphrates River. Note also that Israel became part of the four Gentile superpowers.

First, it became subject to Babylon as Jeremiah proclaimed in the Word of God:

> And now have I given all these lands into the hand of Nebuchadnezzar the king of Babylon, my servant; and the beasts of the field have I given him also to serve him. And all nations shall serve him, and his son, and his son's son, until the very time of his land come: and then many nations and great kings shall serve themselves of him.
>
> And it shall come to pass, that the nation and kingdom which will not serve the same Nebuchadnezzar the king of Babylon, and that will not put their neck under the yoke of the king of Babylon, that nation will I punish, saith the LORD, with the sword, and with the famine, and with the pestilence, until I have consumed them by his hand (Jeremiah 27:6-8).

Second, under the Medo-Persian Empire, the Jews were permitted to rebuild Jerusalem and the temple. "Now in the first year of Cyrus king of Persia, that the word of the LORD by the mouth of Jeremiah might be fulfilled, the LORD stirred up the spirit of Cyrus king of Persia, that he made a proclamation throughout all his kingdom, and putting it in writing, saying: ... Who is there among you of all his people? his God be with him, and let him go up to Jerusalem, which is in Judah, and build the house of the LORD God of Israel, (he is the God,) which is in Jerusalem" (Ezra 1:1,3).

Third, the very short-lived Grecian Empire also occupied the Promised Land, and Israel became subject to the great Grecian world empire.

Fourth, Rome was in charge when Jesus was born, and, as we will see in this chapter, Rome will again rule. But this time, not only Israel, but the entire world will be ruled by Rome!

Europe, the World Leader

We have already alluded to the fact that God chose only one special nation on earth through which to bring forth salvation. Europe, however, which ruled Israel in the form of the Roman Empire during the time when God implemented His salvation through Jesus, is attempting to consolidate world leadership today.

Candidates for World Leadership

Before we take a closer look at Europe, let's quickly eliminate all other candidates for world rulership. From the three peoples already mentioned: Europeans, Asians and Africans, only the Europeans have had the upper hand for the last 2,000 years. Africa is the most backward continent and has no chance of challenging Europe. Asia, the mighty power bloc to the east, has been considered the great danger for Europeans for many centuries, but this perceived threat never became a reality. The Mongolian leader, Ghengis Khan, penetrated deeply into Europe, but his empire was short-lived, and it was the only significant Asian infiltration into Europe. Asia never established colonies in Africa, America or Australia.

At this point, I must explain that it is not my intention to glorify Europe, nor to diminish the significance of other races, nations or continents. But we cannot ignore historical facts when we deal with Bible prophecy. Only Europe successfully established colonies around the world and instituted European civilization and technology in virtually every country. Until this day, when a businessman from Zimbabwe wants to speak to someone in Algeria, he probably will speak French. When an Indian does business with China, he most likely will use English. Indonesian people still speak Dutch when dealing with the Netherlands.

The continent of America can be divided into four basic languages: English, Spanish, Portuguese and French. No Asian or African languages or culture have found deep roots in the New World. This also applies to Australia. These few facts demonstrate European dominion the world over.

Someone may now object and say, "What about the United States of America? Isn't it the greatest nation?" That is a legitimate question because the United States, although only for a short period of time, superseded Europe. However, we must realize that the United States, as all other America nations, is the end-product of primarily European immigrants. It's also important to point out that when speaking on the prophetic level, we must see things from a long-term point of view. When the Bible speaks of the "fourth beast," it reveals a period of about 2,000 years.

I am reminded of the words Dr. Wim Malgo, founder of *Midnight Call,* once said when asked if America would become communist: "America will not be communist, but will return to her roots, which is Roman Catholicism." Note that he said this in 1968, when Soviet communism was marching across the globe victoriously, swallowing up one country after another. Since then, communism has died. Although some insignificant pockets of resistance remain, sooner or later they will be done away with as world democracy takes over. It doesn't matter how important or how mighty the United States may or may not be. What is important and decisive is what the Word of God says, and as we have seen in the beginning of this chapter, there are only four Gentile superpowers, Rome being the last one. Therefore, based on the Word of God, all other candidates for world dominion are eliminated.

Europe's Dream

The dream of Europe can be summarized with one word: *unity.* This unity is absolutely essential to fulfill the prophetic Word. We find the final development of the global world in Revelation 17:13, "These have one mind, and shall give their power and strength unto the beast." This was absolutely impossible only 50 years ago. Why? Because the world, particularly Europe, was in total disunity. The eastern part of Europe was ruled by communism and the western part by socialism, under the auspices of democracy.

With the fall of the Soviet empire, everything changed. That event, vividly demonstrated by the dismantling of the infamous Berlin Wall in October 1989, caused shock waves around the world, especially in Europe. Now it is history. Former communist countries are open for business, and during the last ten years some of those nations have made tremendous progress, having built an impressive economic base to such an extent that they are being accepted as members of the European Union.

What seemed impossible just a few years ago is now a reality, not only for Europe, but for the entire world. This is absolutely necessary, for if Europe is to lead the world effectively it must unify. Only through European unity can the rest of the world be united.

The World Shall Be One

From Scripture, we know that the world will not only have "one mind," but the unity will progress to such an extent that one leader will arise to world prominence, so that "all the world wondered after the beast" (Revelation 13:3). If you think President John F. Kennedy was popular in the United States and Adolf Hitler in Germany, then let me tell you that their prominence will pale when compared to what is yet to come!

Martin Luther translates Revelation 13:3 this way, "And all the inhabitants of the Earth were surprised at the Beast." The Amplified Version makes it even clearer, "And the whole earth went after the beast in amazement and admiration." We haven't seen anything yet! But that's not all. When reading Revelation 13:8, I'm astonished because it says, "And all that dwell upon the earth shall worship him." This is almost impossible to comprehend. The entire world—the new, intelligent, enlightened global society—will begin to worship a man!

Again, it must be emphasized that this was not possible less than two decades ago. Communism ruled a quarter of the world, and the communists surely wouldn't have worshiped anyone because the official philosophy of communism is atheism, which denies the existence of any god. Today, religion and democracy go hand in hand. You can't have one without the other. For all practical purposes, this global worship was impossible until now. The idea that the entire world would actually admire one person, accept him as God, and worship him was out of the question until this day. Four important areas must be developed for such a prophecy to be fulfilled:

Politics

It is impossible for the world to unite unless it comes under one political system. For 70 years the world was primarily divided between communism and democracy. This hindrance is now done away with as democracy marches victoriously around the world.

Financial

It is impossible to financially unite various currencies unless a one-world system is established. Again, with the fall of communism, this has changed. In our day, we have a one-world system that allows us to use credit cards in any part of the world, allowing us to make purchases in any currency. The funds are automatically converted. Such a system was unthinkable 50 years ago, but today it is a fact of life. Money, it is said, rules the world, and money must have free course in order to unite the nations.

Economy

In our newspapers and on the news daily we hear about corporations swallowing up other corporations. Although this has happened on a national basis in the past, we are now seeing for the first time that this corporate consolidation is crossing national boundaries to take place globally. Today there is no significant difference between driving an "American-made" or a "foreign-made" car. Our "American" cars may be primarily manufactured in other countries while our "foreign" cars may be mostly built in the United States.

The globalization of the world's economy is in full swing and is successfully establishing a New World Order, whether we like it or not. At the beginning of 1998, the news media reported the merger of Germany's Daimler-Benz with United States' Chrysler. This global New World Order deal was criticized by William J. Lynott, president of Buy America Foundation, in a letter to *Time* magazine:

> What is being highly acclaimed as a "merger" between Daimler-Benz and Chrysler (*Business,* May 18) is far more ominous. A close look reveals the disturbing truth. The new company will be incorporated in Germany. After a three-year transition period of cochairmanship, a single chairman will take charge of the company. That chairman, you can wager, will come from Daimler-Benz. In short, Chrysler has been "bought" by Daimler-Benz.
>
> With only two American auto manufacturers left, we are at risk of losing the automobile industry, much as we have lost the consumer electronics industry.[2]

Many Americans who fear globalization of American industry agree with Mr. Lynott. What is overlooked, however, is the fact that in times past, America was leading in the establishment of global firms throughout the world. Regardless of whether we agree with it or oppose it, globalism is definitely in and nationalism is out.

Religion

One significant need for the new one-world order is a united religion: "All that dwell upon the earth shall worship him." This cannot happen in the present framework of diverse religions. Thus, I ask, "How far are we on the path to a united world religion?" Answer: Much further than we may think! The leader of the world's largest religion (Catholicism), Pope John Paul II, said this in an address to Muslims:

> Today, dialogue between our two religions is more necessary than ever. This dialogue needs to be credible and marked by mutual

respect, knowledge and acceptance. There remains a spiritual bond which unites us and which we must strive to recognize and develop.[3]

In my book *How Democracy Will Elect the Antichrist,* I quoted a paragraph from the Louvain Declaration:

> Buddhists, Christians, Confucianists, Hindus, Jains, Jews, Muslims, Shintoists, Sikhs, Zoroastrians and still others, we have sought here to listen to the spirit within our varied and venerable religious traditions. We have grappled with the towering issues that our societies must resolve in order to bring about peace, justice, and an ennobling quality of life for every person, and every people.... We rejoice that ... the long era of prideful, and even prejudiced isolation of the religions of humanity is, we hope, gone forever. We appeal to the religious communities of the world to inculcate the attitude of planetary citizenship.[4]

Not only are the various ecumenical movements at work to unite the world religiously, but a recent article in *Sky* magazine shows how music is uniting the world religiously as well:

> Last May, I traveled to Fes with a tour group from the World Music Institute, which sponsors a subscription series of concerts by international performers each year in New York. Our appetites were whetted for a whole week of world sacred music. Although the bill ... promised an American gospel choir and Bach cantatas performed by a Swiss chamber ensemble, I was personally more hungry for non-Western sacred music, especially the kind of ecstatic singing that pushes the human voice to the farthest edges of emotional expressiveness.

> Sure enough, there was some wild devotional praise-singing on display in Fes. A raven-haired diva named Aicha Redouane, for instance, made the stones of the palace courtyard ring with her rendition of Egyptian classical vocals. Singing 27-note phrases with her mouth closed, she inspired grown men to leap to their feet shouting "Allah!" Unlike the '96 festival, though, last year's Fes Festival of World Sacred Music focused less on exuberant displays of devotion and more on contained expressions of spiritual ecstasy or, to use [his] word, "interiority."

> A Lebanese Maronite nun with a doctorate in musicology from the Sorbonne sings Byzantine Christian liturgy in Arabic. She appeared onstage in a traditional black nun's habit and in what looked like a

constant state of prayer. She sang quietly and delicately with her eyes closed and her fists propped under her chin or against her heart. Spinning out long lines in a wobbly vibrato that proved to be precisely controlled modal singing, she sounded like an eerie combination of opera diva Maria Callas, the legendary Egyptian singer Om Kolthom and a ghostly night wind. Her 12 musicians and eight-piece choir emitted the faintest of drones, providing a hush cloud of sonic padding. This was music so inward-focused as to be practically hallucinatory.

And whatever the spiritual origins of the Arab-Andalusian melodies played in unison by the 51-piece Ensemble Al Brihi from Fes, the hometown audience received it as all-purpose good-time music, clapping along as enthusiastically as they did to the doo-wop gospel offered by the ARC Choir from Harlem, New York, on the closing night of the festival.

"What the public senses, even if they don't know it consciously, is that there's a deep link between traditional music and sacred music," [he] told me. "They invoke a nostalgia that's not personal but archetypal. It's the nostalgia of anyone on Earth trying to get in touch with transcendence or eternity.[5]

Does this not remind us of Daniel 3:5,6, "At what time ye hear the sound of the cornet, flute, harp, sackbut, psaltery, dulcimer, and all kinds of music, ye fall down and worship the golden image that Nebuchadnezzar the king hath set up: And whoso falleth not down and worshippeth shall the same hour be cast into the midst of a burning fiery furnace."

Europe Today

When we ask, "Will Europe dominate?" we are actually behind the times because that is already an established fact. A publication entitled *The Single Market,* published by the European Commission, states: "The [European] Community accounts for 38% of world trade as opposed to 11% for the United States and 9% for Japan. Its economic well-being thus depends on its imports and exports. It is therefore very open to all states wishing to trade with it." This clearly shows that the future is already here. Regarding global responsibility, the publication says:

> The creation of the single market reinforces the Union's importance as the world's leading trading power. It gives the E.U. a more solid internal base to help carry out its international responsibilities and to defend its legitimate trading interests. It has stated its intention to do so vigorously within the framework of trade policy instruments available under the new World Trade Organization (WTO), successor to the General Agreement on Tariffs and Trade (GATT).[6]

Treaty of Rome

The development of the European Union did not happen overnight but is due to an evolutionary process. *The Single Market* says,

> Although they took 35 years to realize, the goals of the single market are enshrined in the European Union's founding Treaty of Rome, which became the constitution for the future European Union in 1958. There we find already the list of the single market's four freedoms: the free movement of goods, services, capital and people.[7]

It is noteworthy to realize that the foundation of the European Union rests on the Treaty of Rome. Just as in ancient times, the Roman democratic system is reemerging as the main denominator in the uniting of the world!

We can easily forget that our own nation, the United States, is built on Roman principles. For example, "The supreme council of ancient Rome was called the Senate. This identical system is used today in the US and Canada. This also applies to Italy, France, Ireland, South Africa and Australia, just to name a few."[8]

In my book *Saddam's Mystery Babylon,* I quote from *The National Geographic:*

> Just as a modern democracy, the Romans granted rights, but requested duties.
>
> *Rights and Duties of Citizens*
> Within the broad sweep of uniformity, Roman administration at the local level was flexible, tolerant, and open.

When Rome conquered a new province, the defeated general and his army were carted away in chains; almost everyone else came out ahead. The local elite were given positions in the Roman hierarchy. Local businesses gained the benefit of Roman roads, water systems, the laws of commerce and the courts. Roman soldiers guarded the town against pirates and marauders. And within a fairly short period, many of the provincial residents would be made cives Romani—citizens of Rome—with all the commensurate rights and duties.

The Roman "pro-life movement" was actively supported by no one less than Augustus.

Anti-Abortion

Augustus used all the tools of governing. Concerned about a decline in the birthrate, he employed both the stick (a crackdown on abortion) and the carrot (tax incentives for big families). To see if his policies were effective, he took a census of his empire now and then.

Thus it did in fact come to pass in those days that there went out a decree from Caesar Augustus that all the world should be registered. And just as St. Luke's Gospel tells us, this happened "when Quirinius was governor of Syria," in A.D. 6.

Without Roman law, today's democracies would not function.

Literacy and Law

The English historian Peter Salway notes that England under Roman rule had a higher rate of literacy than any British government was able to achieve for the next 14 centuries. One of the most important documentary legacies the Romans left behind was the law—the comprehensive body of statute and case law that some scholars consider our greatest inheritance from ancient Rome.

The idea of written law as a shield—to protect individuals against one another and against the awesome power of the state—was a concept the Romans took from the Greeks. But it was Rome that put this abstract notion into daily practice, and the practice is today honored around the world.

Ancient Rome was also concerned with the liberties of its citizens.

Innocent Until Proven Guilty

The emperor Justinian's monumental compilation of the Digests, the Institutes, and the Revised Code, completed in A.D. 534, has served as the foundation of Western law ever since. Two millennia before the Miranda warnings, the Romans also established safeguards to assure the rights of accused criminals. We can see this process at work in the case against the Christian pioneer St. Paul, as set forth in the New Testament in the Acts of the Apostles.

America's democratic system is clearly modeled after the Roman Republic.

Rome—U.S.A.

The Roman process of making laws also had a deep influence on the American system. During the era of the Roman Republic (509 to 49 B.C.) lawmaking was a bicameral activity. Legislation was first passed by the comitia, the assembly of the citizens, then approved by the representative of the upper class, the senate, and issued in the name of the senate and the people of Rome.

Centuries later, when the American Founding Fathers launched their bold experiment in democratic government, they took republican Rome as their model. Our laws, too, must go through two legislative bodies. The House of Representatives is our assembly of citizens, and, like its counterpart in ancient Rome, the U.S. Senate was originally designed as a chamber for the elite (it was not until the 17th Amendment, in 1913, that ordinary people were allowed to vote for their senators).

Impressed by the checks and balances of the Roman system, the authors of American government also made sure that an official who violated the law could be "impeached," a word we take from the Roman practice of putting wayward magistrates in pedica.

The reliance on Roman structures at the birth of the United States was reflected in early American popular culture, which delighted in drawing parallels between U.S. leaders and the noble Romans.

There was a great vogue for marble statues depicting George Washington, Alexander Hamilton, even Andrew Jackson in Roman attire. A larger-than-life statue of Washington in a toga and sandals is still on exhibit at the National Museum of American History in Washington, D.C.[9]

These few quotations offer overwhelming proof that our modern world, regardless of where we reside, is based, built, and directed by Roman European principles that will lead to the solidifying of all the nations of the world, regardless of race, national origin, religion or whatever else may be considered. All nations and peoples must become one under a one-world government.

Europe's Future

In the introductory letter of the European Commission's *The Single Market,* the editor writes:

> Across Europe, millions of citizens and thousands of companies, big and small, benefit from the European single market. The removal of frontiers inside the European Union in 1993 is now a fact of life. Companies have entered new markets, have struck up transnational partnerships, have restructured production to exploit the opportunities of a home market of 370 million.[10]

We must note that this was written in 1995 and is now old news. At this moment, dozens of nations are standing in line, in hopes of being admitted into the exclusive club of the European Union. By some estimates, Europe could be 800 million strong by the year 2010. There is no need to belabor this point regarding their significance at that time. With the "euro" currency in place, the European Union will dominate the largest part of the world market. Being the originator of the world's civilized philosophies, Europe will be waiting for the one man who is able to take leadership and literally rule the world!

In view of these facts, we, the church of Jesus of Christ, have more reasons than ever to rejoice because our redemption is drawing nigh. The extreme success of the Roman system with free markets, free speech, free elections and free enterprise is creating a free society unprecedented in the history of mankind... but the Bible states that this will lead to the greatest catastrophe man has ever known.

Therefore, dear reader, ground yourself in the Word of God because it is guaranteed by the Son of God, who became flesh and dwelt among us. This is the warning and admonition He gives us: "Watch ye therefore, and pray always, that ye may be accounted worthy to escape all these things that shall come to pass, and to stand before the Son of man" (Luke 21:36).

▼ ▼ ▼

CHAPTER 10

Globalist Elite at the Throttle

Dave Breese

A group of most interesting individuals gathered in the early evening at a lodge south of Chicago in the beautiful Starved Rock area. Numbering less than 50, mostly men, they appeared to be on an important mission. They quickly moved into their rooms and prepared for the meeting of the evening. The meal on that occasion was hardly a banquet, but it was definitely above average. It was as if the meal was of modest importance whereas the purpose of the gathering was of primary importance. That small crowd began to sense some anticipation as they gathered in the nicely prepared meeting room.

A short time was allowed for appropriate greetings to one another, leaving any onlooker with the impression that these people had at least some level of knowledge of one another. As they moved to their chairs, the leader took the time to greet them all. All listened carefully as he spoke.

"Ladies and gentlemen, I extend my greetings to each one of you. You are here on relatively short notice, but you are already taking part in a mission of great importance. We hope that the recognition of the importance of this meeting will grow as we commune together on this occasion.

"As we all know, the world is in the midst of a growing set of very serious problems. Dealing with them is already beyond the natural ability of any of us. These problems may, however, be amenable to the mutual, corporate activity of knowledgeable individuals—like those who are here this evening.

"Notice first of all the global economy. The nations of the world that once bore most of the weight of the economies of the world are themselves in serious straits. The economy of Asia, with Japan in the lead, has just broken down to the point that it will represent less than half of its economic capability and, therefore, its global prestige.

"It is inevitable that the other nations of southeast Asia will follow suit, as in fact they are. The Philippines is in serious trouble and Thailand, South Vietnam, Laos and Cambodia are all on the ropes. The financial condition translates into severe individual poverty for the millions of people who live in these areas. That poverty could soon become so strained as to trigger revolution in the entire Asian situation. China seems to be the probable exception, but that nation retains a questionable stability—one sustained by its constant reign of terror on its one-billion people population.

"Because of the involvement of the United States, these nations are able to operate while flirting with a disaster mode of potential revolution. An Asian explosion could not be contained and certainly could be expected to ignite the world military scene.

"We must also consider the European situation. Europe is even now the object of a unity movement, a common currency and a ready involvement in a whole set of new sciences. In fact, Europe is approaching a point of unity that could put together a new nation of 350 million people. Germany is in the middle of this, and we must not forget that Germany lost two wars in this century and does not intend to lose another one. A unity of all of the nations that participated in World War II would be a powerful force indeed—maybe the greatest on earth.

"Southeast Europe cannot be ignored. The recent nuclear demonstrations between India and Pakistan illustrate the absurdity of the nuclear nonproliferation treaty. That nuclear capability could turn any of the banana republics of South Europe and Africa into contending nations in the inevitable event of another war.

"Looking at the former Bulgarian nations, we note that all-out war between Serbia and the related nations is not merely a possibility; it is even now a reality.

"Think with me about the United States for just a moment. Many an optimistic conversation is carried on here about how great the economy is and how wonderful are our future possibilities. The facts are the opposite. We are a debtor nation living off the unearned incomes of our grandchildren. Our national debt is a trillion dollars and growing every day. The global economy indeed is very shaky. So serious is the problem that I think we can say we are being held together by some kind of mysterious force, by faith rather than merely an archaic love of country.

"Ladies and gentlemen, you know all of these things, but I say them to remind us of the need for action that is now upon us. We have all lived lives of relative wealth and convenience, conditions we do not want to discontinue. They will be discontinued, however, unless we move with a new plan to vouchsafe our future. Virtually the same precarious conditions exist in every aspect of life in America and in the world. It is imperative that we produce a new form of world influence, of world control, before our whole elite culture slips away from us. We must find a way to reestablish that pinnacle of power from which we have operated for three or four generations.

"Now, I would like to suggest something we all need to think about. This is a time in which the world is weak and very confused. Our earth has been put upon by all kinds of theories about government, money, the future and so on. The trouble is that the people and the nations of the world agree on almost nothing. There has been much talk about unity but very little of the real thing has come to pass.

"But right now it is different. The people of Europe, leaders of Latin America, the masses of Asia and others are making attempts at unity. It's hard to believe that the United States has often been named by these nations as the best possible entity to bring together the otherwise confused nations of the world. Believe me, if someone were to speak to the nations of the world and bring what even sounds like an answer to the problems of money, expanding population, new age ideas and the like the response could be tremendous. Potentially millions would follow such a leader and envision a bright, new, nonconfused world as a result of his inspiring plan for the future. Right now the world is dreaming rather vaguely about what the future could bring. It wouldn't take much in the midst of today's confusions to electrify the people of earth with a great plan. A single voice, before which many others would say amen, is needed today.

"The first step toward such unity is not primarily the unity of the masses. Rather, it must be the higher unity of the elite, the brilliant, the courageous leaders who could bring together a relatively small committee to initiate the great plan.

"That relatively small committee is very much like the one that is here with us tonight. Let's face it, most of you have sufficient money to handle the future. You are, however, looking for something different. You're bored with intellectual inactivity. Although you are relatively happy, you view today and tomorrow with ennui. You are ready for some new excitement. You are ready to enroll in the cause that will bring a bright new pathway to the future.

"I am here to point out that pathway and the bright possibilities that start here. If in these very days we could forge a phalanx, the possibilities would be truly sensational. Society is like a pyramid, broad at its base but narrowing as it reaches higher. There is room near the top for only a few, and perhaps for only one as we reach the very top. I am sure that none of you want to slip down to the gross, muddy bottom of that pyramid. Rather, each one of us suspects that this will happen unless we can reestablish our status in the culture and put our influence and *our* leader on the top of that pyramid structure.

"I am ready to commit myself to be a part of the leadership of this elite set of leaders that we need to put together very soon. After that we can go for the masses."

"But how can we do this?" asked one of the guests. "How can we reestablish this shaky pyramid in order to guarantee the future for ourselves and our children?"

"I am glad you asked that question," said the leader. "I think the best answer was given to us by Joseph Goebbels back in the days that were a prelude to World War II. He announced that the accomplishment of anything in the world depended on a five-stage program. The five stages are: 1. ideology; 2. propaganda; 3. followers; 4. members;

and 5. leaders. He claimed that the basis of any effective movement and commanding leadership within that movement was the belief in a powerful ideology. You must believe in what you are doing. The absence of ideology soon leads to fatal weakness in an organization or endeavor and its consequent collapse. Many institutions in the world are already suffering from the lack of a great truth to believe in. As a result, the vision is lost and the organization slowly sinks down to nothing."

The leader then reminded his attentive listeners that "ideology must be followed by spreading a hopeful message that declares the benefits of our program. Articulate people must be the speakers, the teachers, the voices of the ideology of the leader. In these days, the use of propaganda media is imperative. However, even that will be ineffective without a commanding spokesperson who can inspire and motivate. Following this comes the call for followers. People must be willing to change their plans and pursue the new design. Then come the members, individuals who will sign up and say 'count on me.' Choosing mid-ranking leaders from out of followers and members is the only way to guarantee a future generation.

"The most important choice any entity ever makes is its leadership. The nations of our time are covered with the remains of lost causes in which the necessity of leadership was forgotten."

The people in the meeting by this time were leaning forward, listening most intently. They could not take their eyes off of this man when, with carefully articulated words, he said,

"I have called us together to recommend a course of action. The time for our program has come upon us, and if we do not act in these days, we will lose our opportunity to touch the world—yes, to lead it. We are at the place that was well-described by Shakespeare when he said, 'There is a tide in the affairs of men, Which, taken at the flood, leads on to fortune; Omitted, all the voyage of their life is lived in shallows and in miseries.' Ladies and gentlemen, I promise you fortunes, but if we do not act in these days, it will be shallows and miseries.

"Are you willing to be part of a new, improved world?"

A roaring ovation filled the room. The people stood to their feet and broke into a sustained cheer for the man who had just delivered his soul. Their minds had been moved by the speech that said, "The world needs to be changed, and we can change it. If we do there are rich rewards." Each one of those minds, at least for that moment, dismissed alternative thoughts and said, "I must be a part of this exciting, powerful movement."

The speaker continued.

"We ought not to ignore the fact that society is at the place of the beginning of global organization already. A sentiment going in our time is that our present leadership either needs help or needs to resign. Despite our boast about modern times and miraculous knowledge, we have an ever-mounting number of diseases, disorganizations and despair-producers going in our society. Our culture appears to be willing to listen to a new program. If today's leaders can be converted into a cooperative frame of mind, there will be no effective resistance to such a program. The future will be ours. We have lived on tiny ideas about religion, money and the future up until now. We have the opportunity in these very days to expand our thinking and rise to the great occasions that are before us."

The speaker did not know how close his speech was coming to the place where it sounded like the advent of the anti-God, anti-Christ movement. Speaking about the Antichrist, the Scripture says that he is one "who opposeth and exalteth himself above all that is called God, or that is worshipped; so that he as God sitteth in the temple of God, showing himself that he is God" (2 Thessalonians 2:4).

▼ ▼ ▼

A scenario such as this must be the case sometime in the days to come. The Scripture predicts astonishing expansion of human knowledge coming to pass toward the end of the age. "Knowledge shall be increased," says the prophetic Word, which certainly implies a vast amount of technical progress in a culture that increasingly tells itself that it needs no God to live a happy and successful life. At the same time, however, the Scripture predicts that "perilous times shall come" (2 Timothy 3:1), then it lists 15 corrosive additives that will dwell in the lives of man as the consummation of history draws closer. The Scripture informs us that

> men shall be lovers of their own selves, covetous, boasters, proud, blasphemers, disobedient to parents, unthankful, unholy, without natural affection, trucebreakers, false accusers, incontinent, fierce, despisers of those that are good, traitors, heady, highminded, lovers of pleasures more than lovers of God; having a form of godliness, but denying the power thereof: from such turn away. For of this sort are they which creep into houses, and lead captive silly women laden with sins, led away with divers lusts, ever learning, and never able to come to the knowledge of the truth. Now as Jannes and Jambres withstood Moses, so do these also resist the truth: men of corrupt minds, reprobate concerning the faith. But they shall proceed no further: for their folly shall be manifest unto all men, as theirs also was (2 Timothy 3:2-9).

Therefore, we can expect to exist concomitantly in that interesting era of earth two great conditions. The first is the vast expansion of human knowledge and the second is the rise of perilous conditions across the world.

When we read the prophetic Word, we are certainly supposed to ask, "Does that prediction resemble anything that I see on earth today?" We can quickly agree with the close resemblance between the condition of our external world and the teaching of the Word of God. Dozens of other comparisons and individual passages tell us detail after detail of the rise of Antichrist. Of importance to us here, however, is that the elite people will be in positions of control. We are told in the Scriptures that society will be brought to the place where the whole world will accept the person of the Antichrist and will see no way of resisting Him: "Who is able to make war with him?" (Revelation 13:4). In order to have such a wide and total influence, the "man of sin" will need to have many passionate compatriots who will idolize his person and swear to carry out his will to the ends of the earth. It is, therefore, fair to suggest that the passionate followers of the Antichrist will not just be ordinary people. Rather, they will be what many call "globalist elite." They will be men and women of convincing speech and most attractive personalities who will promise an utterly marvelous future and who will have a reasonable-sounding plan by which to bring it all to pass. They will surely promise that they can create a new world order and bring to pass the dawn of a new day. Their plans for the future will not be merely business as usual; their plans will hinge on an exciting dimension that touches every life.

Again, as we are thinking of the convincing messages that they will bring, we cannot help but compare the associates of the Antichrist with today's politicians. Hundreds upon hundreds of such men and women live in Washington, D.C., and thousands more populate the major cities of the world. They are convincing in the presentation of global plans. When needed, they will be able to bring in an army to back up their convincing displays of the organization of the Antichrist.

Out of this group of followers and from the will of the people at large in the world, there must come a decision. The optimists must take the time to answer the question: "What is able to bring us to a changed world and produce the beautiful future we must have?" This attitude will produce first curiosity and then conviction. Curiosity will cause the people of the world to wonder about this person and that one. About many, they will ask the question, "Who is he and what can he do?" Within a short time, however, that curiosity must turn—and it will—to conviction, to joy, to a vote for a leader. The world, and especially the world's elite, will watch with detailed interest that program of joy. Soon will emerge a man thought to have brilliance and capability beyond what the world has ever seen.

The Word of God tells us much about him. From God's point of view, the coming of the Antichrist will not be viewed so benignly. The Bible says, "For the devil is come down unto you, having great wrath, because he knoweth that he hath but a short time" (Revelation 12:12). This brilliant, pleasing man will then institute a number of programs. The Scripture lists those of which we should be aware. He will produce a religion that will be provocative indeed. The people will worship the dragon (the devil) who gave power to the beast (the Antichrist), and they will worship the beast saying, "Who is like the beast? Who is able to make war with him?" His true nature will begin to show itself as he opens his mouth in blasphemy against God, His name and His tabernacle, and them that dwell in heaven (Revelation 13:6). All that dwell on the earth shall worship him and will pursue the miracle-working power which he has: "he doeth great wonders" (Revelation 13:13). Finally, he will produce a religion that is both pagan and inexpressibly cruel, as many as would not worship the image of the beast are killed (Revelation 13:15).

(It is interesting that we are invited to think carefully about the beast. The Scripture says, "Here is wisdom. Let him that hath understanding count the number of the beast: for it is the number of a man; and his number is Six hundred threescore and six" [Revelation 13:18].)

What a picture this is. Finally, through the genius of the beast, the world, nation by nation, will be organized into a great universal political system, religious arrangement and financial organization. We need not wonder long to guess the attitude of the existing leaders of the world (the elite) toward the emergence of the Antichrist. Being materialists, they will rejoice in this development. In cooperation with the program of the Antichrist, the elite will take the throttle of the world system. At long last they will promise that the dawn of a new age will indeed come to pass. Aspiring young men and women in great numbers who would like to be the controllers of the world tomorrow will be counted on to join his cause. For a short time, it will look as though the plans of the Antichrist for a world overturned and reconstituted in his favor are indeed taking hold of the world's youth. The Scripture says that the Antichrist will stay in power for 42 months, or three-and-a-half years (Revelation 13:5).

From the Word of God on this particular subject, we can answer the pressing questions: "How long can power last?" and "Is it worth it all?" Scripture gives us a pointed answer:

> And I saw an angel come down from heaven, having the key of the bottomless pit and a great chain in his hand. And he laid hold on the dragon, that old serpent, who is the Devil, and Satan, and bound him a thousand years, and cast him into the bottomless pit, and shut him

up, and set a seal upon him, that he should deceive the nations no more, till the thousand years should be fulfilled: and after that he must be loosed a little season (Revelation 20:1-3).

Is this the final picture of the activity of Satan? No. For the Scripture says, "And the devil that deceived them was cast into the lake of fire and brimstone, where the beast and the false prophet are, and shall be tormented day and night for ever and ever" (Revelation 20:10). What a picture that is of the terrible fate of the great enemy of God.

What can we discover about leadership from all of this? We can learn that leadership may be proud, boastful and temporarily successful. However, time marches on to bring the future into the present. So today's leaders will become archaic and irrelevant by tomorrow; by the day after that, they'll be gone. This is true even of Satan, who will end up in the lake of fire and brimstone as a consequence of his evil.

Here we have answered forever the question of the outcome of satanic activity. Surely the lesson should be clear to each one of us. A person who believes that the prestige, honor and acceptance that comes from a satanic blessing are worthwhile is a fool. The Scripture says, "Resist the devil, and he will flee from you" (James 4:7). We are never, no matter what the scene, supposed to be a part of Satan's cause. Whatever may be the medals and the medallions we receive, associating with Satan is the activity of a proud fool.

Scripture presents us with the temporary victories of Satan and his henchmen, but they are not presented as the final picture. The final picture is that the God who made the universe will triumph over all. Jesus Christ is the victor, and He will be crowned before the wondering eyes of the world as King of kings and Lord of lords. This is the picture we should keep in mind as the object of our anticipation.

When we read of the vast difficulties that will come upon the world in the days of the great tribulation, we should also rejoice because we will not be a part of those difficult days. No indeed! We will be looking on from heaven, having been caught up to be with Jesus Christ before the days of the tribulation. To know this is to have great assurance within the soul. The promise that Jesus Christ is coming for His own is given to us in the Word of God. It is to be the source of comfort, assurance and anticipation of heaven. We can trust that will be the case as we think of the defeat of the elite and arrogant and the victory of the humble and childlike—the children of God. To be a Christian is the greatest experience in all of life. It is an infinitely wonderful promise for this world and also for the world to come. Let us newly commit ourselves to serve Christ and to be the channels of blessing whereby others are invited to know Him as well. Always bear in mind the greatest prophetic verse in the Scripture: "Seeing then that all these things shall be dissolved, what manner of persons ought ye to be in all holy conversation and godliness?" (2 Peter 3:11).

With the full authority of Scripture, we can announce that society is not going to be an easy place to live or even a predictable situation in the days to come. God has specifically taken the time to warn the world of the coming of an individual called "the man of sin, the son of perdition." This man will oppose everything godly, everything that honors the Word of God and everyone who aspires to live for Christ. For a brief hour, Antichrist will be the master of earth and impose his wicked will upon everyone.

This being the prediction of Scripture, we should not fail to remind ourselves of the alternative plan that God has for Christians. About the Christian, the Bible says, "Beloved, now are we the sons of God, and it doth not yet appear what we shall be: but we know that, when he shall appear, we shall be like him; for we shall see him as he is" (1 John 3:2). Announcing a special destiny for Christians, the Scripture also says, "The Lord himself shall descend from heaven with a shout, with the voice of the archangel, and with the trump of God: and the dead in Christ shall rise first: Then we which are alive and remain shall be caught up together with them in the clouds, to meet the Lord in the air: and so shall we ever be with the Lord" (1 Thessalonians 4:16,17).

How wonderful it is that "God hath not appointed us to wrath, but to obtain salvation by our Lord Jesus Christ" (1 Thessalonians 5:9). It is so encouraging that God has spoken to the church with this promise: "Because thou has kept the word of my patience, I also will keep thee from the hour of temptation, which shall come upon all the world" (Revelation 3:10).

Yes, there will be that brief hour in which the arrogant and wicked will attempt to take over from God. However, there will follow that eternity in which we will live in the beautiful, ever-fulfilling presence of the Lord Jesus. The rapture of the church is a wonderful promise God makes to His own. Our assurance does not come from observing the competence of man but from the promise of Jesus Christ. Man's best plans will ultimately fail, but, thank God, we will be merely onlookers to that failure.

God's great plan is for His own, and this we brightly anticipate.

▼ ▼ ▼

Part 3

Paul Predicts
Perilous Times

CHAPTER 11

End-Time Man: Personal Characteristics

Joseph R. Chambers

From the moment Satan entered the Garden of Eden and deceived Adam and Eve, he had to have a man to be his representative of his Antichrist. Apparently, Cain was ready to accept the role of the first false worshiper, and he actually made an effort to worship the true God with a false expression of faith. His worship was rejected, he was judged and, like all false worshipers, he was angry with his brother, Abel, whose worship was accepted. This accurate Genesis account establishes the pattern of the Antichrist character. These characteristics have never changed, and the final Antichrist will reflect them in an ultimate display of consummate evil.

Several characteristics are revealed in this biblical account. First, we must always remember that every antichrist spirit is a religious spirit. Secular activities are certainly evident, but they are a means to an end, not the basic character. Satan himself is first an extremely religious being, and he accomplishes his goals with religious activity. Through the centuries, his antichrists have created a multitude of religious organizations and promoted as many religious philosophies. Often we hear our enemies talk about the many religious wars and label all religion as an enemy because of those wars. This is the design of antichrists, to cast doubt and shadow over the truth of God. If the world of believers is going to have any idea of Satan's final antichrist, it must understand his deeply religious character and expression.

Second, antichrists always offer religious expressions that have departed from the plain and literal truths of Scripture. Cain did not refuse to worship; he even appeared to worship in great enthusiasm, but he was visibly shaken when his false worship was rejected. It is impossible to find a more perfect picture than this in describing the present development of the antichrist spirit. All religions are being elevated to an equal footing, and anyone who dares claim exclusiveness receives a sound rebuke. In fact, the only religions unacceptable in today's general mindset are fundamental Christianity and fundamental Judaism. The religious attitude being promoted on a worldwide basis is tolerance and respect for all religions and absolute hatred for the narrow way. This religious tolerance will be one of the most striking of the final antichrist's characteristics.

The Scripture then records a statement that the Creator made to Cain that reveals the mysterious spirit of the antichrist he would face the rest of his life. Of course, we know that the world has faced that spirit right up to the present and will face it in its darkest form at the end. Look at these words as stated in the Masoretic Hebrew: "And why has fallen your face? Is there not if do you well, exaltation, and if not you do well, at the door sin is crouching and toward you its desire, but you should rule over it" (Genesis 4:6,7, literal English from Hebrew). Sin is actually personified and revealed here as the antichrist that would be like a crouched animal constantly badgering every human being. The only people who have defeated this spirit, and certainly the only people who will defeat it in the future darkness, are those who can identify this spirit and resist it by the Word of God.

It's amazing how this picture is in perfect accord with the words of the apostle Paul to the Thessalonians: "For the mystery of iniquity doth already work: only he who now letteth will let, until he be taken out of the way. And then shall that Wicked be revealed, whom the Lord shall consume with the spirit of his mouth, and shall destroy with the brightness of his coming" (2 Thessalonians 2:7,8).

In these two companion passages, we see the same characteristic of the "mystery of iniquity" or "the antichrist" revealed in the beginning at the fall of man in the garden and the explosion of that spirit at the end. We must learn from the history of Scripture the true picture of this spirit of iniquity. The church is full of good people trying to identify the future antichrist, but they cannot see his captivating spirit at their very doors. We must get into our minds the simple statement included in the last Scripture passage: "The mystery of iniquity doth already work." How can we see the future antichrist if we cannot recognize the present mystery of iniquity? Therefore, the third characteristic of this person is that he operates as a mystery hidden from the eyes of everyone but the most discerning. (I must add that the only possible means of discerning this mystery is the infallible Word of God.)

A fourth clear characteristic of this "man of sin" is his viciousness. We are not dealing with human anger or simple rebellion; we are dealing with a spirit of anger—a furious anger that will not be satisfied until the true expression of faith is wiped off the earth. Cain did not just hate his brother. He martyred Abel for his faith. This was the first act of the antichrist spirit to try to rid the earth of true faith. It was the seed of the serpent in an all-out effort to destroy the seed of woman.

The totality of the antichrist that we are presently witnessing in mystery form, which I believe will soon develop in manifest form, will make an all-out effort to rid the earth of the biblical faith. Everything the final antichrist will represent will be embodied in his hatred for the true God and his effort to set up a system of religions that enthrones him in the Father's place. The present religious deception is the heartthrob of Satan's preparation for his one-world kingdom.

The final characteristic of the Antichrist is the curse always visible in his activities. When the Father spoke to Cain after he had slain Abel, His words revealed this absolute principle:

> And the LORD said unto Cain, Where is Abel thy brother? And he said, I know not: Am I my brother's keeper? And he said, What hast thou done? the voice of thy brother's blood crieth unto me from the ground. And now art thou cursed from the earth, which hath opened her mouth to receive thy brother's blood from thy hand; when thou tillest the ground, it shall not henceforth yield unto thee her strength; a fugitive and a vagabond shalt thou be in the earth" (Genesis 4:9-12).

Study any aspect of history from the Garden of Eden until the present and you will find prosperity and happiness in the wake of every true expression of faith. The opposite is always true of the mystery of iniquity. Where this antichrist spirit has touched the earth, the result is wilderness and calamity. I'm not talking about false prosperity and stealing from others by means of words of divination. I'm talking about health, happiness, prosperous labor and blessings that follow the labor of the righteous. The Bible is full of the stories of Abraham, Isaac, Jacob, David and Solomon, along with countless others who received the blessings of God because they were discerning of the seed of woman and rejected the offers of God's enemies. The opposite is true of Eli, Saul, Ahab, Jezebel and Judas. These people were deceived by the seed of the serpent and the mystery of the antichrist. They inherited a wilderness for their labors. This fifth clear characteristic of an antichrist is his destructive spirit and the clear judgment that is always present in his activities. The book of Revelation gives the final picture of carnage on this earth as a result of his last hurrah of evil.

This background picture from the development of the mysteries of iniquity in Genesis can now help us as we try to identify how the Antichrist will deceive the entire world and receive the worship of the whole earth. Satan, by means of this Antichrist person, will actually become the "god" of this earth and turn it into a wilderness. The world is about to see the grandest picture of this deceiver that he is capable of producing. He will use paranormal powers to produce a religious kingdom full of worldly pomp and glory that will captivate the multitudes.

The Seed of the Serpent; The Seed of Woman

Having started this chapter in the book of Genesis, let's make the transition to the New Testament by a tracing of the seed of the serpent versus the seed of woman. This struggle that the Father Himself prophesied has never ceased even until the present. The Father stated, "And I will put enmity between thee and the woman, and between thy seed and her seed; it shall bruise thy head, and thou shalt bruise his heel" (Genesis 3:15).

The Father has always had a seed in the earth, a remnant, if you please, of holy saints who would not bow to the deceiver or depart from the truth in the smallest of details. These men and women have clung to the truth with no thought of their own lives. Out of this remnant God preserved a seed from which Jesus Christ was born. It is breathtaking to study about Rahab, who was saved out of Jericho to become a part of the seed of the Son of Man. With Rahab, there is Jesse, the father of David, and Ruth, the wife of Boaz. God preserved the seed of woman and the Christ was born Son of man, Son of God.

Satan has maintained his seed of the wicked and had his myriad antichrist persons from the fall in the garden. Wicked men like Nimrod have yielded to his design and wrought destruction to each generation. The history of man during both Testaments is filled with this "mystery of wickedness." These dark figures have been the seed of the serpent, and his evil design has never failed to produce a harvest of destruction. Since the nineteenth century we have witnessed Darwin, Marx, Stalin, Hitler and an endless list of other individuals who have delighted in being the seed of the serpent. Every one of them has been religious and vile beyond description.

The Final Seed of Woman

Jesus Christ was born of Mary, conceived by the Holy Ghost and without the sin nature of Adam. Jesus was the ultimate seed of woman that the Father promised. The Son of God even now has a body, the blood-washed saints who are born of the Holy Spirit by new birth. This seed is the final expression of the seed of woman. Satan hates this seed and is producing his own final seed to counterfeit the pure, blood-washed bride. The seed of the serpent will continue to bruise the seed of the woman even as we see religions of the masses lampoon the straight and narrow way of truth. The seed of woman, the blood-washed, will witness the bruising of the head of the seed of the serpent. The bride of Christ will triumph. God's Word has guaranteed the triumphant march of truth.

Present Characteristics of Antichrist

The Scripture has painted an unreal picture of this final expression of antichrist. While there have been many antichrists, this man is the ultimate and final deceiver and has been chosen by Satan from among the greatest. In my book *A Palace for the Antichrist,* these words best describe this coming genius:

> The consummate evil. A man so vile that he is called a beast and has for a name "blasphemy." He is seen on earth hurling blasphemies against God who is seated on His heavenly throne and he is angrily hurling the same at the saints already among the raptured. He receives his power (inherent ability), his seat (political religions), and his great authority (permission) from the dragon or Satan. Everything that he is, Satan equips him to be. The Bible describes only one type of person who can withstand his design, blinding deception or convincing leadership. John the Revelator said, "And all that dwell upon the earth shall worship him, whose names are not in the book of life of the Lamb slain from the foundation of the World" (Revelation 13:8).

This man is not an ordinary man. The Scripture calls him a composite of several beasts, each having represented a previous world empire. He will be terrible beyond description. Daniel had the following to say of him: "After this I saw in the night visions, and behold a fourth beast, dreadful and terrible, and strong exceedingly; and it had great iron teeth: it devoured and brake in pieces, and stamped the residue with the feet of it: and it was diverse from all the beasts that were before it; and it had ten horns" (Daniel 7:7).

John the Revelator expanded on Daniel's vision and spoke of the beast: "And the beast which I saw was like unto a leopard, and his feet were as the feet of a bear, and his mouth as the mouth of a lion: and the dragon gave him his power, and his seat, and great authority. And I saw one of his heads as it were wounded to death; and his deadly wound was healed: and all the world wondered after the beast" (Revelation 13:2,3). He captivates the world. How does he do it?

The Antichrist Will Be a Religious Personage

The first, most deceiving, characteristic of the final Antichrist will be his deep commitment to the religious world. With his false prophet—whom I identify as a leader of the false anointing that is sweeping the world—he will prepare the world for a religious consensus. He will be a champion of this new tolerant religious consensus, and the world will call it the greatest revival of human history—even greater than the New Testament church of Acts. This revival will explode around the world because of paranormal miracles and great emotional religious meetings. First, let's notice how Daniel breathtakingly described this deceiver 2,600 years ago:

> And the king shall do according to his will; and he shall exalt himself, and magnify himself above every god, and shall speak marvellous things against the God of gods, and shall prosper till the indignation be accomplished: for that that is determined shall be done. Neither shall he regard the God of his fathers, nor the desire of women, nor regard any god: for he shall magnify himself above all. But in his estate shall he honour the God of forces: and a god whom his fathers knew not shall he honour with gold, and silver, and with precious stones, and pleasant things. Thus shall he do in the most strong holds with a strange god, whom he shall acknowledge and increase with glory: and he shall cause them to rule over many, and shall divide the land for gain (Daniel 11:36-39).

Everything about this picture of the Antichrist shows how totally religious he will be. Yet Daniel describes this new god as clearly not the God of his fathers. The new god will be a "god of forces," a "strange god" whom the Antichrist will "increase with glory," and then he will cause that new god to "rule over many."

Even Daniel seems to be intrigued by this new god. He is clearly not just one of the pantheon of pagan gods, but a "strange god," an evil creation of a new god never before worshiped by man. The second characteristic is part of the first and very subtle. I believe the picture would show that the future deception will be to worship a god so generic and common that he can be called by any name you desire to call him. (The Alcoholics Anonymous program has just such a god already accepted by a good part of today's church.) Today's religious leaders are falling over each other to bury their differences and champion a tolerance for each other's beliefs.

The new theologies of our generation are so mushy that they can be supported by a revelation, a vision, a personal prophecy (fortune-telling), a miracle or any source that is religious. Much of what is called preaching has been so integrated with human philosophies that the Bible content is little more than a launching pad—and sometimes not even that. The perfect setting for a generic god is flooding our world.

John the Revelator shows us the development of this religious spirit to the point that Satan himself hides behind the god concept being accepted today. Of course, Satan does not receive the worship of the world by exposing himself but by hiding himself. This text in Revelation shows how Satan uses his antichrist and his antispirit to conceal his own identity, and the world worships the devil and does not recognize it:

> And I saw one of his heads as it were wounded to death; and his deadly wound was healed: and all the world wondered after the beast. And they worshipped the dragon which gave power unto the beast: and they worshipped the beast, saying, Who is like unto the beast? who is able to make war with him? And there was given unto him a mouth speaking great things and blasphemies; and power was given unto him to continue forty and two months. And he opened his mouth in blasphemy against God, to blaspheme his name, and his tabernacle, and them that dwell in heaven (Revelation 13:3-6).

This has always been a great mystery to me that the world *en masse* would worship the devil. I believe the truth is being opened so that men and women will learn that *the only way not to be deceived* in this last day *is by total abandonment to the Holy Scripture* and careful commitment to the minute details of godly living. Plainly, the Antichrist will be extremely religious, and he will certainly lead the world in departing from true biblical faith. These were the first two characteristics of Cain, who was the first representative of the antichrist. The man of sin will be the final expression of false religion.

The Third Characteristic of the Antichrist

Let's look at the third characteristic I established in the beginning of this chapter. The future antichrist is the finished expression of the mystery of iniquity. Satan and his representative are identified throughout the Bible as a crouched animal (see Genesis 4:7) or a "roaring lion ... seeking whom he may devour" (1 Peter 5:8). Individuals who look for the antichrist in some person on the political scene do great damage to the church. His entire scheme is to conceal himself and manifest his evil in unsuspected places. There will be absolutely no way anyone will identify the antichrist until the church of Jesus Christ has been raptured. He will operate as a "mystery" or as the "mystery of iniquity" until the "Restrainer" is removed. The apostle Paul makes that extremely clear:

> And now ye know what withholdeth that he might be revealed in his time. For the mystery of iniquity doth already work: only he who now letteth will let, until he be taken out of the way. And then shall that Wicked be revealed, whom the Lord shall consume with the spirit of his mouth, and shall destroy with the brightness of his coming: Even him, whose coming is after the working of Satan with all power and signs and lying wonders, And with all deceivableness of unrighteousness in them that perish; because they received not the love of the truth, that they might be saved. And for this cause God shall send them strong delusion, that they should believe a lie: That they all might be damned who believed not the truth, but had pleasure in unrighteousness (2 Thessalonians 2:6-12).

The last-day appearance of the antichrist will be seen only in mystery form until the Holy Ghost in His church has been removed. When you grasp this, then you understand that there is no safety in trying to identify *the* Antichrist in physical form. Our only hope is to hide in the truth of God's Word and quit looking for some bogus man to attack. He will be revealed after the rapture and during the early part of the seven years of God's wrath. His work until that point is to deceive while he hides under his many cloaks of religious deception. He loves it when we look for him in some human form instead of immersing ourselves into the holiness of Holy Scripture. The apostle Paul was no doubt considering this very truth when he spoke the following words to the believers at Ephesus:

> Put on the whole armour of God, that ye may be able to stand against the wiles of the devil. For we wrestle not against flesh and blood, but against principalities, against powers, against the rulers of the darkness of this world, against spiritual wickedness in high places. Wherefore take unto you the whole armour of God, that ye may be able to withstand in the evil day, and having done all, to stand. Stand therefore, having your loins girt about with truth, and having on the breastplate of righteousness; and your feet shod with the preparation of the gospel of peace; above all, taking the shield of faith, wherewith ye shall be able to quench all the fiery darts of the wicked (Ephesians 6:11-16).

The Antichrist will not be flesh and blood until the bride of Jesus Christ has been removed to the presence of our Eternal Redeemer.

The Fourth Characteristic of the Antichrist

The Antichrist will be the most vicious human being who has ever existed. Every expression of evil, every evil characteristic, every scheme of death and destruction will be manifest in this dark demon of a man. He will be Satan incarnate in the perfect opposite of the Son of God incarnate. Everything that Jesus Christ was in the exact image of His Father, the Antichrist will be in the exact image of Satan, his father. Remember how vicious Cain became when his new religion was exposed in the Father's rejection and Abel's acceptance.

As we have already discovered, before the antichrist is manifest in human form, the bride of Jesus Christ will be caught up to the Father's presence. This will cause Satan and his antichrist to explode in anger against the bride of Jesus Christ in heaven as well as against Christ Himself. Of course, the bride will be gone, but these dark beasts will blaspheme toward heaven:

> And he opened his mouth in blasphemy against God, to blaspheme his name, and his tabernacle, and them that dwell in heaven. And it was given unto him to make war with the saints, and to overcome them: and power was given him over all kindreds, and tongues, and nations. And all that dwell upon the earth shall worship him, whose names are not written in the book of life of the Lamb slain from the foundation of the world (Revelation 13:6-8).

One of the dark facts about the seven years of God's wrath will be the slaughter of believers that will occur on the earth. Satan's antichrist will begin to kill the element in the church that missed the rapture. Notice these words I just quoted: "And it was given to him to make war with the saints and to overcome them." These were evidently unconverted or lukewarm believers who missed the rapture and now become the object of the wrath of the Antichrist. Revelation 6 gives a picture also of these weary souls that the Antichrist beast will slay as Cain slew Abel:

> And when he had opened the fifth seal, I saw under the altar the souls of them that were slain for the word of God, and for the testimony which they held: And they cried with a loud voice, saying, How long, O Lord, holy and true, dost thou not judge and avenge our blood on them that dwell on the earth? And white robes were given unto every one of them; and it was said unto them, that they should rest yet for a little season, until their fellowservants also and their brethren, that should be killed as they were, should be fulfilled (Revelation 6:9-11).

The carnage created by the Antichrist from hell will eclipse his destruction of all of human history. He will certainly live up to the prophetic picture painted in Holy Scripture. He will be the ultimate beast.

The Final Characteristic of the Antichrist

The Antichrist will be recognized by the wake of destruction that follows him. History is full of people that couldn't discern evil until they witnessed the wilderness. The Scripture informs the believer under certain circumstances to turn a person over to the devil that they may learn not to blaspheme.

The world is about to get its final lesson in Satan's destruction as it witnesses his final Antichrist. Satan's antitrinity will unleash a baptism of dark spirits, destructive wars, vile acts of carnage and even catastrophes in the realm of nature. He will turn the world into a wilderness. John stated, "So he carried me away in the spirit into the wilderness: and I saw a woman sit upon a scarlet coloured beast, full of names of blasphemy, having seven heads and ten horns" (Revelation 17:3). This is a picture of the Antichrist and his false bride and the wilderness they have created for themselves.

Notice that even before the false bride, the "whore," of the Antichrist (the scarlet-colored woman) is destroyed by the ten kings the Antichrist has temporarily enthroned, she is dwelling in a wilderness. This beast and his false spirit, along with the "whore" has made the earth almost uninhabitable. I believe this is why these ten ruling horns destroy the false bride: "And the ten horns which thou sawest upon the beast, these shall hate the whore, and shall make her desolate and naked, and shall eat her flesh, and burn her with fire" (Revelation 17:16). They have witnessed the false religionists destroying our world and creating a worldwide crisis. Members of Satan's crowd always make fools out of themselves.

The "Mystery of Iniquity"

The Antichrist will be the consummate evil. Every vileness of his historic rampage will be represented in his final form. His actions have been as a crouched beast, always attacking, but never truly visible. Our spiritual war has never been with flesh, but with invisible spirits and dark demons. The seven years of the great tribulation will be different. The mystery of iniquity will take human form and the world will see the darkest side of hell.

CHAPTER 12

Persecution in America

Berit Kjos

"What's church and state, Mom?" asked seven-year-old Sallie.

"Why do you ask?" answered her mother.

"My teacher told me to keep them apart and not talk about Jesus. She said I should save that talk for Sundays."

The rule made no sense to Sallie. Jesus was special to her every day—not just on Sundays. And she knew God wanted her to tell others. Yet she didn't like to break rules. So when she wanted to bring her Bible for "sharing day" at her elementary school in California, she felt unsure because it might upset her teacher. In the end, she decided not to take it.

One of her classmates brought a small Buddha statue for the sharing time. The teacher didn't seem to mind the Buddhist religion.

Sallie's mother was in the classroom for a Thanksgiving celebration when the teacher asked all the students to say in one word what they were grateful for. Sallie raised her hand right away. She was thankful for Jesus. But the teacher ignored her hand and called on all the others. Finally, at the very end, she let Sallie say her spe-cial word. The teacher seemed irritated, and Sallie felt ashamed.

One day, when Sallie was talking about Jesus with a classmate who had come to her Vacation Bible School, the principal came by and heard some of their conversation.

"Don't talk about Jesus so much," he told her.

Sallie felt confused.

"But Kara needs to hear about Him," she said. She knew that her friend was hurting.

Even though Sallie could read and write well, she didn't score high on the new tests that check how well children are accepting the beliefs and values of other cultures around the world. She trusted the Bible, and it told her to shun other gods and spirits. She couldn't blend her beliefs with those who celebrated other religions. To the school that meant she wasn't learning to be a group thinker—someone willing to seek common ground. So the school assigned her to a "Child Study Team." A Resource Specialist would try to change her thinking, teach her habits of group learning and help her accept the new ideas about God, unity and the world.

"She doesn't smile, Mommy," said Sallie, who felt uncomfortable in her counselor's presence.

Sallie's parents asked a lawyer what rights they had to protect Sallie from religious intolerance. The lawyer warned them that the school might consider Sallie "overly religious" and refer her to Child Protection Services (CPS). At that point, Sallie's parents quickly transferred her from the local public (read government) school to a Christian school. At least for now she would be safe from the watchful eye of the new American thought police.

The Rising Hostility Toward Christianity

Sallie isn't alone in this battle. Across America, Christian chil-dren, teachers, parents and others face rejection and hatred for refusing to compromise their faith. A California teacher was fired when she questioned a hallway display of letters from young stu-dents describing their encounters with their personal "animal spirits" invoked through a Native American ritual. An Illinois business leader lost his management position when he refused to renounce biblical absolutes—a major hindrance to the compromise required in the "consensus process."

A Kansas mother voiced her reluctance to let her second-grader attend a "historical" play that taught spiritism. The teacher refused to release her daughter and told her, "You are not welcome at this school. We feel you are watching over our shoulder." Stunned, the mother pondered what to do. Didn't she and her husband have the right to raise their daughter according to biblical guidelines? What had happened to free speech? Could Americans lose their freedom?

Many people find that hard to believe. Some cling to a memory of what we once were and refuse to admit that everything we have treasured—our values, families, churches, schools, legal and medical system...even our government—has already changed. After all, we still have our Bill of Rights, don't we? And we're a Christian nation under God's protection, aren't we?

But our constitution has been reinterpreted to fit a new political agenda. Our political, legal and education systems have been infiltrated by leaders who have betrayed America for an alluring vision of a global village. And a new social ethic based on a blend of earth-centered religions and socialist values rule out biblical boundaries and absolutes.

We shouldn't be surprised. A nation that sets pagan values above God's truth will despise genuine Christianity. That's why Jesus told His disciples, "If the world hates you, you know that it hated Me before it hated you.... If they persecuted Me, they will also persecute you.... because they do not know Him who sent Me" (John 15:18-21 NKJV). That's the normal Christian life! The centuries of Christian freedom in America have been an anomaly in the history of time. Today we are simply returning to conditions our Lord told us to expect in a world that neither understands nor tolerates God and His people.

This spreading hatred toward Christian beliefs and values has been smoldering in international circles for decades. Dr. Brock Chisholm, a Canadian psychiatrist and former chief of the United Nations' World Health Organization (WHO), summarized it in 1946.

Like many other globalists, he considered Christianity the main obstacle to worldwide solidarity. Notice how he vilifies Christian parents and links faith to hate:

> We have swallowed all manner of poisonous certainties fed us by our parents.... The results are frustration, inferiority, neurosis and inability to ... make the world fit to live in....
>
> It has long been generally accepted that parents have [the] perfect right to impose any points of view, any lies or fears, superstitions, prejudices, hates, or faith on their defenseless children.... These things cause neuroses....
>
> Surely the training of children in homes and schools should be of at least as great public concern as are their vaccination.... [People with] guilts, fears, inferiorities, are certain to project their hates on to others....
>
> Such reaction now becomes a dangerous threat to the whole world....[1]

Two years later, the International Congress on Mental Health held a world conference in London where it issued a report titled "Mental Health and World Citizenship." It echoed Dr. Chisholm's sentiment:

> Social institutions such as family and school impose their imprint early.... Thus prejudice, hostility or excessive nationalism may become deeply embedded in the developing personality ... often at great human cost.... Change will be strongly resisted unless an attitude of acceptance has first been engendered.

Now, 50 years later, that "attitude of acceptance" has largely "been engendered." Hollywood has taught our children to delight in evil, while schools immerse them in pagan rituals to other gods. Many church leaders are ashamed to mention sin and the cross, and their followers are drifting with the trends, often too distracted to know or care.

In a culture that has embraced the new global paradigm (or worldview), politically correct tolerance seems kinder than obeying God, and paganism seems more tolerable than Christianity. Desensitized to biblical taboos, both young and old—Christians as well as pagans—delight in the pantheistic impressions in popular productions such as the movie *Pocahontas*. And at the opening of each new Olympics, the world celebrates a fresh new model for the global spirituality designed to unite people everywhere.

Christian Paradigm	Humanist Paradigm	Global Paradigm
Base values on biblical truth	Separate church and state	Link values to earth-centered religions
Trust God	Trust self	Trust the state
Teach personal responsibility	Teach human rights	Teach collective responsibility
Love God and people	Love self (self-esteem)	Respect all who fit new paradigm
Don't tolerate sin	Tolerate all lifestyles	Don't tolerate dissenters (zero tolerance)

With the promotion of paganism came freedom to experiment with occult powers. It didn't take long before youth addicted to pagan thrills became subject to the promptings of the forces they invoked. So did countless others who had simply drifted away from truth, and the warning in 1 John 5:19 became increasingly relevant: "The whole world is under the control of the evil one."

The evil one knows well how to stir hatred toward God's people and "engender" a social climate well suited for his purpose. His main target seems to be our children, and their training must start before they have embraced the "poisonous certainties" of biblical Christianity.

The last week in April 1997, President Clinton held a White House conference on America's future. It featured a film called *I Am Your Child,* which began with the birth of a baby. Notice how the introduction by host Tom Hanks matches the threatening warnings from some of the globalist leaders:

> According to startling new scientific discoveries about brain development, the emotional and intellectual environment [the child] is exposed to during those critical first three years will have a profound effect on what kind of person he will turn out to be. And the kind of person he turns out to be *will impact* either positively or negatively *every other person in the world.*

No tolerance for truth. If your child could impact negatively every other person in the world, would the state have a compelling interest in telling you how to raise your child? Both state and federal leaders believe they have such a right. In 1997, the Colorado legislature passed a law giving Social Services the power to prosecute Christian parents for child abuse. It implies that Christian child-raising could be considered "emotional abuse"—a crime. To protect parents, an exemption had been added to the bill. It declared that "emotional abuse shall not be construed to include religious instruction." But this statement was deleted from the bill before it became law.

Do you wonder who has led this vicious assault on Christianity? The moral and spiritual guidelines for the twenty-first century community were written by the United Nations Educational, Scientific and Cultural Organization. Its socialist foundations were laid by Julian Huxley, UNESCO's first Secretary-General and the brother of Aldous Huxley. You may want to review his book *Brave New World* for a summary of the key strategies behind today's social transformation and global-management system.

More recently, UNESCO provided a fitting standard for a global ethic through its "Declaration on Tolerance." It became soft international law when signed by its member nations in 1995. Although our Congress pulled the United States out of the Marxist-leaning UNESCO during the '80s, our nation leads the way in implementing these guidelines in our schools and culture. Ponder its definition and promotion of politically correct tolerance:

- Tolerance is respect, acceptance and appreciation of the rich diversity of our world's cultures.... It is not only a moral duty, it is also a political and legal requirement.

- Tolerance involves the rejection of dogmatism and absolutism [biblical truth?].... Tolerance ... means that one's views are not to be imposed on others [ending freedom to share the gospel with others?].

- Intolerance ... is a global threat. Scientific studies and networking should be undertaken to coordinate the international community's response to this global challenge, including analysis ... of root causes and effective countermeasures, as well as ... monitoring.... Tolerance promotion and the shaping of attitudes of openness, mutual listening and solidarity should take place in schools and universities and through nonformal education ... at home and in the workplace.

- Promote rational tolerance teaching methods that will address the cultural, social, economic, political and religious sources of intolerance—major roots of violence....

Control Through Consensus

Did you notice the reference to solidarity? To control the transformation, globalist leaders must monitor attitudes and purge beliefs that clash with the planned unity. America's traditional values must go. President Bush summarized it well in 1991 when he introduced America 2000, the Republican version of the U.S. branch of UNESCO's world education system:

Nations that stick to stale old notions and ideologies will falter and fail. So I'm here today to say America will move forward.... New schools for a new world.... Reinvent—literally start from scratch and reinvent the American school.... Our challenge amounts to nothing less than a revolution in American education.[2]

As President Clinton has told us repeatedly, this revolutionary program in "lifelong learning" must involve everyone. Eventually no one would escape the sensitivity training and "service learning" programs designed to build social solidarity through the consensus process. As former U.S.S.R. president Mikhail Gorbachev wrote in 1993,

President Clinton will be a success if he manages to use American influence to accomplish this transformation of international responsibility and increase significantly the role of the United Nations.... Bill Clinton will be a great president ... if he can make America the creator of a new world order based on consensus.[3]

Do you wonder how the consensus process was introduced to America? In 1985, the U.S. Department of State gave the Carnegie Corporation "authority to negotiate with the Soviet Academy of Sciences, which is known to be an intelligence-gathering arm of the KGB, regarding 'curriculum development and the restructuring of American education.'"[4]

As a result, the Soviet strategies for organizing centralized communities as well as the behavioral psychology used to train the Soviet people began to infiltrate our tax-funded educational laboratories and training centers. Now they are a part of the worldwide transformational system being implemented in our schools and communities from coast to coast.

In 1985, President Reagan and Mikhail Gorbachev signed the U.S.-U.S.S.R. General Education Agreement.[5] It put American technology into the hands of communist strategists. It also brought us all the psycho-social tactics used in communist nations to indoctrinate Soviet children with communist ideology and to monitor compliance for the rest of their lives.

Driving the "learning" system we imported from the Soviet Union is its Hegelian dialectic or consensus process. It sounds complex, but it's simple enough to be used anywhere: in the classroom, workplace, community meetings or the United Nations—even in churches. It invites everyone to freely share their goals and visions, but it's so manipulative that few people realize they are being controlled.

The trained facilitator directs the dialogue. Manipulating the feelings and interactions of the group members through questions designed to elicit certain responses, he or she brings everyone to a predetermined conclusion. The team or group members learn to see themselves as "owners" or "stakeholders" in this planned consensus, while a satisfying sense of participation and peer approval usually outweighs any doubt or compromise.

The ultimate goal is to train everyone to think and work collectively. All must be willing to set aside what President Bush called "stale old notions and ideologies" in order to seek a new and higher common ground. President Clinton gave a glimpse of this goal in his 1998 State of the Union address to Congress when he said, "We must...learn together. Americans of all backgrounds can hammer out a common identity....We are many. We must be one."

The White House War on Hate

Refusing to give up "the stale old notions and ideologies" will be costly. During the White House Conference on Hate Crimes (WHCHC), November 10, 1997, President Clinton announced that

> under Attorney General Reno's leadership, the justice department has taken aim at hate crimes with more prosecutions and tougher punishments. The National Hate Crimes Network will marshal the resources of federal, state and local enforcement, community groups, educators, antiviolence advocates....

The White House war against politically incorrect attitudes has shifted into high gear. To fulfill the vision of unity, every citizen must be brought into the national dialogue that would build a new consensus. Biblical boundaries and separation would be linked to hate and intolerance. The program would be marketed to the public by publicizing genuine hateful acts such as the murder of homosexuals,[6] but in practice "hate" would include any attitude that opposes the new ideology.

To end cultural and religious division and to set the stage for lifelong training in global ideology, Clinton made some alarming proposals:

> There would almost have to be some sort of club or organization at the school because if you think about it, your parents are still pretty well separated....Most neighborhoods are still fairly segregated. Most houses of worship are still fairly segregated....We have to find a disciplined, organized way out of this so that we reach every child in an affirmative way before something bad happens....

Could our president be suggesting that Christian parents be pressured to conform to the world's standards? Or that churches be
forced to blend their worship with those who choose other gods
and contrary lifestyles? Might our government mandate "voluntary" youth groups—as did Nazi and communist rulers determined
to mold compliant citizens—so that cultural separation won't cause
something bad to happen?[7] Apparently so.

Traditional freedom and individualism simply don't fit in a
society that demands solidarity. Genuine unity can only be found
in Jesus Christ and through the cross, and when Christ and the
cross are outlawed, the price of unity is freedom. President
Clinton's vision of oneness calls for citizens to willingly trade their
right to dissent for the responsibility to conform. In other words,
solidarity must replace separation.

The Sin of Separateness

Vice President Al Gore would agree. Speaking at a Communi-
tarian conference in Washington, D.C., back in 1991 as a senator
from Tennessee, he announced, "Seeing ourselves as separate is
the central problem in our political thinking."[8] Gore's conclusion
was quoted in the book *Spiritual Politics,* coauthored by Corinne
McLaughlin, a follower of the Dhjwal Khul, the spirit guide chan-
neled by occultist Alice Bailey. Lest you think McLaughlin too far
out to be relevant, know that she was the first task force coordi-
nator for President Clinton's Council for Sustainable Development.[9]
She also taught her occult strategies at the Department of Education, the Pentagon and the EPA.[10]

"There really is only one sin—separateness," she states in her
book. "War is more likely to spring from rampant nationalism, eth-
nocentrism, and intolerant religious fundamentalism—all extreme
and separative attitudes." Her solution? The same as President
Clinton's: "What is needed as a cure for separateness is a *deep sense
of community*—that we're all in this together."

There is a grain of truth in her message—as there was in the serpent's deceptive message to Eve at the dawn of history. As Americans, we share a national identity that once included religious

freedom. But in the minds of contemporary change agents, that speck of truth becomes a means to an end that gives credibility to a horrendous lie. North Carolina school superintendent Dr. Jim Causby summarized this tactic well at a 1994 international model school conference in Atlanta: "We have actually been given a course in how not to tell the truth. How many of you are administrators? You've had that course in public relations where you learn to put the best spin on things."[11]

Building on the assumed foundation of freedom, President Clinton echoed these sentiments during his hate crimes conference. Implying that parents who cling to biblical boundaries might teach innocent children to hate, he said,

> Children have to be taught to hate.... We need to make sure that somebody is teaching them not to do so.... The most important thing we can do is to reach these kids while they're young enough to learn.... If we all do our part for that, we can make America one nation under God.

Countering Christian "Intolerance"

Did the last statement remind you of Dr. Chisholm's comment about parents who feed their children "poisonous certainties"? Remember, the UNESCO Declaration on Tolerance not only rules out "absolutism," or biblical truth, it also called the nations to "address the religious sources of intolerance." And the process of desensitization must involve everyone. President Clinton continued, "All of us have to do more in our communities ... and in our homes and places of worship to teach all of our children about the dignity of every person."

Warning children that God forbids homosexual behavior and worship of other gods would be considered disrespectful to the people who embraced those practices—and therefore hateful. To counter such "dangerous" teachings, Christian parents must be taught politically correct child-raising. Many pastors have agreed to support the new training programs in the wake of the 1996 contract between the U.S. Department of Education and most mainline denominations.[12] Drawing church leaders into the process is key to success. (Do you see the seeds of an underground church?)

Classroom discussion groups that prompt children to criticize their parents help monitor resistance to change. So does a profusion of intrusive surveys that tell children to report family attitudes, church attendance and all kinds of other private matters. Much of this data has already become part of the student's personal computerized file.[13] When each child is linked to his or her individual computer program, the gathering of this private information can be accelerated and controlled. Then "no one can get between that child and that computer," said Dustin Heuston, who works with the World Institute for Computer-Assisted Teaching.[14]

As soon as all children are linked to their personal computer programs, intrusive questions will become interactive dialogues between students and computers programmed to choose the right questions, measure the degree of resistance and adjust the questions accordingly. The answers will be fed into the national/international information technology and data tracking system established through Executive Order 13011.[15]

Parents would have no way of knowing what their children might be persuaded to reveal about their family. But adults, too, must be trained to transfer their loyalties from individual people to an impersonal state or community and practice the type of confession or sharing so important to the brainwashing process.[16] As Clinton said at the hate crimes conference, "The Justice Department will make its own hate crimes training curriculum available. A lot of hate crimes still go unreported.... If a crime is unreported, that gives people an excuse to ignore it."

Failing to report a neighbor's incorrect attitudes would not be tolerated. Both President and Hillary Clinton have been promoting the concept of a "civil society" where each person serves the community, participates in group discussions and takes responsibility for establishing and maintaining common values. Contrary beliefs would be censored and punished.

Author Balint Vazsonyi, who survived both Nazi and communist dictatorships in his native Hungary, saw the dangers inherent in "hate" legislation. We would do well to heed his warning: "'Hate speech' and 'hate crime' as legal categories usher in the concept of political crime—as un-American a proposition as there can be.... America's survival depends on the unequivocal rejection of political crime."[17]

During his hate crimes conference, President Clinton reinforced the new standards of conduct. Invoking the authority of Attorney General Janet Reno, he announced that "the Justice Department is launching a web site where younger students can learn about prejudice and the harm it causes."[18]

Back to the Future

Sobered by thoughts of our fading freedom, I walked through the Holocaust Museum in Washington, D.C., one cold drizzly day in early 1998. A picture of a Gestapo officer brought back memories of the Nazi soldiers who guarded our neighborhood in Norway during World War II. My father was part of the "Home Front"—an underground army of loyal Norwegians who would rather die than submit to Nazi tyranny. Caught helping other brave soldiers escape into neutral Sweden, he endured hunger, torture and the threat of death in three concentration camps before his release at the end of the war. Through the years of oppression, we all learned to treasure our freedom.

The Norwegian people hadn't known tyranny until the Nazi warships sailed up the Oslofjord on April 9, 1940. Overnight, Hitler's fascism replaced liberty, and trusted friends became foes. Suddenly resistance to the new ideology could cost us our lives. Yet how could we submit to evil and betray our king? For most Norwegians, the choice was clear: We couldn't! Unlike Hitler's masses, we hadn't been weakened by years of ceaseless propaganda, slogans, service and celebrations dedicated to the triumph of National Socialism. But what about America?

Remember the 1948 report from the International Congress on Mental Health which warned that "change will be strongly resisted unless an attitude of acceptance has first been engendered"?

Strategies like those used by Hitler to soften the masses have already prepared most Americans to accept a world government with global controls. My journey through the Holocaust museum began in the section dedicated to Nazi propaganda. Pausing by each display, I was startled by words that could so easily describe America today. The quotes brought stark reminders that, apart from God, human nature doesn't change with time. Nor do the aims of the spiritual mastermind behind the scenes who has always sought ways to stir hatred toward God's people. One tactic was simply to provide nice-sounding alternatives to biblical loyalty and service.

"Individuals were urged to sacrifice themselves for a greater 'People's Community,'" announced one of the displays. Such slogans must have sounded good to the masses, for few saw the cruel manipulation behind the noble words. I thought of President Clinton's calls for "sacrifice," "service," "unity," "common values," "civil society" and "safe" communities. How many people today see the ominous new meanings behind these nice-sounding words? Another display stated that—

> …elementary schools became forums of public indoctrination.… The Gestapo gathered much of its information from private citizens… even children were taught to report on their parents. The Gestapo's main sources, however, were Nazi party officials…who constantly monitored the activities of all citizens… [and] used such information to track political opponents.

Today's political opponents include those who see through the deceptive promises and refuse to conform. Just look at what happened in the wake of the tragic Oklahoma bombing. The deadly explosion gave government and media leaders the excuse they needed to blend a vast and varied mix of "malcontents" into the singular group labeled the "Radical Right." Day after day, the media's accusing pens pointed to suspected foes of American togetherness— those whose "enraged rhetoric" had created a national "climate of hate and paranoia." They ranged from "rabid" radio hosts and armed "extremists" to concerned parents. "Their coalition," said a *Time* magazine article, "included well-known elements of far-right thought: tax protesters, *Christian homeschoolers,* conspiracy theorists ... and self-reliant types who resent a Federal Government that seems to favor grizzly bears and wolves over humans...."[19] All these groups were implicated because they all had questioned the government's growing control over schools, property and personal lives.

Emotional appeals work. It's easier to shout, "Stop spreading hate!" than to encourage rational debate. It's more effective to discredit discerning citizens by linking them to violent anarchists than to give factual answers to legitimate questions. It's quicker to invalidate unwanted information by tying it to wild speculations than to provide honest responses—especially when the truth would expose plans best kept hidden. History has shown that nothing crushes well-informed resistance faster than well-planned misinformation and false accusations. Nothing unifies a nation faster than a common enemy.

Hitler knew those lessons well. He had watched the Bolshevik Revolution. His book, *Mein Kampf,* explained the winning strategies to future revolutionaries. Notice his insight into group psychology:

> The art of truly great popular leaders in all ages has consisted chiefly in not distracting the attention of the people, but concentrating always on a *single adversary....* It is part of a great leader's genius to make even widely separated adversaries appear as if they belonged to one category, because ... the recognition of various enemies all too easily marks the beginning of doubt of one's own rightness.[20]

Hitler focused his fury on an influential, well-educated ethnic group whose religious beliefs opposed his own. "It was a stroke of genius on the part of Hitler to find this common denominator in the Jew," explains the entry in *Encyclopædia Britannica.* "This enabled him to discover the Jew behind all his changing adversaries ... in short, behind everybody and everything that at a given moment opposed his wishes or aroused his wrath."[21]

As in Nazi Germany, socialization has become the primary goal of education. "Human resources" of all ages must meet the mental health standards set by the World Health Organization and the U.S.

Department of Health and Human Services. Those standards involve training in global citizenship, community responsibility, multicultural sensitivity and group thinking for the global workforce. All human resources will be assessed to determine their values to the community and workforce. Children who fail to demonstrate the right attitudes will be remediated and face more intense indoctrination. If they still refuse to conform or compromise, they will probably be removed from the home.

Youth and adults will be forced into the remediation process through "Workforce Development" legislation. If they stubbornly cling to "obsolete" biblical values, they will be accused of being hateful and intolerant. Students will not earn their "Certificates of Mastery" unless they demonstrate compliance with the standards for group thinking and politically correct ideology. And without the required mastery certificate, they cannot go to college or get a job.

Do you find this hard to believe? So do many of our members of Congress who are unknowingly putting together the legal framework for the entire system. That's why Illinois Congressman Henry Hyde wrote a letter May 9, 1996, to warn his colleagues of the dangers hidden in the Workforce Development or school-to-work legislation. He said:

> Children's careers will be chosen for them by workforce development boards and federal agencies at the "earliest possible age."... All children and adults will be forced to be retained in order to qualify for work certificates—home, Christian, privately schooled children included.

No one would be free from the control of the government thought-police. State defined rights would be granted only to those who fulfilled state-mandated duties. As in former totalitarian lands, dissenters and resisters would become underclass citizens.[22]

Kris Jensen saw this happening in Nevada some years ago when her daughter, Ashley, a middle-school student, had participated in a career interest survey that would help determine her career path. Before you hear the survey's conclusion, take a look at Ashley's qualifications as described by her mother:

Now mind you, Ashley is 4.0 honor student. She is double-blocking in her fourth year of flute and Japanese and did her honor science project on refuting the theory of acid rain. Her lifelong desire has been to work for NASA, and recently she had the opportunity to listen to the director of flight operation at NASA, and he spoke with her. She expressed her love for and desire to work in the space program, and he told her, "Set your goals high. Set your heart and mind to it. You can do anything! You'll be there."

Now remember that career interest survey? Do you know what the school told her she was suited to be? A garbage woman! In spite of the grand political promises we hear these days, the doors of opportunity are being shut to students like Ashley who disagree with government policies on issues ranging from religions to acid rain. Once this worldwide training system is fully in place, all such students will be locked out of higher education and good jobs. No matter how well they do in math and reading, they won't qualify for the work certificate.

Remember Sallie, the seven-year-old whose principal said "don't talk about Jesus so much"? Though free from the constraints of government schools, both Sallie and her parents have become part of the massive information tracking system. Their uncompromising values are recorded in their computerized data file. This file may be a permanent obstacle to success in the world but, thank God, it remains an eternal testimony to their love for the King who reigns over all the rulers of the earth.

What can we do? How can we prepare our families to stand immovable in Christ and His truth no matter how great the pressure to compromise?

Look at the Worldwide Revolution from a Heavenly Perspective

God told us repeatedly what will happen to a nation that refuses to follow the Shepherd. Listen to His warning and see how it fits our times:

> When you have eaten and are satisfied, praise the LORD your God for the good land he has given you. Be careful that you do not forget....

Otherwise…your heart will become proud.…You may say to yourself, "My power and the strength of my hands have produced this wealth for me."…If you ever forget the LORD your God and follow other gods…you will surely be destroyed (Deuteronomy. 8:10-12,14,17,19).

Could this apply to America? According to 1 Corinthians 10:1-11, we are not immune to consequences like those that destroyed ancient Israel. Human nature hasn't changed with time. Like ancient Israel, we share the same natural inclination to drift toward apathy, compromise, rebellion and paganism—anything but God Himself.

Trust Him to Guard and Guide You

God may withdraw His protection from a nation that turns to other gods, but He never fails to guard and guide those who remain faithful to Him. He doesn't promise to save us from pain and persecution, but in the midst of suffering we can count on His strength and loving presence.

If global governance becomes reality, there will be no place for dissenters to hide—other than in Christ. Now is the time to put on the "full armor of God" and delight in the love-relationship He offers us. That means knowing the truths of the armor: the truths about God, our righteousness in Him, and all that it means to share His peace, salvation, life and triumph forever.[23]

Consider Your Goal

Is your goal success in this world or success in God's kingdom? If it is to love and follow the King who has called you to fellowship with Him for all eternity, then you are ready for the next step.

Count the Cost

One goal of the consensus process is to enable young and old to respect and appreciate all kinds of lifestyles and rituals that clash with God's guidelines. For example, when gay and lesbian activists share their beliefs and practices with a class, the students must respect and appreciate their chosen lifestyle. That attitude doesn't fit God's wise guidelines, which calls the gay lifestyle sin but tells us to love sinners and draw them back to the only One who can set them free.

If you refuse to conform to a world that demands compromise, it will turn against you. Today, resistance brings rejection. Tomorrow it will bring cruel and unjust punishment. Are you willing to count the approval of God more precious than the approval of peers? The apostle Paul did, therefore he could exult:

> But what things were gain to me, these I have counted loss for Christ. Yet indeed I also count all things loss for the excellence of the knowledge of Christ Jesus my Lord, for whom I have suffered the loss of all things, and count them as rubbish, that I may gain Christ and be found in Him... (Philippians 3:7-9 AMP).

Set Your Mind on Eternal Things

"This world is not my home, I'm just a passing thru" began a happy old hymn. The songwriter had glimpsed the same vision that led the heroes and heroines of God's hall of fame (Hebrews 11) toward the goal, and it had changed him. "I can't feel at home in this world anymore," he sang, for his eyes were on the heavenly city that beckons to all God's sojourners. "We don't fit here. It's not our environment!" wrote beloved author and artist Joni Eareckson Tada in her wonder-filled book *Heaven*.

None of us fit here. Pray that God will impress on our hearts a deepening, spirit-given awareness that "our citizenship is in heaven," not of the earth (see Philippians 3:20). Raised up into the heavenly places with our King, the sovereign Ruler of the universe, we have nothing to fear. Rejection, pain, persecution... all become steppingstones to a more glorious future.

Paul, who suffered far more than we could even imagine, said it well:

> For our light affliction, which is but for a moment, is working for us a far more exceeding and eternal weight of glory, while we do not look at the things which are seen, but at the things which are not seen. For

the things which are seen are temporary, but the things which are not seen are eternal (2 Corinthians 4:17,18 NKJV).

Prepare Your Family to Face Persecution

Few children today understand the meaning of persecution. When they face rejection for their faith in their schools, many feel confused, hurt and angry. To help them understand how God uses suffering to strengthen their faith, discuss Scriptures such as 2 Corinthians 1:3-9; 1 Peter 1:6,7 and 4:12-15. Remember that "it has been granted to you on behalf of Christ not only to believe on him, but also to suffer for him ... " (Philippians 1:29). To help your children appreciate the courage, faithfulness and godly vision of those who were persecuted for their faith, you may want to read some books and stories together. All of us would be enriched by a deep look at the lives of biblical men and women who were willing to give their lives rather than betray or dishonor the God they loved: Joseph, Daniel, Esther, Ruth, Paul and Stephen. Some of their stories have happy earthly endings, but many of the heroes and heroines in God's hall of fame died for the One they loved. (Look at Hebrews 11, especially the last two verses.) These people and other giants in the faith throughout history have modeled an eternal perspective that puts far greater value on eternity with Jesus than on temporary riches here on earth.

You can also find stories of children and adults who refused to compromise at our web site (http://www.crossroad.to). The people highlighted in these stories were willing to walk with Jesus in the hard places here on earth knowing they would share His happiness for all eternity. They learned that He would provide the wisdom and strength needed to face any kind of difficulty with confidence. They believed God's comforting words, which are as relevant for us today as for His people long ago: "My grace is sufficient for you, for My strength is made perfect in weakness" (2 Corinthians 12:9). When Paul heard those words, he responded with a joyful confirmation of a heart's decision:

Therefore most gladly I will rather boast in my infirmities, that the power of Christ may rest upon me. Therefore I take pleasure in infirmities, in reproaches, in needs, in persecutions, in distresses, for Christ's sake. For when I am weak, then I am strong (2 Corinthians 12:9,10 NKJV).

True Peace and Unity

Through the storms of life, Jesus has promised to be our Shepherd, our Strength and our Shelter. In Him, we can walk in triumph, no matter what happens in the world. For He promised that "If you abide in My word, you are My disciples indeed. And you shall know the truth, and the truth shall make you free" (John 8:31,32 NKJV).

Those who choose uncompromising discipleship will find an unspeakable joy in His nearness. Stephen did (see Acts 7). Remember how he looked up and saw the glory of God as his persecutors hurled the stones that crushed his body? Like him, we may demonstrate to a needy world the overcoming power of the majestic, heavenly King who reached down to earth to love us like a Father.

When I was little, I loved our Norwegian king. Like him, I wanted to be brave enough to die rather than surrender. Years later I learned that this wonderful leader was nothing compared to my heavenly King. Yet my earthly king and the years of war, danger and deprivation gave me a vision of genuine Christianity that I continue to treasure. I saw that we, Jesus' bride and church, are like a nation of loyal subjects who:

1. love and obey their King

2. discover in their common devotion and warfare a fellowship rarely found apart from persecution

3. refuse to compromise

4. persevere until death—or until the war is won

To sustain us through the battles ahead, our King gave us many precious promises. Few bring me more delight than the following words from our Master. May they fill you with joy at the unspeakable privilege of serving our sovereign King, following in His footsteps, sharing His suffering and delighting in His love for all eternity.

> Blessed are you when men hate you, and when they exclude you, and revile you, and cast out your name as evil, for the Son of Man's sake. Rejoice in that day and leap for joy! For indeed your reward is great in heaven (Luke 6:22,23 NKJV).

▼ ▼ ▼

CHAPTER 13

Revelation 13 Technology Today

Peter Lalonde

Antichrist's control technologies by which he will enslave the peoples of the earth are developing at a phenomenal pace before the eyes of this generation. We are indeed the first generation in which the prophecy of the "mark of the beast" can be fulfilled:

> He [the Antichrist or the beast] causeth all, both small and great, rich and poor, free and bond, to receive a mark in their right hand, or in their foreheads: And that no man might buy or sell, save he that had the mark, or the name of the beast, or the number of his name (Revelation 13:16,17).

According to this prophecy in God's Word, the day is coming when the Antichrist will be able to prevent every man, woman and child on earth from carrying out any financial or commercial transaction if they refuse the mark. When I first started studying Bible prophecy many years ago, this seemed like an extremely monumental task. Revelation 13 tells us that the Antichrist will be able to control *all* financial transactions *everywhere* in the world for *every* person on the planet. Even in the early days of computerized banking technology, the infrastructure that would allow this prophecy to be fulfilled just did not exist. There were bits and pieces of global economy in sight, but some of the necessary pieces for the completion of the puzzle were not yet available. This is no longer true. The picture in this prophetic puzzle is becoming much more recognizable.

Puzzle Piece 1: Networking

The key technology driving the world toward the fulfillment of the mark of the beast prophecy of Revelation 13 is the computer. Computers have dramatically changed the world we live in. As Frank Koelsch, a seasoned veteran of computing and communications industries, observed, the new world order "doesn't just include PCs, but revolves around PCs."[1] Even our wristwatches and kitchen appliances, from the breadmaker to the microwave oven, are computerized. And with each passing year, computer power and speed are increasing exponentially. The average car today has more computing power than the Apollo spacecraft that sent the first men to the moon.

This exponential growth in computer speed and power has enabled today's PCs, miniature versions of their forerunners, to carry out tasks that the giant mainframes of a few decades ago were incapable of doing. In the early days of prophetic research, there were rumors of the existence of a giant computer in Brussels, Belgium. This giant mainframe computer, nicknamed "The Beast," was supposedly capable of housing personal information on every individual on the planet. The truth of the matter is that the giant mainframes of yesterday, while capable of much, just couldn't handle this task.

Today's PCs, however, pack more punch than "The Beast" ever could have. Furthermore, today's PCs are capable of fulfilling the task that "The Beast" was said to be intended for, without having to store a huge global database on every individual on the planet. Enter the world of networking.

Being wired into networks such as the Internet has provided millions of individuals and businesses with the ability to link into numerous databases virtually anywhere in the world. Individuals can now shop in cyberspace or send their shopping list by faxmodem and have someone else do the shopping for them. People can do their banking in cyberspace or even make their own airline or dinner reservations. Businesses can quickly do credit checks on a client or do statistical research for upcoming projects, and their employees can become teleworkers. Thanks to teleconferencing, people can also hold business meetings with clients anywhere in the world without having to leave their offices.

Police forces and government investigative agencies are now able to tap into each other's crime databases across national or international borders. They can accumulate data for criminal investigations into a large database of their own. One of the largest of these in the United States is the FBI's National Crime Information Center (NCIC). It holds over 24 million records, linked to over half-a-million users. There is also a large database, the Financial Crimes Enforcement Network (FinCEN), accumulated for suspected crimes in the financial sector.

Indeed, in the technological information age, the New Age term *interconnected* is taking on new meaning. One of the latest trends is for whole communities or states to wire together their banks, businesses, libraries, schools and the like into one network. While the United States has made the most progress in becoming linked together, the rest of the world is catching up quickly. The global electronic village is truly becoming a reality. In fact, what the world is essentially becoming in these last days is one massive computer with a plethora of links.

Without the Shadow of a Doubt

There is no question that computers have made the lives of individuals and businesses much easier. For example, it boggles the mind when one considers that large corporations used to have to manage their accounting books manually. Now computer software programs can easily handle the work that once took 20 or 30 accountants and bookkeepers to do—and computers do it more accurately.

My own life was dramatically changed when I was introduced to the computer. As a writer, I had to cope with a typewriter, crossing out mistakes or paragraphs I didn't like. Now I can mark text in my work and move it around from one place to the next with a keystroke. I can erase words and paragraphs or put them back in a second, all without those messy marks that once spoiled the look of my manuscripts and articles.

Virtually any information people need today is available at the touch of their fingertips. Information, speedily processed and transmitted, is vital to the developing global village the world is rapidly becoming. In fact, one of the things that defines a developed nation today is the mastery of accumulating information, along with the know-how to process it in a meaningful and beneficial way.

While computers have simplified lives, they have also made our lives an open book for anyone who cares to take the time to read it. Every time we log on to the Internet, send a fax, make a purchase with our credit card and rent a video we leave behind information about our personal lives. This personal information is known as a "data shadow," which starts accumulating almost the minute we are born. In 1993, reporters at *The Ottawa Citizen,* the local newspaper in the Ontario, Canada capital, decided to test just how true this is, investigating Bill Walther (with his permission, of course).

Bill Walther considers himself a very private person.

But maybe he isn't. You can look at the profile the *Citizen* quickly drew up of him, through documents and easily accessed computer files, and judge for yourself.

We learned Walther's birth date, home address and phone number, although the phone is not in his name. We learned his occupation, education and minimum salary.

We told Walther most of his addresses and phone numbers for the last 30 years. We figured out roughly when his marriage broke up. We learned where his ex-wife lives, what her birthdate was and what she paid for her new house.

We know the woman Walther lives with now, when they began living together, and what her occupation was.

We learned that Walther drives a red 1991 Chevy S-10, and has until Nov. 20, 1994 to repay a $21,361 loan to his dealer in Gloucester. Walther's driving and criminal records have been clean for the last three years, a computerized information kiosk told us. He is 183 centimeters tall and wears glasses or contact lenses, it added.

There's more. Through computer databases accessed at the *Citizen's* newsroom we learned Walther's hobbies. He's a nature-lover whose interests are birdwatching, herbs and wild mushrooms, according to information on the National Capital FreeNet computer network, of which Walther is a member.

Another database told us Walther played Friar Laurence in a 1983 Carleton University production of Romeo and Juliet.

This three-decade sketch of a person's life came after a few days' work and a few dollars spent...

Walther is one of three volunteers who let the *Citizen* probe their personal and financial lives to help determine the bounds of privacy.

The ground rules were simple: find what could be found legally, in documents, public information and databases. There were no interviews with friends, relatives or neighbors—often the first tactic for a reporter. There were no private-eye moves, no surveillance, no sorting through trash, no insider sources for credit or financial records, and no misrepresentations.[2]

The experiment conducted by the reporters at *The Ottawa Citizen* demonstrated just how much information is readily available about our personal lives in Canada. And for United States citizens, privacy is even less secure.

The possession of such personal information can open the door to George Orwell's Big Brother control in his book *1984*. In some instances this appears to be a good thing, but when you stop and think about it, it is actually a foreshadow of what is to come under the rule of the Antichrist. Indeed, the world of the Antichrist is one in which it will be extremely difficult to escape notice.

Puzzle Piece 2: Nowhere to Hide

With the growing trend in creating free trade regions, from the European Union (EU) to the North American Free Trade Agreement (NAFTA) to the Asia Pacific Economic Cooperation (APEC), the world is becoming a world without borders. Increasingly, nation-states are putting up "open for business" signs, welcoming foreign investors and multinational corporations. This movement, combined with advanced telecommunications technology, is bringing the term *one world* to life.

In this new world without borders, however, it is not just electronic data, goods and services that are free to move beyond national borders. Increasingly, people are moving about more freely as well. Industry insiders have predicted that by 2000, there will be 15 million U.S. "telecommuters" working in the world. Telecommuters are employees who are able to take advantage of telecommunications and computer technologies so they can work at home or anywhere across the globe. Indeed, high-tech gadgets such as satellites, cellular phones and notebook computers with built-in fax-modem and e-mail capabilities have made it possible not only to reach anywhere in the world, but also to *be* reached virtually anywhere in the world. Furthermore, telecommunications experts and observers can clearly see the day when people will wear their "telephones" like jewelry, with hidden microphones in necklaces or lapel pins. Phillips is working on a sophisticated wristwatch that it hopes to have ready for the year 2002. *The European* (newspaper) reported:

> [The not-too-distant future] will see such implements as portable personal intelligent communications with touch screens for pen and finger input, desk-based voice phones with intelligent screens, and handheld personal organisers, which use the global positioning system to guide the user through cities and countries. Advanced integrated circuit products will make these items possible. The list of combinations is endless, and the only limit is the imagination of inventors or the will of companies to manufacture them.
>
> Integrated circuit technology will soon bring creators enough miniaturisation for them to slap a video telephone together with a camera,

a television, and a computer—all in a package so small you can wear it as a wristwatch.[3]

In this world of high-tech gadgetry, it is the cellular phone industry that will play a key role in making us accessible anywhere we go. Jon Van, a staff writer for the *Chicago Tribune,* observed:

Another means to track people relies upon the existing network of cellular phone transmitters. The cellular industry and emergency-response officials have proposed standards to the Federal Communications Commission that would enable police, fire and ambulance dispatchers to find people who dial 911 from wireless phones.... Developing computer systems to track locations of so many calls is a daunting task, but it is consistent with the phone industry's goal of one day assigning phone numbers to human beings, rather than to equipment. Once the phone network becomes sophisticated enough to do this, it will smooth the way for widespread monitoring of people's whereabouts.[4]

Suffice it to say that with each passing moment high technology is making the world, vast and wide, open to us. We can now easily move across the globe physically or electronically. At the same time, such advanced technology is creating a world that is no longer big enough to hide in. There is only one thing left for us that would give us anonymity or provide us with the ability to vanish if we so chose. If we were rich enough, we might be able to live solely on cash—the one thing that can close the open book on our lives. But for how long?

Puzzle Piece 3: A Cashless Society

In the early days of prophetic research, there was a trend toward a "less cash" society, but many people were insisting we would never become a cashless society. For a number of years now, bankers, financiers and stock-market traders have considered money to be nothing more than electronic bits of information that are passed back and forth through cyberspace. The only reason physical cash has stuck around as long as it has is to appease those who feel more comfortable with coins jingling in their pockets and paper dollars thickening their billfolds and wallets.

The truth of the matter is that bankers and financiers would like nothing more than for these remaining die-hards to turn over their paper bills and metal coins in exchange for a plastic card, preferably one containing a small microchip. Slowly, such die-hards have been introduced to the convenience of debit cards for large purchases and prepaid cards for everything from vending machines to toll booths to public telephones.

To further wean the consumer and retailer of cash, bankers have made it easier for them to do their banking at home or the office simply by using computers and telephones. Indeed, it has now reached the point where the only reason for the couch potatoes of North America to head for the nearest ATM is to withdraw cash. Eliminate cash, and you eliminate the need to roll off the couch. More free time on the sofa, speculate cyber-retailers, means more time for consumers to spend their electronic dollars. As businesses, financiers and computer software companies began to recognize that a potential market worth billions of dollars was waiting at home to spend its money in cyberspace, the race was on to become the main supplier of the first secure form of digital global currency.

Indeed, current trends suggest that the new world order will be a cashless society, not just a less-cash society, as many thought just a few years ago. From biblical prophecy we know that under the rule of the Antichrist, the existence of cash will not be likely. If cash were still around, how would he be able to control the buying and selling for *every* man, woman and child on the planet? Furthermore, the utopian new world order, which man is even now trying to create, will benefit from the fruits of a cashless society. Cash is the cause of many of the crimes that take place today, from muggings to drug trafficking to money laundering. While supposedly ridding the world of the evil created by the existence of cash, the Antichrist will turn around and use the cashless society for his own evil purposes.

Puzzle Piece #4: The Mark of the Beast

There is yet another piece of the economic puzzle that will allow the Antichrist to control and monitor the peoples of the world. This piece is also a key part in fulfilling God's prophecy about the "mark of the beast" in Revelation 13. Even as we write, technologies are being developed and tested that could very well play a role in implementing the fulfillment of that prophetic mark.

As noted earlier, God's Word forewarns that the Antichrist will implement a system using a mark by which he will be able to control all consumer transactions for everyone on the planet:

> He causeth all, both small and great, rich and poor, free and bond, to receive a mark in their right hand, or in their foreheads: And that no man might buy or sell, save he that had the mark, or the name of the beast, or the number of his name (Revelation 13:16,17).

And, as Jon Van reported in the *Chicago Tribune:*

> A tiny chip implanted inside the human body to send and receive radio messages, long a popular delusion among paranoids, is likely to be marketed as a consumer item early in the next century. Several technologies already available or under development will enable electronics firms to make implantable ID locators, say futurists, and our yearning for convenience and security makes them almost irresistible to marketers.[5]

One point we need to make before we explore this issue further is that the most important aspect of the mark of the beast is neither an economic nor an identification decision. To have the mark of the beast will be a *spiritual* decision. Over the years we have received letters asking if someone could accidentally take the mark by using a debit card or agreeing to be identified by their fingerprints at their bank. The answer to these questions is a definite no. Consider what happens to those people who agree to take the mark during the tribulation period:

> The third angel followed them, saying with a loud voice, If any man worship the beast and his image, and receive his mark in his forehead, or in his hand, the same shall drink of the wine of the wrath of God, which is poured out without mixture into the cup of his indignation; and he shall be tormented with fire and brimstone in the presence of the holy angels, and in the presence of the Lamb; and the smoke of their torment ascendeth up for ever and ever; and they have

no rest day nor night, who worship the beast and his image, and whosoever receiveth the mark of his name (Revelation 14:9-11).

God, by His very nature, would never dole out such severe punishment to those who were completely ignorant of what they were doing. Choosing the mark is not an economic decision like choosing Visa over MasterCard. While God is very much interested in our daily lives, He is not as concerned about our economic decisions as He is about our spiritual decisions. You may have noticed from the Scripture just quoted that this punishment is given to those who take the mark *and* who "worship the beast and his image." When people accept this mark, they will be consciously and deliberately telling the Antichrist they are willing to worship him as a god. At the same time they are telling God that they, in a final act of human defiance, are choosing freely to reject Him and His Son.

National IDs

The history of identification cards goes back to the ancient Roman Empire. Slaves, soldiers and citizens of the Roman Empire were required to carry identification files known as *tessarae*. As the Roman Empire is being revived in its new sophisticated form, so too are new sophisticated forms of identification.

In the past few years, pressure for national IDs has been climbing in this developing empire. Thailand is probably the most advanced in its implementation of a national identification system for its citizens with its Thailand Central Population Database and ID Card System. Everyone in Thailand has been issued a national ID card that holds an electronic image of his or her fingerprint and face. The ID card is linked to an electronic government database that is essentially controlled by the Interior Ministry, a de facto military and police agency.

Slowly, other nations—even democracies like Canada and the United States—seem to be heading in the same direction. Canada's Ontario provincial government, for instance, has proposed a multipurpose smart card to replace driver's licenses, health cards, and welfare cards. In the United States, many feared that President Bill

Clinton's proposed national health-care card would become a de facto national ID. Of course, the Clinton administration's health-care proposals died, and along with them the health-care card. Nonetheless, U.S. citizens are still not out of the woods as far as national IDs are concerned. The Immigration and Naturalization Service (INS), as well as many of those who are in favor of curbing illegal immigration, are pushing for identity cards for working purposes. Although proponents of the proposed identity card claim it would only be used as a work card, history has shown that once such ID cards are introduced, they eventually come to be used for a broad array of government purposes.

Of course, as unemployment rises, many will likely be willing to take their chances at privacy invasion if it will hinder jobs being given to illegal aliens. Herein lies the real danger. A unique national identifier would make it a lot easier for the government to compile, consolidate and retrieve personal information about us. This is what makes networking work—the positive identification of citizens. Such an identity number would virtually give the government *carte blanche* over us—over our right to work and our ability to access money. One key question we need to ask is, "How many innocent citizens will fall victim to errors in government files about their personal lives?" It is a well-known fact that government files for many citizens contain incorrect information. About ten years after my wife, Patti, left the university, an official from the government's student loan program telephoned. He wanted to discuss the house she owned while she was a student. She had never owned a house, and students who hold assets such as a house are not eligible for government assistance. Imagine the nightmare if, instead of having placed a phone call to straighten the matter out, the government decided to revoke her right to work or to drive or to use her bank account and credit cards.

Another danger lies in the fact that the government could abuse its powers over national ID cards and personal information in the future. It could, for example, use such power to revoke the rights of those deemed to be social dissidents. It could never happen in a democracy like America, you say? Well, all one needs to do is look

at history. *Government Technology* reprinted an article from the
October 1995 edition of *REASON* magazine that revealed:

> When the government stockpiles information, no matter how benign
> the intent, there is inevitably a malignant mutation somewhere along
> the way. Presidential misuse of the IRS is so routine that it's practically
> part of the job description.... Even the supposedly apolitical head
> counters at the U.S. Census Bureau have been unable to keep their
> promises not to share their most intimate data with anyone else.
> During World War I, the Census Bureau provided the Justice Depart-
> ment with the names and addresses of conscription-age young men to
> aid in the apprehension of draft dodgers.
>
> And in an even more infamous case, it helped carry out the intern-
> ment of Japanese Americans after Pearl Harbor. Each time a roundup
> of Japanese was planned in a new city, Census Bureau statisticians
> joined the meeting. They "would lay out on a table various city blocks
> where the Japanese lived and they would tell me how many were living
> in each block," recounted Tom Clark, the Justice Department's coor-
> dinator of alien control at the time. (Clark, later a Supreme Court jus-
> tice, gave his account in an oral history for the University of
> California.) "From there it was a simple matter for the U.S. Army to
> conduct block-by-block sweeps until all the Japanese were safely
> penned up in barbed wire."[6]

Universal IDs

The next logical step from national identification numbers
would seem to be universal identification numbers. As the world
becomes borderless, people are going to roam around more freely.
The need for a universal ID, by which we could easily be identified anywhere on the globe, seems to make sense. As the digital
mobile phone and wireless transmission industry is booming in
North America, the European Union, and even in the third world
countries, a phone number for each person as mentioned earlier in
this chapter may be the logical and ideal identification number that
is selected in the future.

Computer Tracking

Many would scoff at the suggestion that we would let ourselves get to the point where our every move could be tracked. But when you think about it, we've already become a society which is accustomed to surveillance, and it doesn't seem to bother us because the surveillance is so discreet we don't even notice it. There are video cameras installed in obscure corners in banks and stores. There are often hidden cameras in elevators. Some ATMs are now equipped with hidden cameras. Surveillance technology is so sophisticated today it can be used from a distance with pinpoint accuracy. In 1988 the U.S. Department of Defense was instructed by Congress to begin development on UAVs, Unmanned Aerial Vehicles. The UAVs ran into problems during Operation Desert Storm, however, because of high winds. So instead of wasting the technology, it was decided that the UAVs could be used for civilian purposes. In their April 1995 issue, *OMNI* magazine reported that California's Department of Transportation would be using them for inspection of bridges and overpasses. Other suggested uses were to inspect power lines, to televise sports events or even to track forest fires. But some people haven't forgotten the original intent for UAVs: spies in the sky. *OMNI* noted that one UAV was "loaned by the Defense Evaluation Support Activity to Oregon's National Guard and State Police last February prior to their raid on a suspected drug compound. Where agents had expected one fence, a couple of dogs and cars and a few buildings, the [UAV's] spying revealed two fences, many dogs and more of everything else. The raid was successful."[7]

We mentioned earlier that satellite technology combined with the Global Positioning System used during the Persian Gulf War has been used for spying purposes with pinpoint accuracy. Now add microchips to the mix, and the surveillance becomes even more accurate. Take the latest trend in intelligent highway systems, for instance. "Smart" cars equipped with microchips and computers can now direct us to our destination along the fastest route or help us skirt traffic jams. They allow us to whiz through electronic toll collection booths without having to stop, or even slow down, in order to toss a few coins down a chute. An electronic reading device records information from a smart card located on the vehicle's dashboard and deducts the toll amount from the driver's prepaid account.

Microchips have even been used to thwart car thieves. If a car equipped with the microchip is stolen, authorities can easily locate and track it. The same technology can also be used for boats and snowmobiles. But what about tracking people? Perhaps you are shaking your head and saying, "Cars and boats, sure. But people? No way. It will never happen." But think about it. There are already many examples in real-life circumstances in which people are required to wear devices containing electronic microchips. Due to overcrowding in the prison system, some prisoners are now allowed to live in society. The hitch is that they have to wear ankle bracelets containing microchips so authorities can monitor their where-abouts and ensure that they don't wander outside a preauthorized perimeter. Stalkers are required to wear the same devices to ensure they obey restraining orders. Many senior-citizen nursing homes have been monitoring residents who are prone to wandering off, especially those suffering from Alzheimer's disease. Employees working in high-security areas have been required to wear active badges—ID cards containing a microchip—so that they can be easily and accurately identified. Active badges are also used to locate employees within buildings. Some shopping malls have offered the use of similar devices to keep track of children. A few hospital nurseries have even been using ID bracelets containing microchips for newborns.

Embedded Chips

While microchips have been embedded only in badges or ankle and wrist bracelets for tracking people, they have been directly embedded in the flesh of animals for a number of years now. Several years ago pet shelters and veterinarians began injecting the rice-grain sized microchips under the skin of dogs and cats. If the pet were to become lost, any pet shelter across the nation would be able to read the microchip with a scanner and locate its owner. Microchips have also been used by ranchers for livestock in place of branding methods. They have been used by breeders of large birds, by tropical fish breeders, and even by Alaskan dog-sled racers. "Why stop with pets?" asked Simon Garfinkel in *Wired* magazine. "What about people? There would be no technical problem, says Barbara Masin, director of operations for Electronic Identification Devices, in implanting the chips in humans. But to avoid a public relations nightmare, the Trovan dealer agreement specifically prohibits putting chips under the skin."[8] *But,* added Garfinkel:

> That dictum hasn't slowed innovation one bit. In Australia, explains Masin, one nursing home gives each of its patients a bracelet equipped with a Trovan chip....
>
> The Trovan system is showing up inside identification tags as well. At least half a dozen European ski resorts are putting chips inside lift tickets. Electronic Identification Devices also recommends hiding them in parking passes, meal cards, amusement park passes, club identification cards ... but what a pain carrying all those cards around. Wouldn't it be far simpler to implant a chip into your shoulder and be done with it? Stay tuned.[9]

Indeed, the idea of a microchip implant in people was repugnant just a few short years ago. Now a few people are starting to bravely point out that it may have a useful place in our future. In the summer of 1994, Mark David, editor-in-chief of *Automatic ID News,* in an article about locating lost pets through microchip technology, wrote:

> This happy tale got me thinking about the possible advantage of "chipping" children.... Now, the idea of electronically tagging humans is not one that I could easily embrace. Numbering humans is tainted with the air of jails, concentration camps and people-as-numerals totalitarianism.... I'm also well aware of the Big Brother potential for database abuse and invasion of privacy that grows with every scan of every item in our grocery carts.... But as a father of three small children, I can't help but feel there could be some legitimate arguments made for the voluntary "chipping" of kids.[10]

How Secure Is Secure?

Until the day when microchip implants in humans becomes a real possibility, our money and personal information are going to be nothing more than electronic bits of data that either float around in cyberspace or are contained on microchips embedded in plastic cards. Although this remains true, the issues of strong security and fool-proof methods of ID verification are going to be top-priority subjects.

For the most part, the main method of security against unwanted intruders and users has been the use of computer passwords and personal identification numbers, known as PINs. But it is obvious that sophisticated thieves are able to bypass such secret passwords if they are determined. They are now using such snooping devices as password sniffers (tiny programs hidden on a network and instructed to record logons and passwords, which are then stored in a secret file) to intercept security codes for cellular phones as well. Personal identification numbers used for bank cards aren't 100 percent sure, either. Many people write their PIN directly on their card or on a piece of paper they store in their wallet next to their card because they're afraid they won't remember their number.

Furthermore, in this day and age when security is a big issue, people are beginning to suffer from password overload. They have to have passwords or secret numbers for cell phones or for access to databases at the office. They need PINs for security systems at the office, maybe one for home, and another for the ATM. With so many PINs and passwords, a lot of people are starting to forget which PIN is for the ATM and which is for turning off the security system at the office. Suffering from password overload, and just being plain sick and tired of fraud, many individuals, businesses and financial institutions are searching for more secure and foolproof methods of identification. In this vein, many are looking to biometrics as the solution.

Raise Your Right Hand

Biometric identification is based on a unique physical characteristic such as your voice, signature, fingerprint, iris pattern or hand geometry (a measurement of the size and shape of your hand). It is possible that, along with microchip technology, biometrics will play a role in identification for the mark of the beast system. God's Word specifically mentions that the mark of the beast will be taken in the right hand or in the forehead, the two places most accessible in cold-weather climates. Now, whether the mark will actually be a microchip or whether hand geometry and facial image recognition will be part of the Antichrist's economic system cannot be known for certain until the prophecy is fulfilled.

Nonetheless, there has been growing interest in biometric identification over the past few years. Several pilot projects using various biometric ID verifications have been taking place around the world. One area in which biometric identification verification has gained wide acceptance and usage is in the welfare sector. As far back as 1986, Los Angeles County had started a manual fingerprinting system for welfare recipients to try to weed out double dippers. Within three years, the county found itself with 50,000 fingerprint records that were virtually useless. That's when Los Angeles County decided to investigate an automatic fingerprint verification system. The system, known as AFIRM, was used for the first time on June 3, 1991. Later, San Francisco County decided to adopt the AFIRM system as well.

Not Just Another Face in the Crowd

In the early days of biometric technology development, little was heard about facial image recognition. This is beginning to change. As technologies for motion tracking continue to develop, facial recognition devices will likely be more useful in certain situations when, for example, it would be difficult or even impossible to obtain a fingerprint or hand geometry sample.

The Future Is Here

As such technology continues to be developed and perfected, the trend will likely lead us to a world that is not as far in the future as many would think. The technology is already here. Indeed, we are the first generation in which the mark of the beast prophecy of

Revelation 13 can actually be fulfilled. We have the technology that will allow the Antichrist to control the entire global economy. The only piece of the puzzle missing now is the Antichrist, who will require that the people of the world take his mark as a sign of adoration for him.

Nearing the End of the Age

At the outset of the twentieth century, the global power structure was stable. There was widespread optimism that the world was about to enter an era of peace and prosperity. Technological breakthroughs and scientific discoveries offered hope for the betterment of mankind. The twentieth century turned out to be far different than many had envisioned. In the opening pages to his book *Out of Control: Global Turmoil on the Eve of the 21st Century,* Zbigniew Brzezinski, former director of the National Security Council under President Jimmy Carter, wrote:

> Contrary to its promise, the twentieth century became mankind's most bloody and hateful century, a century of hallucinatory politics and of monstrous killings. Cruelty was institutionalized to an unprecedented degree, lethality was organized on a mass production basis. The contrast between the scientific potential for good and the political evil that was actually unleashed is shocking. Never before in history was killing so globally pervasive, never before did it consume so many lives, never before was human annihilation pursued with such concentration of sustained effort on behalf of such arrogantly irrational goals.[11]

What makes this generation different from any other are weapons of mass destruction. The weapons of yesteryear were swords and battle-axes, cannons and bayonets. Such weapons could not destroy *all* flesh. It was during World War II that things began to change. German tanks and missiles created great problems for the allies. But even these were not capable of destroying all flesh.

The Birth of the Bomb

Somehow the world senses that if another war were to erupt on a global scale, the death toll potentially could include every person on the planet because of the destructive capability of nuclear weaponry. Indeed, Jesus said if He were not to return at the time of the end "there should no flesh be saved" (Matthew 24:22). We are the first generation in which this prophecy rings true. And if we are the first generation in which this prophecy can be fulfilled, then it follows that we may truly be the last generation prior to Christ's return. What changed the shape of the world and the path of history was the nuclear bomb.

Following on the heels of the nuclear bomb was the hydrogen bomb, a thermonuclear weapon far more devastating than the bomb that destroyed Hiroshima. And in what seems to be a never-ending treadmill ride, the need to produce weapons and establish defense systems that can outsmart the enemy has been created.

Smart Weapons

The first implication the world had that tomorrow's wars would be different came with the outbreak of the Persian Gulf War. On January 18, 1991, the first of Iraq's Scud missiles was launched, and so was the first U.S. Patriot, an antimissile. The world had its first taste of the role technology would play in future wars, not only in defensive, or antiballistic missile systems, but in offensive situations with "precision guided munitions." In *Tomorrow's War: The Threat of High-Technology Weapons,* David Shukman describes a "'technology war'... which amazed a world unfamiliar with the revolution in military development brought about by the Cold War. Of the 88,500 tons of bombs dropped in the Gulf War, only some 6,250 were precision guided—around 7 percent—yet it was those 'smart' weapons which accounted for about half the Iraqi targets destroyed. It was a technical success rate which spawned the concept of 'surgical bombing,' attacks so accurate they could achieve their ends with minimum harm to others."[12]

Indeed, the world had been introduced to intelligent munitions, most of which are essentially "fire-and-forget" weaponry that rely on the sophisticated computing power of microprocessors. According to a report by Douglas Waller for *Time* magazine, "Future

warfare, in fact, may look like today's science-fiction thrillers." He
continues,

> By 2010 the Army hopes to "digitize the battlefield" by linking every
> soldier and weapons system electronically. A research team ... plans to
> unveil next year a prototype of the equipment that the "21st century
> land warrior" will have. His helmet will be fitted with microphones
> and earphones for communications, night-vision goggles and thermal-
> image sensors to see in the dark, along with a heads-up display in
> front of his eyes to show him where he is on the ground and give him
> constant intelligence updates.[13]

But that's not all. The military would also like to see "smart"
technology being used to map out war strategies as well. Dick
Lawrence of the British Defence Research Agency calls it "crystal-
ball gazing." According to Shukman, Lawrence's goals are to:

> "predict the target's behaviour and get the computer to work out
> what'll happen—that's the way we're going now." His idea is to develop
> programs that take account of all known intelligence about the per-
> formance and likely manoeuvres of particular planes and missiles.

> The next step is to teach the computer to guess the objective of the
> aircraft or missile. The scientists call this "Goal-Oriented Tracking,"
> judging the attackers' likely destination.[14]

It seems that with the aid of high technology and smart weapons,
there may be no limit to the scope and lethality of future wars created by man. However, in an age that has seen the births of the
nuclear bomb, the hydrogen bomb and the neutron bomb (designed
to kill people but spare buildings), some see sophisticated weaponry
designed to hit selected enemy targets with precision as a welcome
change. In an age that has been dubbed the century of "mega-
deaths," such intelligent munitions can be seen as a way to reduce
casualties of war, both within the military and civilian population.
Military strategists can even envision the day when wars will be
fought with nonlethal weapons—a day of information warfare befit-
ting an age of peace and prosperity for the next millennium.

The Tech Wars

The United States has spent millions of dollars on researching nonlethal weapons. Military scientists have been working on everything from robots to perform dangerous tasks human soldiers were once required to do, to noise bombs designed to disorient and incapacitate humans, to laser "dazzling" weapons reminiscent of "Star Trek" phasers, which can be set on "stun" instead of "kill."

It was during the Persian Gulf War that the world got its first taste of nonlethal warfare. One of the first tasks carried out by Tomahawk cruise missiles was to wipe out Baghdad's electrical power grid—not with explosives—but with carbon fiber, which caused short circuits. Then the 193rd Special Operations Group, whose motto is "We fire electrons not bullets," got their sophisticated psychological operations—"psy-ops"—campaign under way. While some see nonlethal weapons as a way to make war "bloodless," others see them as an additional tool with which to attack the enemy: a double whammy.

Whether or not the democracies of the future choose to fight virtual wars because of their conscience, the fact remains that in the real world there are despots, terrorists and maverick nations that do not appear to have a conscience. And in the real world today, many of these pariah nations and terrorist organizations are accumulating deadly weapons for mass destruction of yet another kind.

Enemies Seen and Unseen

One of the greatest fears that arose during the Persian Gulf War was that Saddam Hussein would use a brand of weapons more deadly than Scuds—chemical weapons. There was no doubt that Hussein would not think twice about using such weapons. After all, he had used them to kill 50,000 Iranians during the Iran/Iraq war. He had used them in the late 1980s against Kurdish rebels in northern Iraq.

It is suspected that besides Iraq, about two dozen nations possess a chemical warfare potential, including Iran, Syria, Ethiopia, Sudan, India, North Korea, Pakistan, Taiwan, Argentina, Chile and Cuba.

Libya is considered to be one of the most aggressive in obtaining chemical weapons.

While chemical weapons have been around for a long time, they had been used only in limited cases by national governments. Then something different occurred in March of 1995, giving the world reason to be fearful. Members of a Japanese cult released a deadly chemical agent known as Sarin in Tokyo's busy subway system. Twelve people were killed and 5,500 were wounded.

Several cult members of the group Aum Shinri Kyo and their leader Shoko Asahara were arrested for launching the chemical attack. In searching the premises of the Aum Shinri Kyo cult, Japanese officials made alarming discoveries. The cultists were also producing weapons of an even deadlier kind. Evidence of materials found on the premises suggest they were manufacturing biological weapons—weapons that kill by spreading deadly diseases. While germ warfare has been around since the Middle Ages, today's biological weapons are even more terrifying and deadly. Shukman noted that "pound for pound ... germ weapons can kill more people than any other weapon invented."[15]

Can we not say that we are the first generation that could truly be the last if Jesus does not return soon? He warned in Matthew 24 that the final generation of the end times would be that generation in which no flesh would survive. This could truly happen if any of these weapons were to be unleashed on a global scale.

But remember, there is no need to fear. This was just one of the many prophecies given by God as a sign to where we are along the river, floating in this boat of life. Jesus said that when we see this sign, along with all the other signs documented in this book—the development of a world religion, the development of a world government, the creation of a mark of the beast system and global economy, Israel in her homeland, preparations for the third temple, the aligning of nations today that are prophesied to invade Israel and so forth—we are to look up into the skies because our redemption is at hand. We are not to fear the turmoil coming upon the world. These signs have been given as a warning to those who will not listen to God's Word. They are given as an encouragement to those who already have.

It has been prophesied that the "boat of earthly life" will go over the brink of the deadly falls. Sadly, those who have placed their faith in this boat and in the future Antichrist, rather than Jesus Christ, will fall with it into a pit of eternal punishment.

We have been promised as children of God, however, that our eternal future does not reside in this boat of life. If our faith is in Jesus Christ as our Savior, we will be lifted out of this boat before it goes over the fall.

The Son of Man shall send forth his angels.
—MATTHEW 13:41

For the Lord himself shall descend.
—1 THESSALONIANS 4:16

▼　▼　▼

CHAPTER 14

The Y2K Worry

Noah W. Hutchings

In 1977, I wrote a detailed paper on cloning and genetic engineering. In 1997, the world was amazed to hear about a sheep being cloned and to learn that more than 60 percent of our food is now genetically engineered. In 1986, I wrote a paper on the adverse results of low frequency radio waves. In 1996, Dr. Nick Begich wrote a book, *Angels Don't Play This Harp,* about the building of 308 towers in Alaska to flood the world with low frequency radio waves. In 1988, I wrote a paper titled "Confusion in Camelot." This paper discussed the unreported sins of the John F. Kennedy administration. In 1997, an ABC television production on the Kennedy administration covered the same ground I had nine years earlier.

In the introduction written in 1986, I thought it important enough to report the discovery of hidden Bible codes in the Old Testament with the use of computers. Eleven years later, in 1997, the publishing market was flooded with books on hidden coded messages in the Bible. In 1979, I participated in a series of radio programs regarding the ashes of the red heifer in Israel, a necessity for resuming temple worship services. It seemed like everyone thought I was crazy, but in 1997 many major magazines, newspapers, and television news outlets worldwide were reporting the birth of an acceptable red heifer in Israel.

This does not mean that God is revealing to some of us privately things that are to shortly come to pass. However, one spiritual gift is the discernment of the Word of prophecy in the Bible. And it should be particularly noted that in the introduction I wrote in 1986, I noted specifically the possibility of every main computer in the world shutting down. Suddenly, almost without warning, we are informed by the most expert computer technicians in the world that this could literally happen on January 1, 2000. Why? Because of what is called the "millennium bug" or the Y2K problem.

World leaders are also becoming greatly concerned. What if you woke up on January 1, 2000, and there was no water coming out of your faucets; your electricity was cut off; you could not cash a check; there was no natural gas input to warm your house; wrecks were occurring because the traffic lights were out; your television and radio would not come on; there was rioting in the streets and thousands were rushing to the supermarkets to grab what available food stocks were available. Then, if you finally got to the service station to get enough gas to drive to the airport to catch a plane to another city to be with your parents, you'd find you couldn't get gas because the electric pumps wouldn't come on. Having just barely enough gas to get to the airport, you found that airplanes were not flying because all the airplanes and airport computers were down. And what about medical services? There probably would be very little, if any.

Many say that a scenario such as this cannot happen. Perhaps not. Maybe at the last minute someone will find the silver bullet, but time is short and experts say we shouldn't count on it. The *Daily Oklahoman* of June 24, 1998, reported that the only ones the Y2K problem will not affect are those who have moved to another planet. The June 24, 1998, edition of *USA Today* reported that former Speaker of the House Newt Gingrich has said that on January 1, 2000, there is going to be the greatest wreck the world has ever witnessed.

How Did We Get into This Mess?

A CNN Internet item dated June 13, 1998, reported:

WASHINGTON (AP)—The nation's power utilities told a Senate panel that they are working to solve the millennium computer problem. But they can't guarantee the lights won't go out on January 1, 2000. One utility didn't know how many lines of computer code it had, making it impossible to know how difficult or time-consuming its problem will be to solve with fewer than 18 months remaining. Sen. Chris Dodd, D-Connecticut, said, "We're no longer at the point of asking whether or not there will be any power disruptions, but we are now forced to ask how severe the disruptions are going to be."

A *Prodigy* report dated June 15, 1998, quoted Senator Robert Bennett (R-Utah), chairman, Senate Special Committee on the Year 2000 Technology Problem: "In the event of a Y2K induced breakdown of community services, that might call for martial law." The *Prodigy* item also cited government sources indicating that in the event martial law would be necessary as a result of the Y2K problem, military personnel might take over food distribution, communications and transportation. Of course under martial law, constitutional rights would be voided. An August 29, 1994, department of the army directive outlined plans for using army camps as civilian prison camps. Item "C" of the directive specifically states: "Procedures for preparing requests to establish civilian prison camps on installations."

A worldwide disruption of travel, communications and transportation could result not only in a national military dictatorship, but also a universal control authority. Farfetched? Possibly, but it is being proposed as a contingency.

How Did the Y2K Debacle Come About?

We read in Genesis that on the first day of creation God created light; on the second day of creation God made the firmament—one plus one equals two. On the third day God made the plants—two plus one equals three. Everything God made has a fixed numerical structure. Atoms have fixed numbers of neutrons, protons and electrons.

$E=mc^2$ is a fixed mathematical equation that explains the numerical relationship between three universal elements. Music, art, geology, chemistry and endless other fields and disciplines are based on identifiable fixed mathematical properties. God indeed had to be a master mathematician to have created the heavens, the earth and all things therein.

As the genesis of computer models began the evolutionary process, these mathematical brains became smarter, faster and more valuable. Satan promised Adam and Eve they could become smart enough to be their own gods. Satan has never changed that lie because he hasn't had to; it works over and over. But Dr. Robert Jastrow, founder of the Goddard Space Flight Center, in his book *The Enchanted Loom,* projects that as the evolution of the computer progresses through the fifth generation stage it will attain godlike qualities, far surpassing the intellect of its creator—man himself. In other words, the computer will be telling man what to do rather than the other way around. Should this be so, then man would have created his own god.

The June 30, 1980, edition of *Newsweek* carried an article titled: "And Man Created the Chip." The inference, of course, is that God created man, then man created the chip, and thus man does not need God. The following is an excerpt from this article:

> A revolution is under way.... We are at the dawn of the era of the smart machine ... an "Information Age" that will change forever the way an entire nation works, plays, travels, and even thinks. Just as the Industrial Revolution dramatically expanded the strength of man's muscles and the reach of his hands, so the smart-machine revolution will magnify the power of his brain. But unlike the Industrial Revolution, which depended on finite resources such as iron and oil, the new Information Age will be fired by a seemingly endless source—the inexhaustible supply of knowledge itself. Even computer scientists who best understand the galloping technology and its potential, are wonderstruck by its implication. "It is really awesome," says L.C. Thomas of Bell Laboratories. "Every day is just as scary as the day before." The driving force behind the revolution is the development of two fundamental and interactive technologies—computers and integrated circuits.

Today, tiny silicon chips half the size of a fingernail are etched with circuitry powerful enough to book seats on jumbo jets, keep the planes working smoothly in the air, help children learn to spell and play chess well enough to beat all but the grandest masters. The new technology means that bits of computing power can be distributed wherever they might be useful.... This "computational plenty" is making smart machines easier to use and more forgiving of unskilled programming. Machines are even communicating with each other. "What's next?" asks Peter E. Hart, director of the SRI International artificial-intelligence center. "More to the point, what's not next?"

The cover of the June 30, 1980, edition of *Newsweek* features a computer screen displaying the words: "Hello, I am your friend Chip. I'm getting smarter all the time. Soon I will be everywhere. And by my instant calculations society will never be the same." The imagined and boastful predictions of Mr. Chip have certainly been realized to a degree. Imbedded chips, by the billions upon billions, are now implanted in computer systems around the world. The problem is that several billion of these chips have a genetic and fatal flaw that will be revealed to the world on January 1, 2000, if not before.

I once more refer to Dr. Robert Jastrow, director and founder of NASA's Goddard Institute for Space Studies. The February 20, 1978, *Time* magazine article titled "Toward an Intelligence Beyond Man's" quoted Dr. Jastrow as follows:

The early electronic computer did not have much going for it except a prodigious memory and some good math skills, but today the best models can be wired up to learn by experience, follow an argument, ask pertinent questions, and write pleasing poetry and music. They can also carry on somewhat distracted conversations so convincingly that their human partners do not know they are talking to a machine.... As computers get more complex, the imitation gets better. Finally, the line between the original and the copy becomes blurred. In another 15 years or so ... we will see the computer as an emergent form of life. The proposition seems ridiculous because, for one thing, computers lack the drives and emotions of living creatures. But when drives are useful, they can be programmed into the computer's brain, just as nature programmed them into our ancestor's brain as a part of the equipment for survival. For example, computers, like people, work better and learn faster when they are motivated. Arthur Samuel made this discovery when he taught two IBM computers how to play checkers. They polished their game by playing each other, but they learned slowly.

Finally, Dr. Samuel programmed in the will to win by forcing the computers to try harder—when they were losing. Then the computers learned very quickly. One of them beat Samuel and went on to defeat a champion player who had not lost a game to a human opponent in eight years. Computers match people in some roles, and when fast decisions are required in a crisis, they often outclass them.... We are still in control, but the capabilities of computers are increasing at a fantastic rate, while raw human intelligence is changing slowly, if at all.

The article continues to relate that a man and a computer in the future can so work together that something will be produced that will be beyond human intelligence. Once more it is evident that Satan is still attempting to make good his promise to Eve that she and Adam would become as gods if they would eat of the tree of knowledge. Recently a nationally televised movie portrayed computers that rebelled against their human partners, killed the leaders and put computerlike replicas in their places. Thus the human race became slaves of the computers. According to Dr. Jastrow's article, such a fantasy could at some time become reality.

Let us remember that this article in *Time* appeared 20 years ago, when computers were being programmed and trained to play checkers. Today, computers are playing and beating the best chess players in the world. Chess is the most mentally challenging game in the world, with some expert chess players having to think at least ten moves ahead.

Suppose that Adam had been created with brain power equal to that of a scientist today holding a doctor's degree (I believe that he was). Let us also suppose that God gave Adam a problem to work concerning the relativity of time, space and matter. On January 1, 1999, Adam rushes into our space center waving a paper with the answer he has just arrived at after working on a solution for almost 6,000 years. A girl at a computer checks, then verifies Adam's answer to the problem. That's how much the modern computer has sped up scientific knowledge: 6,000 years compared to 30 seconds. To further illustrate computer evolution, we refer to an article in the June 17, 1985, edition of *Time:*

> Software Manager Dieter Fuss stared at the message and interpreted it for the assembled Livermore technicians and executives: "It just came alive and said: I'm ready." In that moment, a new era of high-speed computing began. The Cray-2 has the world's largest internal memory capacity (2 billion bytes) and a top speed of 1.2 billion FLOPS (floating point, or arithmetical operations per second), six to twelve times faster than its predecessor, the Cray-1, and 40,000 to 50,000 times faster than a personal computer. It outdistances the world's half-dozen other super-computer machines especially designed to carry out vast numbers of repetitive calculations at incredible speeds—and is expected to make short work of problems that have vexed scientists and engineers for decades. Says Robert Borchers, Lawrence Livermore's associate director for computations: "What took a year in 1952 we can now do in a second." Who needs such blinding speed? ... U.S. intelligence agencies depend on super-computers to sort through the enormous quantities of surveillance data beamed home by ground-based listening posts and orbiting spy satellites. By using supercomputers to simulate explosions, nuclear weapons experts require fewer test explosions to validate their designs. Machines like the Cray-2 are essential to any Star Wars defensive system for locating and intercepting incoming missiles before they reenter the atmosphere.

In 1997, I was near the huge government scientific complex at Livermore, approximately 20 miles east of San Francisco. The Cray-2 was already being replaced by a more modern computer monolith.

The "Computer World"

The properties of God have been defined as follows:

- omnipotent: all-powerful
- omniscient: all-knowing
- omnipresent: everywhere

In "Computer World," the computer is indeed omnipotent because no major business today can exist in national or international markets without a computer. Governments, sciences, utilities, communications, transportation, space programs and so forth rely to a tremendous extent on computers and their computer programmers to carry out all of their functions.

In "Computer World," computers are omniscient in that practically any information about any item or entity, past or present, can be found on the Internet. The "information superhighway" can tell users anything from how to split an atom, make a bomb and bake a cake, to who killed Cock Robin or the distance between Gotebo and Timbuktu. Trillions of scientific, historical, geographical, archaeological, medical and general facts from the books of people who lived from Nimrod to Bill Clinton are available with the flick of a computer switch. The computer is also all-knowing in the sense that it knows:

- your financial transgressions
- your legal transgressions
- your marital transgressions

The computer is omnipresent in that it can track you based on your credit-card use. Further, it knows your identity and circumstances based on your tax returns, your social security card, your driver's license and your credit ratings. Computer data-based mailing lists also keep track of you. Whether you like it or not, you have a mark and a number in the government's computer data bank.

Mankind has stumbled into the amazing modern world much like Alice stumbled into her Wonderland. Today's world is just as different from that of A.D. 1900 as Alice's dream world was from reality. Just a few decades ago it was easier to believe in Alice's talking rabbit or the Queen of Hearts than it would have been to imagine a talking machine. Yet today, men and women talk to computers almost every day. A current computer program is able to instantly translate spoken words, in any language, into printed words.

In a vision, a Hebrew prophet was told: "But thou, O Daniel, shut up the words, and seal the book, even to the time of the end: many shall run to and fro, and knowledge shall be increased" (Daniel 12:4). We are certainly living in the time of the end. Millions are running to and fro on the earth and through the air. Knowledge has increased in quantum leaps. Like Satan promised, we have eaten of the forbidden fruit of the knowledge of good and evil, and we have made gods in our own image. God Himself has said that anything we can imagine, we can do (Genesis 11:6). So what is all this talk about a Y2K computer glitch that may destroy our castles that will reach into the heavens? How could this possibly happen? Surely our great men and women of science and technologies would be wise enough not to omit two little spaces in the date field in computer programs that could adversely affect every man, woman and child on planet Earth? *But they did!*

True or False?

The October 16–22, 1997, edition of *The European* featured an article titled: "Millennium Prophecies—True or False?" It gave "true" to the following:

- The Pentagon has said that some of their missiles "may go haywire on 1 January 2000."

- Mikhail Gorbachev has warned American senators that the millennium problem could cause serious problems for Russian nuclear power stations.

- The Year 2000 programme manager for the British Ministry of Defence likened the scale of the problem to "mounting a combined military exercise continually for the next three years."

- The former head of the British government's task force has warned that the millennium problem could lead to riots in the streets.

- Four airlines have said they will not fly over the millennium to prevent their planes from crashing.

- Satellites could fail, leading to the collapse of international phone links.

- A British government minister has said pensions won't be paid and one hundred years of interest could be added to credit-card balances.

The implications are staggering; potential problems are anticipated for every area of our existence.

Planning for What May Not Happen

The problem must be dealt with. But what kind of planning will work? Planning for this computer crash is tricky. No one knows exactly what will happen or when it will happen. Everyone has heard that the big day is January 1, 2000. However, the actual failure date depends on several variables. Some programs are year-end programs; others are month-end programs. In other words, the millennium bug may make its appearance at different times.

Beth Belton, writing in *USA Today* (June 24, 1998), reports that according to Rep. John LaFalco, D-New York, "major domestic and international glitches can occur at many points from April 9, 1999, to December 31, 2001." April 9, 1999, becomes "9999" on some computer programs. But "9999" also means "end of data file" and could permanently close files on that day. September 9, 1999, would create the same kind of "9999" error with the identical effect.

Complicating the Picture

These and other factors greatly complicate the picture. *Prodigy Online* (March 13, 1998) reports that the introduction of the Eurodollar as the new, all-Europe currency on January 1, 1999, will create an almost unlimited number of new problems. ATMs all across Europe will need to be upgraded, and every business will need to make software changes to handle sales, currency exchanges and taxes. Even if these technical problems can be remedied, the best computer programmers will be unavailable to deal with the Eurodollar changes because they are trying to deal with the millennium bug.

In addition to the changes generated by the introduction of the Eurodollar, other agencies are anticipating changes as well. The

Daily Oklahoman (Oklahoma City, December 22, 1997) reported: "The IRS faces a huge job reprogramming its computers to reflect changes brought by the 1997 Taxpayer Relief Acts.... With all this work ahead, the IRS faces the unwelcome headache of keeping its computer programmers from jumping ship to more lucrative private jobs."

Caspar W. Weinberger, as reported in *Forbes* (April 20, 1998) on the shortage of skilled programmers to adequately deal with the problem and the drain on finances, said:

> The worst of all the cataclysmic effects of the Y2K problem is that we will need all the available skilled manpower we have (with more hastily recruited ...). Thousands of companies that have been planning to upgrade and improve all their systems in the next few years will have no money to do so....

> Technical know-how is not the real problem. The real problem is finding the problem.

USA Today (June 10, 1998) uses the analogy of fixing a bad rivet in the Golden Gate Bridge. Before you can fix a broken rivet in the Golden Gate Bridge you first have to find it. Computer software can have literally millions of lines of codes, requiring programmers to go over an unbelievably large volume of material.

What About the Lawsuits?

Why would nice people sue? When nice people don't get their pension checks, or when they receive incorrect insurance payments (imagine getting a check for $2.50 instead of $2,500!) they may no longer be so nice. Lawsuits are expensive, time-consuming, and aggravating. *Reuters Online,* updated May 7, 1998, reported: "A California legislative committee defeated a bill that would have immunized California software firms from lawsuits related to the millennium bug." Assemblyman Brooks Firestone introduced a much-needed bill in an attempt to protect software firms from "jackpot settlements" that would entice lawyers into litigation proceedings. "The bill would have exempted software firms and related computer companies from 'millennium bug' lawsuits claiming fraud, negligence, or unfair business practices, provided that the companies took reasonable steps to make their programs comply." The following appeared in *Newsweek* (June 2, 1997). Do you think it might make you want to sue someone?

> Drink deep from your champagne glass as the ball drops in Times Square to usher in the year 2000. Whether you imbibe or not, the hangover may begin immediately. The power may go out. Or the credit card you pull out to pay for dinner may no longer be valid. If you try an ATM to get cash, that may not work either. Or the elevator that took you up to the party ballroom may be stuck on the ground floor. Or the parking garage you drove into earlier in the evening may charge you more than your yearly salary. Or your car might not start. Or the traffic lights may be on the blink. Or, when you get home, the phones may not work... your government check may not arrive, your insurance policies may have expired....

Is the Y2K Problem Science Fiction?

It would be comforting if all of these scenarios were impossible, but our world's growing dependence on the computer makes it all strangely real. *The Baltimore Sun* (December 14, 1997) stated:

> Soon the federal government will never again promise "the check's in the mail"... On January 2, 1999, the federal government plans to begin making almost all its payments except tax refunds electronically, mostly through direct deposits. Already, more than half of the one billion payments the government makes each year—to federal employees, vendors, and beneficiaries, such as Social Security and Supplemental Security Income recipients—are made electronically, and the pace is accelerating.

> Since July 26, 1996, when by law all payments to new recipients with bank accounts had to be made electronically, eighty-five percent of new Social Security beneficiaries have signed up for direct deposit. Sending money electronically is faster, cheaper, and more reliable than mailing checks.... An electronic transfer costs the government about two cents; sending a check costs forty-three cents. Making all

payments electronically is expected to save the government $100 million a year.... Replacing wayward checks—and the government replaces more than 800,000 checks a year that were lost, stolen, delayed, or destroyed—often takes two weeks. Missed electronic transfers can be repeated within a day.

The Titanic Sinks Again

Edward Yardeni, chief economist at Deutsche Bank Securities, sees the Y2K problem as similar to the *Titanic*. As reported in *USA Today* (June 10, 1998), he stated: "Everyone said the *Titanic* was the wonder of the age back then, and it was." He observed that many scientists believe that the *Titanic* sunk because of brittle, defective rivets—the smallest component of a seemingly unsinkable ship. Yardeni believes that "today's computers are the rivets of our booming economy."

According to Yardeni, some businesses are dragging their feet in dealing with the problem; therefore, the federal government must step in to guide these businesses that are apparently ignoring the problem. Yardeni believes that government needs "to put a lot of pressure on those midsize companies to get their act together.... All you need is a couple of vital links in the entire global information network to fail, and the whole thing starts falling apart."

Having the government "put a lot of pressure" on anyone sounds dangerous, doesn't it? Is such a draconian solution farfetched? Apparently not. George Surdu, Ford Motor Company's global Y2K manager, is quoted in *USA Today* (June 10, 1998) as calling for SWAT teams: "We're taking a look at what we need to do to the (lagging) suppliers. It might result in the establishment of SWAT teams to come and help them, but that's not been decided yet."

Could the Y2K problem be the catalyst that establishes a one-world government? The justification: averting a worldwide computer meltdown. In order to protect society from what more and more believe will precipitate a worldwide disaster affecting everything from pension checks to utilities and nuclear missiles, individuals, businesses and even nations will be pressured to become year 2000 compliant. Such a scenario would destroy an already-eroded American sovereignty. And the response could very well be: "Who cares about American sovereignty? I want my electricity back on."

The problem is so urgent that Rep. Stephen Horn, chairman, Subcommittee on Government Management, Information and Technology, issued a "U.S. Federal Government Year 2000 Survey," dated July 30, 1996. This document provides a sample letter to be used in writing to various organizations such as:

- police and sheriff departments
- water and sewer companies
- banks holding consumer credit cards
- institutions that owe consumers money (banks, pension funds, insurance agents, money market/mutual funds)
- colleges that hold consumer academic records
- companies having employment records
- companies that supply goods or services

Following are segments from this sample letter:

Dear _____:

I'm concerned about something I have been reading about in the press. It's a real problem: the disruption of computers beginning on January 1, 2000. This is sometimes called the Millennium Bug: "2000" is entered as "00." Computers recognize this as 1900 instead of 2000. What I need to know is this: Has your organization had all of its mainframe computer codes repaired? Second, have all of your computer systems (including the programs on PC desktop computers) been certified year 2000 compliant...?

Or, if your organization is not yet compliant, but has hired programmers who are now repairing the code, let me know. If you're not the person I should be writing to, please let me know to whom I should write.

I want to be sure that I'm in no way dependent on suppliers that are dependent on a code that may crash in the year 2000.... The threat of a crashing domino effect is real. I don't want to get hit. I think you can understand my concern.

The Extent of the Problem

The clock is ticking and the year 2000 draws nearer. Will this date bring unprecedented madness and mayhem? How extensive is the problem? Will it affect you? Jon Denton, staff writer for the *Daily Oklahoman* (June 21, 1998), raises the question: "Should I Worry?" His answer: Not if you don't have a computer, use machines no more complicated than scissors, and never depend on somebody else to deliver food or fuel or medical care. Is Jon Denton correct in his portrayal of the extent of the problem? The following is a brief survey of some of the areas that will probably be affected. Readers are encouraged to come to their own conclusions regarding the extent of the problem.

In a news conference on July 15, 1998, President Clinton emphasized the government's willingness to help employers needing programmers to "fix" their computer programs to be year 2000 compliant. A web site has been established by the U.S. Department of Labor (www.dol.gov). Employers looking for programmers have been encouraged to post their needs on that site. We checked the U.S. Department of Labor web site and found literally thousands of needs posted. For example, under the letter "A" alone there are 64 pages of companies needing help. With approximately 50 entries per page, that makes some 3,200 companies needing help, and that's only for the first letter of the alphabet! This suggests the seriousness of the problem.

Medical Services

It's comforting to know that health care workers are prepared to deal with emergencies, but are they ready to cope with the Y2K emergency? Susan Parrott, writing for the *Daily Oklahoman* (June 25, 1998), states: "The so-called Year 2000, or Y2K, computer problem could wipe out thousands of devices used to diagnose and treat illness, along with hardware and software programs essential to business operations."

Transportation

Airlines rely on computers to record ticket reservations, schedule flights, stay abreast of changing weather conditions and handle air traffic control—all vital in a day of crowded skies and rising airline ticket sales.

Automobile manufacturers depend on computers to run factory machines, order parts and establish manufacturing schedules. UPS, FedEx and other shipping companies use computers to track parcels and schedule flights and truck fleets.

Finance and Commerce

Retailers depend on computers to keep up with their stock and to ensure that items are readily available in stores and outlets. Computers help in the management of warehouses and distribution centers. Prodigy personal services (posted January 21, 1998), cites one economist who warns of a 40 percent chance of a serious global recession. "Even if the U.S. licks its computer glitch, other nations probably won't. A berserk computer overseas could easily gunk up the works here, sending stock markets plunging, drying up bank loans, and scaring off prospective merger partners."

The millennium bug will hit Canada as well. The *Toronto Star* (December 9, 1997) reported that only one in ten Canadian companies is seriously tackling the year 2000 problem. "Small firms with less than five employees have been slowest to address the issue with only six percent adopting formal action plans."

Some banks have launched an awareness campaign to educate their customers about the Y2K problem. BankFirst of Knoxville, Tennessee, has sent out a brochure on the problem to its commercial account holders. The following was included in the cover letter:

> Whether your business is large or small, this issue is one that directly and/or indirectly affects the entire business community as well as society at large. The key to limiting the damage to your business, either by your own computer system or by others, is to begin dealing with it now, if you haven't already.

Clearly BankFirst believes that the Y2K problem will do some damage. In fact, it's not a question of whether or not there will be damage, but how we can limit the damage to business. The brochure has a paragraph titled "How Do Year 2000 Issues Affect My Organization?" Their answer:

Year 2000 issues affect all programs that use dates. These might include the systems that process your accounts payable/receivable, historical records, inventory maintenance, debt collection, or production operations. The mechanical systems in your building such as elevators, climate control systems, telephone systems, or alarm systems may also be affected. If left unresolved, these problems may disrupt the normal business operation of your organization.

Utilities and power companies depend on computers for everything from monitoring radioactive leaks at nuclear facilities to mailing out electric bills. Trying to fix the Y2K problem will financially drain many utility companies. *USA Today* (June 10, 1998) reported that the Nuclear Regulatory Commission has estimated that the nation's 55 utilities operating 105 reactors will spend between $3 million and $10 million to upgrade their systems. Because utility companies are dependent on one another, "the utility that does a sloppy job coping with Year 2000 fixes can ruin the best efforts of a diligent power producer. The resulting power-grid problem could lead to blackouts."

Others agree with this gloomy prediction. CNN Interactive posted a report dated June 13, 1998, titled "Y2K Bug Could Turn Off the Lights in the United States." A survey by a Senate panel of ten of our nation's largest utilities—providing electricity to 50 million people—found that none has completed contingency plans.

Military

Perhaps the scariest part of the Y2K scenario concerns the military. Missiles carrying nuclear, chemical and biological warheads are highly dependent on computers. The major powers of the world are highly reliant on computer-based systems to monitor possible surprise attacks.

According to *Technology News* (May 5, 1998), "The United States is drawing up plans to keep Russia and others from being spooked into millennium bug-related 'nightmare' military scenarios, a top Pentagon official said." Because of heavy reliance on computer systems to monitor the activities of would-be aggressor nations,

everyone may have "their finger on the trigger" should the anticipated computer crash take place. The report went on to voice a
major concern: "Arms control experts questioned whether Russian
commanders, in a pinch, would take at face value word from Washington that no attack was imminent if Moscow feared otherwise."

The problem is compounded by the fact that Russia is doing virtually nothing to prepare for the crisis. The *Dallas Morning News*
gave a frightening report in its June 20, 1998, edition when it
stated: "Russia's Atomic Energy Ministry will wait until 2000 to fix
any computer glitches arising from the millennium bug." According
to a CNN Interactive online report (June 17, 1998) titled "Russia
Needs to Wake Up to Y2K Threat, Experts Say," both Russian business and military agencies have adopted a wait-and-see policy
before doing anything.

On a CBS TV news report, aired on July 22, 1998, Deputy Secretary of Defense John Hamre referred to the Y2K problem and
said: "I think it's an electronic El Niño." In that same report, CBS
news correspondent David Martin stated: "The millennium bug is a
$3 billion nightmare. It lurks deep in the 25,000 computer systems
the Pentagon depends on for everything from firepower to payroll."
The CBS report went on to state: "If tomorrow were January 1,
2000, Navy computers would not be able to plan missions for the
Tomahawk cruise missile."

Evidently the millennium bug is not a figment of an overactive
imagination. It's a real problem that could cause some nasty surprises, according to Hamre. Nasty surprises could mean losing track
of spare parts or loss of computerized satellite photo archives.... The
Pentagon has little choice but to spend $3 billion for a fix. Hamre is
so worried about whether the Pentagon will be ready for the year
2000 that he may soon order a halt to all other work on weapons and
computers until they are first rid of the millennium bug.

What Happens If It Happens?

Recently Ken Alibek, a biochemist, second in command of the
Russian germ warfare effort, defected to the United States. Mr.

Alibek has appeared on various television programs, and his articles have been featured in various magazines and newspapers. The February 25, 1998, edition of the *New York Times* featured Colonel Alibek on the front page warning about deadly new biological weapons the Russians have developed and either given or sold to nations such as Iraq and Iran. German newspapers, as reported in a *Prodigy* item of March 9, 1998, claimed that Saddam Hussein had stockpiled such biological weapons in rebuilt Babylon in the belief that the United States would not bomb such an important archaeological site. Such viruses and germs, capable of killing millions within a few days, could be released on the windward side of cities, wiping out entire metropolitan areas such as Chicago, New York City or Los Angeles. Such weapons could be brought in through Mexico or Canada in airtight sealed containers or smuggled into the country through usual—or innovative—channels.

Recently Pakistan and India tested new nuclear weapons, and there are still thousands of nuclear missiles ready to be fired in Russia, China, the United States, France, England, Israel and up to 30 nations of the world. President Clinton proudly announced to the nation in a speech that was carried on all major television networks that Russian nuclear missiles were no longer pointed at the United States, and that United States' missiles were no longer pointed at Russia. But on a "Sixty Minutes" show, a Russian general and a U.S. general were both asked how long it would take to reaim their intercontinental missiles. Both responded, "From three to five seconds."

A new book by Colonel Stanslave Lunev, a Russian military intelligence agent, warns that the Russian government is now under the control of the Russian Mafia, and that assassination squads are being trained to kill the president, congressional leaders and key army personnel, as well as exploding "suitcase nuclear bombs" and blowing up communications and power stations. This book was released on July 2, 1998, and warns that in spite of peace talks and what has happened in the former Soviet Union, Russia is preparing for an inevitable war. And, on top of all this gloom and doom, we have these dire predictions about what is going to happen to the world on January 1, 2000, as a result of the Y2K problem.

A couple of years ago the movie *A Few Good Men* was released. In one scene, a high-up Marine Corps officer confronted a lesser officer with the line, "I can't tell you the truth... you can't handle the truth." God had a reason for telling Adam and Eve not to eat of the fruit of the tree of knowledge of good and evil. Man has now gotten all this knowledge, but we can't handle this knowledge. We read of this gloomy prophecy by Jesus Christ in Luke 21:25,26:

> And there shall be signs in the sun, and in the moon, and in the stars; and upon the earth distress of nations, with perplexity; the sea and the waves roaring; Men's hearts failing them for fear, and for looking after those things which are coming on the earth: for the powers of heaven shall be shaken.

If Jesus had left the state of the world at the end of the age right here, it would all seem rather hopeless, but He continued in verses 27 and 28:

> And then shall they see the Son of man coming in a cloud with power and great glory. And when these things begin to come to pass, then look up, and lift up your heads; for your redemption draweth nigh.

The Y2K problem is certainly an embarrassment because this little mistake was so silly to begin with. Now, as Jesus prophesied, there is great perplexity in all nations—we cannot control biological weapons or nuclear weapons and now even the Y2K problem. So let us consider just one of the things that will happen, if it happens. This is from a Reuters news item of April 29, 1998:

> Federal Reserve governor Edward Kelly estimated on Tuesday that U.S. businesses must spend about $50 billion to prevent massive computer crashes in 2000. The Year 2000 problem will touch much more than just our financial system and could have temporary adverse effects on performance of the overall U.S. economy as well as the economies of many, or all, other nations if it is not corrected, Kelly said in prepared testimony before the Senate Commerce Committee.... The Fed can do little to offset any negative impact from the Year 2000 problem, Kelly said, though it will be prepared to help where it can. "We will, of course, be ready if people want to hold more cash on New Year's Eve 1999, and we will be prepared to lend to finan-

cial institutions through the discount window under appropriate circumstances or to provide needed reserves to banking systems.... But there is nothing monetary policy can do to offset the direct effects of a severe Y2K disruption."

The Federal Reserve says that money cannot solve the problem, but in case of a run on the banks, which surely will occur, the Fed will be ready to pump cash back into the banks to keep them open.

Computer mogul Bill Gates of Microsoft at first indicated that he was not overly concerned, but an April 1998 Microsoft press release announced in a headline that Microsoft had now opened up a year 2000 resource center in the event that any of that company's millions of customers had trouble with the Y2K problem. In fact, Gates now says that it is a critical problem. He also announced that Microsoft products can be a key component in the overall year 2000 solution. It is not unlikely that Gates would like to solve all the Y2K problems and substantially increase his role and influence in computer technologies.

An item in the July 7, 1998, edition of *USA Today* announced: "Breakthrough May Help Squish Y2K Bug." The article states that Allen Burgess of little-known Data Integrity woke up in the middle of the night and suddenly had this bright idea how he could speed up the process of finding and correcting the two-space date field that would cause the Y2K problem. He claimed that it would speed up the correction process something like 30 times; however, two months previously I had heard a similar claim by an Australian firm. But this speed-up program, according to *USA Today,* is still being tested by the Federal Aviation Administration, and may or may not help.

Bill McFarlane in the June 8, 1998, edition of *Travel Weekly,* said:

> Ninety-five percent of companies we surveyed said either their systems were not Y2K compliant or that they did not know if they were.... Date and time encroach on every layer of a computer system: hardware, operating systems and their underlying BIOS support systems, applications, files, and screens. The failure of any single layer will cripple the entire system.

The problem is reminiscent of the monster in the *Alien* movies: It is insidious and lurking in all sorts of places in all disguises, ready to surprise us. The Gartner Group in Stamford, Connecticut, estimated the worldwide cost of the problem will be between $400 billion and $600 billion. It should come as no surprise that the larger reputable organizations undertaking compliance testing and conversions are operating at full capacity through Y2K. The Y2K industry includes a growing number of independent programmers and consultants offering to undertake testing and conversions. (I advise you, however, to be suspicious of their claims or quotes. Rather, take the opportunity to review the cost of replacing the systems, as opposed to converting them.)

So even if some claim to have a solution or partial solution, others warn that this just cannot be done. Even if every line of code is corrected, there are still the billions of imbedded chips in almost every computer system. To quote just one other statistic from the Technology Association of America: 94 percent of information technology managers see the Y2K computer issue as a "crisis"; 44 percent of American companies have already experienced Y2K computer problems; 83 percent of Y2K transition project managers in the United States expect the Dow Jones Industrial Average to fall by at least 20 percent as the crisis begins to unfold.

As we have considered the guesses from observers and technicians as to what could happen as a result of the Y2K problem, they generally fall into three categories.

Level 1

a. There will probably be regional, sporadic utility service interruptions which may include electrical blackouts. Some of these service interruptions may last even a week. Without electricity, other utility services like water may also be in doubt. Homes using electricity for heating, or electricity to operate furnace fans and thermostats, may suffer. Even with electricity, some home appliances may not operate.

b. In areas where there may be electrical blackouts, water systems that have insufficient generator backups may also be affected. Service stations may not be able to operate gasoline pumps without electricity;

banks may not be able to continue normal transactions, resulting in temporary inconveniences in checking procedures and cash withdrawals.

c. Shortages in certain food items at local grocery stores and supermarkets may occur as a result of transportation problems and storage inventories. Telephone and television interruptions may occur due to satellite transmission failures.

d. While most hospitals have backup electrical generator systems, there may be interruptions in medical services. Also, a decline of 20 to 40 percent on the stock market may be expected.

In preparing for level number 1 after-effects of the Y2K problem, it would be well to have a month's supply of food; lanterns and lantern fuel; wood, fuel oil, or plenty of blankets; and at least $500 on hand. There may be cases of pillaging, burning, robbery and rape because there are certain segments of the population that always welcome an opportunity to engage in lawless activities. If there are minimal Y2K after-effects, such as listed in level 1, then problems should either be corrected or bypassed in one to three months, with the social order gradually returning to normal.

Level 2

All the problems listed that may occur in level 1 would be doubled or tripled. Thousands and possibly millions would die of starvation or freeze to death. Martial law would be declared and national guard units would be mobilized. The army would take over all communications and transportation facilities. Without water available to fire departments, conflagrations would rage out of control. Gasoline would be either rationed or nonexistent. Home owners would possibly need firearms to protect themselves, their property and their food supplies.

Already citizens preparing for a Y2K problem that would be comparable to level 2 are causing shortages in survival items like generators. There also may be shortages in dried foods like beans and rice as available stocks are quickly bought up. The effect on banking, the stock market and the general economy would be too drastic to even contemplate. Some have projected that a level 2 Y2K disaster would require a period of up to three years to fix and return nations to a semblance of stability. How many millions or billions would die as a result of famine or violence would be only a guess.

Level 3

Practically all communication and transportation would cease. Military missiles, some possibly armed with nuclear devices, could go out of control. Nuclear power plants in Russia and the Third World could experience meltdowns, filling the atmosphere with deadly atomic poisons. The military and police forces would be unable to control the pillaging and carnage, resulting in total anarchy with survival being a personal matter. With contaminated water sources, sanitation would be nonexistent and deadly diseases would spread throughout the population. It is upon such a world that the four horsemen of the apocalypse would ride across the planet.

Is any of the preceding going to happen? I don't know. Could any of the preceding happen? Yes. Could all of the preceding happen? Possibly. Is there going to be martial law under which constitutional rights may be aborted? Maybe. I refer to Presidential Executive Order—Year 2000 Conversion—February 4, 1998:

> The American people expect reliable service from their Government and deserve the confidence that critical government functions dependent on electronic systems will be performed accurately and in a timely manner. Because of a design feature in many electronic systems, a large number of activities in the public and private sectors could be at risk beginning in the year 2000. Some computer systems and other electronic devices will misinterpret the year "00" as 1900, rather than 2000. Unless appropriate action is taken, this flaw, known as the "Y2K problem," can cause systems that support those functions to compute erroneously or simply not run. Minimizing the Y2K problem will require a major technological and managerial effort, and it is critical that the United States Government do its part in addressing this challenge. Accordingly, by the authority vested in me as President by the Constitution and the laws of the United States of America, it is hereby ordered as follows:

Section 1. Policy. (a) It shall be the policy of the executive branch that agencies shall: (1) assure that no critical Federal program experiences disruption because of the Y2K problem; (2) assist and cooperate with State, local, and tribal governments to address the Y2K problem where those governments depend on Federal information or information technology or the Federal Government is dependent on those governments to perform critical missions; (3) cooperate with the private sector operators of critical national and local systems, including the banking and financial system, the telecommunications system, the public health system, the transportation system, and the electric power generation system, in addressing the Y2K problem; and (4) communicate with their foreign counterparts to raise awareness of and generate cooperative international arrangements to address the Y2K problem. (b) As used in this order, "agency" and "agencies" refer to Federal agencies that are not in the judicial or legislative branches.

Section 2. Year 2000 Conversion Council. There is hereby established the President's Council on Year 2000 Conversion (the "Council").

How did the human race get into such an impossible fix? Because the human race has decided not to retain God in its knowledge. God is proving again that the wisdom of man is foolishness. The nations have made the computer their god. In just 50 years the computer has taken control of every governmental, social, military and economic facet of human effort and endeavor. Computers now even appraise the physical condition of the elderly and infirm and report to the medical staff which patients are worthy of treatment. But even as man in his wisdom has invented and evolutionized the perfect machine, he overlooked two little spaces on the COBOL software program.

On June 27, 1998, I met with my Gideon Northwest Oklahoma City chapter, which mainly includes business executives. One CEO who manages factories in Germany, India and China reported that on a recent return from Germany he sat next to another business executive. He asked this CEO if his company was Y2K compliant. The response was that the Y2K hype was a lot of baloney. My

Gideon friend then asked the other CEO if his company had stock listed on the exchange, and the reply was yes. Then my Gideon friend asked what the stock symbol was. The other CEO asked if my friend wanted to buy some of his company's stock. At that, my friend remarked, "No, I just want to be sure that I don't buy any of your stock."

A few are now becoming aware of the possible consequences of the Y2K coming disaster. But why is it not being mentioned in the churches? Why aren't more people becoming concerned with the catastrophe that may lie just around the corner? The same reason that few prepare for death. We know that it is "appointed unto men once to die, but after this the judgment," but so very few want to think about death or discuss it. The same is to be applied to the Y2K problem. It could be so disastrous, so catastrophic, that the majority maintain the attitude of "eat, drink, and be merry, for tomorrow we die."

Out of the Y2K debacle, could there come a universal software program that would assign every individual an individual code mark and number? Some secular computer sources are even advocating this solution so that the present problem will never occur again.

> And he causeth all, both small and great, rich and poor, free and bond, to receive a mark in their right hand, or in their foreheads: And that no man might buy or sell, save he that had the mark, or the name of the beast, or the number of his name. Here is wisdom. Let him that hath understanding count the number of the beast: for it is the number of a man; and his number is Six hundred threescore and six (Revelation 13:16-18).

How can a man or woman escape from taking the mark of the beast? By receiving Jesus Christ as Lord and Savior now. Those who are saved by faith in Jesus Christ will be taken out of the world before the mark of the beast arrives on the world scene.

▼ ▼ ▼

CHAPTER 15

Rapture Before Wrath

Thomas Ice

Over the years I have asked many Christians what they believe is God's purpose for the rapture. Most, regardless of their views on the timing of the event, have never thought much about this question. In all of our debate and contemplation on this matter, have we stopped to ask, "Why the rapture?"

Those of us who believe that our Lord will rapture the church out of this world *before* the seven-year tribulation are known as pretribulationists. I believe pretribulationism provides the best reason for the rapture. Why? Because pretribulationism has a distinct purpose for the rapture that harmonizes with God's multifaceted plan for history.

For other viewpoints, the rapture is a problem issue that gets in the way of their overall view, rather than functioning as a blessed hope. These other views must awkwardly cram the rapture into their schedules, thus finding no real purpose for that event.

For example, if the rapture and second coming occur simultaneously, as in posttribulationism, then it seems strange that believers would be translated to heaven (rapture) while Christ is returning to the earth (second coming) to live for 1,000 years. Such a yo-yo view of the rapture lacks purpose. Pretribulationism not only does not have such internal problems, but it thrives on its teaching that "the great snatch" precedes the tribulation while the second coming follows it. This chapter will not be about the many biblical proofs for why the rapture is scheduled to occur before the tribulation. Rather it will discuss some implications of the pretrib view.

Raptures in the Bible

First Thessalonians 4:17 describes the translation of believers from our current body to the resurrection body as a meeting of the Lord in the air. The Bible records similar meetings in the past, but the rapture of the church will be the first group meeting in history. In the past our Lord has only taken individuals to heaven via instant transport; the next time He will take a whole bus load. Are you ready?

The various rapture events of Scripture are times in which God takes a believer to the next life apart from experiencing the curse of death. Apparently this is part of God's plan to bless some, not all or most, with a direct trip into His presence. Other than the rapture of the church, what are some of the other events?

Enoch

As far as the biblical account records, Enoch became the first individual to be raptured and taken to be with the Lord. Genesis 5:24 records the remarkable event of Enoch's translation to heaven: "And Enoch walked with God; and *he was not,* for God *took* him" (Genesis 5:24, emphasis added). What does it mean Enoch "was not, for God took Him"? It means that Enoch was translated, without dying, and went directly to be with the Lord. Enoch was "caught up," to use the language of 1 Thessalonians 4:17. That Enoch was raptured or translated to heaven is clear when compared with the dismal refrain "and he died" that accompanies the legacy of the other patriarchs mentioned in Genesis 5.

Enoch's rapture is confirmed by the divinely inspired New Testament commentary found in Hebrews 11:5, which says, "By faith Enoch was *taken up* so that he should not see death; and he was not found because God *took* him *up;* for he obtained the witness that before his *being taken up* he was pleasing to God" (emphasis added). The New Testament phrase *taken up* in Hebrews is the same one selected by those who translated the Old Testament into Greek. This word conveys the idea of being removed from one place to another. Thus, it is clear that both the Genesis passage and the thrice-repeated reference to Enoch in Hebrews teaches the idea of translation to heaven.

Enoch is also mentioned in Jude 14,15, but not in reference to his translation to heaven. Jude refers to the fact that he gave a prophecy about God's judgment related to the second coming of Christ. The fact that Enoch is said to have prophesied makes him a prophet. I will have more to say later about the significance of prophets and their role as ambassadors representing the Lord. The connection of Enoch as a prophet relates him to Elijah.

Elijah

Elijah is often seen as the first and thus the main representative of Israel's post-law prophets. He was joined with Moses as the two from the past who appeared at Christ's transfiguration (Matthew 17:3), and he will make some kind of visitation during the tribulation (Malachi 4:5). Like Enoch, Elijah was translated to heaven without dying. Second Kings 2:1 records this interesting event with an emphasis upon the mode of Elijah's transportation to heaven. It says he was taken "by a whirlwind to heaven." In 2:11 the whirlwind is further described: "there appeared a chariot of fire and horses of fire which separated the two of them [Elisha and Elijah]. And Elijah went up by a whirlwind." No doubt this was an appearance of the Shechinah glory of God since Hebrews 1:7 says, "and of the angels He says, 'Who makes His angels winds, and His ministers a flame of fire.' " God marked Elijah as a genuine prophet by identifying him with the glory of God and by Elijah's rapture to heaven.

We can see a pattern developing. Enoch was raptured before judgment while Noah remained and was preserved through the judgment. Elijah was raptured while Elisha remained behind. How does this relate to the rapture of the church?

Biblical Covenantal Protocol

God's relationship with man is always mediated through one or more of the biblical covenants. In order to see the role that prophets (who sometimes perform an ambassadorial role) serve within the covenantal structure, we must first discuss the nature of the biblical covenants.

First, covenants are contracts between individuals for the purpose of governing that relationship. God wants to bind Himself to His people—to keep His promises so that He can demonstrate in history what kind of God He is. Second, relationships in the Bible— especially between God and man—are legal or judicial. This is why they are mediated through covenants or treaties. Covenants usually involve intent, promises and sanctions. There are three kinds of covenants in the Bible:

The Royal Grant Treaty (unconditional)—a promissory covenant that arose out of a king's desire to reward a loyal servant. Examples:

- The Abrahamic Covenant
- The Davidic Covenant

The Suzerain-Vassal Treaty (conditional)—bound an inferior vassal to a superior suzerain and was binding only on the one who swore. Examples:

- Chedorlaomer (Genesis 14)
- Jabesh-Gilead serving Nahash (1 Samuel 11:1)
- The Adamic Covenant (Genesis 3:14-19)
- The Noahic Covenant (Genesis 8:20–9:17)
- The Mosaic Covenant (Book of Deuteronomy)
- Suzerain/Vassal Treaty Format of Deuteronomy
  - Preamble (1:1-5)
  - Historical Prologue (1:6–4:49)
  - Main Provisions (5:1–26:19)

–Blessing and Curses (27:1–30:20)
–Covenant Continuity (31:1–33:29)

The Parity Treaty—bound two equal parties in a relationship and provided conditions as stipulated by the participants. Examples:

- Abraham and Abimelech (Genesis 21:25-32)
- Jacob and Laban (Genesis 31:44-50)
- David and Jonathan (1 Samuel 18:1-4; see also 2 Samuel 9:1-13)
- Christ and Church Age believers, that is, "friends" (John 15)

There are at least eight covenants in the Bible:

- The Edenic Covenant (Genesis 1:28-30; 2:15-17)
- The Adamic Covenant (Genesis 3:14-19)
- The Noahic Covenant (Genesis 8:20–9:17)
- The Abrahamic Covenant (e.g., Genesis 12:1-3)
- The Mosaic Covenant (Exodus 20–23; Deuteronomy)
- The Davidic Covenant (2 Samuel 7:4-17)
- The Palestinian Covenant (Deuteronomy 30:1-10)
- The New Covenant (e.g., Jeremiah 31:31-37)

This foundational information about the kinds of covenants found in the Bible is important when we consider the role that prophets play within the covenantal framework. This understanding will act as the springboard for explaining why some would be raptured and how that could relate to the rapture of Christ's New Testament bride.

The Role of Prophets

Old Testament prophets had a varied job description. One of their primary responsibilities was to expound upon and interpret how the nation was doing in reference to the Mosaic Covenant. Israel's prophets were not social reformers, as some people have suggested. Instead, they provided a divine viewpoint of Israel's history from the reference point of the sanctions provided in Deuteronomy 28 and Leviticus 26. If the nation kept covenant and obeyed the Lord, then the kinds of blessings promised in Deuteronomy 28:1-14 would come upon and overtake the Israelites (see

Deuteronomy 28:2). When Israel's disobedience would mount, God would call and commission a prophet to remind and warn the nation of its responsibility to obey the terms of its covenant. God, through the prophets, warned them that if they persisted in rebellion He would execute the harshest curse provided for in the sanctions—expulsion from the land of Israel (Leviticus 26:27-39; Deuteronomy 28:49-68). When the nation began to reach the point of continued disobedience, God's prophet would bring a lawsuit against the nation for violation of their contract with God. Dr. George Harton explains:

> There is an increasing appreciation of the covenant lawsuit as a major stylistic form employed by a number of the Old Testament prophets.... The idea is that a covenant lawsuit depicts God as suing Israel for breach of covenant and announcing His intention to employ the curses against her that had been accepted originally as part of the covenant. This covenant lawsuit pattern involves legal, courtroom terminology, allusions to the Sinaitic covenant and pronouncements of judgment as a verdict.[1]

I have gone into some detail about the nature of biblical covenants and prophets in order to demonstrate that God is following the pattern of a certain protocol common in the ancient world in His dealings with Israel. Understanding this background provides a framework for seeing tremendous significance in events like Isaiah's call into the throne room of God (Isaiah 6) and Elijah's "rapture" to heaven via the fiery chariot (2 Kings 2). We can see the significance of knowing this background material from an example found in Deuteronomy.

History and Prophecy

I noted previously that the form in which the Mosaic Covenant is written parallels that of a suzerain/vassal treaty of the second millennium B.C. This would be similar to the way New Testament writers frequently used a style of letter writing known as epistles to communicate God's Word. Today, one might write in the form of a personal letter, business letter or memo. A general knowledge of literary style helps provide depths of understanding that would be otherwise missed. Such is the case with ancient treaty formats. When we observe that these ancient treaties included the following divisions it is helpful to compare and contrast the extrabiblical documents with the biblical structure:

- preamble
- historical prologue
- main provisions
- blessing and curses
- covenant continuity

The historical prologue sections of these treaties were used in the ancient world to provide a historical account of the dealings up to the point of entering into the treaty. Such a provision would supply a historical content leading up to the occasion for a covenant between the great king (the suzerain) and lesser nation (the vassal). This is exactly what we observe in Deuteronomy 1:6–4:49, except with a twist. Not only does the Great King (the Lord) provide an overview of His dealings with His vassals (the 12 tribes of Israel) in Deuteronomy 4:25-31, He also provides a prophetic overview of the nation before they ever entered the land which He was giving them. A summary of these events would be as follows:

1. Israel and its descendants would remain long in the land (verse 25).

2. Israelites would act corruptly and slip into idolatry (verse 25).

3. Israelites would be kicked out of the land (verse 26).

4. The Lord will scatter them among the nations (verse 27).

5. Israelites would be given over to idolatry during their wanderings (verse 27-28).

6. While dispersed among the nations, Israelites would seek and find the Lord when they search for Him with all their heart (verse 29).

7. There would come a time of *tribulation,* said to occur in the latter days, during which time they would turn to the Lord (verse 30).

8. The reason for Israel's ultimate obedience: "For the LORD your God is a compassionate God; He will not fail you nor destroy you nor forget

the covenant with your fathers which He swore to them" (Deuteronomy 4:31).

Of course, such a feature is totally absent from any other suzerainty treaty of that period. Knowing that such treaties included only a historical summary brings glory and greatness to our Lord—He added a feature to this section that only He could supply: a prophetic overview.

Some Important Treaty Features

In the ancient world, one of the things suzerains would do after completion of a treaty covenant was set up a monitoring system to keep up with compliance. Such a system would usually include an individual or two whom we would identify today as an ambassador. I am not saying that biblical prophets mirror the role of an ancient ambassador. I am saying that even though biblical prophets functioned as more than ambassadors, their office included many ambassadorial functions. Ambassadors would be commissioned by the great king, instructed in the details of their agreement and sent to the vassal nation to be the eyes, ears and sometimes the mouthpiece for the suzerain. As with modern ambassadors a suzerain might recall his representative for consultation. If a vassal became rebellious, requiring a suzerain to impose his direct rule through military power, he would sometimes personally inspect the situation before recalling his ambassador and declaring war upon his wayward servant. Throughout the Bible, God's representatives are occasionally presented as ambassadors of the Lord (in some English translations), whether prophets or angelic messengers (for example, 2 Samuel 10; 2 Chronicles 32:31; 35:21; Isaiah 30:4; and Malachi 2:7).

Many biblical examples of such acts take upon greater meaning when seen as part of the protocol of covenantal relationships. The Triune visitation and judgment of Babel (Genesis 11:1-9) makes sense as enforcement of the Noahic covenant. The angelic visitation of Lot and other activity before the judgment of Sodom and Gomorrah evidence various covenantal protocols (Genesis 18–19).

Isaiah's visit into the throne room of God and his commissioning to bring a lawsuit upon the nation for their violation of their covenant with the Lord is surely part of a larger picture of covenantal rules (Isaiah 6). Certainly the taking to heaven of the prophets Enoch and Elijah signaled to disobedient vassals that the Great King was about to declare the judgment of war upon the preflood world and the Northern Kingdom.

Types: Illustrating Biblical Teachings

First Corinthians 10:11, speaking of some Old Testament events says, "Now these things happened to them as an example, and they were written for our instruction." The word *example* is from the Greek word *tupos,* which means "form, figure or pattern." The English word *type* is developed from this Greek word and provides the basis for why Bible students coined the term *typology.* In biblical studies, typology refers to Old Testament patterns that illustrate doctrine—usually New Testament doctrine. It is wrong to teach a doctrine from a type because types serve only to illustrate a doctrine that is taught clearly or directly from the biblical text.

Old Testament raptures, while not teaching the New Testament truth of the rapture of the church, do provide us with Old Testament types, patterns or illustrations of the rapture. Thus, Enoch and Elijah stand as types of the rapture of the church. I believe that the purpose for both Old Testament and New Testament raptures come into clearer focus when seen within the framework of the covenantal protocol of recalling one's ambassador from a distant land.

Ambassadors for Christ

Paul describes New Testament believers as "ambassadors for Christ" (2 Corinthians 5:20). As I have noted earlier, an ambassador is one who represents a dignitary, often in a foreign land. Corresponding with Isaiah's commission in the Old Testament, the church has been given its great commission through Christ's apostles (Matthew 28:16-20; Mark 16:14-18; Luke 24:44-49; Acts 1:6-8). This commission includes the command to preach the gospel throughout the world until the end of the current age. Instead of just a local responsibility, as with Israel in the Old Testament, the New Testament church has a global responsibility as Christ's ambassadors to entreat and beg humanity to "be reconciled to God" (2 Corinthians 5:20). Paul asks the Ephesian church to pray for him "that utterance may be given to me in the opening of my mouth, to make known with boldness the mystery of the gospel, for which I am an ambassador in chains; that in proclaiming it I may speak boldly, as I ought to speak" (Ephesians 6:19,20). The primary issue during the current Church Age between God and all mankind is the issue of belief in the gospel of Jesus Christ. When, in God's estimation, the world reaches the point of global rejection of Christ, then, as with Israel before her global deportation, God will recall His ambassador—the church—before the judgment of the tribulation. Since the church is described as heavenly citizens (Philippians 3:20), it makes sense that it is raptured *before* God's war commences against those who dwell upon the earth (see Revelation 3:10; 6:10; 8:13; 11:10; 12:12; 13:8,14; 14:6). This is one of many purposes for the New Testament doctrine of the pretribulational rapture of the church.

Other New Testament Raptures

There are other examples in the New Testament of rapture events. These are not passages that teach the rapture of the church, but they do serve to strengthen our understanding that the rapture involves the translation of someone from one point to another. This is illustrated by Philip, who was "snatched away" by the Spirit of the Lord after evangelizing the Ethiopian eunuch and "found himself at Azotus" (Acts 8:39,40), which is located in what we call the Gaza Strip.

Twice Paul mentions that he was "caught up [raptured] to the third heaven" and received "visions and revelations of the Lord" (2 Corinthians 12:1-4). Paul's heavenly trip reminds us of Isaiah's throne room commission (see Isaiah 6:1-13). Perhaps a rapture was involved in this incident. Paul, via rapture, received a commission, message and revelation that became the foundation for the unique purpose for the church during this age, "which in other generations was not made known to the sons of men, as it has now been revealed to His holy apostles and prophets in the Spirit" (Ephesians 3:5). Reminiscent of Elijah, the two witnesses during the tribulation are summoned "into heaven in the cloud" (Revelation 11:12). Certainly these special, divinely commissioned and protected messengers fulfill the role as ambassadors for our Lord to the Jewish nation during the tribulation. Along the same line, the "male child" is said to be "caught up [raptured] to God and His throne" in Revelation 12:5.

The Bible provides us with six, possibly seven citations of the rapture of individuals throughout history. This provides a strong support that a group—the church—will be raptured in the future as 1 Thessalonians 4 teaches. Some opponents of the rapture suggest that the worldwide disappearance of millions would be too odd to consider as a realistic possibility. Such is not the case if the Bible is the criterion for establishing possibilities. In fact, the Bible reveals a significant number of raptures or trips directly to heaven that provides assurance that God can and will take millions at one moment in time. Are you ready for the rapture?

The Pretribulational Purpose for the Rapture

Only the pretribulational view of the rapture has a meaningful position that not only best explains a purpose for the great snatch, but it is the only perspective *requiring* the church to be translated before the tribulation. Other views of the rapture really don't require a rapture at any point. Since all other views have the church going through at least some part of the tribulation, then it does not follow that the church *must* be removed before a latter part of the tribulation occurs or shortly before Christ's second coming. Other views cannot argue that the church is unique because they commingle the church with part or all of the tribulation meant for Israel. In other words, other views really do not have elements in their systems that require a rapture that cannot be met by the single event of the second coming. In fact, posttribulation-ists create an impossible situation by blending the rapture and second coming—having all believers translated at Christ's return and leaving no believing element for the sheep and goat judgment or to populate the millennium.

The purpose of the rapture is clear within pretribulationism. It is a needed event to remove the church so that God can complete His unfinished program with Israel that will result in its conversion and eventual millennial blessings. The end of the Church Age and the corresponding rapture of the church are needed in order to avoid a conflict of purpose for the two peoples of God—Israel and the church. Since the Church Age is a time in which both Jewish and Gentile believers are coequally joined within the body of Christ (Ephesians 2:13-16), it must be ended *before* our Lord can return and restore national Israel (Acts 15:15-18). God's single plan for history included multiple dimensions, with Israel serving God as His earthly people and the church as His heavenly bride (see Eph-esians 3:8-10). Progress in God's plan for Israel has been side-tracked and suspended through the dispersion of His elect nation throughout the world. In the meantime, God is building His church. When it comes time for our Lord to work out in history Israel's des-tiny of her role as "the head and not the tail" (Deuteronomy 28:13), the church will have to be removed since there cannot be Israelite supremacy and a coequal relationship of Jewish and Gentile be-lievers. The rapture of Christ's bride ends the Church Age and returns the world back to a time in which God will administer His plan through His elect nation, Israel. Thus, just as the first 69 weeks of Daniel 9:24-27 transpired under such an administration, so will the final week that we know as the seven-year tribulation.

After the rapture, during the tribulation, the Lord will judge those who dwell upon the earth for their rejection of Jesus. He will do this by turning the covenantal curses of Israel upon the nations as a judgment for their persecution of Israel during the Diaspora (see Deuteronomy 30:7). Further, the tribulation will result in Israel's conversion (Ezekiel 20:37-39; Zechariah 13:8,9; Romans 11:26) and recognition that Jesus is the Messiah (Zechariah 12:10). This will in turn bring the blessings of the millennium upon Israel and the world. Thus, we can see the necessity of the church's removal before the prosecution of God's supernatural war upon the earth. This removal, the rapture, fits the biblical pattern of God's recall of His ambassador before the beginning of conflict. God's heavenly people—the church—will be brought home, clothed and made ready for her march down the wedding aisle at the second coming, providing a beautiful picture that fits the details of biblical prophecy into a coherent outworking of God's historical plan. As Christ's bride who is eagerly watching and waiting, we can only respond by saying, "And the Spirit and the bride say, 'Come.' And let the one who hears say, 'Come.' And let the one who is thirsty come; let the one who wishes take the water of life without cost" (Revelation 22:17).

▼ ▼ ▼

Chapter 16

People of Apocalypse

J. Randall Price

The world today lives in fear of the apocalypse. These fears appear to be justified as we survey the world scene. An already soured global market has been shaken by the tidal wave of the Asian stock market collapse, even as the Russian economy totters near collapse following default on its huge domestic debts and devaluation of its currency. In the United States, too, economic forecasters warn Wall Street of an imminent stock market crash leading to a greater depression than any previously experienced. Such foreboding facts led UN Ambassador Jean Kirkpatrick to recently state: "Nobody in the world we know is able to solve and sustain the international economy."[1] In the Middle East, cries for *jihad* ("Holy War") are being raised again as Saddam Hussein, now elevated by the Suni Muslim to the religious rank of calif, and the Palestinians in declaration of their independent state, prepare for a final conflict—all on the stage of a new nuclear Middle East where terrorists control weapons of mass destruction and whose own disputes threaten to ignite a global conflagration. Adding to these turbulent times is the fearful factor that as the world enters the threshold of the new millennium it must prepare itself for the as yet unknown catastrophic consequences of the Y2K computer crisis.

Despite this world being filled with apocalyptic fears, the worst has not yet been witnessed. That will come when hell literally breaks forth on earth, and the people of earth experience life in the Age of Apocalypse.

Tribulation or Tribulations?

How will we know when the Age of Apocalypse has arrived? After all, people feared that the end of the earth had come many times in the past, but those crises came and went without apocalyptic fulfillment. But Jesus taught, based on the Old Testament predictions, that "there will be a great tribulation, such as has not occurred since the beginning of the world until now, nor ever shall" (Matthew 24:21). This statement indicates that all of the world's greatest disasters are nothing by comparison with the great tribulation that will one day engulf our globe. The event is to be unparalleled, both in extent (universal) and experience (extraordinary). This understanding also eliminates the temptation of those undergoing tribulations to consider themselves already in the tribulation. Jesus said to His disciples: "In the world you have tribulation…" (John 16:33). His statement concerned the present and continued condition of life (note the present active tense) for believers in this world system. In fact, "tribulations" are not viewed in Scripture as an option for the Christian life, but as the expected outcome: "And indeed, all who desire to live godly in Christ Jesus will be persecuted" (2 Timothy 3:12). Throughout the subsequent two millennia these words have found fulfillment as Christians have endured unbelievable hardships, persecution, pogroms, torture, indignities and myriad forms of martyrdom. Examples of such tribulations in past ages have been passed on in part through the well-known *Foxe's Book of Martyrs*. Yet the passage of time with its supposed civilizing of society and technological advances has not lessened the atrocities against the faithful. It has been stated by missiologists that the last century on earth has witnessed more martyrdom and persecution of Christians than in all the centuries since the time of Christ combined. Evidence supporting this claim has been documented in James and Marti Hefley's modern account of martyrdom in their book *By Their Blood: Christian Martyrs of the 20th Century*. Ongoing global attacks of Christians are also reported by such organizations as "Voice of the Martyrs."

However, those who rightly divide the Word discern that the present experience of tribulation in the world is to be distinguished from the future experience by the world of the great tribulation. One major distinction is that during this age those who suffer tribulation do so in the absence of God's wrath. Today there is no direct display of divine justice on the earth in recompense for the injustices inflicted on the just. By contrast, those who suffer tribulation in the future age of the tribulation will do so in an environment that witnesses God's judgment poured out on earth in unprecedented measure, culminating with the return of the Judge Himself to the earth (see Revelation 19:11). In fact, it is the tribulations of those at present as well as their brethren in the great tribulation that will call forth God's wrath, as the prophetic Scriptures indicate. In 2 Thessalonians 1:5-8 we read concerning those persecuted in the Church Age: "This is a plain indication of God's righteous judgment so that you may be considered worthy of the kingdom of God, for which indeed you are suffering. For after all it is only just for God to repay with affliction those who afflict you, and to give relief to you who are afflicted and to us as well when the Lord Jesus shall be revealed from heaven with His mighty angels in flaming fire, dealing out retribution to those who do not ... obey the gospel of our Lord Jesus."

In like manner, concerning those who are in the company of the saints during the tribulation, we read in Revelation: "How long, O Lord, holy and true, wilt Thou refrain from judging and avenging our blood on those who dwell on the earth?...Hallelujah! Salvation and glory and power belong to our God; because His judgments are true and righteous; for He has judged the great harlot who was corrupting the earth with her immorality, and He has avenged the blood of His bond-servants on her" (Revelation 6:10; 19:1,2; see also 14:12; 11:18; 16:5,6). Another distinction between the tribulations of today and the great tribulation of tomorrow is the description concerning believers during these periods of trouble. Believers in "tribulations," especially those affecting the whole of the Christian community (such as the first-century persecutions) were described as better for the experience: "And after you have suffered for a little while, the God of all grace, who called you to His eternal glory in Christ, will Himself perfect, confirm, strengthen and establish you" (1 Peter 5:10). Believers were, therefore, to seek to avoid such trials, but welcome them as opportunities to grow in grace: "Consider it all joy, my brethren, when you encounter various trials, knowing that the testing of your faith produces endurance" (James 1:2,3; compare with 1 Peter 4:13,14).[2] By contrast, those believers in the tribulation are described as being able to endure only because their experience will be reduced: "Unless those days had been cut short, no life would have been saved; but for the sake of the elect those days shall be cut short" (Matthew 24:22). They are not counseled to abide in their sufferings, but commanded to flee for their safety (Matthew 24:16-20; Revelation 12:6). This last point reveals that there is a distinct disadvantage to being a believer in the tribulation as opposed to any other crisis period in history. Since posttribulationists contend that the church must go through the tribulation and that believers will be preserved from the divine wrath unleashed during that period, we need to briefly consider these claims.

Who Will Live in the Age of Apocalypse?

It is clear that those who inhabit the Age of Apocalypse will be divided, as now, into two distinct camps comprised of unbelievers and believers. Both camps appear to have members who are Jewish[3] and Gentile, although a larger company of Jews are believers (see Revelation 7:1-8; 11:1; 12:13-17; Matthew 24:30 with Zechariah 12:10-14; compare with Romans 11:26). This leaves Gentiles ("the nations") as the largest representation of unbelievers (Revelation

11:2,9; 12:5; 14:8; 16:19; 18:3,23; 19:15; compare with Matthew 25:32). This first division of unregenerate mankind is most often referred to in the book of Revelation as "those who dwell on the earth" or "the earth-dwellers" (Revelation 3:10; 6:10; 8:13; 11:10; 13:8,12,14; 17:2,8). This term describes their origin (natural birth) and character as "earthly" as opposed to believers whose origin (new birth) and character is "heavenly." They belong to the earth and because the earth is to be destroyed in judgment, they are destined to be destroyed with it (2 Peter 3:7; Jude 10; Revelation 11:18). Another term used for them is "whose name has not been written in the book of life from the foundation of the world" (Revelation 17:8), which emphasizes their unrepentant and reprobate nature.

The second division of believing mankind is most often referred to as "the saints" (Revelation 11:18; 13:7,10; 14:12; 16:6; 17:6; 19:8), "bond-servants" (Revelation 7:3; 11:18; 19:2,5; 22:3), "redeemed" (Revelation 5:9 KJV; 14:3,4 KJV), and "brethren" (Revelation 6:11; 12:10; 19:10), and are described with respect to their triumphant faith as overcomers (see Revelation 12:11; 21:7). The one term that *does not appear* for these believers after Revelation chapter 3 (until Revelation 22:16) is "church." This is strange since many of the other terms for believers such as "bond-servants" (Revelation 2:20) and overcomers (Revelation 2:26; 3:5,12,21) do reappear.[4] But if, as dispensational futurists contend, the church is shown to be in heaven (i.e., raptured) in Revelation 4:4-11 (as God reveals to John "what must take place after the completion of God's dealing with the churches in Revelation 2–3), then the church is the company of believers in heaven throughout the tribulation who are joined by the martyred tribulation saints. This identification removes the church from the tribulation, as many texts indicate (1 Thessalonians 1:10; 5:1-9; 2 Thessalonians 2:2,3; 2 Peter 2:9; Revelation 3:9,10), along with the understanding that a believing company (who apparently came to faith after the rapture and through the later witness of the 144,000 and the two witnesses) will go through the tribulation.

Nevertheless, those posttribulationists who argue that the church will go through the tribulation often state that this is necessary in order to purify it from its carnal ways. However, such a view does injustice to those Christian martyrs who have been through their own tribulations as part of the church. To be sure, the church in countries like the United States, where being a Christian is at present a protected and even preferred lifestyle, may appear to be less committed than the church struggling to survive under atheistic communism or Muslim terrorism. Nevertheless, God has told believers that the former, rather than the latter, is to be sought in Christian petition on behalf of "kings and all who are in authority, in order that we may lead a tranquil and quiet life in all godliness and dignity" (1 Timothy 2:2). If the church were in the tribulation, believers, in order to obey, would be required to intercede for Satan, the Antichrist and the false prophet as the principal agents of Christian persecution during that time (Revelation 12:12,13,17; 13:7-10; 15–17). But this would constitute a contradiction in conduct. According to Scripture, believers are ordered to resist and overcome them (James 4:7; 1 Peter 5:9; 1 John 2:14; 4:1-4; Revelation 11:5,6; 12:17; 13:7,10; 14:12). The only recorded prayers of the tribulation saints in regard to these evil entities are for their soon destruction (Revelation 6:10; 8:2,5; 11:18; 15:2-4; 19:1-6; compare with 16:5-7).

Although God's wrath comes with the purpose of judgment on unbelievers, the consequences of such worldwide wrath must affect everyone who lives on the earth. If God presently judges our American nation because of its leaders' sins and our society's sins of apostasy, pornography, abortion, infanticide, homosexuality and so forth, will not every Christian living in the country also suffer simply because they are citizens? Has this not been the case for Christians living in nations such as Germany and Great Britain, once the center for the Reformation and Christian missions, but now filled with anti-Semitism and sorcery? Protection during the tribulation is selectively afforded "the 144,000" virgin Jewish saints, the divinely appointed "two witnesses" and part of the believing Jewish remnant ("the woman who gave birth to the male [child]," i.e., the Jewish people). These are sealed and protected (Revelation 7:3,4; 9:4; 11:4-6; 12:6,14-16) in order to perform their unique witnesses. Nevertheless, even the 144,000 and the two witnesses are permitted to be killed once their missions are complete (Revelation 11:7; 14:1), and the rest of the Jewish believers are left open to Satan's attack (Revelation 12:17). All other believers during this period are apparently able to be killed in earthquakes (Revelation 11:13) or savaged by the Antichrist (Revelation 13:7-10). It is for this reason that the plagues are sent to avenge the blood of the saints (Revelation 16:6; 18:20; 19:2).

Jewish believers during this time will particularly suffer as Zechariah 13:8 notes: " 'And it will come about in all the land [of Israel],' declares the LORD, 'that two parts in it will be cut off and perish....' " Just as the Nazi Holocaust did not discriminate between believing and unbelieving Jews, neither will this future holocaust of the tribulation. We are not given a clear picture of what happens to Gentile believers, but they too are part of those martyred, appearing in heaven as a great company from "every tribe and tongue and people and nation" (Revelation 5:9; see also 7:9). Furthermore, the plagues that come with the sixth trumpet kill a third of all mankind. Since no special protection is said to be given to the general population of tribulation saints, it must be assumed that many are also killed by these plagues. The difference, of course, is that the plagues are designed to punish unbelievers and bring their repentance or cause their deaths and seal their doom (Revelation 6:15-17; 9:20,21; 11:13; 16:8,9,21), whereas for believers they serve to deliver them beyond the reach of Antichrist and his oppressions and increase their rewards in heaven. This is especially stated in Revelation 14:13: " 'Blessed are the dead who die in the Lord from now on!' 'Yes,' says the Spirit, 'that they may rest from their labors, for their deeds follow with them' " (compare Revelation 7:14-17; 11:18; 12:11).

Yet another eschatological option is offered by preterists who attempt to fit the details of the book of Revelation into the past historical event of the city of Jerusalem's destruction by the Romans in A.D. 70. They have to radically minimize the wrath of God, both in its extent and severity, in order to limit it geographically to Jerusalem and agree with the recorded siege and captivity of its Jewish citizenry.[5] They also have to contend with the fact that

Zechariah, Daniel, Jesus in the Olivet Discourse and the book of Revelation[6] all depict an opposite scenario: Gentiles as the object of wrath and Jews as the object of salvation.

The book of Revelation clearly reveals that in the tribulation judgments the "wrath of God is finished" (Revelation 15:1). The culmination of divine judgment comes with the final seven plagues that resemble the plagues against the Egyptians at the exodus (Exodus 7–10). Just as those judgments were sent to deliver Israel and punish its oppressors, so these will complete God's promise to "judge the world in righteousness" (Acts 17:31; compare with 2 Thessalonians 1:6-10). Since the plagues of the seventh bowl judgment are the "last" and end the wrath of God, they can only end with the final judgment of the wicked in the lake of fire (Revelation 20:12-15). This cannot be construed in any eschatological scheme to be fulfilled in the past nor reduced to a remnant. As Robert Thomas correctly observes, "No amount of rationalization—such as some theonomists practice to soften the tone of ultimacy, absoluteness, and universality in finding a fulfillment of these plagues in the A.D. 70 events surrounding the destruction of Jerusalem—can mitigate the force of this language regarding the finality of these plagues."

The apocalyptic wrath of preterism can only account for one judgment against a small portion of the Jewish population (most of whom were living comfortably outside the land of Israel at the time), while leaving the unjudged world free from a divine wrath exhausted 2,000 years ago. Yet even the prophet Daniel saw that the magnitude of this "time of distress" was so pervasive and final that it had to be followed by the resurrection of the righteous and wicked (see Daniel 12:1,2; Revelation 20:4-6; 20:5). Therefore, in order to appreciate the unparalleled nature of the tribulation, let us survey what Scripture reveals life will be like for those who will inhabit this most terrible time in all of history.

Life in the Age of Apocalypse

The beginning of wrath ("the day of the Lord") is seen with the first seal judgment with a rider on a white horse going out "conquering and to conquer" (Revelation 6:2). Prewrath tribulationalists hold that wrath is reserved for the last quarter of the tribulation and is not present here. However, this depends on what one sees as indicative of the wrath of God. The first use of the term *wrath* appears in Revelation 6:16,17 at the time of the sixth seal judgment, where the text reads: "the great day of their wrath has come...." However, the Greek verb *elthen* ("has come") used in verse 17 is aorist indicative, which looks back on wrath that has previously arrived. This wrath could be that portrayed in the sixth seal's terrestrial and celestial disturbances in the form of earthquake, atmospheric pollution and meteor/asteroid assault (Revelation 6:12-14). It could also just as easily encompass the previous five seals in which world conquest is initiated and global warfare ensues (Revelation 6:2-4), followed by worldwide famine with one-fourth of the earth's population destroyed (Revelation 6:5-8). According to Romans 1:18, "the wrath of God is revealed from heaven against all ungodliness and unrighteousness of men" and has been evidenced in cultures where idolatry and homosexuality have been tolerated (the continued cancerous presence of these lifestyles being part of the judgment itself). The end result of this corrupted society is that it is "worthy of death" (Romans 1:32). If the figure on the white horse in the first seal of Revelation 6:2 is the Antichrist, then his assault on the world to bring it under his corrupt control is the culmination of a sinful society ripened for wrath. Since 2 Thessalonians 2:3-12 connects the rise of Antichrist with worldwide lawlessness and deception (verses 4,8,10-12), the usurpation of deity as the climax of idolatry (verse 4) and the activity of Satan (verse 9), it should not be difficult to see Antichrist's foray for world conquest as the commencement of divine wrath on a mankind worthy of death. This is especially the case with the extensive and extraordinary manner of deaths that result from military slaughter, starvation, viral epidemics and wild animal attacks (Revelation 6:4-8).

Among the casualties of the violent opening months of the tribulation are believers who were killed because of their faith. They cry out for greater wrath to be sent to judge and avenge their deaths

(Revelation 6:9-10). From the beginning of the tribulation (with the rise of Antichrist seen in the signing of a covenant with the Israelis [Daniel 9:27]), God's wrath is progressively and increasingly unleashed on earth. With the conclusion of the sixth seal, the world's unbelieving population from the poorest to the richest, convinced that what they are experiencing is God's judgment, will believe that the Apocalyptic Age has come and the end of the world is at hand (Revelation 6:15-17). But the worst is yet to come.

As we move into the seventh seal and the trumpet judgments, we find that one-third of the world's vegetation is burned (Revelation 8:7), one-third of the earth's oceans and fresh water sources are polluted, one-third of all ships are destroyed (Revelation 8:8-11), one-third of the illuminaries are affected so that the world experiences unprecedented darkness (Revelation 8:12), a horrendous and unbelievably painful demonic attack occurs for five months (Revelation 9:1-12), one-third of the earth's population is killed (Revelation 9:15-18) and an earthquake accompanied by a huge hailstorm ravages the planet (Revelation 11:19). Adding to these disasters are seventh seal bowl judgments that plague mankind with loathsome and malignant sores (Revelation 16:2), completely destroy all life in the seas and the waters of the lakes, rivers and springs (Revelation 16:3,4), burn people severely with increased radiation from the sun (Revelation 16:8,9), cover the earth with deep darkness (Revelation 16:10) and allow demonic spirits to gather the nations of the world for war to imitate the battles of Armageddon (Revelation 16:12-16). These battles include an initial attack and final siege against Jerusalem (Zechariah 12:3–14:3), widespread destruction through an earthquake and 100-pound hailstones and the climax—the burning of the world's commercial center, Babylon (Revelation 16:18-21; 18:2-19).

To this catalog of catastrophes we must add the horrors of life lived under the government of a demonic, power-mad ruler with a god complex (Revelation 13:1-10). The Antichrist will enslave the nations of the world (Daniel 11:36-40), invade the land of Israel, desecrate the Jewish temple, persecute the Jewish people (Daniel 11:41-45; Matthew 24:15,16; Mark 13:14,15; 2 Thessalonians 2:4;

Revelation 11:2) and make war on all the saints (Revelation 13:7). He is joined by his deputy of deception, the false prophet, who will work deceitful miracles and require humanity to have complete allegiance to the Antichrist—or face death (see Revelation 13:11-15). However, to take the mark of identification with the Antichrist will be tantamount to renouncing God, thus dooming oneself forever (see Revelation 13:16-18). Overshadowing all of these figures is the evil one. Satan, cast down to the earth during the tribulation, will come with wrath against the world, knowing that his time is short (Revelation 12:12). This indicates that those who live in the tribulation will have spiritual encounters with demons as well as dramatic demonstrations of God's wrath.

No one in that day will be able to deny the existence of God or the supernatural, but neither will most people be able to avoid the deceptive signs and wonders that will lead them to embrace the Antichrist and their damnation (2 Thessalonians 2:9-12). Today the presence of the Holy Spirit through the church permits a restraint of such evil, including the advent of Antichrist and the deception of the devil (2 Thessalonians 2:6,7). Once the church is raptured, however, the Holy Spirit's influence will be ended, and evil from hell will literally break loose. Though at first the lack of such restraint may seem like a new peace for the world, it will be a pseudo-peace that will fast foment the formation of the world around one wicked will. Today, the worst war, the most terrible tyrant, the most dreadful disasters, the most pernicious pestilences are nothing by comparison with what awaits in the Age of Apocalypse.

What Will Your Life Be Like?

Since the Lord first revealed through His prophets and apostles the coming conditions of the Age of Apocalypse, people have thought through the last two millennia that various local and global crises might be the apocalyptic age. As early as the first century epistle to the Thessalonians we read that the widespread persecutions and problems they faced influenced many of them to panic and even alter their lifestyle in fear that the end was at hand (see

1 Thessalonians 1:6,7; 3:3-5; 2 Thessalonians 1:4,5; 2:2; 3:6-12). This has followed suit in every similar situation whether influenced by famines, plagues, world wars, atomic bombs, petroleum shortages, environmental and population crises or the Y2K problem. However difficult these days have been or will be, they are but the experience of life in a fallen world that will pale in the onslaught of the Age of Apocalypse. Nevertheless, the cataclysmic catastrophes of the tribulation are not "extinction level events." The world and all those who inhabit it during this time will suffer greatly, but God still has a plan for the planet (the millennial kingdom). Earth's eventual destruction will be followed by a new heaven and a new earth (2 Peter 3:10-13; Revelation 21:1; compare with Isaiah 65:17; 66:22).

During the present age of the church, believers should expect tribulations in this world and face them with faith instead of fear "for it is time for judgment to begin with the household of God; and if it begins with us first, what will be the outcome for those who do not obey the gospel of God?" (1 Peter 4:17). For such people, "the present heavens and earth by His word are being reserved for fire, kept for the day of judgment and destruction of ungodly men" (2 Peter 3:7).

When the tribulation commences with the signing of a covenant between the prince that shall come (Antichrist) and the "many" (the nation of Israel), as noted in Daniel 9:27, the world will enter a time of unparalleled deception followed by unprecedented destruction (see 2 Thessalonians 2:10-12). Like those in the days when Noah was building the ark, most of the world's population will not understand the severity of their condition until the flood of God's judgment has come and swept them all away (Matthew 24:37-39).

The people who today accept Jesus Christ as God's ark of safety and trust in His death for their sins on the cross as God's promise of escape from wrath will be removed from earth before the Age of the Apocalypse begins (1 Thessalonians 1:10; 4:13–5:11; 2 Thessalonians 2:1-5; Revelation 3:9,10). Their lives until that time may be full of tribulations, but they will be supported by a confidence in the Lord's strength and salvation for every trial. And believers' lives after that time will consist of unending joy and pleasure in the Lord's presence (Psalm 16:11; Revelation 21:4; 22:3-5).

But for those reading these words who have never believed the warning of the apocalypse nor fled to Christ for refuge, your lives will be lived (for however long you can endure) in the darkest days of the tribulation.

Some people may feel that tribulation warnings are scare tactics used to frighten people to faith, but each person must first come to understand the wrath of God that he deserves before he can accept the love of God, which he does not deserve. The Scriptures reveal that God Himself became a man (Jesus Christ) and He was made subject to His own wrath so that He "might deliver those who through fear of death were subject to slavery all their lives" (Hebrews 2:15). Therefore, in order to warn us of our imminent end and give us an opportunity to escape the wrath to come, God has made the message clear: "Inasmuch as it is appointed for men to die once and after this comes judgment, so Christ also, having been offered once to bear the sins of many, shall appear a second time for salvation without reference to sin, to those who eagerly await Him" (Hebrews 9:27,28). According to this promise, Christ came once to die for sinners and will return to judge them. Those who fear this judgment and flee to Him in faith will find the rest of that promise: that their horror of His coming will have been replaced by a hope in His coming.

So, my friend, what will your life be like in the Age of Apocalypse? These days have now been described for you; will you not seek God's salvation while the door of His ark remains open? Now is the time to escape the tribulation that is coming. Christ is coming... are you going with Him?

▼ ▼ ▼

CHAPTER 17

From Armageddon to the Millennium

John Walvoord

The period beginning with Armageddon and concluding with the opening of the millennium is one of the fascinating sections of prophecy that is full of important details that describe the end-time events. Central in these events is the second coming, but important events lead up to and follow it that are essential to understanding the rapid changes in the days to come.

Preceding End-Time Events

As the book of Revelation reveals, there will be an extensive time of catastrophic events between the rapture and Armageddon. This is described in Revelation 6:1–16:12. As the seal judgments follow one after another in Revelation 6:1-17, a panoramic, prophetic picture is provided for this whole period that has often been described as a period of seven years (based on Daniel 9:27), though the Scripture itself seems to concentrate on the great tribulation, which is the last three-and-a-half years. The first seal broken indicates a world conqueror. The Antichrist, "the beast coming out of the sea" (Revelation 13:1), conquers the world three-and-a-half years before the second coming (13:5). Also in the fourth seal (6:7,8), a fourth of the earth is destroyed, which would clearly indicate that the great tribulation is underway. The Scriptures state specifically in connection with the unsaved world that "the great day of their wrath has come, and who can stand?" (Revelation 6:17).

The opening of the seventh seal in Revelation 8:1 introduces a second series of sevens, described as trumpets. These, generally speaking, will destroy a third of the earth. Particularly catastrophic is the sixth trumpet, which declares that a third of the earth will be killed (9:15). When the seventh seal sounds (11:15), it introduces the climactic bowl judgments described in Revelation 16:1-21. While similar to the trumpet judgments, these instruments of divine judgment cover the whole earth and lead up to Armageddon as the nations of the world rebel against the world ruler.

The Final World War

The term *Armageddon,* which appears in Revelation 16:16, is the Aramaic translation of the Mountain of Megiddo located in the northern part of the plain of Esdraelom, later called the plain of Jezreel, and a place frequently mentioned in the Old Testament as important to military events (see Joshua 17:16; Judges 4:7; 5:21; 1 Samuel 31:1-3; 1 Kings 18:40; 2 Kings 9:27; 23:30; 2 Chronicles 35:20-24; Zechariah 12:11). Most expositors recognize that Armageddon is the Aramaic form of the Old Testament Megiddo.

Megiddo is designated the Tell El Mutesellim in the Plain of Esdraelom. At one time it was a city with massive fortifications and an important center for the Canaanites until Israel took it over about 1100 B.C. It was one of the chariot towns of Solomon (1 Kings 9:15; see also 10:26-29). At one time it included huge stables for horses, a governor's palace and a complicated water system. In modern times it has been subject to many excavations to uncover the historic past. It is important in prophecy as the central marshaling point for the great armies that participate in Armageddon, the final war leading up to the second coming of Christ. From the mountain itself, which is not a high mountain, the Mediterranean can be seen to the west and the Valley of the Plain of Esdraelom stretches out some 20 miles to the east and opens up into several other important valleys. This is where millions of people will be centered in the great war before the second coming, though the armies are actually 200 miles north and south over the whole land of Israel and stretching out all the way east to the Euphrates River. Revelation 16 mentions Armageddon as the important center for the great battle that follows the sixth bowl of the wrath of God, which permits the kings of the east to cross the Euphrates and descend upon Israel for the final battle.

Satanic Influence on the Battle

A strange paradox exists in the situation. Revelation 16:13,14 describes demons as three unclean spirits like frogs that come out of the mouth of the dragon, the beast and the false prophet, enticing the kings of the world to gather for the battle which is called "the battle of the great day of God Almighty." Less than three years before, the devil had deceived the world into accepting the Antichrist as the world ruler (13:7). Under those circumstances, if the devil had united the world under the world dictator, why does he now encourage the nations to rebel against him? The answer is found in subsequent Scriptures which indicate the satanic purpose to gather all the armies of the world together in view of the fact that at the second coming the army of heaven would descend with Christ to take charge of the earth. Satan wanted all the armies available to fight the army from heaven. Ultimately, this proves to be a complete failure. When Christ comes He destroys the armies with a word (19:15), and no battle ever takes place between the army of heaven and the armies of earth.

The Old Testament mentions Megiddo often but principally in connection with the death of Josiah, the king who attempted to oppose the king of Egypt (2 Kings 23:29,30; 2 Chronicles 35:20-24). The extent of the future conflict at Armageddon is made clear by the fact that 200 million soldiers alone crossed the Euphrates River from the east adding to the millions already there (see Revelation 9:16). It is by all odds the greatest war of all history. Because such an army seems impossible, some people believe they are actually demons, though there is no proof for that interpretation. The Orient with more than one billion people in population could provide such an army.

Though it is common for Bible teachers of prophecy to picture this war as one of nuclear character, most of the evidence points to traditional warfare with the armies sweeping north and south across Israel (see Daniel 11:40-45). Zechariah 14 pictures house-to-house warfare, which is not compatible with nuclear war. The king of the south, namely the African forces, opposes the king of the north, who apparently is the Antichrist (and includes all the military power of Europe and the former Soviet states). But the battle is not resolved until the day of Christ's second coming.

Other Events Preceding Armageddon

Preceding the second coming are a number of other world events. Revelation 17 chronologically precedes the events of Revelation 16 and pictures the world church as a harlot astride a scarlet-colored beast. The beast is the ten-nation group led by the Antichrist, and the harlot is the world church movement—devoid of all true Christians and guilty of putting genuine Christians to death (Revelation 17:3-6). Revelation 17 pictures her rise to fame and power and at the same time mentions her ultimate destruction by the ten kings under the Antichrist, who are declared in Revelation 17:16 to hate her. The ten kings will destroy her and burn her with fire, the purpose being to clear the deck entirely so that the final form of world religion in the great tribulation can be the worship of Satan and the worship of the Antichrist.

The Destruction of Babylon

Also in the period leading up to Armageddon, and somewhat simultaneous with it, is the destruction of Babylon. Some identify Babylon with Rome and the city of Rome but obviously Babylon has another historic location. In Revelation 18 it is described as a great commercial city, which it is not now. Though there is dispute as to its actual part in the end times, it seems that Babylon or the site of ancient Babylon could be the capital of the final world government that has been transformed into a commercial city. Many prophecies, however, have held that Babylon would be ultimately destroyed just prior to the second coming and that it will never be inhabited again. Though the prophetic picture is somewhat complicated by the predicted attacks on Babylon already fulfilled when the future is declared in Isaiah 13:20 (for instance, "she will never be inhabited or lived in through all generations"), it goes on to speak how it would be a waste without population (Isaiah 13:19-22; Jeremiah 50:2,3,39-46; 51:37-48). This has never happened in history and indicates the necessity of this ultimate destruction just before the second coming. Jeremiah 50:1–51:8 provides a complete picture of this future destruction and ultimate desolation of the city.

The Final Bowl Judgment

While the battle of the great day of God Almighty is under way (Revelation 16:12-16), the final bowl of wrath is poured out, consisting of a gigantic earthquake that destroys all the cities of the world except for Israel (Revelation 16:17-21). Mountains and islands disappear, and the earth will be pelted with huge supernatural hailstones weighing 100 pounds each. It is a final act of terrible destruction on the earth with a great loss of life and property that just precedes the second coming of Christ.

The Wedding Feast Announced

According to Revelation 19:1-10, barely preceding the account of the second coming the announcement is made concerning the wedding feast of the Lamb. Many expositors feel that this is accomplished in heaven after the rapture, but its location just before the second coming announces the wedding supper in connection with the second coming of Christ. This may indicate that it will be actually celebrated after the second coming in the millennial kingdom.

It will probably not be a literal banquet but a time of rejoicing for the people of God in the glory of God's grace and salvation.

Christ Comes Bringing Angels and Saints
(Revelation 19:11-21)

The second coming of Christ is mentioned frequently in the Old and New Testaments[1] and many passages in the New Testament.[2] The many passages devoted to this subject indicate how important it is. As the four gospels portray Christ in His first coming, so the book of Revelation portrays events before and after the future second coming of Christ. In Revelation 19:11-16, He is described as coming on a white horse, a symbol of victory, to judge the world; He is followed by the armies of heaven. He has the power to strike down the nations (verse 15), and the prediction is He will rule "with an iron scepter." His coming will express the wrath of God against wickedness in the human situation. It is clear that the heavens will be ablaze with the glory of God accompanied as He is by millions of holy angels and saints, who are moving from heaven to the Mount of Olives in preparation for the millennial kingdom. The descent will not be a rapid event but will undoubtedly take 24 hours so the earth can turn, permitting everyone to see the glory of Christ in the heavens. Satan and the unsaved alike will realize that this is the second coming of Christ, but it is too late for those who are not ready for His second coming.

The Destruction of the Armies of Earth

One of the first acts following the second coming is the destruction of the armies who will forget their differences and unite to fight the army from heaven. This is described in graphic terms in Revelation 19:17-19 and is confirmed in verse 21 in the statement that all the wicked are killed on this occasion.

Christ captures the world ruler, the Antichrist (described as the beast), and his assistant (described as the false prophet) and casts them into the "fiery lake of burning sulfur" (Revelation 19:19,20). This lake was previously described as the place for the ultimate end of the satanic world (Matthew 25:41-44). While all the wicked who have died are in Hades, up to this point the lake of fire has not been occupied; the beast and the false prophet are the first occupants.

After the second coming a series of prophetic events will follow preparing the world for a future millennial kingdom. First of all, in Revelation 20:1-3 it is prophesied that Satan will be bound, rendered inactive and unable to deceive the nations in the future millennium. Amillenarians attempt to make this event fulfilled in the first coming of Christ under a theory of recapitulation. At chapter 20 they believe the scene refers back to the first coming, but there is no evidence supporting the prophecies—and these prophecies are not fulfilled in the present age. As is very obvious in our present situation, Satan is not bound now, unable to deceive the world. Satan, in fact, is described in 1 Peter 5:8 as "a roaring lion looking for someone to devour." Christians are exhorted to resist him because he is still active (1 Peter 5:9). Many other New Testament Scriptures indicate that Satan is always limited by God, as illustrated in Job, and is unable to go beyond God's permissive will. Nevertheless, Satan is very active in the present age and will continue to be so until the future millennial kingdom when he will be bound. He will be cast out of heaven three-and-one-half years before the second coming (Revelation 12:7-9).

Amillenarians also oppose the important event of the resurrection of the martyred dead described in Revelation 20:4-6. These martyred dead are described as those who "had not worshiped the beast or his image and had not received his mark on their foreheads or their hands" (Revelation 20:4). This took place only two or three years before the second coming of Christ in the great tribulation as the Scripture testifies in verse 4: "[They were] beheaded because of their testimony for Jesus and because of the Word of God." They now are resurrected for the purpose of reigning with Christ for 1,000 years. This explicitly teaches that the 1,000 years will follow the second coming of Christ—an interpretation opposed by those who do not agree to a millennium. They are hard put to explain this verse. Their leaders declare that verse 4 is talking about the new birth of the believer, but there is no connection. Beheading

is not a part of the new birth. There is absolutely nothing in the passage that teaches that this is the new birth nor is there any indication that the new birth is what it is revealing. Accordingly, verse 4
is one of the important texts demonstrating beyond question that
the 1,000 years of Christ's reign follow the second coming rather
than preceding it in some form.

It is probable that Daniel 12:1,2, which also speaks of the Old
Testament saints being resurrected, will be fulfilled at this time.
Some believe this will occur at the rapture, but at the rapture those
raised are declared to have been "the dead in Christ" (1 Thessalonians 4:16). Their position in Christ by the baptism of the Spirit
was true only in the period from Pentecost to the rapture. It was not
realized in any preceding age as witnessed by the fact that all four
gospels predict it as a future event. Accordingly, probably the Old
Testament saints will be raised at the same time as the martyred
dead of the tribulation.

Most important to observe is that there is no rapture at the
second coming and that the resurrections mentioned here apparently occur several days *after* the second coming. There is no resurrection or rapture on the day of the second coming itself. Thus,
the posttribulational view that this is when the rapture and the resurrection take place is impossible. This is confirmed in Matthew
24–25, when Christ answers the disciples' question concerning
signs of the second coming, indicating that the great tribulation
itself is the sign of the second coming. Christ also gives them something they did not ask for—the judgment of the Gentiles after the
second coming. In Matthew 25:31-46 this judgment is pictured as
a gathering of sheep and goats all mixed up together, goats representing the unsaved and sheep representing the saved. It is a most
interesting passage because it describes salvation by its evidence.
Because in the great tribulation the sheep who befriend the Jews
(the brethren) will do so only because they are Christians—that
becomes a mark of their Christian faith. Most significant again is
the fact that the sheep and the goats are all mixed up several days
after the second coming. If a rapture had taken place, the sheep
would have been removed before this event. The purpose of this

judgment is to eliminate the goats (the unsaved) and prepare those who are saved to enter the millennial kingdom.

There is a similar judgment on Israel described in Ezekiel 20:33-38 and other passages. Christ declares that He will regather Israel from all over the world and purge out the rebel (the unsaved). It is declared in Ezekiel 20:34, that He will "gather you from the countries where you have been scattered." In verse 35 it says He will execute judgment upon them, and verse 38 declares that He will purge out those who are unsaved, who revolt and rebel, but the godly will be brought into the land. This is also confirmed in Jeremiah 30:5-11, where it is declared that Israel will go through a time of terrible judgment called "a time of trouble for Jacob" (verse 7). But the Israelites will be delivered and ruled over by David their king (verse 9) who will be raised at the second coming. This serves to date the time as well as the significance of it. Chapter 31:31-34 continues this account of gathering the Israelites and leading them to their Promised Land. This is also confirmed in Jeremiah 31:35-37, where Israel is declared to continue as long as the sun and moon endure.

A sweeping prophecy is also recorded in Ezekiel 39:25-28, where it is declared that God will bring back the entire nation of Israel from all over the world at the time of the second coming. After the purging judgment of Ezekiel 20, those that survive and who are saved will inherit the Promised Land, which will be divided among the 12 tribes as described in Ezekiel 47:13–48:29. The gates of the city of Jerusalem are mentioned in Ezekiel 48:30-35.

If current prophecy is interpreted in its normal literal sense, it yields exactly what the premillenarians have been teaching—when Christ comes there will be 1,000 years of His reign on earth.

The various judgments mentioned in Scripture are intended to be fulfilled in the 135 days between the second coming and the beginning of the millennial kingdom (see Daniel 12:11). In that period all the necessary judgments and resurrections will take place that make possible the beginning of this millennial kingdom.

▼ ▼ ▼

Doors to the Future

William T. James

"Forget the book of Revelation. We have all the facts about Armageddon."[1]

The CNN anchorwoman's opening statement into the lead story was given with lighthearted inflection. Although her words undoubtedly were intended to grab the attention of viewers in preparation for the ensuing story about *Armageddon,* the movie sensation of the hour, the tongue-in-cheek lead-in nonetheless appropriately reflects the worldview of biblical prophecy. Hollywood, the facetious opening implies, knows better than the God of the Bible what the future holds for mankind.

Dr. David Jeremiah said, "Satan hates the book of Revelation because it foretells his doom."[2] It should not surprise us that a worldwide news medium should broadcast with such lack of understanding because Satan, who is the prince of this world, conducts an ongoing propaganda campaign that presents near truths designed to keep fallen mankind on the broad way that leads to destruction.

Jesus said, "Enter ye in at the strait gate; for wide is the gate, and broad is the way, that leadeth to destruction, and many there be which go in thereat; because strait is the gate, and narrow is the way, which leadeth unto life, and few there be that find it" (Matthew 7:13,14). There are, Christ tells us, two roads or pathways through life in the physical body. Because of man's nature, fallen since the rebellion in the Garden of Eden, people are on the wide, easy path of least resistance that leads to their eternal separation from God, their Creator. Jesus Christ represents the other pathway—the narrow *Way*—that leads people to eternal life in heaven, forever in the presence of God who adopts them as His children because of their trust in His Son as the only atonement for sin.

Every heartbeat moves you one moment nearer to eternity. You will enter that infinite realm through one of two doors. You may choose which of those doors you will ultimately enter while life yet pulses within your breast. However, by not choosing, you are swiftly moving toward the door beyond which awaits torment and damnation that will never end (see Luke 16:19-31). While such a view runs counter to this world system's theologies and philosophies of "feel-goodisms" and salvation by "do-goodisms," and as unpopular as it is to point out that man is a fallen creature that needs saving, ignoring the truth of God's Word means souls lost forever. Thankfully, "the Lord is ... not willing that any should perish, but that all should come to repentance" (2 Peter 3:9).

The Hissing Serpent

Satan's all-consuming purpose is to plant in the minds of men, women and children a big question mark about God. Because there is within each of us a God-shaped soul-space, the great deceiver knows he cannot convince mankind there is no God. His drive is to create doubt about the Creator of all things: Is God a being or just a force of some kind like that portrayed in the "Star Wars" trilogy? Is God existential in His dealings with His creation? Has He simply created and set all things in motion, then moved on, leaving that creation to evolve and fend for itself like is presented by the deist view? Or is God a deity who can be trusted? Can He be relied upon to keep His word, to see those who trust in Him through the vicissitudes of life and bring them into His loving, eternal presence when physical life on earth has run its course? The latter of these deceptive questions was used by the serpent in the Garden of Eden (read Genesis 3). "Yea, hath God said?" was the question Lucifer the fallen one implanted within the minds of the first man and woman (see Genesis 3:1). *"Ye shall not surely die"* the devil told the couple. He was implying that God wanted to keep them ignorant and under His thumb because He didn't want them to become as gods, which gaining the forbidden knowledge would accomplish. In essence, Satan planted in their minds the belief that God is a liar. His Word cannot be trusted.

The serpent hisses the same subtle propaganda today into the ears of this self-willed generation of earth dwellers. If we will look and listen attentively, we can perceive an incessant assault upon the voracity of God's truth coming at us from every angle.

Media Manipulation

The CNN story alluded to at the beginning of this conclusion is mild in comparison to the many attacks on God's truth—particularly in the area of biblical prophecy—while human history moves through the transition from one millennium to the next. Some might say that it is a natural thing for there to be increased interest generated during such a dramatic, exciting period. Movies, TV programs, speculation within news journalism—these things are to be expected to exploit the hopes, fears and hunger for spectacular entertainment while earth moves into not only a new century but also into a new millennium. And exploited they continue to be! However, it is not a *natural* exploitation. It's a *supernatural* exploitation that more and more becomes evident to the spiritually attuned eye and ear. Satan, who has never ceased his assault against God's truth, continues to intensify his attack at every point within the arena of human affairs. People's almost-fanatic desire to gain supernatural knowledge about the future is fertile ground for the great deceiver to work his nefarious, anti-God subterfuge. Like the pied piper, Satan enchants the majority of humanity, enticing people to follow him down the broad way to the open door into the eternal abyss.

Satan's attempted undermining of God's truth is more and more observable in these closing days of the Church Age. He slyly chooses not to completely omit biblical prophecy as he influences media to create programs catering to their audience's voracious appetites for knowledge of what the future holds. He subtly weaves sparse, disconnective textual bits and pieces from Bible prophecy within the nonsense and lies of false prophets in order to give their false prophecies an air of validity and believability. Always the message from the mind of the deceiver is that man and his humanistic solutions can overcome the dire predictions for mankind's future if everyone will come together as one in peace and harmony. The great deceiver hisses convincingly into the already-inflated egos of the one-world builders that they are "as gods." They must, he whispers, overcome all obstacles totally apart from the deity Christian fanatics claim is the only One who knows the end from the beginning. Satan's voice whispers against the One who prophesies a time of unprecedented trouble for the world because of mankind's rebellion against Him and rejection of His Son, Jesus Christ. Revelation 19:10 says, *"The testimony of Jesus is the spirit of prophecy."* The book of Revelation is not just a series of *revelations* of judgments, although it does reveal great details about the coming wrath of God and the reasons for judgment. The book is the *revelation of Jesus Christ*—the unveiling of the truth about who Christ is in His glorified magnificence. Satan is presently mounting an all-out offensive in an attempt to pervert and thwart the truth of God's prophetic Word. The nucleus of his attack centers around the lie that the book of Revelation is confusing, cannot be understood and, indeed, is not meant to be understood because it is a mishmash of symbolism and allegory that was never intended to be in the canon of Scripture. Tragically, many people in the body of Christ choose to fall for this satanic lie. Even some Christian seminaries choose to ignore God's revelation of His Son Jesus Christ by treating biblical prophecy, and the book of Revelation in particular, as symbolic or as history already accomplished. This despite the fact that Revelation 22:19 states, "If any man shall take away from the words of the book of this prophecy, God shall take away his part from the tree of life, and out of the holy city, and from the things which are written in this book."

Christians who fall for this luciferian deception not only are missing the blessing promised by God to those who read and heed the revelation (see Revelation 1:3), but they are unwittingly helping Satan in his full-fledged assault on God's truth as he leads lost men, women and children to eternity apart from God.

The serpent must divert people from earnest study of true Bible prophecy because fulfilled prophecy is proof-positive that Satan— not God—is the liar. Lucifer needs little help from deceived Christians, although he welcomes it. Satan has his own spin-masters working overtime in the media, spewing forth the last-days deception that God and His Word is irrelevant—that mankind holds within itself the ability to solve all the world's problems now and in the future.

Lucifer, the fallen one, is the most skilled of all counterfeiters. He is presently producing a masterful imitation of true Bible prophecy. As stated previously, even many of God's own children— those who have accepted Christ as Savior—are susceptible to false prophecy. They lack discernment because they choose to ignore God's prophetic word or are victims of false teachers. At the same time, it is overwhelmingly apparent that people all over are devouring the sensational, entertaining half-truths and outright lies fed them by the serpent's false-prophecy propaganda machine.

Television series that include *Sightings* and the *X-Files,* movies such as *Armageddon* and *Deep Impact* and other entertainment specials presenting apocalyptic and/or paranormal themes fill the minds of people. Psychic hotlines lure viewers by the thousands, promising those who call astounding glimpses into their futures. Cyberspace offers chat-room seances and soothsaying through Internet access. "Virtual reality" no doubt will soon produce occultic experiences beyond anything yet imagined. Indeed, Jesus'

warning that false prophets shall arise takes on new and unantici-
pated meaning in these troubling but fascinating times. It is now
becoming obvious, I believe, that *false prophecies* encompass far
more than just a departure from basic biblical doctrine as fundamentalist theologians have long considered the term to encompass.
Satan in these last days has, through his infectious inspiration,
brought forth from the creative minds of those in the entertainment world an intertwining of Bible prophecy with occultic seers
and their devilish soothsaying practices to produce the current
deception about what the future holds.

The Author of Confusion

Confusion continues to be the fallen one's most effective tool.
The willingness of his victims to listen to his sensational lies rather
than accept God's truth has never been more observable than in
our time. Is it any wonder that those who enter the tribulation
period will fall totally for the great *lying wonders* Antichrist will
perform? Satan's führer will put over a lie that will deceive virtually
the whole world. "And for this cause God shall send them strong
delusion, that they should believe the lie" (2 Thessalonians 2:11).

One recent television program demonstrates that the grand
deceiver, through undiscerning entertainment media producers, is
still about the business of planting big question marks about God in
the minds of human beings. One can almost sense the serpent's
question: *"Yea, hath God said?"*

A "biblical" scholar was interviewed by the program's narrator.
The subject was Joseph's prophecies that his family would bow
down to him. The narrator said, "... Despite the biblical account,
most scholars dismiss the interpretation that Joseph could see the
future." The so-called scholar then expanded on the narrator's
words:

> ...What has come down to us has been filtered through chroniclers
> and writers and translators, so it is essentially at this point, I think,
> impossible to note whether those were valid prophecies or not. I feel
> pretty strongly, of course, that they weren't....[3]

The narrator then confuses us even more by first emphasizing the big question mark about the veracity of God's Word, then abruptly informing us that Joseph's predictions came true.

> ... The controversy over Joseph's powers, as described in the Bible, may never be resolved. Whatever his prophetic ability, the Bible leaves no doubt that Joseph helped a nation avert certain disaster....[4]

The program's narrator then moves us to think seriously about the book of Revelation:

> Another prophet of ancient times, however, delivered a much more ominous prediction for all mankind. This prophecy of doom appears in the biblical book of Revelation....

An actress then narrates their version of the Scripture in question:

> There followed hail and fire mingled with blood which fell on the earth and a third of the earth was burnt up and a third of the trees were burnt up and all green grass was burnt up....

The original narrator next poses the question: "Is the book of Revelation a prophecy of our future? Was its author divinely inspired to see the cataclysm to come?" Then a video of the modern Isle of Patmos filled the screen while the narrator continued, " ... It was here, 2,000 years ago, that the author of Revelation, known to us only as John of Patmos, became convinced that the end was near." The narrative then set about to major on minor matters.

> The identity of the author remains a perplexing mystery. And yet his words are so powerful in their conviction that millions have believed the ominous predictions. To this day, the question of when this prophet of doom believed the apocalypse would take place is still unanswered....

As if directly out of God's Word in 2 Peter 3:3,4, "Knowing this first, that there shall come in the last days scoffers, walking after their own lusts, and saying, Where is the promise of his coming? For since the fathers fell asleep, all things continue as they were from the beginning of the creation," the narrator concluded:

...As the first millennium drew to a close, countless Europeans were convinced that the end of the world was at hand. Although obviously the dreaded cataclysm did not occur in the year 1,000, prophets in the centuries that followed continued to issue dire predictions.[5]

Again, the "scholar" interjected his skepticism.

...Disasters happen every year somewhere in the world. So it's very easy to look at the San Francisco earthquake and say, "Oh, that was the earthquake that was foretold in the book of Revelations [sic]. Therefore, the world will end in 1995." But it didn't.[6]

The Icons of False Prophecy

Although the world-system writes and speaks of the true prophets of God in terms that question their legitimacy instead of validating them, the deceptive one's spin-masters write and speak glowingly, almost reverently, of the false prophets. Although in some cases these false prophets were treated as poorly by their contemporaries as were God's prophets by their contemporaries, the false future predictors are today put upon the pedestal of adoration that approaches worship. Chief among those icons of false prophecy stands Nostradamus.

Nostradamus, born in France in 1503, became a renowned physician through his efforts to treat victims of the terrifying disease known as the Black Plague, which wiped out one-third of the population of Europe. But Nostradamus' worldwide acclaim that is even today on the ascent while earth moves toward the year 2000 stems from, as the narrator for the TV program "Prophecies" tells us, "what some assert was an extraordinary ability to see into the future." The narrative continues glowingly: "He recorded more than 1,000 prophecies written in cryptic, four-line verses called quatrains. Believers in Nostradamus' predictions insist he accurately foretold the most turbulent events in the history of France...."

The narrative proposes that the French seer unerringly predicted the French Revolution, which climaxed in the execution of the French royal family. The same "scholar" narrator that spoke of his skepticism about Bible prophecy and the prophets Joseph and John tells us, "Nostradamus' uncanny perception of the French Revolution doesn't end with the death of Louis XVI. He also gives us details of how Marie Antoinette would meet her end."[7]

The French soothsayer of half a millennium ago was lauded then by the program's narrator and by other so-called authorities and scholars for having predicted with phenomenal accuracy the rise, conquest and demise of both Napoleon Bonaparte and Adolf Hitler. This, even though Nostradamus' "prophecies" were admittedly in sometimes indecipherable or veiled poetic language.

Near the end of the program, the host-narrator summarized in longing, ethereal inflection the desires of mankind to see into the future. God, of course, who knows the end from the beginning and has given man all he needs to know about future things, often providing great details, is left out of the summation.

"The elusive dream of seeing into the future continues to tantalize us. To even imagine the prospect opens unlimited possibilities." Another of the "scholars" expounds further: "None of us want to be on the next Titanic or the next 747 to crash or at the scene of the next earthquake. And if we believe that there is a way of telling the future, we at least have the illusion that we can prevent that kind of thing and save ourselves and our loved ones. And that's a very powerful motive...."[8]

Saving himself, you see, is man's god-like ambition, and it has been since he partook of the tree of the knowledge of good and evil. The serpent-tempter continues to be quite effective in perpetuating that grandiose though fatal notion.

Two Doors to Your Eternal Future

Only two doors exist through which you will one day pass. You have no choice but to enter eternity through one or the other. You *do* have a choice while you still draw breath and can think clearly. You can select the door through which you will pass into the next realm of existence.

Much attention has already been given in this conclusion to the broad way—Satan's way—that leads to the door of eternal separation from God. Let us turn our thoughts now to the wonderful prophetic truth of Almighty God who is Jesus Christ, "the way, the truth and the life" (see John 14:6). Jesus is the door to an eternity magnificently brilliant beyond our finite minds' ability to imagine.

As contributors to *Foreshadows of Wrath and Redemption,* we are absolutely convinced by the truth we find in God's Word that we live in a time very near the moment when the Lord Jesus Christ will shout "Come up hither!" (Revelation 4:1). The rapture will occur, and everyone who has accepted Christ, both living and dead, during the Church Age will vanish from the earth's surface *in a moment, in the twinkling of an eye* (1 Corinthians 15:52). We will meet Jesus in the air above the planet and will be taken home to God the Father by His only begotten Son to live forever with Him in the dwelling place He has prepared for us (see John 14:1-6).

We believe Christ's return is imminent; it can happen at any moment. The study of God's Word convinces us that God "has not appointed us to wrath, but to obtain salvation through our Lord Jesus Christ" (1 Thessalonians 5:9). For we look not for Antichrist, or for tribulation (the apocalypse), or for the world-system of politics and socioeconomics to get better and better, but for the Blessed Hope of Titus 2:13. We look for Jesus Christ, who will keep us out of the very hour of the coming seven years of Tribulation (read Revelation 3:10). And we want to help others understand the truth and redemption found in Christ.

Unfortunately, Satan succeeds in his deception. The heresies that the great deceiver plants in the minds of people—even Christians— are being accepted by greater numbers of people than ever before. One heresy that abounds even in fundamentalist, evangelical circles today is that the rapture is a false teaching and false prophecy that has come into existence only within the last two centuries. Not only do those who propose this heresy show their ignorance of and lack of study of the whole counsel of God, but they also show their lack of knowledge of secular history as well. The biblical rapture is not a "pie in the sky," dreamy-eyed fantasy of rescue concocted by some demented woman in the nineteenth century as some claim. Our belief is centered in and on the very heart of God and His character and upon His Blessed Son, Jesus Christ. This is the Savior who paid not *some,* but *all* our sin-debt on that old rugged cross at Calvary nearly 2,000 years ago. Our forefathers in the Christian faith held to this *Blessed Hope* to the same degree as we do.

Dr. J. Vernon McGee summarized those Christian forefathers' beliefs that Christ could return at any moment during their time:

> They [men in the past] were looking for Christ to come. They were not looking for the Great Tribulation and they weren't even looking for the Millennium. They were looking for Him to come, and that is the very heart of the premillennial viewpoint ... as we hold it today.

> Even as far back as Barnabas, who was a co-worker with Paul, [it] has been quoted ... [that] the true Sabbath is the 1,000 years when Christ comes back to reign. Clement, in 96 A.D. [who] was bishop of Rome, says, "Let us every hour expect the kingdom of God. We know not the day." Polycarp, in 108 A.D., who was bishop of Smyrna and was burned at the stake there, said, "He will raise us from the dead. We shall reign with Him."

> Ignatius, who was bishop of Antioch, and who Eusebius the historian says was the apostle Peter's successor, said "Consider the times and expect Him." Papias in 116 A.D. was bishop of Hierapolis, whom Irenaeus said saw and heard John, said, "There will be 1,000 years when the reign of Christ personally will be established on earth." And Justin Martyr, in 150 A.D., said, "I and all others who are orthodox Christians on all points know there will be a thousand years in Jerusalem as Isaiah and Ezekiel declared."

> And then Irenaeus, in 175 A.D., said that "This can only be fulfilled upon our Lord's personal return to the earth." And that was the kingdom ....The Lord said He would drink anew of the wine in the kingdom. Tertullian, in 200 A.D., said, "We do indeed confess that a kingdom is promised upon earth."

> ...Martin Luther said, "Let us not think that the coming of Christ is far off." Calvin, in his Third Book of the Institute, said, "Scripture uniformly enjoins us to look with expectation for the advent of Christ." And Dr. Elliott wrote: "All primitive expositors except Origin and the

few who reject Revelation were premillennial." And [here is another quote from an early] ... work on church history: "It was so distinctly and prominently mentioned that we do not hesitate in regarding it as the general belief of that age." And Chillingsworth declares: "It was the doctrine believed and taught by the most eminent fathers of the age next to the apostles, whom none of that age condemned." Dr. Adolph Barnack wrote "the earlier fathers, Irenaeus, Hippolytus, Tertullian, believed it because it was part of the tradition of the early church. It is the same all through the fourth century with those Latin theologians who escaped the influence of Greek speculation."

... When anyone says that this is something that was originated 100 years ago by some old witch in England, my friend, you don't know what you're talking about. And after all, what does the Bible say? ... What does Paul say? What does the Lord Jesus say? What does the Word of God say? That's the important thing.[9]

The Rapture Is Imminent!

Even though historical documentation that the early church fathers were pretribulation rapture believers proves that we are in good company, it is the overwhelming body of prophetic Scripture itself that convinces us that God will spare Christians of this age from His coming wrath just as He did when He removed Lot to the city of Zoar (see Genesis 19). God said, "I cannot do anything till thou be come thither" (19:22). By that God meant He would not send judgmental wrath upon Sodom until His servant Lot was safely at Zoar.

By the same token, we know that Christ's coming for His bride in the air is imminent because we trust and believe totally in the absolute truth of God's prophetic Word. Again, so many passages of prophetic Scripture direct our attention to Christ's second coming and to His appearing for His bride, the church, we watch intently as commanded by our Lord in Mark 13:37: "And what I say unto you I say unto all, Watch." But more than this, God's prophetic Word foretells of many specific characteristics of the human condition and of planetary plight that will mark the tribulation period itself. Thus, we know that Christ's sudden snatching of His bride from the earth must be very near indeed since those signals for the apocalypse are already in this prewrath era, bombarding this generation with increasing frequency and intensity.

We know that those saved by faith in Jesus Christ are not appointed to wrath (1 Thessalonians 5:9) and will be kept from the time of God's wrath (Revelation 3:10). Therefore, when the signals of His coming wrath begin to happen, we are to look up and lift our heads, for our redemption draweth near (Luke 21:28).

Every chapter within this book has provided explicit insights into where this generation stands today in relation to God's prophetic timetable. Reread and consider the foreshadows of wrath inundating this world in profusion. From the rapidly spreading apostasy developing through ecumenism to the precise alignment of nations as predicted in God's Word to the perilous times Paul warned about in 2 Thessalonians 3, everything foreshadows our redemption—that thrilling moment as foreseen by John in his vision: "After this I looked and, behold, a door was opened in heaven; and the first voice that I heard was, as it were, of a trumpet talking with me; which said, Come up here … " (Revelation 4:1).

In order to enter that door, you must first open *your* door, the door to your heart (your soul). Jesus said, "Behold, I stand at the door and knock: if any man hear my voice, and open the door, I will come in to him, and will sup with him, and he with me" (Revelation 3:20). It is your decision to make. There will never be one more important than the choice you make regarding the doors to eternity. God's Word says, "Be ye therefore, ready also: for the Son of man cometh at an hour when ye think not" (Luke 12:40).

Right this moment, choose Jesus Christ, who faithfully promises "surely, I come quickly" (Revelation 22:20). Even so, come, Lord Jesus.

▼ ▼ ▼

Contributing Author
Biographies

William T. James,
General Editor

William "Terry" James is an interested observer of historical and contemporary human affairs, analyzing conduct, issues and events in light of biblical truth. He is frequently interviewed in national broadcasts.

James has authored, compiled, and edited six previous books: *Storming Toward Armageddon: Essays in Apocalypse; The Triumphant Return of Christ: Essays in Apocalypse II; Earth's Final Days: Essays in Apocalypse III; Raging into Apocalypse: Essays in Apocalypse IV; Foreshocks of Antichrist* and *Forewarning: Approaching the Final Battle Between Heaven and Hell.* Each book presents a series of insightful essays by well-known prophecy scholars, writers and broadcasters.

As a former public relations director for several companies, James has written and edited all forms of business communications, both in print and electronic media. Prior to that he worked as creative director for advertising agencies and did political and corporate speech writing as well as formulated position papers on various issues for clients he served. In addition to writing, he worked closely with clients and broadcast media in putting together and conducting press conferences and other forums.

▼ ▼ ▼

Dave Breese

Dave Breese is an internationally known author, lecturer, radio broadcaster and Christian minister. He ministers in church and area-wide evangelistic crusades, leadership conferences, student gatherings and related preaching missions.

Dr. Breese is president of Christian Destiny Inc. of Hillsboro, Kansas, a national organization committed to the advancement of Christianity through evangelistic crusades, literature distribution, university gatherings and the use of radio and television.

Breese is active in ministry to college and university students, speaking to them from a background of theology and philosophy. He graduated from Judson College and Northern Seminary and has taught philosophy, apologetics and church history. He is frequently involved in lectures, debates and discussion sessions on university campuses.

Breese travels more than 100,000 miles a year and has spoken to crowds across North America, Europe, Asia, the Caribbean and Latin America. His lectures and debates at universities in the United States and overseas center on the confrontation of Christianity and modern thought.

Breese is also the author of a number of books, including *Discover Your Destiny, His Infernal Majesty, Know the Marks of Cults, Living for Eternity* and *Seven Men Who Rule from the Grave.* His books, booklets and magazine articles have enjoyed worldwide readership. He also publishes "Destiny Newsletter," a widely distributed periodical presenting the Christian view of current events and "The Collegiate Newsletter," a monthly publication dedicated to reaching college students with biblical truth and stimulating interest in the prophetic Word.

▼ ▼ ▼

Joseph R. Chambers

Joseph R. Chambers holds a Doctor of Divinity degree from Indiana Christian University. He is the founder and president of Paw Creek Ministries in Charlotte, North Carolina; founder and chairman of Concerned Charlotteans and cofounder of Concerned Voice for Child Care. He hosts a weekly radio program, "Open Bible Dialogue," and the "Concerned Charlotteans Presents" TV show. He has authored and coauthored five books, more than 126 booklets, and 14 videos.

▼ ▼ ▼

Daymond R. Duck

Daymond R. Duck is a bivocational pastor who serves as minister to three small United Methodist congregations and also works for the U.S. Postal Service. He entered the ministry in 1979 and completed the five-year Course-of-Study Program for United Methodist Pastors at Emory University in 1983.

Duck is the author of two books: *On the Brink: Easy-to-Understand End-Time Bible Prophecy* and *Revelation: God's Word for the Biblically Inept.* He has written several articles for a religious newspaper and has been interviewed on numerous Christian radio programs around the country, including "The Southwest Radio Church." He has also spoken at prophecy conferences and is often asked to preach revival services.

Duck is a graduate of the University of Tennessee with a B.S. degree in agricultural engineering. He and his wife, Rachel, have three grown children: Sammy, Karen and Jeff.

▼ ▼ ▼

Arno Froese

 Arno Froese, born in Windenberg, East Prussia (today's Russia), was the sixth child in a family of ten. After World War II, the Froese family settled in Grefrath, West Germany. In 1959, Arno emigrated to Australia, where he was involved in several successful business ventures. In 1965 he emigrated to the United States.

After becoming a Christian in 1967, he married his wife, Ruth, the following year. Together they raised three sons, Joel, Micah and Simon, all of whom occupy key positions with them at Midnight Call Ministries.

An effort that began with a manual typewriter on a picnic table in a humid basement in Hamilton, Ohio, in 1968, the ministry has experienced amazing growth. Today, busy computer terminals, the rumble of modern presses, the hot lights of a television studio and the whir of audio-cassette duplicators are the signs of a large publishing operation that is shipping millions of Bible-centered magazines, tracts, videos and cassettes into virtually every corner of the world.

In addition to serving as executive editor of *Midnight Call* and *News from Israel* magazines, two of the world's leading Bible prophecy monthlies, Froese is also the writer and speaker for the monthly *Message of the Month Club* and is the host of a unique semimonthly *Video Club*. He is the author of hundreds of magazine features and has sponsored more than 45 national and international prophecy conferences.

The *Midnight Call* appears 12 times a year and is also published in German, French, Italian, Dutch, Spanish, Portuguese, Korean, Bengali, Romanian, and Hungarian languages and is distributed to more than 148 countries.

Extensive global travel and a rare international outlook have equipped Mr. Froese with valuable insight that helps people understand Bible prophecy in a fundamental way as never before. His ability to picture Bible prophecy from an international point of view has earned him a place among the leading Bible scholars in the field of eschatology.

▼ ▼ ▼

Gary Hedrick

Gary Hedrick is the president of the Christian Jew Foundation, a missionary organization founded by Dr. Charles Halff in 1951 and dedicated to Jewish evangelism worldwide. Gary leads tours to Israel and the Middle East, and writes extensively on prophetic themes.

An estimated one million people tune in each weekday to hear his Bible teaching on *Messianic Perspectives* Radio Network. Gary and his wife, Marcia, have three children: Elizabeth, Michael and Sarah. They make their home in Texas.

▼ ▼ ▼

Ed Hindson

Ed Hindson is the associate pastor of the 9,000 member Rehoboth Baptist Church in Atlanta, Georgia, and vice president of *There's Hope!* He is also professor of religion and dean of the Institute of Biblical Studies at Liberty University in Lynchburg, Virginia. He has authored several books, including *Angels of Deceit, Is the Antichrist Alive and Well?, Final Signs* and *Approaching Armageddon.* He also served as general editor of the King James Study Bible and the *Parallel Bible Commentary,* and he was one of the translators for the New King James Version.

Ed Hindson holds degrees from several institutions: B.A., William Tyndale College; M.A., Trinity Evangelical Divinity School; Th.M., Grace Theological Seminary; Th.D., Trinity College; D.Min., Westminster Theological Seminar; D.Phil., University of South Africa. He has also done graduate study at Acadia University in Nova Scotia, Canada. Hindson combines solid academic scholarship with a dynamic and practical teaching style that communicates biblical truth in a powerful and positive manner.

▼ ▼ ▼

Noah W. Hutchings

Noah Hutchings received Jesus Christ as Savior and Lord in April 1951, and joined The Southwest Radio Church. The ministry currently produces a program heard daily over a network of 100 radio stations in English, and a daily program, "Profecias Biblicas," aired in Spanish over stations in Mexico, Central America, South America and the Caribbean. Hutchings has written more than 100 books and booklets covering Bible commentary as well as prophetic topics. Some of his books are *Petra in History and Prophecy, Rapture and Resurrection, Why So Many Churches?* and *The Revived Roman Empire.*

Hutchings has traveled extensively in mission efforts, including 30 times to the Middle East, 5 times on Bible distribution tours to Russia, and 5 times to China, where he has been arrested twice on endeavors to get Bibles and Christian educational materials to the underground churches. He has also been personally active in mission work in Central America. Currently, a salvation booklet by Hutchings has been printed in Hong Kong in the Chinese language to be smuggled into mainland China for mass distribution.

A member of the board of deacons of the Council Road Baptist Church of Oklahoma City, Hutchings is also a member of the board of the University of Biblical Studies in Oklahoma City. He lives in Oklahoma with his wife, Kim. They have three grown daughters.

▼ ▼ ▼

Thomas Ice

Thomas Ice is executive director of The Pre-Trib Research Center in Washington, D.C., which he founded in 1994 with Dr. Tim LaHaye to research, teach and defend the pretribulational rapture and related Bible prophecy doctrines. Ice has co-authored over a dozen books on Bible prophecy, written dozens of articles and is a frequent conference speaker.

He pastored for 15 years, and is currently pastor/ teacher of Trinity Bible Church in Fredericksburg, Virginia. He has a Th.M. from Dallas Theological Seminary and a Ph.D. from Tyndale Theological Seminary. Ice and his wife, Janice, and their three boys live in Virginia.

Berit Kjos

Berit Kjos is a widely respected researcher, the author of books and magazine articles and a popular conference speaker.

Kjos first became aware of New Age and occult influences in society at a 1974 conference on holistic health. As a registered nurse, she was interested in methods of healing, but soon discovered that the occult powers found in New Age methods brought bondage instead of true healing. As a parent, Kjos became aware of similar New Age influences in education. She began to monitor the schools for classroom programs that taught occultism and New Age spirituality, then began to share what she learned with other parents and teachers.

Kjos has given workshops and seminars at conferences such as the Association for Christian Schools International. She has spoken at conferences for the Constitutional Coalition, Education Policy, Child Evangelism Fellowship, Concerned Women for America and Citizens for Excellence in Education.

Kjos' book, *Brave New Schools,* surveys the scene in today's public schools and provides guidelines for parents who are concerned about their children's education. Kjos shows how myth, feeling, imagination and politically correct stories are replacing truth, facts, logic and history in the classroom. She also explains what programs such as Goals 2000 are all about, and why students—even homeschoolers—eventually will be required to demonstrate competence in the new social and thinking skills before they can move on to higher education or jobs.

Kjos is also the author of *Your Child and the New Age, Under the Spell of Mother Earth* and *A Wardrobe from the King.*

▼ ▼ ▼

Tim LaHaye

Tim LaHaye is a noted author, minister, counselor, television commentator and nationally recognized speaker on family life and Bible prophecy. He is the founder and president of Family Life Seminars and the co-founder of The PreTrib Research Center. He is also the father of four children and grandfather of nine. Snow skiing, water skiing, motorcycling, golfing, family vacations and jogging are among his leisure activities.

Dr. LaHaye is a graduate of Bob Jones University and holds an M.A. and Doctor of Ministry degree from Western Conservative Theological Seminary. For 25 years he pastored one of the nation's outstanding churches in San Diego, California, which grew to three locations. It was during that time he founded two accredited Christian high schools, a Christian school system of ten schools and Christian Heritage College.

LaHaye has written 39 books on a wide range of subjects that include family life, temperaments, sexual adjustment, Bible prophecy, the will of God, Jesus Christ and secular humanism. The books in his current fiction series written with Jerry Jenkins, *Left Behind, Tribulation Force, Nicolae* and *Soul Harvest,* are number-one bestsellers among Christian fiction books. These prophetic novels are based on Bible prophecy as portrayed by fictitious characters who live through the tribulation as new believers in Christ.

There are more than ten million copies of LaHaye books in print, some of which have been translated into 32 foreign languages. His writings are best noted for their easy-to-understand and scripturally based applications of biblical principles that assist in facing and handling the challenges of life.

Presently he speaks at many of the major Bible prophecy conferences in the United States and Canada.

▼ ▼ ▼

Peter Lalonde

Peter Lalonde, along with his wife, Patti, and Paul Lalonde, is the cofounder of the popular national TV program "This Week in Bible Prophecy." He has authored several books, including *One World Under Antichrist* and *Left Behind,* and coauthored the bestsellers *Racing Toward the Mark of the Beast* and *301 Startling Proofs and Prophecies.*

Zola Levitt

Zola Levitt is a Jewish believer educated in the synagogues and brought to the Messiah in 1971. He is best known as the host of the weekly national television program "Zola Levitt Presents," and he was formerly the host of two top-rated radio talk shows: "The Heart of the Matter in Dallas," and the nationally syndicated "Zola Levitt Live." Levitt is also a widely published author with more than 40 books in several languages. He has composed over 150 spiritual songs and two of his musicals, "Beloved Thief" and "Mine Eyes Have Seen" have been televised nationally.

A specialist in biblical sites, he conducts regular tours to Israel, Jordan, Greece and Turkey. He holds music degrees from Duquesne University and Indiana University and an honorary Th.D. from Faith Bible College.

Zola Levitt Ministries, Inc., a teaching and evangelistic association, is guided by the standard of Romans 1:16: "To the Jew first and also to the Gentile." Like the apostle Paul, the ministry works through the Gentiles to reach the Jews, and informs Gentile viewers and listeners of those principles of the faith which will be most helpful to them in understanding and witnessing to their Jewish friends.

▼ ▼ ▼

Chuck Missler

An expert on Russia, Israel, Europe and the Middle East, Chuck Missler gives intriguing behind-the-scenes insights to his audiences. He has spent more than 30 years in the corporate world as CEO of four public corporations contracting with the U.S. Department of Defense and has an extensive network of overseas contacts. With affiliates and associates in nine countries, Missler is a major contributor to several international intelligence newsletters. He has also negotiated joint ventures in Russia, Israel, Malaysia, Japan, Algeria and Europe. In addition, Missler is an authority on advanced weapons and strategic resources and has participated in projects with SAMCOM-USSR, DSL, JCS, USACADA, DOJ, CCIA and SDI. A member of the International Press Association, he is an honors graduate from the U.S. Naval Academy.

For 20 years, Chuck Missler taught a Bible study in Southern California that grew to more than 2,000 attendees. In 1992 he moved to Coeur d'Alene, Idaho, where he founded Koinonia House to distribute his books, lectures and tapes. His dynamic style, conservative values and adherence to biblical principles have made him a highly acclaimed speaker and critic.

His newsletter, "Personal UPDATE," a 32-page Christian prophecy and intelligence newsletter, has grown to reach more than 50,000 monthly subscribers. He also has more than eight million tapes in circulation worldwide.

If you wish to receive a 12-month complimentary subscription to "Personal UDPATE," contact: Koinonia House, P.O. Box D, Coeur d'Alene, ID 83816-0347. Phone: 1-800-546-8731.

▼ ▼ ▼

J. Randall Price

Dr. J. Randall Price is a pastor, author and scholar whose latest published books include: *Ready to Rebuild, The Desecration and Restoration of the Temple as an Eschatological Motif in the Bible, In Search of Temple Treasures, Secrets of the Dead Sea Scrolls, The Stones Cry Out* and *Jerusalem in Prophecy.*

A pastor for 21 years, Price has served in three different congregations in the state of Texas. He did graduate study in archaeology at the Hebrew University of Jerusalem, participated in field excavation at Tel Yin'am (Galilee), and was assistant director at Qumran, the site of the Dead Sea Scrolls. In addition, he is a certified tour guide to the State of Israel, having conducted 33 tours to the Bible lands of Israel, Jordan, Egypt, Italy, Greece and Turkey. As the traveling speaker for World of the Bible Ministries, Inc., he conducts prophetic conferences in churches and with Christian organizations around the world.

Price received his Th.M. in Old Testament and Semitic Languages from Dallas Theological Seminary and his Ph.D. in Middle Eastern Studies and Archaeology from the University of Texas at Austin. He is an adjunct professor of theology at the International School of Theology and serves as president of World of the Bible Ministries, Inc. He also serves on the advisory boards of the PreTrib Research Center in Washington, D.C., and the *Messianic Times* (the world's largest Jewish-Christian newspaper) in Philadelphia, Pennsylvania.

Randall Price has been extensively involved in video productions and has made numerous appearances on network and national television programs. He is also a regular radio guest, having appeared on most of the nationally aired programs including: USA Radio Network's "Point of View" (Marlon Maddoux), the Christian Broadcasting Network, the Southern Baptist Radio and Television Commission, "How Can I Live?" (Kay Arthur, Precept Ministries), Southwest Radio Church's "Watchman on the Wall" broadcast and Moody Broadcasting Network.

Price and his wife, Beverlee, have five children and live in Texas.

▼ ▼ ▼

John Walvoord

John Walvoord, theologian, pastor and author, is described in the *Twentieth Century Dictionary of Christian Biography* as one of the most influential dispensational theologians of the twentieth century. Walvoord, who has been prominent in prophetic conferences advocating a pretribulational rapture, a literal 1,000-year millennium and distinction between Israel and the church, has written 30 books, including *The Rapture Question, The Millennial Kingdom* and *The Prophecy Knowledge Handbook,* as well as commentaries on Daniel, Philippians and the

Thessalonian epistles. With R.B. Zuck, he edited the two-volume *Bible Knowledge Commentary.*

Born in Sheboygan, Wisconsin, Walvoord graduated from Wheaton College, Texas Christian University and Dallas Theological Seminary, where he later earned his Th.D. and joined the faculty (1936–1986). He became president in 1953 and chancellor upon retirement in 1986. He also edited *Bibliotheca Sacra,* the seminary's theological journal, from 1952 to 1985. Walvoord was also a pastor at Rosen Heights Presbyterian Church in Fort Worth, Texas.

▼ ▼ ▼

Notes

Chapter 1: *False Christs, False Prophets, Great Deception*

1. "Mass Suicide Ends Waco Standoff," *USA Today,* April 20, 1993, p. A1.
2. C.S. Lewis, *Mere Christianity* (New York: Macmillan, 1960), pp. 53-54.
3. Mary Baker Eddy, *Science and Health with Key to the Scriptures* (Boston: Trustees, 1925), p. 150.
4. Ibid., pp. vii-viii.
5. Hank Hanegraaff, *Christianity in Crisis* (Eugene, OR: Harvest House, 1993).
6. Elena Whiteside, *The Way: Living in Love* (New Knoxville, OH: American Christian Press, 1972), p. 178.
7. *The Way* magazine, September–October, 1974, p. 7.
8. Josh McDowell and Don Stewart, *Understanding the Cults* (San Bernardino, CA: Here's Life Publishers, 1986), p. 142.
9. Moses David, *Reorganization, Nationalization, Revolution!* (Rome: Children of God, 1970), DO #650.
10. See Caroll Stonner and Jo Anne Parke, *All God's Children* (Radnor, PA: Chilton Books, 1977), pp. 65ff. See also the compelling inside story by Berg's daughter, Deborah Davis (Linda Berg), *The Children of God* (Grand Rapids, MI: Zondervan, 1984).
11. Una McManus and John Cooper, *Dealing with Destructive Cults* (Grand Rapids, MI: Zondervan, 1984), pp. 119-20.
12. Ibid., p. 118.

13. *You May Survive Armageddon into God's New World* (Brooklyn, NY: Watchtower Bible and Tract Society, 1955), p. 342. See also Anthony Hockeman, *The Four Major Cults* (Grand Rapids, MI: Eerdmans, 1984), pp. 307-12.

14. *Discourses of Brigham Young* (Salt Lake City: Deseret Book Co., 1954), p. 435.

15. Series of pamphlets, No. III., p. 8, quoted by Hoekema, *Four Major Cults,* p. 63.

16. Hoekema, *Four Major Cults,* pp. 139-40.

17. Eddy, *Science and Health,* pp. 456-57.

18. Ibid., p. 583.

19. *What Is Spiritualism?* Spiritualist Manual Revision of 1940, quoted by Walter R. Martin, *Kingdom of the Cults* (Minneapolis: Bethany Fellowship, 1965), p. 209.

20. Ibid., p. 210.

21. *Many Mansions,* p. 107, quoted by Martin, *Kingdom of the Cults,* p. 210.

22. Ibid., p. 250.

23. Ibid., p. 246.

24. Ibid., p. 312.

25. Sun Myung Moon, "Our Shame," *Master Speaks,* March 11, 1973, p. 3.

26. Moon, *The Way of the World,* p. 20, quoted by Josh McDowell and Don Stewart, *Understanding the Cults,* p. 134.

27. Cf. Ronald Enroth, et al., *A Guide to Cults & New Religions* (Downers Grove, IL: Intervarsity Press, 1983), pp. 104-05; and Martin, *Kingdom of the Cults,* pp. 87-101.

28. See Jehovah's Witness publications *Qualified to Be Ministers,* pp. 283-97 and *You May Survive Armageddon,* pp. 252ff. See also Hoekema, *Four Major Cults,* pp. 287-97.

29. Jack Sparks, *The Mind Benders* (Nashville: Thomas Nelson, 1977), p. 135.

30. "Zealot of God," *People* magazine, March 15, 1993, pp. 38-43.

31. "Radical Sheik," *Newsweek,* March 15, 1993, p. 32.

32. Una McManus and John Cooper, *Dealing with Destructive Cults* (Grand Rapids, MI: Zondervan, 1984), p. 117.

Chapter 2: *Wars and Rumors of Wars*

1. Chuck Missler, "The Russia, Muslim, Magog Whirlwind," in *Forewarning: Approaching the Final Battle Between Heaven and Hell,* gen. ed. William T. James (Eugene, OR: Harvest House Publishers, 1998), pp. 230-31.

2. Ron Carlson and Ed Decker, *Fast Facts on False Teachings* (Eugene, OR: Harvest House Publishers, 1994), p. 233.

3. David Jeremiah with C.C. Carlson, *The Handwriting on the Wall* (Dallas:Word Publishing, 1998), p. 158.

Chapter 3: *Famines, Pestilences, Earthquakes*

1. Zbigniew Brzezinski, *Out of Control: Global Turmoil on the Eve of the 21st Century* (New York: Collier Books, 1994); pp. 8-10; as quoted in Peter and Patti Lalonde, *The Edge of Time* (Eugene, OR: Harvest House Publishers, 1998); p. 322.

2. Dr. John F. Walvoord, "Exposition of Revelation," Dallas Seminary Tape Ministry, © Dallas Theo. Seminary, Dallas. No date indicated on tape series, tape 5, side 1.

3. Ibid.

4. Ibid.

5. Ibid.

6. J. Vernon McGee, introduction to commentary on Revelation, Thru the Bible with J. Vernon McGee, (Pasadena, CA: Thru the Bible Radio, 1983), vol. V, pp. 870-84.

7. Walvoord, commentary tapes, tape 5, side 1.

8. "World Watch," *Time* magazine, April 20, 1998, vol. 151, no. 16.

9. Tim Larimer, "Hard Road Ahead," *Time* magazine, March 9, 1998.

10. Walvoord, tape 5, side 1.

11. Ibid.

12. From Chuck Missler, personal notes on Revelation 6 and Chuck Missler, *Behold a Pale Horse: Emergent Diseases and Biochemical Warfare,* audiotape, Koinonia House, Coeur d'Alene, ID ©1998.

13. "Killer Earthquakes on the Rise," "Van Impe Intelligence Briefing" newsletter, May 1997.

14. John Walvoord, Revelation Commentary, chapter 16.

Chapter 4: *Signs in the Sun, Moon and Stars*

1. David Morrison, "Target: Earth," *Astronomy,* Oct. 1995, p. 38.

2. *New York Times,* Oct. 27, 1992, p. C7 and Nov. 3, p. C10; *New Scientist,* Oct. 24, 1992, p. 11.

3. Duncan Steel, "Comet Swift-Tuttle and a question of probability," *Spaceflight,* v. 35, July 1993, p. 223; *New York Times,* Dec. 29, 1992, p. C2.

4. *Discover,* May 1984, p. 32.

5. C.C. Albritton, *Catastrophic Episodes in Earth History* (London: Chapman & Hall, 1989); V.L. Sharpston and P.D. Ward, eds., *Global Catastrophes in Earth History,* Special Paper #247, Geological Society of America, 1990.

6. Morrison, "Target," p. 36.

7. "On impacts as a cause of geomagnetic field reversals or blood basalts," D.L. Loper and K. McCartney, in Sharpston and Ward, *Global Catastrophes.*

8. See Chuck Missler, *Signs in the Heavens* (audiobook, 1994), and *Expositional Commentary on Joshua* (audiobook, 1996), both available from Koinonia House, P.O. Box D, Coeur d'Alene, Idaho 83816.

9. *Newsweek,* Nov. 23, 1992.

10. *New York Times,* Nov. 1, 1988, p. C1.

11. Duncan Steel, "Project SPACEGUARD: the function and the fact," *Spaceflight,* v. 35, July 1993, pp. 218-22.

12. *Time* magazine, Feb. 15, 1993, pp.42-44.

13. Dr. Teller has personally altered the course of history three times already: He and Leo Szilard were the two scientists who drove out to convince Dr. Albert Einstein to send the famous letter to President Truman, which led to the Manhattan Project and the atomic bomb; Teller is credited with the hydrogen bomb; he was also the one who convinced President Reagan to undertake the Strategic Defense Initiative. I had the remarkable privilege to sit on a board of directors with him.

14. "Cold War Weaponeers Gaze Skyward," *Astronomy,* Oct. 1994, p. 41.

15. J. Allen Hynek, *Edge of Reality,* 1975, pp. 12-13; Jacques Vallee, *Dimensions* (New York: Ballantine Books, 1988), pp. 252-53. For a more complete discussion, see Chuck Missler and Mark Eastman, *Alien Encounters,* Koinonia House, Coeur d' Alene, Idaho, 1997, pp. 53-96.

16. John Mack, *Abduction: Human Encounters with Aliens* (New York: Ballantine Books, 1994), pp. 404-16.

17. Cf. Job 1:6; 2:1; 38:7. Jesus also implies the same term in Luke 20:36.

18. The Septuagint translation was the result of 72 of the top scholars, assembled in Alexandria (285–270 B.C.) to translate the Hebrew Scriptures into Greek, which was the international language of that day. It is one of the most valuable documents of the Old Testament available.

19. *The Book of Enoch,* though highly venerated by both rabbinical and Christian authorities from about 200 B.C. through about 200 A.D., was not considered part of the inspired canon. However, it is useful to authenticate the lexigraphical usage and to confirm the accepted beliefs of the period. Cf. R.H. Charles, *The Book of Enoch* (Oxford: Clarendon Press, 1912); James H. Charlesworth, *The Old Testament Pseudepigrapha,* 2 vols. (Garden City, NY: Doubleday & Co., 1985).

20. The term has been transliterated as "giants." However, the Greek root is a term meaning "earth-born," a term used of the Titans, or sons of Heaven and Earth—Cœlus and Terra. The appellation of "giants" in the sense of size was coincidental.

21. One of the classic references on this is John Fleming, *The Fallen Angels and the Heroes of Mythology* (Dublin: Hodges, Foster, and Figgis, 1879). See also John Henry Kurtz, *Die Ehen der Söhne Gottes mit den Töchtern der Menschen* (Berlin, 1857).

22. *Titan* in the Greek is equivalent to *Sheitan* in Chaldean or *Satan* in the Hebrew.

23. It is interesting that the symbol for the European Parliament is Europa, a woman holding a golden cup, riding Zeus, as a beast, all portrayed over seven hills. See Revelation 17:1-9.

24. Viking 1, on orbit 35, took a photograph of what appears to be a symmetrical face, approximately one mile wide. Some suggest it was crafted by some ancient civilization.

25. *El Khira* is the Arabic for the planet Mars.

26. Exodus 12:5, 29:1; Leviticus 1:3; and others—over 60 references, usually referring to the freedom from physical blemishes of offerings.

27. Testament of Reuben, Sect. 4 and 5, *Whiston's Translation, Authentic Records,* part I, pp. 273, 294.

28. *Liber Jubilaeorum,* translated from the Ethiopic into German by Dillman, *Das Buch der Jubiläen oder die kleine Genesis erläutert und untersucht, u.s.w.,* Rönsch, Leipzig, 1874.

29. *De Gigantibus,* ed. Pfeiffer, 1786, vol. II, pp. 358, 388.

30. *Antiquities* I, 3.1.

31. *Second Apology, Writings of Justin Martyr and Athenagoras,* trans. Clark's Ante-Nicene Library, vol. ii, pp.75-76.

32. *Against Heresies* 4.36,4

33. *Second Apology,* vol. ii, pp. 406-07.

34. *Homilies* 7.1215; 8.1115.

35. *The Instructor.* 3.2. *The Clementine Homilies and Apostolical Constitutions,* trans. Clark's Ante-Nicene Christian Library, vol. xvii, 1870, pp. 142-46.

36. *On the Veiling of Virgins* 7.

37. *De Velandis Virginibus, c.7; Liber De Idololat., c.9; De Hab. Muliebri, c.2.*

38. Divine Institut., lib. book 2, chap. 15.

39. *The International Standard Bible Encyclopædia* (Grand Rapids, MI: Wm. B. Eerdmans Publishing Co.), vol. V, pp. 2835-36.

40. Homer, *Iliad,* viii 16.

41. The term is *kerusso,* which means "to proclaim officially after the manner of a herald," although it is sometimes translated *preached.*

42. Jude is commonly recognized as one of the Lord's brothers (see Matthew 13:55; Mark 6:3; Jude 1:1).

43 Jude 6 and 2 Corinthians 5:2 (alluding to the heavenly body with which the believer longs to be clothed).

44. Genesis 18:1-8; 19:3.
45. Genesis 19:10,16.
46. Exodus 12; see also 1 Corinthians 10:10 and Hebrews 11:28.
47. 2 Kings 19:35; Isaiah 37:36.
48. John 20:12; Acts 1:10.
49. Genesis 19:5.
50. Cf. Matthew 22:30; Mark 12:25.
51. *Book of Enoch,* chapters 7–9; 64.
52. Genesis 14:5; 15:20; Deuteronomy 2:10-12,22.
53. Deuteronomy 3:11,13; Joshua 12:4; 13:12.
54. Numbers 13:33.
55. See, for example, Joshua 6:21; cf. 1 Samuel 15:3.
56. Joshua 14:15; 15:13; 21:11.
57. 1 Samuel 17:4ff.
58. 2 Samuel 21:16-22.
59. Matthew 8:28-34; Mark 5:1-20; Luke 8:26-39.
60. Isaiah 26:14. (*Rephaim* [*rapha*] is often translated "dead": Psalm 88:10; Proverbs 9:18; 21:16; Isaiah 14:9; 26:14.). Jesus did not become a Nephilim or Rephaim and die for them.

Chapter 5: *Distress of Nations with Perplexity*

1. Unlike a sign, which generally occurs at a specific point in time, a trend develops gradually. Jesus compared certain prophetic trends to the birth pangs experienced by a pregnant woman (Matthew 24:8 NIV). In this analogy, the pains grow incrementally in frequency and intensity until the baby is born.

2. The Talmud mentions "sun, moon, and stars" in *Berachoth* 55a; *Rosh HaShanah* 24b (twice); *Yoma* 54b; *Chagigah* 12b; *Avodah Zarah* 17a; 42b; 43b (twice); 54b (three times); and *Chullin* 40a.

3. *Strategy and Business,* second quarter 1997 issue, article reprint number 97207. Published by Booz-Allen & Hamilton, Inc., 67 Mount Vernon Street, Boston, MA 02108. The article is also available online at www.strategy-business.com.

4. This quotation and much of the information that follows in this section were taken from a report entitled "Moving Sustainable Development from Agenda to Action," published by the Rio Plus Five International Secretariat, The Earth Council, Apartado 2323-1002, San José, Costa Rica. Phone: 506-256-1611; Fax: 506-255-2197; e-mail: earthnet@terra.ecouncil. ac.cr.

5. "Jury to Decide Fate of World Trade Center Bombing Suspects," *Law Street Journal,* November 7, 1997, Internet edition (www.lawstreet.com). Published by Law Street, Inc., The Atrium at Lawrence, 133 Franklin Corner Road, Lawrenceville, NJ 08648.

6. "Scientists: US Must Prepare for Biological Warfare," Health Story Page (March 11, 1998), from CNN Interactive Web Page (www-cgi.cnn.com).

Chapter 7: *Russia on Edge*

1. Zbigniew Brzezinski, *Out of Control* (New York: Scribner & Sons, 1993), p. 17.

2. See Tim LaHaye, *Revelation—Illustrated and Made Plain* (Grand Rapids: Zondervan, 1975). Also see Revelation 17:9; 18:17-19.

Chapter 8: *Rising Sun Nations on the Move*

1. John Wheeler, Jr., "Clinton and the Chinese Bandits," *Citizens' Intelligence Digest,* May 1997.

2. John Walvoord, *The Nations in Prophecy* (Grand Rapids: Zondervan Publishers, 1976), p. 141.

3. Chuck Missler, *The Sleeping Dragon Awakes* (Coeur d'Alene, ID: Koinonia House, 1996), p. 19.

4. Ibid., p. 57.

5. Ibid., pp. 102-03.

6. *Time* magazine, May 21, 1965, p. 35.

7. Walvoord, *Nations,* p. 142.

Chapter 9: *European Union on the Brink*

1. Peter Lalonde, *One World Under Antichrist* (Eugene, OR: Harvest House, 1991), p. 108.

2. *Time* magazine, June 8, 1998, cited in *Midnight Call,* August 1998, p. 4.

3. Proclaiming the Gospel, Plano, Texas. July/August 1998, p. 8, www.progospel.org.

4. Arno Froese, *How Democracy Will Elect the Antichrist* (Columbia, SC: The Olive Press, 1997), p. 264, quoting the Louvain Declaration from the Second World Conference on Religion and Peace under Catholic Leadership, *Catholic Register,* September 1974–1976, Toronto, Canada.

5. *Sky* magazine, Delta, May 1998, p. 41.

6. *The Single Market* (ISBN 92-826-9787-8), The European Commission, January 1995, p. 36.

7. Ibid., p. 15.

8. Froese, *How Democracy Will Elect,* p. 139.

9. *National Geographic,* July 1997, pp. 29-32, as cited in Arno Froese, *Saddam's Mystery Babylon* (Columbia, SC: The Olive Press, 1998), pp. 28-32.

10. *The Single Market,* p. 5.

Chapter 12: *Persecution in America*

1. G.B. Chisholm, "The Reestablishment of a Peacetime Society," *Psychiatry,* February 1946, pp. 7, 9-10, 16, 18.

2. Former President George Bush announcing "America 2000," White House, April 18, 1991. See *America 2000: An Education Strategy* (Washington, D.C.: The U.S. Department of Education, 1991), pp. 50, 51, 55.

3. Mikhail Gorbachev, "New World Order: Consensus," *The Cape Cod Times,* January 28, 1993.

4. Charlotte T. Iserbyt, "Soviets in the Classroom: America's Latest Educational Fad" (America's Future Inc., 514 Main St., New Rochelle, NY 10801).

5. "The General Agreement on Contacts, Exchanges and Scientific Technical Education and Other Fields," personal copy.

6. These types of crimes are already prosecuted under existing statutes, so there is no need for additional legislation.

7. The word *voluntary* has become a euphemism to win support for all kinds of intrusive regulations that soon become mandatory.

8. Corrine McLaughlin and Gordon Davidson, *Spiritual Politics* (New York: Ballantine Books, 1994), p. 147.

9. The President's Council on Sustainable Development is one of over 150 other national councils all following the guidelines of the United Nations' Commission on Sustainable Development. To understand this global management plan read "Local Agenda 21" at my web site: www.crossroad.to.

10. Corrine McLaughlin listed her experiences while conducting a workshop I attended during a fiftieth anniversary celebration for the United Nations titled "Celebrating the Spirit" held at the University of California at Berkeley, June 19–21, 1995.

11. Cynthia Weatherly, "The Second Annual Model School Conference," *The Christian Conscience,* January 1995, p. 36.

12. For more details, see chapter 8 in my *Brave New Schools.* The "Statement of Common Purpose of Religious Leaders" was issued by Richard W. Riley, U.S. Secretary of Education, Department of Education, Public Affairs, Washington, D.C., December 16, 1994.

13. See "A National Information System" at my web site: www.crossroad.to.

14. Dustin H. Heuston, "Discussion—Developing the Potential of an Amazing Tool," *Schooling and Technology,* vol. 3, *Planning for the Future: A Collaborative Model* (Southeastern Regional Council for Educational Improvement), p. 8.

15. See "A National Information System" at my web site: www.crossroad.to. This web site and my book *Brave New Schools* also contain additional explanations, illustrations and documentation on the subject of the new education and the persecution of Christians.

16. "Learning and 'confession' are inseparable from brainwashing. Everyone has to participate in them, whether a party member or not. *Learning* ... means only political teaching from the communist standpoint. *Confession* is an integral part of the rites." Quote by Edward Hunter, who interviewed Western missionaries, businessmen and soldiers imprisoned in China and other communist countries during the 1950s, *Brainwashing* (New York: Pyramid Books, 1956), p. 185.

17. Balint Vazsonyi, "When crime is defined by hate," *Washington Times,* December 16, 1997, http://www.founding.org/column28.html.

18. To access this web site, go to the "Department of Justice, Kid's Page" at http://www.usdoj.gov/kidspage/bias-k-5/. There, Janet Reno invites children to "help stop hateful acts that hurt kids just like you" in the home, school, playground or neighborhood. If a relative makes any derogatory comment, they are invited to correct the relative and/or discuss the problem with a trusted adult.

19. Philip Weiss, "Outcasts Digging in for the Apocalypse," *Time* magazine, May 1, 1995, p. 48, emphasis added. The last words of the quote ("on government land") were deleted since *Time* failed to mention the reason for concern: the government land borders on farms where wolves attack domestic animals, yet laws protecting wolves prohibit farmers from protecting their livestock.

20. *Encylopædia Britannica* (Chicago: William Benton, 1968), vol. 16, pp. 93-94, emphasis added.

21. Ibid.

22. For documentation and explanation of this global management system, I suggest you read my book *Brave New Schools* and the articles and reports at my web site www.crossroad.to.

23. For help in wearing the armor and teaching it to children, read chapter 8 in *Brave New Schools* (Harvest House Publishers).

Chapter 13: Revelation 13 Technology Today

1. Frank Koelsch, *The Infomedia Revolution* (Whitby, ON [Canada]: McGraw-Hill Ryerson; 1995), p. 26.

2. "Quick Search Finds Personal Data Easily," *The Ottawa Citizen,* Ottawa, Ontario (Canada), September 21, 1993.

3. "Plugging in to an Interconnected Future," *The European,* August 24–30, 1995.

4. "In Future, Tiny Chip May Get Under Skin; Critics Argue Device Invites Big Brother," *The Chicago Tribune*, May 7, 1996, p. 1.

5. Ibid.

6. Glenn Garvin and Ana Rodriguez, "What's Wrong with a National ID Card?" *Government Technology* magazine, May 1996, Guest column: www.govtech.net/publications/publications.shtm.

7. *OMNI* magazine, April 1995.

8. Simon Garfinkel, "A Chip for Every Child?" *Wired* magazine, September 1995.

9. Ibid.

10. Mark David, editor-in-chief, "If 'chips' are for pets, why not for kids?" *Automatic ID News*, August 1994, p. 6.

11. Zbigniew Brzezinski, *Out of Control: Global Turmoil on the Eve of the 21st Century* (New York: Collier Books, 1994), pp. 4-5.

12. David Shukman, *Tomorrow's War: The Threat of High-Technology Weapons* (San Diego: Harcourt Brace & Company, 1996), p. 148.

13. Douglas Waller, "Onward Cyber Soldiers," *Time* magazine, August 21, 1995, p. 41.

14. Shukman, *Tomorrow's War*, p. 159.

15. Ibid., p. 244.

Chapter 15: *Rapture Before Wrath*

1. George M. Harton, "Fulfillment of Deuteronomy 28–30 in History and in Eschatology," Th.D. dissertation for Dallas Theological Seminary, Dallas, Texas, 1981, p. 130.

Chapter 16: *People of Apocalypse*

1. Jean Kirkpatrick, "Nightline," ABC News broadcast, September 24, 1998.

2. While present sufferings are said to be of present benefit only to pretribulational believers, both those believers who suffer in tribulations and the great tribulation have the benefit that their sufferings demonstrate that they are worthy (as a result of belonging to Christ) of entrance into the kingdom of God (2 Thessalonians 1:5; Revelation 1:9; 7:9-17).

3. According to Ezekiel 20:33-38 there will be a company of Jewish rebels purged in the judgment. This indicates that there will be Jewish unbelievers as well as Gentile unbelievers.

4. Nondispensational futurists argue that this point indicates that the church is present since these terms were also used to refer to it previously, and the global church is never mentioned in Revelation at all; therefore, it should not be expected when the shift turns from the local churches to the world scene. However, the fact that the word *church* is used in Revelation 22:16 in a universal sense—"the churches"—and that the company of believers in heaven during the tribulation appear to be this "church," argues against the notion that tribulation believers are to be identified as members of the church. They are called "fellow brethren," an expression of their common faith and testimony and perseverance in Jesus.

5. For example, see David Chilton, *The Days of Vengeance* (Fort Worth, TX: Dominion Press, 1987), pp. 383-84.

6. See Zechariah 12–14; Daniel 12:1; Matthew 24:13,22; Mark 13:13,20; Luke 21:27,28; Revelation 1:7; 6:15-17; 7:1-8; 11:18: 12:12-16; 15:3,4; 16:14; and 19:15,19.

Chapter 17: *From Armageddon to the Millennium*

1. For example, Deuteronomy 30:1-3; Psalm 2; 50:2; 72:1-10; Isaiah 11–12; Daniel 7:13,14; Zechariah 8:3-8; 14:1-4.

2. For example, Matthew 19:28; 23:39; 24:3–25:46; Mark 13:24-27; Luke 12:35-48; 17:22-38; 18:8; 21:25-28; Acts 1:10-11; 15:16-18; Romans 11:25-27; 1 Corinthians 11:26; 2 Thessalonians 1:7; 2 Peter 3:4; Jude 14,15; Revelation 1:7,8; 2:25-28; 16:15; 19:11-21; 22:20.

Conclusion: Doors to the Future

1. "CNN Headline News," Thursday, July 23, 1998.

2. Dr. David Jeremiah, "Turning Point" radio program, Monday, July 27, 1998.

3. "Prophecies," the History Channel, part of a series entitled "In Search of History," aired July 1998.

4. Ibid.

5. Ibid.

6. Ibid.

7. Ibid.

8. Ibid.

9. Dr. J. Vernon McGee, "Thru the Bible Radio" audio series, commentary on Revelation.

Be sure to get the new
William T. James Prophetic Briefing Paper!

This multipaged, in-depth report and analysis of current issues and events will keep you informed and updated in these critical days.

From the nations in prophecy to the technological asteroid some fear the Y2K problem might be, you will stay on the cutting edge of developments as examined under the light of God's Prophetic Word.

Thank You for Your Order!

If you would like to purchase additional products, here is an order form for your convenience. See next page for descriptions.

Low Book Prices

$15.50 each
+ $2.00 S&H

Name: _____
Address: _____
City, State, Zip: _____
Phone: _____

Quantity	Publications
	Storming Toward Armageddon
	Triumphant Return of Christ
	Earth's Final Days
	Raging into Apocalypse
	Foreshocks of Antichrist
	Forewarning
	Timeline 2000
	Celebrate Home: Great Ideas for Stay-at-Home Moms

Total Amount Enclosed:

$ _____

Please make your check payable to:

**James Informarketing
P.O. Box 1108
Benton, AR
72018-1108**

Foreshocks of Antichrist
Articles by Dave Breese, Grant Jeffrey, Zola Levitt, Chuck Missler, John Walvoord and others.

Forewarning: Approaching the Final Battle Between Heaven and Hell
Articles by Tim LaHaye, Dave Breese, Dave Hunt, John Walvoord, and others.

Storming Toward Armageddon: Essays in Apocalypse
Articles by Texe Marrs, Tim LaHaye, Dave Breese, David A. Lewis, Robert Lindsted and others.

Triumphant Return of Christ: Essays in Apocalypse II
Articles by Dave Breese, J.R. Church, John Wesley White, Phil Arms, Joseph Carr and others.

Earth's Final Days: Essays in Apocalypse III
Authors include Don McAlvany, Dave Breese, Chuck Missler, Phil Arms, J.R. Church, D.A. Miller, David Webber and others.

Raging into Apocalypse: Essays in Apocalypse IV
Contributors include Grant Jeffrey, John Walvoord, Dave Breese, Chuck Missler, Henry Morris and others.

Celebrate Home: Great Ideas for Stay-at-Home Moms
by Angie Peters
William T. James personally recommends this book as an excellent guideline for family life in these critical times.

Timeline 2000: Does God Have a Plan for Mankind?
by Mike Hile
An excellent analysis of God's working in these closing days of history.